The Dawn of
Religious Freedom
in South Carolina

The Dawn of Religious Freedom in South Carolina

James Lowell Underwood
and W. Lewis Burke

Introduction by Walter Edgar

UNIVERSITY OF SOUTH CAROLINA PRESS

Published in Columbia, South Carolina,
by the University of South Carolina Press

Manufactured in the United States of America

15 14 13 12 11 10 09 08 07 06   10 9 8 7 6 5 4 3 2 1

Library of Congress Cataloging-in-Publication Data

The dawn of religious freedom in South Carolina / edited by James Lowell Underwood and
    W. Lewis Burke.
      p. cm.
    Includes bibliographical references and index.
    ISBN-13: 978-1-57003-621-7 (cloth : alk. paper)
    ISBN-10: 1-57003-621-7 (cloth : alk. paper)
      1. Freedom of religion—South Carolina—History. 2. Church and state—South Carolina—
    History. 3. South Carolina—Church history. I. Underwood, James L. II. Burke, William Lewis.
    BR555.S6D39 2006
    323.44'209757—dc22

                                                                                  2005029340

This book was printed on Natures Natural, a recycled paper with 50 percent postconsumer waste.

Contents

Acknowledgments

THIS BOOK, LIKE OUR EARLIER BOOK, *At Freedom's Door,* grew out of a seminar sponsored by the South Carolina Supreme Court Historical Society during the chief justiceship of Ernest Finney, Jr. Justice (now Chief Justice) Jean Toal and Columbia attorney Richard Gergel, president of the society, were the moving forces behind the organization of the seminar. The quest for religious freedom, like the struggle for racial equal protection, a focal point of the first seminar, is a fundamental drive of human nature. As such it cannot be captured in a short seminar but demands book-length treatment. This volume does not reproduce seminar speeches but instead presents new essays, composed by seminar participants and others, on the evolution of religious freedom and the relationship of church and civil authority during colonial and early state history in South Carolina. Addressing this challenging subject required the help of many people. The skill and professionalism of the staff of the University of South Carolina's Coleman Karesh Law Library was once again quite helpful in a variety of ways ranging from finding obscure material to interlibrary loans. Those lending assistance include Director Steve Hinckley; Joe Cross, who retired as associate director but continues to be invaluable especially through his extensive network of contacts among librarians. Associate Directors Rebekah Maxwell and Pamela Melton continue to delight everyone with their well-honed research skills. Karen Taylor, director of access, was especially helpful as liaison with other libraries. Dr. Michael Mounter of the library staff, a master of historical research techniques, was helpful in locating obscure sources.

The South Caroliniana Library of the University of South Carolina is an impressive repository of older documents and reference works placed in a pleasant architectual setting conducive to historical research. We would especially like to thank Robin Copp, Thelma Hayes, and Brian J. Cuthrell of its staff. The Special Collections unit of the Thomas Cooper Library of the University of South Carolina was a fine source for older religious tracts.

The South Carolina Department of Archives and History is a rich resource for a wide variety of patrons ranging from those tracing their ancestry to scholars conducting in-depth research. Its staff of expert archivists has been of great help to the editors for many years on a variety of projects. Especially helpful on this project were

Marion Chandler, Charles Lesser, and Steve Tuttle, who provided invaluable advice guiding us through the thicket of historical documents.

Other helpful libraries, institutions, collections, and archives include the American Catholic Historical Society, Philadelphia; Beth Elohim Synagogue, Charleston; the University of Chicago; Emory University's Pitts Theology Library; Furman University's Richard Furman Collection; the College of Charleston's special collection on Jewish history; the Archives of the Catholic Diocese of Charleston, especially Brian Fahey, archivist; and Shorter College, Rome, Georgia. The Charleston Library Society's collection of 1790 newspapers afforded greater insight into the activities of the state constitutional convention meeting that year. The South Carolina Historical Society not only has a rich trove of research material but also afforded a quiet sanctuary for scholarly research. Especially helpful were Lisa Reams and Pat Kruger. The Hebrew Union College provided copies of essays about the Charleston Jewish Community. Particularly helpful was Arona Rudavsky

Prof. Desmond Greer of the Law Faculty, Queen's University of Belfast, Northern Ireland, an old friend of one of us (Underwood) from Fulbright professor days, responded to a rather desperate cry for help by sending Irish legal material that showed the atmosphere in which John England, first Catholic bishop of Charleston, grew to manhood.

The administration of the University of South Carolina School of Law has supported this project in many ways, especially by providing logistical aid. Thanks are due to the former dean, John Montgomery, a longtime supporter of faculty research, and the present dean, Burnele Powell. Associate Dean Phil Lacy's skill and dedication in facilitating his colleagues' work is legendary. Our colleague Prof. Herbert Johnson gave a careful reading of the manuscript and offered constructive advice.

Substantial contributions were made to the project by student research assistants. Listing them in chronological order of the time of their participation, we acknowledge Justin Werner, Christopher Newton, Elizabeth Tilley, Barry Thompson, Kori Brett McKeithen, Nicholas Green, Renèe Lipson, and Marie Vermillion.

Great honor and thanks are due to DeAnna Sugrue because her excellent typing skills and consistently gracious manner while dealing with the curmudgeonly editors were essential to this project.

Our distinguished array of contributors has our enduring gratitude. They are Dr. Bernard E. Powers Jr. of the College of Charleston, Dr. W. Scott Poole of the College of Charleston, Dr. Orville Vernon Burton of the University of Illinois, Dr. Alexander Moore of the University of South Carolina, Dr. Walter Edgar of the University of South Carolina, Dr. David Herr of St. Andrews Presbyterian College, Dr. Belinda Gergel and Richard Gergel of Columbia, S.C., and the Reverend Dr. Peter Clarke of North Augusta, S.C.

Introduction

Walter Edgar

SOUTH CAROLINA COLONIAL CHARTERS, Fundamental Constitutions, and early laws promised a safe harbor of religious freedom for the oppressed.[1] This was an appealing inducement to minorities who had been roughly used, such as Protestant dissenters, Huguenots, Quakers, and Jews. The Fundamental Constitution of 1669 generously allowed any seven persons who formed a religious consensus to start their own church.[2] To be sure, there were requirements in the Fundamental Constitution for those wishing to be freemen in Carolina, but these standards merely stipulated belief in God and that God was publicly to be worshipped.[3] But these generous grants of religious freedom were undermined by the preferred position given the Church of England, which was the only denomination to receive government financial support[4] in the 1670 version of the Fundamental Constitutions. Also the grant of religious freedom was less than evenhanded in a 1696–97 law that granted full religious freedom but only for "all Christians" and pointedly excluded Catholics from the circle of liberty.[5] On the whole, however, South Carolina's beacon of religious freedom was among the brightest in the colonies. Even though South Carolina sometimes seemed to submerge individual religious initiative by an intricate set of regulations of the Church of England, the colony escaped the harshness that sometimes occurred in older colonies in the seventeenth century. A 1624 New Amsterdam law required people to practice only the Reformed religion; the famed Maryland Toleration Act of 1649 contained generous protection for religious freedom but limited its cloak to Christians and provided that blasphemy could be punished by death; and mid-seventeenth-century Boston saw the execution of several recalcitrant Quakers.[6]

At first, religious freedom was granted through the tolerance of the monarch and the proprietors rather than as a guaranteed right. What is the difference? Tolerance is a revocable grant that can be canceled at the discretion of the grantor. It is likely to instill a don't-rock-the-boat timidity on the part of the recipient of the boon of tolerance. A right, by contrast, is guaranteed and cannot be revoked legally. In his two introductory essays, James L. Underwood traces the evolution of religious freedom in South Carolina from its somewhat shaky moorings in the Charters and Fundamental Constitutions' religious toleration provisions to the 1790 South Carolina Constitution's grant of "free exercise and enjoyment of religious profession and worship, without discrimination or preference."[7] The 1790 Constitution completed the process of disestablishment begun in the 1778 Constitution,[8] which had provided for the shift from a Church of England establishment—under which the government ideologically and financially sponsored only that denomination—to a general Protestant establishment without financial support but with the granting of incorporation to churches that subscribed to specified beliefs. Since this right was limited to Protestants, Jewish synagogues and Catholic churches could not incorporate.

The 1790 Constitution, with its proscription of "discrimination or preference," granted full equality to Jewish and Catholic synagogues and churches and guaranteed the right of religious freedom to all. James Lowell Underwood discusses the adoption of this provision, which was spurred by the wave of reform following the Revolution, the 1787 federal constitutional convention, and the 1789–1791 debates on the Bill of Rights, including the First Amendment with its protection of free exercise of religion and its prohibition of federal laws "respecting the establishment of religion." Charles Pinckney, a delegate to the federal convention and presiding officer of the 1790 South Carolina constitutional convention, furnished enlightened leadership on religious freedom. Under the principles of equality and freedom of religion embodied in the Constitution of 1790, the Jewish community flourished and energetically participated in civic affairs. But occasional clashes flared, such as the controversy over Gov. James H. Hammond's 1844 Thanksgiving Day Proclamation, which omitted Jews from the circle of those invited to commemorate the occasion. Disputes over the validity of Sunday closing laws were a further irritant.[9]

Against the background of the evolution of religious freedom in South Carolina from toleration to guaranteed rights, this volume discusses experiences of particular minority religions. Richard and Belinda Gergel trace the journey of Jews from the repressive climate of Europe to a welcoming South Carolina, where they established the historic synagogue of Beth Elohim in 1749, engaged in thriving businesses, and enthusiastically participated in charitable and other community activities. The Gergels discuss the development of Jewish political equality from the election of Francis Salvador as a member of the First Provincial Congress in 1774 up through the remarkable flowering of Jewish office holding on both the state and local levels during the antebellum period. A unique perspective is provided on the Catholic experience in the essay by Peter Clarke and James Lowell Underwood on Bishop John England, the first bishop of the Charleston diocese (1820–1842). England was an eloquent advocate of the separation of church and state whose writings and speeches provided the rationale for reconciling the Catholic faith with American democracy. He eloquently refuted nativist arguments that the Catholic Church's hierarchical organization and relationship with the pope, the head of a foreign state, were antithetical to democracy.[10] England contended that the individual Catholic citizen was free to make his own decision on how to vote on civil matters without any dictation from church or civil authorities.[11] England created a model of the virtuous citizen who was to reach his decision on how to vote by a careful perusal of the merits of the candidates and the issues rather than in response to religious or ethnic affiliations.[12]

The history of religious freedom in South Carolina is one of the clash of contending forces, such as the desire of individuals and groups for freedom of conscience colliding with the government's desire to use religion as an instrument of social control. A related conflict is the clash of the desire of some to search for new ways to approach God versus the desire of entrenched power to protect an established church. Another sharp conflict involved the desire of the individual, including slaves, for personal freedom, which may be spurred by exposure to religion, clashing with the desire of masters to make sure that this exposure leads to tractability rather than to revolt. Clarke and Underwood point out that Bishop England, a staunch advocate of individual freedom who considered slavery a great evil, did not challenge the slave system because doing so would create a hostile climate for other aspects of his ministry. Other essays in the volume illustrate how the thrust toward individual freedom collides with the purpose of those in power to use religion as a bulwark of, rather than a challenge to, the established order.

In his essay "Seeking the Promised Land: Afro-Carolinians and the Quest for Religious Freedom to 1830," Bernard E. Powers Jr. traces the struggle of free and slave blacks to shape religious beliefs that served their needs rather than merely providing another tool for white social control that might make the black population more docile. Powers observes:

> For Afro-Carolinians religion and freedom had an important symbiotic relationship. They often used religion and the church to create psychological living space. That space could expand dramatically if Christian instruction provided access to literacy, as it sometimes did. Christian doctrine became a yardstick by which the behavior of the master class could be judged and condemned. Correspondingly—when measured against that same moral standard—the oppressed could build their self-esteem.

Powers traces the struggle to develop such "psychological living space" from early colonial times through the ministry of George Whitefield, who sought improvement in the lot of slaves during his visits to South Carolina in 1738 and 1740. Powers describes the apocalyptic appeal to slaves and warning to whites made by Whitefield follower Hugh Bryan, which created fears of a slave revolt and was especially frightening in light of the Stono Rebellion of 1739. Powers singles out the formation of the Charleston African Methodist Episcopal Church in 1818 by free and slave blacks and the persecution of its members by officials fearful of a slave revolt as a watershed in the development of Afro-Carolinian religious identity, which was underscored by the 1822 insurrection led by Denmark Vesey, who had been a member of the church.

Orville Vernon Burton and David Herr explore the evangelical movement, which with its emphasis on a personal relationship to God in which individuals stand equal before their maker, created a climate for religious tolerance. This was especially true in the backcountry, where Methodist and Baptist itinerants outnumbered the Church of England missionaries, who were more aligned with the status quo and social order than sympathetic to individual spiritual exploration. Burton and Herr point out how the message of the early evangelicals led some to view all souls—men or women, slave or free—as equal before God, an attitude that could have undermined the social order in general and the slave system in particular. The backcountry ministry also blurred lines between denominations. Ministers were scarce in that region. When one arrived in an area he drew audiences that cut across denominational lines. Furthermore, the emphasis of such evangelical meetings on emotional experiences, by which a worshiper reassembles his spiritual personality according to God's will, encourages tolerance toward another's experience as being just as authentic as your own. Fifth Sunday meetings, in which congregations from a variety of backcountry churches came together for a service, also contributed to tolerance by encouraging those from diverse religions to seek modes of worship that were comfortable to all.[13]

Burton and Herr point out that "evangelical theology's egalitarian leanings threatened wealthy planters as converts struggled with the inconsistency of slavery and Christianity." They note that in 1784 a Methodist statement declared that slave ownership was sinful and that "'LIBERTY is the birthright of mankind."[14] This alarmed the slave owners, who feared that a ministry to blacks would incite insurrection. Evangelicals were eager to convert black slaves. The masters exacted a price for access: the message should be one that urged submissiveness rather than dissatisfaction with the bonds of slavery. But the evangelical emphasis on personal conversion and direct communication with God planted seeds of liberty anyway. African Americans proved adept at melding African traditions with the evangelical ethos to form modes of worship that were unique and satisfied their needs in ways that a rote reception of prefabricated white traditions could not. Burton and Herr point out that "evangelical emphasis on oral communication with the supernatural strongly aligned with African traditions," but "while African American evangelicalism emphasized creative expression, white evangelicals did not."

As they entered the nineteenth century, white evangelical churches that had been successful in attracting members became formal and organized and began emphasizing moral rules for individual conduct as much as the personal-conversion experience. Rules against drinking, gambling, and adultery were energetically invoked. Some of the earlier tolerance was lost within particular congregations, but Burton and Herr conclude that "religious tolerance across denominations was secure." What was no longer tolerated was abolitionist attitudes. They observe that "by the late antebellum period the evangelical ethos included defense of slavery and the protection of male supremacy, two fundamental features garnering the white male support necessary to flourish in South Carolina's slave society."

The reformulation of the evangelical ethos from anti- to pro-slavery represented the evangelicals compromise with the system that surrounded them. A dramatically different approach was followed by the Quakers. W. Scott Poole's essay describes the Quaker experience. The Quakers' clash with authority involved: (1) their opposition to swearing oaths; (2) their opposition to violence, which led them to resist military service; (3) their eventual opposition to slavery, which threatened the stability of the slave based economy; (4) their opposition to ceremonial deference, such as removing hats in the presence of officials or in court or legislative assemblies. South Carolina originally provided a welcoming environment to Quakers in the late seventeenth and early eighteenth centuries. Article 90 of the Fundamental Constitution of July 21, 1669, provided that the swearing of oaths was not essential. Groups organizing churches merely had to afford some "sensible way" to attest to the truth. Governor John Archdale, a Quaker himself, obtained passage of a 1696 law that gave him power to exempt Quakers from military service on conscientious objector grounds.[15] However, later the enforcement of compulsory military service became tighter during the time of the Yamassee War, with Quakers being punished by fines or seizure of goods for failure to report for military service.[16] As time went on, officials were less respectful of Quaker opposition to oaths, especially those required for legislative service.[17] Poole notes that unlike many other groups, the Quakers refused to compromise on the slavery issue to blend in more easily with surrounding society. This controversy reached a peak in the late eighteenth and early nineteenth centuries. In 1786 the Bush River Monthly Meeting of Quakers in the Newberry area sent a memorial in opposition to slavery to the legislature, which responded with deafening silence.[18] Their refusal to compromise on the slavery issue led most Quakers to conclude that they should leave the state, with the result that Quakers had largely vanished from South Carolina by the early nineteenth century.

Another group that found refuge from European oppression in South Carolina was the Huguenots. Alexander Moore notes that between 1598 and 1685 this group of French Protestants received partial protection of their religious freedom in a Catholic country by the Edict of Nantes. This document reestablished the Catholic Church but allowed the Huguenots to live throughout the nation and worship in specified places. The revocation of the edict in 1685, preceded by mounting harassment of their worship, forced Huguenots to flee from France to various locations in Europe and the United States, including New York, Massachusetts, and South Carolina. Prerevocation oppression included closing trades and professions to Huguenots, placing Catholic monitors in their worship services, and dragoons in their homes. The revocation directed destruction of Huguenots' houses of worship and ordered that their children be raised as Roman Catholics.[19] Moore points out that, although the Huguenots found a safe refuge in South Carolina, their political problems were not over. They were caught in the middle in the power struggle between the Church of England party and the Protestant dissenters over control of the Commons House of Assembly. The Dissenters viewed Huguenots as allies of the Church of England party and challenged their right to vote on the grounds that they were not fully naturalized.[20]

Thus, many of their difficulties sprang not from laws directly regulating the practice of religion but from the clash of political rivals whose identity was in part defined by their religion. Eventually they were absorbed into the Church of England population because of the difficulty of finding French-speaking ministers and the impossibility of supporting both their own churches through contributions and the Church of England through taxes.[21]

These essays focus on several major issues throughout the book. One is the difficulty of vindicating religious freedom while maintaining a government-supported church that is subjected to intricate regulations and is used by the government for the purpose of social control and not merely to serve the religious goals of its adherents. The evolution from a Church of England establishment to a general Protestant establishment and finally to no establishment shows South Carolina reaching the sometimes imperfectly observed conclusion that religion is freest when government neither finances it or opposes it. The established church was enmeshed in red tape that circumscribed its freedom of decision making, and the other denominations were handicapped by their members having to support the preferred denomination by taxes and then having to scramble for leftovers to support themselves. Until this situation was resolved, the tension between promises of religious freedom that were made to attract settlers and the preference for the established church was significant. Another major theme is the tension between the promise of religious freedom and the slave system, which resulted in a diluted version of that promise going to slaves lest they be inspired to revolt. This tension was handled differently by the various denominations: some muting early abolitionist rhetoric in order to be accepted by the surrounding community but with the Quakers leaving the state rather than compromising. This volume perceptively discusses these issues and provides useful historical information to enhance the reader's understanding.

Notes

1. See Walter Edgar, *South Carolina: A History* (Columbia: University of South Carolina Press, 1998), 49.

2. Article 87 of the Fundamental Constitution of July 21, 1669, in *North Carolina Charters and Constitutions, 1578–1698,* ed. Mattie Erma Edwards Parker (Raleigh, N.C.: Carolina Charter Tercentenary Commission, 1963), 149. See also Edgar, *South Carolina: A History,* 43.

3. Article 86, in *North Carolina Charters and Constitutions, 1578–1698,* ed. Parker, 148.

4. Article 96 of the Fundamental Constitution of March 1, 1670, ibid., 181.

5. See Act No. 154 of March 10, 1696–97, para. VI, 2 S.C. STATUTES AT LARGE 131, 133 (Cooper 1837).

6. Mortimer J. Adler, ed. *The Annals of America,* vol. 1 (Chicago: Encyclopedia Britannica, 1968), 88 (New Amsterdam Law of 1624); Maryland Toleration Act of April 21, 1649, in Donald S. Lutz, *Colonial Origins of the American Constitution* (Indianapolis: Liberty Fund, 1998), 309–13; James Bowden, *The History of the Society of Friends in America;* vol. 1 (1850; reprint, New York: Arno Press, 1972), 184, 201, 214–15.

7. Article 8, Section 1, The South Carolina Constitution of 1790, in *Basic Documents of South Carolina History,* ed. J. M. Lesesne and J. H. Easterby (Columbia: Historical Commission of South Carolina, 1952).

8. Article 38, South Carolina Constitution of 1778, in ibid.

9. Morton Borden, *Jews, Turks, and Infidels* (Chapel Hill: University of North Carolina Press, 1984), 142n2 (Thanksgiving Day Proclamation); City Council of Charleston v. Benjamin, 33 S.C.L. (2 Strob.) 508 (1846) (upholding Sunday Closing law as applied to Jewish merchants).

10. "Rt. Rev. John England, Substance of A Discourse preached in the Hall of the House of Representatives in the Congress of the United States in the City of Washington, Jan. 8, 1826," available in the South Caroliniana Library, University of South Carolina, Columbia.

11. "Letter on Civic and Political Duties to the Roman Catholic Citizens of Charleston," in *The Works of the Right Reverend John England, First Bishop of Charleston*, 7 vols., ed. Sebastian Messmer (Cleveland: Ohio, Arthur H. Clarke, 1908), VI: 352–72.

12. Ibid.

13. Orville Vernon Burton, *In My Fathers House Are Many Mansions: Family and Community in Edgefield South Carolina* (Chapel Hill: University of North Carolina Press, 1985), 22.

14. Robert M. Calhoon, *Evangelicals and Conservatives in the Early South, 1740–1861* (Columbia: University of South Carolina Press, 1988), 125.

15. *An Act for the Better Settling and Regulating the Militia*, 1696, John Archdale Papers 1690–1706 (microfilm), available at the South Carolina Department of Archives and History, Columbia. *Yearbook City of Charleston 1883* (Charleston: News and Courier Book Presses, 1883. Quotes and discussses the 1696 act. The two versions differ somewhat in wording.

16. Mabel L. Webber, "The Records of the Quakers in Charles Town," *South Carolina Historical and Genealogical Magazine* 28 (1927): 30.

17. James Lowell Underwood, *The Constitution of South Carolina*, vol. 3: *Church and State, Morality and Free Expression* (Columbia: University of South Carolina Press 1992), 38 (1766 exclusion of Quaker Samuel Wylly from taking the legislative seat to which he was duly elected when he refused to take the prescribed oath).

18. Jo Anne McCormick, "The Quakers of Colonial South Carolina 1670–1807," Ph.D. dissertation, University of South Carolina, Columbia, 1984, 187–88.

19. See Edgar, *South Carolina A History*, 50–52, 91–92; Milton Viorst, *The Great Documents of Western Civilization* (New York: Barnes & Noble, 1994), 106–8 (setting forth the Edict of Nantes), 146–47 (setting forth the main provisions of the revocation); see also Bertrand Van Ruymbeke, "Minority Survival The Huguenot Paradigm in France and the Diaspora," in *Memory and Identity: The Huguenots in France and Atlantic Diaspora*, ed. Van Ruymbeke and Randy J. Sparks (Columbia: University of South Carolina Press, 2003), 3–4; see also Jon Butler, "The Huguenots and the American Immigrant Experience," ibid, 197; see also Van Ruymbeke, "Escape from Babylon, *Christian History* 20, issue 71 (August 2001): 38; see also Arthur Henry Hirsch, *The Huguenots of Colonial South Carolina* (1928; reprint, London: Archon Books, 1962), 6.

20. Hirsch, 103–30.

21. Ibid., 94, 127.

*The Dawn of
Religious Freedom
in South Carolina*

The Dawn of Religious Freedom in South Carolina

*The Journey from Limited Tolerance
to Constitutional Right*

James Lowell Underwood

THE EVOLUTION OF RELIGIOUS FREEDOM in early South Carolina was not an unbroken line of progress toward liberty. The general movement was from limited to broader tolerance and then from the view that religious freedom was a revocable boon dispensed by the government to the belief that it was a guaranteed constitutional right. Interruptions in the progress were caused by official vacillation between polar opposite policies: the view of religion as a matter of individual conscience and its antithesis, the idea of religion as an instrument of social control that could be used by the government to ensure the loyalty of the people through appeals to the spirit as well as patriotism. The overture of this story is found in the early Charters and Fundamental Constitutions with their provisions for tolerance.[1] The main theme is the establishment of the Church of England; and its counterpoint is the struggle for a more firmly grounded right of religious freedom unshackled by such favoritism.[2] The denouement is the adoption of a strong guarantee of religious freedom without preference in the Constitution of 1790.[3] This essay and the following one will trace the journey from limited tolerance to a constitutional right of freedom of religion. They will also trace the parallel journey from the belief that an established church is essential to the preservation of civilization to the belief that such an establishment must be dispensed with if freedom of religion is to be fully realized.

The Charters and Fundamental Constitutions:
Limited Tolerance as a Magnet to Settlers

The first Charter for Carolina, granted by Charles II in 1663, seemed to be at once parsimonious and lavish in its grant of religious freedom. This ambivalence toward freedom of religion reflected the tensions of the time: Charles II's personal inclination toward tolerance was under constant pressure from Parliament for enforcement of

1

conformity that strengthened the position of the Church of England.[4] In the Charters these tensions found expression in provisions that envisioned a vital role for religion as part of the social glue that held society together but with the government seeking to be simultaneously tolerant and controlling. A vigorous planting of new churches was expected but under the careful control of the Lords Proprietors, who were granted the power to license new churches.[5]

The Charter needed to fly a flag of tolerance because potential settlers had varied beliefs. To this end the Charter permitted the Lords Proprietors to grant relief from conformity to the doctrines of the Church of England to settlers who could not in good conscience embrace them but who remained loyal to the Crown and whose worship did not "in any wise disturb the Peace and safety . . . , or scandalize or reproach the said Liturgy, forms, and Ceremonies" of the Church of England.[6] Such tolerance was feasible, not only because it would be a magnet for settlers, but because the "remote distances" of the colony from England meant that the variety of beliefs it countenanced would not undermine the "unity and uniformity established in this Nation."[7] But it is important to recognize that such nonconformity was permitted by reversible dispensation of the Lords Proprietors rather than as a right. The Charter speaks of "Indulgences and Dispensations" that may exist "for and during such time and times, and with such limitations and restrictions" as the Lords Proprietors cared to impose.[8]

The second Charter, granted to the Lords Proprietors on June 30, 1665, provided a firmer basis for religious liberty. It forbade punishment for "differences in opinion or practice in matters of Religious concernment, [of those] who [did] not disturb the Civil Peace," whereas the first Charter apparently permitted action against those who merely scandalized or reproached the standards of the Church of England.[9] Furthermore, freedom of religion was protected against encroachment by English law; the second Charter announced that religious liberty was granted despite any "usage or Custom of Our Realm of England to the contrary hereof in any wise notwithstanding."[10]

The broad terms of the Charter were reduced to more concrete form in the concessions and agreement of January 7, 1665, between the Lords Proprietors and a group of Barbadian settlers led by Maj. William Yeamans and his father, Sir John Yeamans.[11] This document displayed the same ambivalence to religious freedom found in the Charters: making a lavish grant of religious freedom with one hand and retaining the power to revoke it with the other.[12] The power to revoke freedoms was to be exercisable only as to new settlers who had not come to the colony in reliance on the initial grant.[13] This raised the bizarre possibility of various waves of settlers coexisting with different degrees of religious freedom. The concessions and agreement also furnished evidence of how the proprietors would use their power to license churches. They promised not to exercise this power to dilute "the General clause of Liberty of Conscience."[14] County legislative assemblies were granted the power to create churches and maintain them with public funds.[15] But the assemblies were not to have a monopoly over the creation of new churches. Freedom was granted "to any person or persons to keep and maintain what preachers or Ministers they please," but the implication was that these privately initiated groups were to fend for themselves for funds.[16] This preferential system would give government churches a competitive advantage.

The approach of the Charters to religious freedom—granting liberty but within carefully prescribed limits, making the grant of freedom subject to revision or revocation by the proprietors, and expressing a preference for certain religious beliefs—was refined in the Fundamental Constitutions. These documents, which allocated power and granted rights, were issued by the Lords Proprietors beginning in 1669.[17] The numerous versions of these constitutions subjected religious freedom to such endless tinkering, expansion, contraction, and refinement, that they did not provide a firm mooring for liberty.[18] Since the Fundamental Constitutions were infused with medieval concepts—such as the creation of a rigidly hierarchical set of socioeconomic classes, including the serflike "leetmen"—they were rejected by the people and never completely implemented.[19] Speculation has credited John Locke with authorship of the Fundamental Constitutions, but some scholars have concluded that, rather than reflecting his philosophy, the documents implemented the views of the proprietors.[20] However, Locke's influence may be seen: ideas he later expressed in *A Letter Concerning Toleration* (1689) are foreshadowed, albeit imperfectly, in the Fundamental Constitutions.[21] Locke observed that "neither pagan nor Mohometan nor Jew ought to be excluded from the civil rights of the commonwealth because of his religion."[22] But he argued that toleration should not be extended to those whose religion undermined the moral standards necessary to preserve civil society or to religions that required allegiance to a foreign prince or denied the existence of God.[23] Even though the Fundamental Constitutions were never fully implemented, they furnished the rhetorical weaponry for any disputes over religious freedom.

The balance that the Fundamental Constitutions attempted to strike was to create an aura of sympathetic tolerance to attract settlers but to insist that they adhere to broadly defined core religious principles thought to be essential to a civilized society.[24] Article 86 [61] of the July 21, 1669, version stipulated these bedrock beliefs: "No man shall be permitted to be a Freeman of Carolina, or to have any Estate or habitation within it, that does not acknowledge a God, and that God is publicly and Solemnly to be worshipped."[25] But anyone adhering to these core principles, even if otherwise deviating from orthodoxy, was welcome. To avoid discouraging settlement by those who might fear that their religion was unacceptable, the July 21, 1669, version promulgated a generous policy for the creation of new churches. Article 87 [62] stated that in order

> that heathens, Jews, and other dissenters from the purity of Christian Religion may not be Scared and kept at a distance from [knowledge of] it, but, by having an opportunity of acquainting them selves with the truth and reasonableness of its Doctrines, and the peaceableness and inoffensiveness of its professors, may, by good usage and persuasion, and all those convincing Methods of Gentleness and meekness Suitable to the Rules and design of the Gospel, be won over to embrace and

3

unfeignedly receive the truth: Therefore, any Seven or more persons agreeing in *any Religion* shall constitute a church or profession, to which they shall give Some name to distinguish it from others. (emphasis added)[26]

A similar but less generous provision was contained in Pennsylvania Charter of 1681, granted by Charles II to William Penn. It stated "that if any of the inhabitants of the said Province, to the number of Twenty, shall at any time hereafter be desirous, and shall by any writeing, or by any person deputed for them, signify such their desire to the Bishop of London for the time being that any preacher or preachers, to be approved of by the said Bishop, may be sent unto them for their instruction, that then such preacher or preachers shall and may be and reside within the said Province without any denial or molestation whatsoever."[27] The grant of religious freedom in the Pennsylvania provision was more tightfisted; less room was permitted for local religious inventiveness because all the preachers dispatched at the colonists' request had to be approved by the bishop of London. The Virginia Charters issued in 1606, 1609, and 1611–12 spoke in broad terms, promising settlers that they would "enjoy all Liberties, Franchises and Immunities" as if they were in England but did not focus on religious freedom, perhaps because as A. E. Dick Howard notes, the "settlement grew from neither religious nor political persecution."[28]

As generous as the Carolina provision was, it did not value tolerance in itself so much as it appreciated its effectiveness as a beacon for settlers and as a subtle instrument for evangelism. But such pragmatic tolerance is often the only kind obtainable. A similar tolerance, broad but still constrained by boundaries requiring acceptance of essential religious principles, governed the creation of churches by private parties. While Article 87 [62] permitted "Seven or more persons in any Religion [to] constitute a church," Article 90 [65] required that, to be deemed a church, an organization had to embody in its communion the beliefs that there was a God and that God was "publicly to be worshipped." It also had to provide some mechanism by which its members could vow that testimony they gave in official proceedings was the truth.[29] This theme of tolerance, circumscribed by broad belief requirements, recurs in South Carolina history. More than a hundred years later the Constitution of 1778 proclaimed "That all Persons and religious Societies, who acknowledge that there is one God, and a future State of Rewards and Punishments, and that God is publicly to be worshipped, shall be freely tolerated."[30]

The 1669 Fundamental Constitution, though broadly tolerant, circumscribed the privacy of both the churches and their members by requiring that their membership rolls be maintained by public officials.[31] This was an essential mechanism for enforcing the rule that acceptance of broad monotheistic religious standards was a necessary attribute of citizenship. Groups not complying with the intricate maze of regulations they had to adhere to in order to be deemed a church were viewed as outlaw assemblies that "shall not be Esteemed as churches, but unlawful meetings, and be punished as other Riots."[32] But churches meeting the standards received protection of their worship from those who would disturb it. Article 93 [68] stipulated, "No man of any other [another] Church or profession shall disturb or molest any Religious Assembly," and Article 97 [72] decreed, "No person shall use any reproachful, Reviling, or abusive language against the Religion of any Church or Profession, that being the certain way of disturbing the public peace, and of hindering the conversion of any to the truth by engaging them in Quarrels and animosities, to the hatred of the professors and that profession, which otherwise they might be brought to assent to."[33] The last provision might have been calculated to aid a religiously diverse society in coexisting harmoniously, but it also could have discouraged the theological debate that helps prevent religious atrophy.

Religious debate can be messy, and the Fundamental Constitutions prized order over bruising disputes. This was no where more evident than in the Fundamental Constitutions' attempt to safeguard the government from being undermined by religious dissent. Religious freedom was the beneficiary of broad tolerance, but state security was a higher virtue. This is evident in the stern admonition that "No person whatsoever shall speak any thing in their Religious assembly Irreverently or Seditiously of the Government or Governors or States matters."[34]

To a limited extent even slaves were to share in the largesse of tolerance. Article 98 [73] provided that slaves could choose a church and become members, but this did not exempt them from their masters' dominion.[35] Tolerance did not extend to religious beliefs that would undermine the slaves' status of servitude. The Fundamental Constitutions firmly decreed that "Every Freeman of Carolina shall have absolute Authority over his Negro Slaves, of *what opinion or Religion soever.*"[36] Judged by this language, the slaves' freedom of religion was largely inward; religion could not remove external restraints on them. Yes, the Constitutions purported to give the slaves the right to choose a church, but it is doubtful that such a freedom could exist in isolation without other freedoms to undergird it. Nicholas Trott's 1721 compilation, *The Laws of the British Plantations in America Relating to Church and Clergy, Religion and Learning Collected in One Volume,* assembled as an aid to the Society for the Propagation of the Gospel in Foreign Parts in its work throughout the colonies, highlighted a 1712 South Carolina statute confirming that the master's property rights in a slave were not in any way undermined by a slave's undergoing baptism.[37] The act implied that some slave owners had been reluctant to permit their slaves to be baptized lest the rite would signify that the slave had been freed.

Even though the 1669 Fundamental Constitution had belief requirements that had to be met to qualify as a freeman in Carolina, the standard was more generous and less specific than a 1624 provision governing the colony of New Amsterdam, which required colonists to practice only the Reformed religion to set an example for Indians and other "blind people," but which, despite this restriction, purported to grant "everyone the freedom of his conscience."[38] Freedom of conscience is far less meaningful if its external manifestations must adhere to a specific mode and doctrine.

The South Carolina religious rules also lacked the severe punitive bite of the Maryland Toleration Act of 1649, which despite its harshness, has been described as containing one of the broadest grants of religious freedom of the seventeenth century.[39] Even though this provision guaranteed that no one would be "troubled, Molested or discountenanced for or in respect of his or her religion," this guarantee was limited to those "professing to believe in Jesus Christ."[40] And, even though the provision sought tolerance by punishing those who criticized another's religion, anyone who blasphemed God, by denying that Jesus Christ was the son of God or denying the doctrine of the holy trinity, was punishable by "death and confiscation or forfeiture of all of his or her lands and goods."[41] The Maryland act also provided for punishment by fines or public whipping of those who used "reproachfull words" concerning such revered figures as the Virgin Mary and the Apostles.[42] A Maryland Jew, Jacob Lumbrozo, was prosecuted for blasphemy in 1658 under charges alleging he had said that Jesus was a man rather than the son of God and that Christ had not performed miracles but merely the conjuring tricks of a magician. The defendant replied that he had not pressed his views on anyone but had merely responded to questions and that he had not said anything that scoffed at or derided Christian beliefs.[43] The defendant was bound over for trial but the outcome cannot be ascertained.[44] Despite its belief requirements, the South Carolina Fundamental Constitution of 1669 was not crippled by this vengeful form of evangelism. But a 1703 South Carolina law punished blasphemy by anyone who professed or was educated in the Christian religion when such a person denied that it was the true faith, that the Bible was divinely inspired, or that any person of the holy trinity was God.[45] Although the penalties for a first offense were substantial—including disability to hold civil, military, or ecclesiastical employment—they lacked the severity of the Maryland law.[46] Still, the Fundamental Constitutions did state the favored position of the Church of England in no uncertain terms.

In a new version of the Fundamental Constitutions, issued on March 1, 1670, the proprietors tightened their embrace of the Church of England. Article 96 provided that the Church of England was the "only true and Orthodox" religion so that only it was to be "allowed to receive Maintenance by Grant of Parliament."[47] Such provisions tend to foster the view that the favored church is a mere state functionary. The new document continued the requirement of its predecessor that one must believe in God to be a freeman in Carolina.[48]

This fiscal and ideological endorsement of the Church of England clouded the message of tolerance sent to current and would-be settlers by the Charters and the earlier version of the Fundamental Constitutions and replaced it with a not-so-subtle hint that those who wished to advance socially, politically, and economically should align themselves with the official religion. Government financial support of the Church of England gave it an advantage over its competitors by draining, through taxes, the pool of funds that might otherwise be available for private contributions to other religious bodies, and government funding also dampened the ardor of Church of England followers to contribute to their own religion. One commentator has absolved John Locke of any responsibility for the retrogressive Article 96 by noting that a draft of the July 21, 1669, version in Locke's handwriting contained no such provision and that Locke later claimed Article 96 was included in the new version at the behest of other proprietors and not his patron, Anthony Ashley Cooper, Lord Ashley (later Earl of Shaftesbury).[49]

Two drafts of the Fundamental Constitutions issued in 1682 tightened the religious requirements for being a freeman in Carolina. The January 12, 1682, version stipulated that to be a freeman, one must not only believe in God and that God is publicly to be worshiped, but also that "there is a future being after this Life."[50] Another version, issued later in 1682, contained the stern admonition that the freeman must not only avow a belief in God and that God is publicly and solemnly to be worshiped but also avow a belief in a future life after this one that can be either one of "happiness or misery" depending on the path taken in this life.[51] The official leash on freedom of conscience became tighter and tighter. Curiously, however, this same version temporarily reduced the burden placed on taxpayers by the Church of England establishment.[52] It provided that the public maintenance of the Church of England was to be funded only by contributions by its adherents and that every church but the "Church of Rome" could tax its own members. These levies, however, had to be under a ceiling set by the Constitution, and each church had to open its books for inspection by the authorities.[53]

This Constitution still assumed everyone would be a member of some church. Preference for the Church of England was still evident in the restraint the Constitution placed on the growth of its rivals by limiting the amount that they could collect from their members. It was also apparent in the government's power to inspect the rivals' books, which could have dampened their ardor. Whether the purpose of these restraints was to lighten the load of the taxpayer or to hobble competitors of the established church, these provisions still bespoke the kind of microscopic government scrutiny that could chill nonconformity. The reference to the Catholic Church as the "Church of Rome" and its exclusion from the fiscal powers enjoyed by others showed a fear that the papal state could undermine the power of England over the colony if its religious agents were given a firm foothold. Still, the lightening of the burden on non-Anglicans was a bold departure signaling tolerance.

Further evidence that religion was intended to be the tool of the state rather than its master is seen in Article 102 of the August 1682 Fundamental Constitution. It stipulated that "no ordained minister, or that receives any maintenance as minister of any congregation or Church, shall be member of parliament, or have any civil office, but wholly attend his ministry."[54] This was separation of church and state of a sort: religious officials were to be separated from the levers of state power, but religion was entwined with the state as one of its agents of social control.

The seemingly endless permutations of the Fundamental Constitutions congealed into a final version, issued April 11, 1698. The experiment with assessing only Church of England members for its support had run its course. The final version reverted to language similar to Article 96 of the 1670 draft. Parliament was charged with the duty of providing for the construction of churches and payment of the salaries of ministers, and the Church of England was anointed as the "only true and orthodox, and the National Religion of the King's Dominions."[55]

Even though the Charters and the Fundamental Constitutions sent a mixed message, on the one hand promising broad tolerance and on the other signaling a preference for the Church of England, the overall tone was attractive to settlers of varied backgrounds and beliefs. An early Carolina statute, passed during the 1696–97 legislative session, reaffirmed this enlightened tone by extending to all settlers, whatever their country of origin, the same property rights and rights before the courts as were enjoyed by settlers born in the colony to English parents.[56] The preamble of the statute extended a welcoming hand to all those fleeing religious oppression who would be loyal to the king.[57] But this generous message was muted by provisions in the same law that granted a "full, free and undisturbed" worship but limited the right to "all Christians" and excluded papists.[58]

Despite the vacillation between broad tolerance to all settlers and unflinching preference for the Church of England, the predominant flavor of the Charters and Constitutions was attractive to the religiously oppressed. Barnett Elzas, in his history of the Jews of South Carolina, praised the 1669 Fundamental Constitution by observing that it "was a veritable Magna Charta of Liberty and Tolerance," especially in the Article 87 provision permitting "Seven or more persons of any Religion" to form a church, with the result that in Elzas's view the "persecuted Jews, like the persecuted Huguenot and German Palatine came here to find a haven of rest."[59]

The Huguenots were Protestants who fled from persecution in France in the late seventeenth and early eighteenth centuries, especially after the 1685 revocation of the Edict of Nantes (1598), which had guaranteed tolerance.[60] Jon Butler has described the entire "Huguenot diaspora—the Refuge—the forced flight of several hundred thousand Protestants from France between 1680 and 1700" to various places in Europe and America (including New York, Massachusetts, and South Carolina) as "the largest single population movement and forced religious change in early modern Europe except for the expulsion and forced conversion of Jews in Spain a century earlier."[61] The Edict of Nantes reestablished the Roman Catholic Church in France but permitted Protestants to live throughout the kingdom and worship in designated places.[62] The revocation ordered the destruction of Reformed Protestant Temples, banned RPR (religion prétendue réformée) meetings, excluded its ministers from the kingdom, and ordered Protestant children to be raised as Roman Catholics.[63] Even before formal revocation of the Edict of Nantes, persecution intended to bring about forced conversion to Catholicism persisted.[64] Bertrand Van Ruymbeke notes that King Louis XIV embraced "the powerful 'one King, one faith' principle" in the belief that "the country's stability depended on the monarch and his people all following the same religion."[65] Huguenots were excluded from many trades and professions; Huguenot academies were closed; restrictions were placed on psalm singing; dragoons were quartered in Huguenot homes at the owner's expense; books were burned; and Catholic observers were stationed in Protestant worship services and permitted to interject comments refuting the pastor's message.[66] Van Ruymbeke notes that the revocation of the Edict of Nantes left Huguenots "still living in France three choices: convert, enter the underground church or flee."[67] Those choosing the last two options could receive the death penalty if caught.[68] In recounting the story of Judith Giton, who fled from southern France to Charleston in 1684, Van Ruymbeke identifies "elements common to the Huguenot exodus," including "the quartering of troops [in Huguenot homes], a night flight, a long risky voyage filled with hardships and sorrows—but also survival, hope, freedom, and prosperity."[69] The Huguenots found Carolina to be an attractive destination because, as another commentator observed, there they could "live in comparative innocence, free from the rigid requirements of antiquated religious limitations" in the tolerant atmosphere created by the Charters and Fundamental Constitutions.[70]

Quakers also generally found early South Carolina a welcoming environment.[71] In a 1675 letter to Andrew Percivall, the influential proprietor Lord Shaftesbury announced that a group of Quakers was planning to settle in the colony and that Percivall should "be very kind to them and give them all the assistance you can in the choice of a Place, or anything else that may conduce to theire convenient settlement[.] For they are people I have a great Regard to and am obliged to care of."[72] By contrast Mary Fisher (later Mary Fisher Crosse), who became a prominent Quaker preacher, and her companion Anne Austin, were arrested, banned from the province, and had their books burned when they arrived in Boston as ship passengers in 1656.[73] In an attempt to provide a clearer legal basis for acting against Quakers, Boston authorities passed a statute in 1656 banning Quakers, ordering their publications destroyed, and punishing those who defended them.[74] This was followed by the passage by a narrow vote of a controversial 1658 law banishing all Quakers from the province with the death penalty imposed on those who refused to leave.[75] Inhabitants who defended Quakers or criticized the persecution of Quakers were also subject to banishment enforced with a death penalty.[76] This law was far from a dead letter. In 1659–61 prominent Quakers William Robinson, Marmaduke Stevenson, Mary Dyer, and William Leddra refused to accept banishment, defied the law, and were executed.[77] They continued to preach from the gallows immediately before their execution. William Robinson's final words were "I suffer for Christ, in whom I live, and for whom I die."[78]

Why did a group now viewed as having made so many positive contributions inspire such venom from the civil and ecclesiastical establishment of the mid-seventeenth century? Twentieth-century Quaker philosopher D. Elton Trueblood offers this explanation: "the new breed of preachers were disturbers of the peace. They spoke in church services where they had captive audiences, they shocked officials by treating them as equals rather than with obsequious manners, they treated women as the equals of men, they sang in prison, and they made effective witness behind prison walls."[79] The harsh Boston approach was not followed in South Carolina. The Fundamental Constitution of July 21, 1669, beckoned to the Quakers by a provision that accommodated their aversion to oaths by permitting the organization of churches that met basic monotheistic belief standards so long as they provided some "Sensible way" for their members in legal proceedings to "bear witness to truth" even though it was not an oath symbolized by "Kissing the Gospel" or "holding up the hand."[80]

The Quakers had a well-developed sense of religious freedom and separation of church and state. Writing in 1678, Quaker leader Robert Barclay observed that since "God hath assumed to himself the power and dominion of the conscience," any attempt by civil authorities to coerce beliefs by severe punishments "proceedeth from the spirit of Cain."[81] Religious truth was an inward revelation by the spirit that could not be subjected to external tests from the government or others.[82]

Their pacifist beliefs were accommodated, at least for a time.[83] In 1695–96 Gov. John Archdale, himself a Quaker, engineered the passage of an act that gave him discretion to exempt from compulsory militia duties Quakers who "refuse to beare armes upon a conscientious principle of religion."[84] But this exemption was absent from the 1703 act, which required militia commanders to summon "all and every the inhabitants within the limits of his or their respective company, from the age of sixteen to sixty to appear, completely armed."[85] The act made no mention of the excusal of Quaker members but did exempt "Ministers of the Gospel and their clerks," a term broad enough to include Quaker ministers.[86] The enforcement of compulsory attendance tightened when the security of the colony was threatened. In the Yamassee War various Indian tribes combined forces against the colonists. Quaker Thomas Kimberley reported to the Charleston Meeting in 1719 that in 1716 "in the time of the Indian War," a Captain Green had ordered goods valued at 30 pounds seized as satisfaction of a fifty shilling fine.[87] Kimberley was fined again for failure to bear arms in 1717 with a similar seizure of goods occurring when he failed to pay.[88] But generally the early history of the colony was one of tolerance toward Quakers, Huguenots, and others who sought refuge. Later, toward the end of the eighteenth century and the beginning of the nineteenth, as the Quakers' antislavery position hardened and the society surrounding them became more adamant in defending the institution, the Quakers' situation became untenable because they refused to compromise with what they had come to consider an evil. The result was that by 1807 the Quakers had largely left the state for Ohio and other more hospitable locations.[89]

Robert St. John has observed that although the Fundamental Constitutions did set broad belief standards for those who wished to be a freeman in Carolina—and although all persons above seventeen were expected to choose a church in order to be eligible for places of honor and profit—a generous ambit was still left for individual differences of belief. St. John further noted that, even though the message of tolerance embodied in the Fundamental Constitutions was in part motivated by the missionary goal of gently nudging non-Christians toward conversion, the documents still created an atmosphere of tolerance.[90]

But the Charters and Fundamental Constitutions proceeded on the dubious assumption that religious freedom could exist without separation of church and state. This is demonstrated by the fact that these basic documents set Christian missionary goals as one of the pivotal purposes of colonization.[91] Indeed the Charter of 1663 noted that one of the reasons for the grant to the Lords Proprietors was that they were "excited with a laudable and pious zeal for the propagation of the Christian Faith" as well as by a desire to enlarge the King's empire.[92] Such religious goals commonly formed a part of colonial charters. The 1606 Charter of Virginia declared that one of the purposes of the settlement was "propagating of *Christian* Religion to such people as yet live in the Darkness and Miserable Ignorance of the true Knowledge and Worship of God."[93] Similarly, the Maryland Charter issued to Caecilius Calvert, Baron of Baltimore, in 1632, stated that one reason for its promulgation was the need to colonize the land because it was then "occupied by Savages, having no knowledge of the Divine Being."[94] The language in the 1681 Pennsylvania Charter granted to William Penn also combined the practical goals of economic and political empire building with devout purposes. Charles II commended Penn for his desire "to enlarge our *English* Empire, and promote such useful comodities as may bee of Benefit to us and Our Dominions, as also to reduce the savage Natives by gentle and just manners to the Love of Civil Societie and Christian Religion."[95] With similar proselytizing goals in the Carolina Charter and the preference for the Church of England that permeated the Fundamental Constitutions existing alongside the message of tolerance found in the same documents, a tug of war of competing principles was launched, with the Church of England establishment being the immediate victor but with religious freedom being the ultimate winner when its vigorous exercise was found to be incompatible with a pervasive establishment.[96]

The Established Church:
Caught in a Regulatory Web

The Church of England was the favorite of the law, receiving both ideological and fiscal support of the government. But it paid a steep price by forfeiting much of its freedom of decision making for a dense maze of regulations. An intricate 1704 law—declared null and void by the Queen in Council and repealed and replaced in 1706 by another complex law—shows the extent to which the church became the instrument rather than the partner of government.[97] The statute's goal was to found "a well grounded Christian commonwealth."[98] The statute dictated the content of Church of England services: the Book of Common Prayer, the Psalms of David, and the morning and evening prayers had to be read in every established church.[99] No tolerance was shown for innovative modes of worship in established churches. Church growth was on a legal leash: parish boundaries, the creation of new parishes, and the construction of new churches were all controlled by statute.[100] Primacy of civil authority over religion was seen in the fact that the highest power in church governance was not a group of local or London-based clergymen, but laymen with political clout who were named in the statute.[101] This colony-wide group of church commissioners exercised considerable sway over the composition of the clergy. Even though church rectors were elected by parish residents who were both Church of England members and taxpayers, the rectors could be dismissed only by the commissioners, who held a hearing on a complaint by nine respectable members of the parish.[102] This pervasive involvement of civil government authorities in church affairs provoked complaints by church authorities in London, who viewed the lay commissioners as rivals who were eroding their power.[103]

Impetus for the grant of clergy-removal powers to the commission was given by the case of Dr. Edward Marston, minister of St. Philip's Church in Charleston, whose stinging criticism of legislative and executive officials in sermons and correspondence created intense dislike of him by the targets of his barbs.[104] Marston so incensed the House by impugning its honor that in 1704 it ordered him to present his sermon notes for examination. When he refused, the House censured him, ordered his salary stopped, and, finally, had him brought before the lay commission, which "removed his living."[105] The Marston case dramatically illustrates the treacherous path that had to be trod by a minister of the established church who sought to be a moral critic of the government on which the church was dependent. It is notable that the House was especially infuriated when Marston insisted that his commission came from God not the legislature even though the latter paid his 150 pound per year salary.[106] This is an example of the machinery of an establishment being more preoccupied with the preening of secular officials than with spiritual duties.

Despite these elaborate controls over church personnel, dissent remained. The Reverend George Whitefield was an ordained Anglican priest who became a leader of the Methodist faction that was growing within the Church of England. In 1740 a tribunal of Anglican priests was convened to hear charges by the Reverend Alexander Garden of St. Philip's Church in Charleston that Whitefield had conducted services without using the authorized Book of Common Prayer and that he had preached that salvation could be gained by a sudden conversion without living a life of good works. In a sharp exchange of letters Whitefield maintained that good works flowed from faith but were not a precondition to the justification of a person's soul, while Garden argued that good works must both precede and follow faith.[107] In a 1740 sermon defending Whitefield, Josiah Smith pointed out that Whitefield argued against the idea of justification through good works because this would mean a person's own efforts rather than God's grace had saved him.[108] Whitefield questioned the authority and impartiality of the tribunal. The church court concluded that Whitefield had forsaken the official doctrine he had vowed to obey when he became a priest, and it ordered him suspended as a Church of England priest.

Whitefield ignored the judgment as well as the tribunal and continued his evangelism throughout the colonies, including occasional forays into South Carolina.[109] In January 1741 Whitefield was called before a civil court to answer charges that he had been guilty of editing a statement in which Hugh Bryan had libeled the established clergy. This is one example of the kind of harassment that can occur when civil power takes sides in an essentially religious quarrel. Far from being intimidated by the charge, Whitefield wrote in his journal, "My soul rejoices in it."[110]

Benjamin Franklin heard Whitefield preach on several occasions when the evangelist visited Philadelphia. In his *Autobiography* (1868) Franklin described the impact of Whitefield's preaching on that city: "From being thoughtless or indifferent about religion, it seemed as if all the world were growing religious, so that one could not walk through the town in an evening without hearing psalms sung in different families of every street."[111] The evangelical challenge to the establishment was more than a theological dispute. It created an atmosphere for challenging entrenched authority, whether the established church, the civil government, or even the slave-based economy. Whitefield disciples Jonathan and Hugh Bryan argued passionately for reform in the treatment of slaves, including the need to give them instruction in Christianity.[112] This created fear among the planters that biblical imagery would create ambitions for freedom among the slaves, possibly sparking an insurrection.[113] Hugh Bryan's conduct was especially frightening to slaveholders. In the early 1740s, after undergoing a mystical experience that he believed called him to be a prophet, he predicted that God's wrath, provoked by owners' withholding Christianity from slaves and mistreating them, would result in destruction of much of the colony by apocalyptic vengeance.[114] Coming shortly after the Stono Rebellion of 1739, this message was especially frightening to slaveholders.[115] The Bryans soon abandoned this public challenge to the system in favor of privately giving Christian education to their own slaves.[116] This gave the slaves a measure of religious freedom.[117] The Bryans' intention was not to free the slaves but to convert them to Christianity and improve their condition.[118] The evangelicals were more prone to chart an independent course than the established church not only because of their emphasis on individual conversion experiences and less structured organization, but also because they were not beholden to the state's fiscal support. That support had a downside.

The fiscal resources of the civil government fueled the expansion of the established church, but the price was statutory specification of the mode of church governance and of the pace and direction of church growth. The 1704 statute specified the broad areas in which new churches were to be created, but the exact location was to be decided by the commissioners with the advice of Church of England followers in the area.[119] The commissioners had the power to accept contributions for building new churches. If these were inadequate, the commissioners could use public treasury funds for a project.[120] If public treasury funds were insufficient to pay ministers of the established church, the commissioners could levy an additional tax for that purpose.[121] Gifts and charges due the church were the first source of funds for church repairs. If these were inadequate, the church vestry could assess a tax on "*all* and *every* the inhabitants, owners and occupiers of lands, tenements and hereditaments, or any personal estate" (emphasis added).[122]

Thus the burden was shared by nonadherents of the established church, who might have preferred to devote the money to their own churches or to secular purposes. One historian of the Huguenots who settled in Carolina, after an interim in England, concluded that one reason their Calvinist churches were absorbed into the Church of England was that maintaining a separate existence for their churches was not economically feasible. They did not have sufficient resources both to pay taxes supporting the Church of England and to make contributions for the support of their own congregations.[123] Since the board of a Church of England congregation was in effect the delegatee of the civil government's taxing authority, it is not surprising that the 1704 statute prescribed the form of church governance. Each established church was to have a vestry (a policy-making board of nine elected members) and two wardens, who were given practical tasks such as keeping the church in good repair.[124] The right to vote on vestrymen was restricted to those who met the three standards of being inhabitants of the parish, followers of the Church of England, and taxpayers.[125] Thus not everyone subject to the vestry taxes could have a say in selecting the board's members. So comprehensive was the statute, that it even set the dates of important vestry meetings.[126] Nothing was left to chance. The tolerance found in some portions of the Charters and Fundamental Constitutions was overlaid by a dense network of regulations that gave scant room for innovation even by the favored denomination.

So intimate was the legal relationship between the established church and the civil governments that decisions concerning the distribution of power or responsibility in the religious sphere could affect the balance of secular power and vice versa. This was especially true with regard to parish boundaries since the parish served not only as a religious unit but also as the basis for legislative representation. Parish boundary changes might be needed to improve the churches' ministry, but they might be problematic because they could upset the political balance of power.[127] Before its repeal, the 1704 act was supplemented by another law the same year, which set election procedures for vestrymen and wardens.[128]

Intense objections to the 1704 law's grant of sweeping and arbitrary power to the lay commissioners to remove ministers summarily for a variety of offenses—ranging from immorality to quarrels with their parishioners—were lodged in a petition from merchant Joseph Boone and other inhabitants of Carolina to the House of Lords, which condemned the law as an egregious usurpation of power. The House of Lords argued that this law, and the law excluding Protestant dissenters from the assembly,[129] not only exceeded the powers granted in the Charter and discouraged trade with Carolina but also harmed religion with its heavy-handed tactics, presumably by making it appear to be a mere political tool rather than an independent spiritual force. After the House of Lords conveyed these objections to the queen on March 12, 1705, a Privy Council order was issued on June 10, 1706, declaring the law null and void and threatening legal proceedings to revoke the Charter.[130] This none-too-subtle rebuke resulted in repeal of the law by the colonial legislature. The 1706 statute replacing the original 1704 law, reaffirmed the Church of England establishment, set the Book of Common Prayer as the spiritual standard, and gave authority to a province-wide lay commission, but the new law deleted the controversial provision that had given the commissioners the essentially ecclesiastical power of removing incumbent ministers on petition of church members and vestrymen.[131] In addition to delineating parish boundaries, the 1706 law tightened government fiscal controls of religion by setting a limit on the sums commissioners could take from the treasury to finish church buildings. It also determined the salaries of the rectors and created a system by which all parish inhabitants could be taxed to compensate Church of England priests specified in the act.[132] Taxpayers who balked at the levy could have their goods seized and sold.[133] The 1706 statute provided for modest diversity by permitting rectors in parishes with largely French membership to use a version of the Book of Common Prayer in their native language.[134]

The incessant revision, tinkering with, and supplementation of laws in this area continued with a 1712 statute.[135] This comprehensive statute redefined the authority of the church commissioners, vestry, and wardens; determined the compensation of priests; delineated parish boundaries; and created a provincial library, specifying that it was to be located in the St. Philip's parsonage.[136] This detailed act even defined the circumstances under which the books could be used.[137] This phantasmagoria of increasingly weblike church regulations must have squeezed the juices of spiritual creativity dry. Perhaps that was their purpose. At any rate the established church paid a heavy price in lost independence.

An examination of the church commissioners' minutes from 1717 to 1742 shows the significant involvement of civil government with church affairs.[138] Some members of the commission had substantial power in the secular government. For example, minutes for the October 1, 1717, meeting reflect the election of Gov. Robert Johnson as president of the commission and note that Chief Justice Nicholas Trott was in attendance as a commissioner.[139] The intertwining of church and political hierarchies was increased when the Reverend Alexander Garden, minister of St. Philip's and commissary of the bishop of London, sat as a commission member.[140] The commission had its finger on the financial pulse of the established church. Minutes for 1717 and 1722 note that the commission approved the allocation of funds for the annual expenses of particular churches.[141] After this intimate involvement with fiscal affairs of individual churches during the early years covered by the minute book, the commission's interest in financial matters focused more on province-wide issues, such as granting a request by the clergy that their salaries be paid in "proclamation money" according to a rate of exchange with the currency that was to be set by the commission.[142] One power exercised by the commission was fraught with political significance. The commission had the responsibility of resolving parish boundary disputes, which—because of the use of parishes as election units—had implications for the exercise of secular as well as religious power.[143] Beginning in 1739 the commission addressed a boundary dispute involving St. Philip's and St. James's Goose Creek.[144]

Perhaps the most frequently recurring items on the commission agenda were requests from Church of England congregations that the commission order the holding of an election to choose a minister for the congregation. Even though the 1717–42 minutes do not reveal commission involvement in the removal of ministers, a controversial practice that had helped fuel opposition to the 1704 church law discussed above,[145] the commission was often involved in the selection process.[146] This involvement was not as initiator of the selection process, or as ultimate decision maker, but as a group whose permission was needed before an election could be held and whose confirmation was needed after the congregation had acted. A few examples will illustrate the commission's role. At a November 22, 1717, meeting the commission granted the request of the vestry of St. Philip's in Charleston that a precept for the election of a minister be issued.[147] The commission order described those who were entitled to vote: inhabitants of the parish who conformed to the Church of England and were freeholders or were taxpayers in some other capacity.[148] The order set the day for the election and required that notice be published at the church on the two Sundays immediately preceding the election.[149] The election results were reported to the commission.[150] As a prelude to issuing an order for a 1718 election at Christ Church that had been requested by its vestry, the commission asked the candidate to present his credentials.[151] The commission often examined the credentials of Church of England ministers on their arrival in the province.[152] When election results were returned to the commission showing that the candidate was successful, the minutes would often contain an entry that since no objection had been made to the election, the results were "ratified and confirmed."[153]

Despite its broad-ranging activities, it is significant that the commission minutes do not reflect any decision making concerning churches that were not Church of England established congregations. However, such monocular attention from a group dominated by politically powerful laymen carried significant risks for the religious groups whose fate was influenced by the commission's decisions. Among these risks was a possibility that decisions concerning them could be motivated more by political than spiritual considerations. Looking back at the movement for disestablishment throughout the country, the U.S. Supreme Court in 1970 and 1971 decisions labeled such "active involvement of the sovereign in religious activity" as one of the "main evils" against which disestablishment was directed.[154]

When a government establishes and financially aids a church, it can find itself diverting funds from uses of benefit to the public in general to the needs of the preferred church. When the church shares in the state's fiscal bounty, it may find itself in unseemly competition with secular uses for a larger share of the fiscal pie. In 1757 a South Carolina statute sought to bolster an inadequate appropriation for finishing a steeple and spire at St. Michael's by diverting funds from construction of a beacon near Charleston Harbor.[155] The funds came from sources that, from a latter-day perspective, would be considered morally compromising: taxes on the importation of slaves and liquor.[156]

The government was not always a benign benefactor of the church; sometimes it was a hard-nosed creditor. A 1768 statute provided an interest-free loan, repayable in three years, rather than a grant for constructing a new parsonage at St. Michael's.[157] Although the terms were generous, the creditors' remedy in case of default was harsh; the public treasurer could sell the church pews.[158]

In addition to financial support and ideological endorsement of its beliefs, a third dimension existed in the relationship of an established church to the state: it served as the instrument for the performance of certain state functions. In South Carolina the established church played important roles with regard to education, aid to the poor, and the conduct of elections.[159] The church's educational role was a logical extension of its traditional responsibility for instruction in ethical standards. The

Society for Propagating the Gospel in Foreign Parts did pioneering work in organizing schools in eighteenth-century South Carolina.[160] The comprehensive 1712 church law, discussed above, is an example of the use of the church to dispense knowledge, providing for a provincial library and stipulating that it be located in St. Philip's.[161] When the government undertook the responsibility of educating indigent children in a 1710 statute, it did so in a manner that recognized the educational leadership of the established church. In addition to being knowledgeable in Latin and Greek, the instructor had to be a member of the Church of England, and religious instruction was required as well as art, science, and grammar.[162]

The role assigned the established church in administering government assistance to the indigent was a logical projection of the church's biblical duty to minister to the poor.[163] A 1712 statute assigned the church vestries the duty to raise and distribute aid to the poor.[164] The vestries were directed to nominate two overseers for the poor, who were to share with the church wardens the task of distributing the aid. Like its 1704 predecessor, the 1712 law spread the financial burden for Church of England programs beyond the Anglican community. If funds from fines and gifts designated for the poor fell short, the vestry could name three assessors to impose a tax "equally upon the estates real and personal of *all* and every the inhabitants, owners and occupiers of lands tenements and hereditaments, or any personal estate, within the several parishes" (emphasis added).[165] As in the case of the church-repair assessments mentioned above, the use of the word *all* in the statute meant that non-Anglicans were subject to the tax even though they could not participate in choosing the vestrymen who could initiate it.[166]

Church officials were assigned the task of conducting elections, and parishes served as the unit of legislative representation as well as determining the boundaries of a spiritual community.[167] This responsibility of ensuring honest elections was a natural coordinate to the church's traditional role in setting standards of probity. With the church being a key instrumentality for delivering government services such as education, aid to the poor and the conduct of elections, and with the government granting fiscal support and ideological endorsement to the established church, it is not surprising that religion played a role in the qualifications to participate in the political process as an officeholder or voter.

Religious Qualifications for Political Participation

Attributing superior religious wisdom to a particular denomination can lead to attributing superior governmental judgment to the same group, especially if doing so also serves practical political goals. Such an approach underlay a 1704 act that drove Protestant dissenters from the Commons House of Assembly.[168] This law stipulated that all persons elected to Commons who had not participated in the rite of the Lord's Supper according to the ritual of the Church of England should do so in a public ceremony immediately after worship; certification of such participation should be given by the minister and two witnesses and presented to the speaker in an open session of the assembly.[169] As an alternative, a Church of England member who did not think he was spiritually prepared to participate in the sacrament at that time could attest that he was regular in church attendance, believed in the rite of the Lord's Supper, was a faithful adherent of the Church of England, and would diligently work for its interest in the legislature.[170] The preamble to the act attempted to strike a lofty tone by claiming "that the admitting [into the legislature] of persons of different persuasions and interest in matters of religion . . . hath often caused great contentions and animosities in this Province, and hath very much obstructed publick business."[171] One commentator has described more mundane political maneuvering that led to passage of the law.[172] Although a comfortable equilibrium of power between the Church of England adherents and Dissenters had existed from 1670 to 1700, this balance was disturbed when Queen Anne began her reign and started energetically to press Anglican interests. The waters were further roiled when Lord John Granville, the palatine (leading proprietor), tried to manipulate both factions to his advantage.[173] The situation became even more tense when Gov. James Moore maneuvered to undermine his opponents in the assembly, largely Dissenters, by charging that they were trying to corner the trade with the Indians. The Dissenters answered with similar charges against Moore. The feud grew bitter when the governor found that Dissenters were blocking appropriations for his expedition to repulse a Spanish threat from Florida. The quarrel became even more virulent under Moore's successor, Nathaniel Johnson, who became determined to remove the Dissenter blight from the assembly. He resorted to a parliamentary trick to obtain passage of the 1704 statute excluding from Commons all who could not certify that they had participated in the Lord's Supper in accordance with the Church of England ritual. He quickly called the Commons House of Assembly into a special session and hurried the bill's passage before the Dissenters arrived to cast their vote.[174] The covert nature of this ploy furnished ammunition for those seeking to have the statute voided. Opponents of the measure hired Daniel Defoe, later author of the novel *Robinson Crusoe* (1719), who was then a literary mercenary, to use his verbal swordsmanship to argue for reversal of the law.

In *Case of the Protestant Dissenters in Carolina* (1706) Defoe argued that liberty of conscience was the most important freedom because it related to one's fate in the afterlife.[175] Every man should be free to believe and act as he sees fit so long as he does not disturb the public peace.[176] Any system by which a legal preference is given to any particular religion undermines the freedom of all, including followers of the favored religion since the preference could shift as the political tides change and a newly favored group uses the government to retaliate against those who were previously preferred. Defoe argued that the only certain protection for any religion was "Universal and Absolute Toleration" of all peaceful denominations.[177] Eligibility for a seat in Commons was akin to a property right that had vested in the Dissenters by virtue of their reliance on earlier standards making them qualified for such seats. Disqualifying the Dissenters had stripped them of their dignity, had made them objects of derision, and had inspired mob attacks on the Dissenter members of the Commons who were thought to have undermined the policies of the executive branch.[178] Defoe argued that, since all rights are interrelated, banning Dissenters from the assembly could lead to the demise of their right to vote and property rights lest these be the instruments by which the Dissenters regained parliamentary power.[179] The Dissenters had not been antagonistic to the Church of England and did not deserve such shabby treatment. In 1698 Gov. Joseph Blake, a Dissenter, had encouraged Anglican priests to settle in the colony and Dissenter members of the legislature had supported these efforts.[180] Such generosity had been the product of the previous system of mutual tolerance, which should be resumed. Defoe made practical arguments that might appeal to the economic self-interest of those whose influence could bring about repeal of the statute. Religious strife was bad for trade. It diverted attention from the creation of wealth. The Dissenters composed about two-thirds of the population of the colony, including some of its wealthiest inhabitants. Creating a hostile climate that might drive them out of the colony would cripple the economy.[181] Religious nonconformists would be discouraged from settling in Carolina.

Not just the exclusionary act but the entire system of intermingling secular and spiritual power earned Defoe's ire. Another 1704 law gave too much power over church affairs to the province-wide board of lay commissioners.[182] A minister beholden to civil authorities for his job, his salary, and approval of expansion plans for his church would be unlikely to comment candidly on the morality of his benefactors' conduct.

Defoe argued that the exclusionary act contravened the broad-gauged tolerance of the Fundamental Constitutions and the Charters. Even though the Fundamental Constitutions had not been ratified by the people at large, they had been accepted by each colonist as a condition of settlement and were as binding on the proprietors as on the colonists.[183] The exclusionary act was unconstitutional since it had not been passed according to the procedure set in the Charter of March 24, 1663, which stipulated that new laws could be passed only "with the advice, assent and approbation of the Freemen of the said Province, or of the greater part of them, or of their Delegates or Deputies."[184] A law adopted by a mere rump faction of the legislature fell short of those standards. Since the Charters had been granted to the proprietors on the condition that they practice religious tolerance, the intolerance of the exclusionary act jeopardized the continued legitimacy of the proprietors' holdings.[185]

The legal issue was joined when a Carolina merchant petitioned the House of Lords in England to invalidate the exclusion of Dissenters from the legislature. The petition contended that: (1) the statute had not been passed according to correct procedure because (a) the advice and consent of the freemen or their delegates had not been obtained as required by the 1663 Charter, (b) only a partisan fragment of the legislature had had an opportunity to vote on it, and (c) many members of the rump faction that had passed the law had been illegally elected at a 1703 contest in which unqualified voters had participated; (2) to be valid a law had to be in accord with sound reason and the customs of England, but the statute defied reason by excluding from the assembly a majority of the population; and (3) the proprietors usurped the role of the sovereign by sanctioning a law contrary to the king's Charter. According to the merchant's petition, an even more fundamental defect of the statute was that it broke the promise made to settlers in the Charters and Fundamental Constitutions of relief from Old World religious oppression in Carolina. Even if the colonists were not direct parties to the Charters, they were beneficiaries of the promises in them and had relied on them in deciding to come to, or stay in, the colony.

The House of Lords endorsed the petition in an address to Queen Anne. In addition to accepting the petition's assertions that the exclusion law was contrary to English customs and the Charters, the House of Lords gave practical reasons why the law was bad policy: it would frighten away potential settlers, deter trade, and transform a vigorous economy into a wasteland. On a less mundane level the House of Lords concluded that the law might undermine religion and encourage atheism, presumably because it was such a cynical political ploy hiding behind a religious facade. The queen responded at first with regal vagueness: "I Thank the House for Laying these Matters so plainly before Me; I am very Sensible of what Great Consequence the Plantations are to England, and will do all that is in My Power to Relieve My Subjects in Carolina, and to Protect them in their just Rights."[186]

This statement was followed by a June 10, 1706, order by the Queen in Council, which declared the exclusion act and the 1704 church act null and void.[187] Since the queen's order in council threatened legal action to revoke the charter, enormous pressure was placed on provincial authorities to repeal the law.[188] The exclusionary law was repealed in a 1706 statute, and the Dissenters returned to their role as a potent political force.[189]

Ironically, during the last decade of the seventeenth century and the first two years of the eighteenth century, the Dissenters had led an effort to block Huguenot voting out of fear that this group of French Protestants would be a pivotal swing vote that could throw elections to the rival Church of England party.[190] The anti-Huguenot bias was spawned by a combination of political, religious, language, and nationality differences, which set them apart from British settlers.[191] The proprietors sought to alleviate this prejudice by passage of an act during the 1696–97 assembly that granted to aliens who petitioned the government and swore allegiance to the king the same rights as those born of English parentage, including the right of free exercise of religion to all Christians, except "papists."[192] A 1705 law ensured aliens that met age, residency, and property-holding standards the right to vote, but it prohibited their membership in the General Assembly.[193] However, as Jon Butler has observed, "by the 1720s Huguenots were being elected regularly to the Assembly."[194]

Even though repeal of the ban on Protestant dissenter service in the legislature signaled a growing consensus behind a broader range of participants in the governing process, the political scene still had a decidedly Christian, and sometimes a Protestant, character. This quality is found in laws passed both before and after the repeal. In 1702 the Commons House of Assembly voted in the affirmative on the question of "whether Roman Catholics have Right to Vote in Elections of members of Assembly."[195] However, one commentator asserts that this resolution was not passed by a properly constituted assembly because (1) it consisted only of Dissenters because the Church of England party had withdrawn, (2) the resolution did not represent the general opinion in the colony, and (3) it was inconsistent with other official positions on the issue.[196] Whatever the motive for the resolution, it was probably not tolerance but political maneuvering. At the same session in which the pro-Catholic resolution was passed, the assembly issued a directive commanding a group of voters with predominantly French names, presumably Huguenots, to appear before the Grand Committee to respond to allegations that they had voted illegally as aliens who had not registered the certificates necessary to become qualified voters.[197]

A 1716 law, repealed in 1718 by the proprietors, required that voters be Christians.[198] The law did not explicitly require that legislators be Christians but did stipulate that they must swear on the holy evangelists that they met the property ownership requirements for service.[199] A 1721 act that replaced it also required that voters be Christian and that legislators swear on the holy evangelists.[200] A tug of war was fought over the requirement of a 1745 law that legislators swear on the "holy evangelist" that they had met the standards for their office.[201] Some Protestant dissenters objected to this form of oath and pressed for a change, which was made in a 1747 law admitting that the earlier provision had kept "many Protestant dissenters in the Province of good estates and sufficient abilitys" from serving in the legislature even though they had faithfully performed the duties of citizenship, such as jury service.[202] The new law permitted them to take an oath "according to the form of their profession."[203] Even though this law may have attempted to stop an internecine war of oaths among Protestants, it did not signal the end of religious requirements for voting or holding office. A 1759 law lent a private-club air to the voting list. To qualify to vote for members of the General Assembly, one had to be a free white male Protestant of at least twenty-one years of age who had resided in the colony for at least a year prior to issuance of the election notice and the owner of a freehold estate worth at least sixty pounds.[204] The legislators themselves also had to be Protestants, and the property holdings they had to have approached the princely, presumably as a means of weeding out those who might be inclined to high taxation and promiscuous government spending. The legislator was required to have "a settled plantation or a free-hold estate of at least five hundred acres of land and twenty slaves over and above what he shall owe" or have houses, town lots, or other land valued at a thousand pounds more than his debts.[205] On December 26, 1761, the Commons House of Assembly received notice from Gov. Thomas Boone that the 1759 statute had been disallowed by the king on advice of the Privy Council.[206] The Assembly elected under the disallowed law was dissolved.[207] However, since the law is listed by Statutes At Large editor Thomas Cooper as having passed all of the provincial stages of the legislative process, including passage by the House and Council and assent of the governor, the law probably reflected local attitudes if not those in England.[208]

The commitment to religious tolerance in colonial South Carolina was uneven; periods of tolerance were followed by periods of rigidity; then the pendulum would swing back again and again. The problem of the legislator's oath on the holy evangelists continued to bedevil some sects even in the decade just before the Revolutionary War. In a December 23, 1683, letter to Friends in Charleston, George Fox, founder of the Quakers (Society of Friends), admonished them that "My desire is, that you may prize your liberty, both natural and spiritual, and the favour that the Lord hath given you, that your yea is taken instead of an oath; and that you do serve both in assemblies, juries and other offices, without swearing, according to the doctrine of Christ: which is a great thing, worth prizing."[209] This philosophy is based on Matthew 5: 33–35, which states: "again, ye have heard that it hath been said by them of old time, Thou shalt not forswear thyself, but shalt perform unto the Lord thine oaths; But I say unto you, Swear not at all; neither by heaven; for it is God's throne. Nor by the earth; for it is his footstool: neither by Jerusalem; for it is the city of the Great King."[210]

A dramatic confrontation, with religious freedom the loser, occurred in 1766 with regard to Samuel Wylly (or Wyly), a respected Quaker gentleman who had been elected to represent St. Mark's parish.[211] The journals of the Commons House of Assembly for January 25, 1766, noted that when he was asked to take the oath "Mr. Wylly being one of the People called Quakers declared he could not take the oath on the Holy Evangelists without doing a violence to his conscience."[212] This recalcitrance prompted passage of a resolution denying Wylly his seat, probably because reform laws such as the 1747 statute were disallowed by the king, and the legislature had to follow the old oath on the holy evangelist procedure of the 1721 election law.[213] Not only was Wylly denied his seat; those who voted for him were denied their choice of representative.

Such oath requirements followed the tradition of the infamous English Test Act of 1677, which not only disqualified papists from sitting in Parliament but also required that before taking his seat a member of Parliament had to take an oath renouncing belief in the adoration of the Virgin Mary and the transubstantiation of the bread and wine of the Lord's Supper into the body and blood of Christ. Not only did the statute bar someone who refused to take the oath from Parliament, it also barred him from other public offices, acting as a guardian of a child or as estate executor, suing in court, or receiving a gift or legacy.[214]

Even though the election laws insisted that the legislators be Christian and the holy evangelists oaths had a New Testament focus, as the Revolutionary War approached and talented men were needed for public service regardless of their religion, such restrictions did not always control. Francis Salvador (1747–1776) was born in London into a family of Portuguese Jewish descent. His father had been a wealthy merchant, but after business losses young Salvador moved to South Carolina, where he assumed management of his father-in-law's land and acquired extensive holdings of his own. The *Biographical Directory of the South Carolina House of Representatives* credits him with being the first Jewish member of the legislature.[215] In 1775 he was elected to represent the Ninety Six District in the First Provincial Congress and again was chosen for the Second Provincial Congress (1775–76) and the First General

Assembly in 1776.[216] He was active in a wide range of public services, including negotiations with the Indians and militia service in the Cherokee campaign, and died of battle wounds in 1776.[217] Earlier, in 1762, Moses Lindo, a Jew who migrated from London, was appointed by Gov. Thomas Boone, on the recommendation of prominent citizens and officials, to be surveyor and inspector general of indigo, a position that involved the grading of the product for the guidance of customers.[218]

The shattering of the sense of political community caused by such laws as the English Test Act, the exclusion of Protestant dissenters, and the requirements that legislators swear on the holy evangelists before they could take office may have prompted Charles Pinckney, an influential South Carolina delegate to the Federal Constitutional Convention, to propose on August 20, 1787, the insertion in the U.S. Constitution of a provision that stipulated, "No religious test or qualification shall ever be annexed to any oath of office under authority of the U.S."[219] On August 30, 1787, he broadened the language of his proposal so that it would state "but no religious test shall ever be required as a qualification to any office or public trust under the authority of the U. States."[220] With only minor changes in language, this provision became Article 6, section 3, of the U.S. Constitution.[221] Not only do religious qualifications for public office collide with the religious freedom of the would-be officeholder, they are also antithetical to democratic debate by presuming certain political doctrines to be divinely ordained and thus beyond challenge.

Establishment and the Lord's Day

The establishment not only affected the structure and functions of both church and state, it also affected the personal routine of individuals, especially the way they spent Sunday. South Carolina's early Sunday laws followed the example of a 1677 English law, the Sunday Observance Act.[222] This law required everyone to spend the "Lords day" in "the dutyes of piety and true religion"; forbade "worldly labour" or any other "ordinary calling upon the Lords day" except for works of "necessity and charity"; and mandated that "noe person or persons whatsoever shall publickly cry shew forth or expose to sale wares merchandizes, fruit, herbs goods or chattel's whatsoever upon the Lords day."[223] Sunday travel was also forbidden except in extraordinary occasions when permission could be obtained from the justice of the peace.[224] Practical necessity forced relaxation of the monocular focus on religion on Sunday by permitting families to prepare meals and "inns cookeshops or victualling houses" to sell food "for such as otherwise cannot be provided" and by permitting perishable items, such as milk, to be sold early in the morning or late in the afternoon, presumably at times that would not conflict with church services.[225] Service of legal process could not be made on Sundays except for treason, felony, or breach of peace, all of which were offenses that sometimes required swift action to avoid the offender's flight or the commission of fresh wrongs.[226] Church and state authority intermingled in the enforcement of the law; church wardens as well as civil officers could seize goods sold on Sunday.[227]

A 1691 South Carolina Sunday law took an approach similar to this English precedent.[228] It emphasized the duty to spend Sunday in worship rather than in the idle and profane pursuit of pleasure. It stated:

> Forasmuch as there is nothing more acceptable to Almighty God than the true sincere performance of and obedience to the most divine service and worship, which although at all times, yet chiefly upon the Lord's Day, commonly called Sunday, ought soe to be done, but instead thereof many idle, loose and disorderly people doe wilfully profane the same in tipling, shooteing, gameing, and many other vicious exercises, pastimes and meetings, whereby ignorance prevails and the just judgement of Almighty God may reasonably be expected to fall upon this land if the same by some good orders be not prevented.[229]

This harsh judgment could be avoided if the people spent the Lord's Day in "exercising themselves of piety and true religion."[230] "Worldly labour," the sale of goods, and travel were forbidden on Sunday.[231] Intoxicating beverages could not be sold on Sunday "unless it [was] for necessary occasions for lodgers or sojourners."[232] The 1691 law also contained religiously based morality standards that applied to every day conduct, not just Sunday deportment. The act observed that drunkenness was growing widespread in the province; since it was "the roote and foundation of many other enormous sins," those guilty of the offense were subject to being fined five shillings.[233] Because "profane swearing and curseing [were] forbidden by the word of God," those guilty of that offense would be fined "seaven pence halfepenny" for each "oath or curse."[234] Enforcement mechanisms grew more draconian. In addition to the traditional sanction of seizure and sale of goods that had been marketed on Sunday, the 1691 statute provided for the humiliation of those who could not pay fines by having them placed in the public stocks for two hours and encouraged people to watch their neighbors closely by providing for diversion of one-third of a fine or the sales price of forfeited goods to those who informed on an offender if the magistrate thought such a reward to be justifiable.[235] But the South Carolina law, like its English precursor, sometimes softened in the face of the realities of life and commerce. Milk could be sold before noon or after four on Sundays; family meals could be prepared and taverns; and victualing houses could prepare and serve meals for those who could not otherwise be provided for.[236]

The Sunday system did not merely provide for a day of rest; it mandated a day of worship. A 1712 law went beyond directing everyone to abstain from worldly work and to participate in "true religion, publickly and privately"; it further required them to "resort to their parish church, or some other parish church, or some meeting or assembly of religious worship, tolerated and allowed by the laws of this Province, and shall there abide orderly or soberly during the time of prayer and preaching, on pain and forfeiture for every neglect the sum of five shillings current money of this Province."[237] Thus the act went beyond mandating worship to require that it be done in part through a group mode—that is, at "some meeting or assembly of religious worship"—and required that one not express his displeasure with the sermon by leaving before its conclusion. This approach goes well beyond that of an earlier document, the Fundamental Constitution of July 21, 1669, which stipulated that to be a freeman in Carolina one must believe in God and that "God is publicly and Solemnly to be worshipped," to prescribe, to a degree, the mode of that worship.[238] However, the 1712 law still appears to tolerate a variety of denominations as satisfying the worship requirement so long as they are recognized by provincial law.[239]

The provisions in the 1712 law with regard to Sunday travel were more elaborate than in its predecessors. The general ban on Sunday travel did not apply when the purpose of the travel was to comfort the sick or when an emergency arose and permission to travel was obtained from officials.[240] If a trip did not fit one of those exceptions, it had to cease on Sunday even if the traveler was already on the road.[241]

The 1712 law banned rowdy pastimes that were likely to disturb the quiet atmosphere of worship that the law sought to foster on Sundays. It mandated: "That no publick sports or pastimes, as bear baiting, bull baiting, foot-ball playing, horse-raceing, enterludes or common plays, or other unlawfull games, exercises, sports or pastimes whatsoever, shall be used on the Lord's Day by any person or persons whatsoever, and that every person or persons offending in any of the premises, shall forfeit for every offense the sum of five shillings current money."[242]

By excluding competing activities such as sports, the law increased the likelihood that the colonists really would spend Sunday in worship. The aggressive character of the law's enforcement provisions is seen in the grant of police power to Charleston church wardens, as well as the regular constabulary, to search the "publick houses" for those who might be "drinking or idly spending their time on the Lord's Day." If the tavern was locked, they were empowered to "break open" the doors.[243]

What the law dictates and what it actually achieves may be quite different. Several observers have noted that Sunday in eighteenth-century South Carolina was not always the oasis of quiet worship contemplated by the Sunday laws. Charles Woodmason, Anglican missionary to the backcountry during the 1760s, was an especially shrewd observer of religious practice or its lack. In an 1768 diary entry he noted, "The open profanation of the Lords Day in this Povince [*sic*] is one of the most crying Sins in it—and is carried to a great height—Among the low Class, it is abus'd by Hunting, fishing fowling, and Racing—By the Women in frolicing and Wantonness. By others in Drinking Bouts and Card Playing—Even in and about Charlestown, the Taverns have more Visitants than the Churches."[244]

Another trenchant observer was Josiah Quincy, a visitor from Massachusetts, who was especially adept at painting the hues of social life. In 1773 he observed that the "Sabbath is a day of visiting and mirth with the rich, and of license and pastime and frolic for the negroes."[245] The scene Woodmason described was far from one of forced church attendance. He complained that the Sabbath was not observed because the people were so exhausted from dancing, trading, litigating, partying, and drinking on Saturdays that they could not rouse themselves for worship on Sundays. As a remedy, he proposed extending the prohibition of worldly activities on Sunday to Saturday, an impractical proposal that would have had serious economic consequences and fed resentment of the establishment.[246]

Despite the picture of nonworshipful conviviality, revelry, and dissipation painted by Quincy and Woodmason, enforcement of the Sunday laws was still pressed. Resentment of the church wardens' Sunday law-enforcement powers helped fuel demands for disestablishment of the Church of England and its replacement by a general Protestant establishment in the Constitution of 1778.[247] George Rogers has noted that zealous Charleston church wardens halted drovers, butchers, and servants who were suspected of transporting goods in violation of the Sunday laws.[248] Such actions, along with ousting idlers and tipplers from public houses, may have meant to some that the government hand in support of the established church had grown too heavy and changes were needed.

The Lingering Illness and Death
of the Established Church

The Constitution of 1778 replaced the Anglican establishment with a general Protestant establishment with intricate regulations. Changes in the mood of the body politic led to this fundamental shift in the relationship of church and state. Resentment of the governmental powers of the established church, such as the Sunday law-enforcement authority of the church wardens, was but one of the complex matrix of reasons leading to the decline and ultimate demise of the established church. One reason was the growing perception of the dangers of an established church. The downside to fiscal and ideological support by the government was the assumption by government officials that they could use the church as a tool of social control. In the 1760s Charles Woodmason muttered in his diary about the indignity of being given a sermon topic by Lt. Gov. William Bull.[249] In accordance with this directive, Woodmason drafted a sermon using as his text I Thessalonians 4:11, containing the phrase "and that ye study to be quiet," which was calculated to soothe the disgruntled backcountry population into a more submissive state of mind.[250] Woodmason complained that he could not leave the province without legislative consent.[251] He carped about non-Anglican Protestants gaining clout in the legislature and, through the dissembling of their leaders—a group of conniving lawyers—blocking legislation that would have been favorable to the Church of England.[252] He argued that backcountry growth of the established church was stymied because it would have involved creating new parishes, and, since parishes also served as the unit for apportionment of legislators, officials were reluctant to take that step for fear of altering the geographical balance of political power.[253] He complained that legislative attention to the Stamp Act controversy had sidetracked appropriations that would have redressed salary inequities between town and rural ministers.[254] The church was being smothered more with regulations than riches.

The shocking realization dawned that once the habit of establishing churches became entrenched, there was no guarantee that one's own church would continue to be the favored one. The shock was administered by British passage of the Quebec Act in 1774.[255] The statute is most accurately viewed as a dual establishment of the Protestant and Catholic religions in Canada and a declaration of the freedom of Catholics to practice their religion. In a realistic recognition of the great concentration of French Catholics in Quebec, the statute gave Catholic priests the right to "hold, receive, and enjoy, their accustomed dues and rights, with respect to such persons only as shall profess the said religion."[256] It is notable that this provision did not impose taxes on non-Catholics to support the Catholic Church. Furthermore, it provided "for the encouragement of the protestant religion, and for the maintenance and support of the protestant clergy."[257] Even though the act provided for the support rather than the stifling of the Protestant religion, it sparked fears of a Catholic establishment in all Britain's North American colonies and the specter of Catholic troops pouring across the border from Canada to quell unrest. The South Carolina Constitution of 1776, more a revolutionary litany of complaints than a traditional fundamental law, addressed the issue in the following terms: "The Roman Catholic Religion (although before tolerated and freely exercised there [Quebec]) and an absolute Government are established in that province, and its limits, extended through a vast tract of Country so as to border on the free Protestant English settlements, with design of using a whole People differing in Religious principles from neighboring Colonies, and subject to arbitrary power, as fit Instruments to over-awe and subdue the Colonies."[258]

Similar concerns were expressed by the noted Baptist leader and advocate of disestablishment Richard Furman in his celebrated *Address on Liberty* (1775) when he argued that the English had "established the Roman Catholic religion, and made it a Military, Arbitrary, and Tyrannick government" with Canadian troops poised to "subdue" the other colonies and if they succeeded "we have nothing to assure us, but the Popish religion may be established in all the colonies."[259] The shocked reaction in South Carolina to the Quebec Act was described by Judge John Drayton, who said that its passage "sunk deep into the minds of the people."[260] This view that linked the Catholics with a threat of foreign intervention could have been one of the reasons why the extension of religious freedom to Catholics was slower than it was to non-Anglican Protestants. But the main impact of the Quebec Act was the alarming realization to Anglicans that establishment did not always mean one's own religion would be the favored one.

The growing disenchantment of Anglicans with the establishment converged with Dissenter dislike of having to support someone else's religion through taxes and government endorsement. Together they created more impetus toward dismantling or altering the establishment. Various formal and informal groups compiled lists of grievances against the establishment. The High Hills of Santee was the scene of an interdenominational meeting in March 1776 called by the Reverend Richard Furman and a prominent Charleston Baptist minister, Oliver Hart, to compose a list of grievances against the establishment.[261] The grand jury of the Ninety Six District provided a more secular and somewhat official platform for citizen discontent. In a

1776 presentment the grand jury recommended that the legislature "put all Sects and Denominations of true Protestants in this State on equal Footings."[262] This language foretold that the Revolutionary War era wave of reform of church-state relations would benefit non-Anglican Protestant denominations more than Catholics and Jews. Even though dissenting Protestant groups had enjoyed generous freedom of worship, their development was retarded by several features of the establishment. The grand jury particularly complained of the tax burden shouldered by non-Anglicans in support of the priests and building programs of the Church of England, which meant that their own churches had difficulty raising money through voluntary contributions from the fiscal scraps left after the taxes.[263]

Another bitter point of contention was the Church of England's attempt to monopolize the performance of certain basic rites, especially the marriage ceremony. Charles Woodmason noted in a January 25, 1767, diary entry that even though only the Church of England could perform a licensed marriage, the scarcity of Anglican ministers in remote areas meant that many couples were living together in sin without the benefit of any form of marriage, or, just as bad, they were united by an ersatz marriage performed by non-Anglican ministers.[264] This feature of the establishment undermined the stability of families and the legitimacy of children. However, some of these marriages may have been recognizable as common-law marriages.[265]

Resentment of the establishment finally overflowed into a petition presented by the Reverend William Tennent of the Independent, or Congregational, Church in Charleston on behalf of Dissenters to the Commons House of Assembly on January 11, 1777.[266] Tennent first sought to diminish the opposition to change by assuring Anglicans that he respected the Church of England and did not seek to deprive it of property it had already gained through government aid; he opposed only continuation of its preferred position, including new acquisitions of property with government assistance.[267] No particular church should be government sponsored no matter how admirable it might be morally. Government establishments "amount to nothing less, than the legislature's taking the consciences of men into their own hands, and taxing them at discretion."[268] Tennent contended that a man's relation to God was the product of a personal spiritual search, not of a legislative edict; the state could not interfere with that individual religious odyssey unless that personal search did concrete injury to others.[269] He considered such a legislative edict to be theologically presumptuous, as trespassing on the domain of a "higher tribunal."[270] The government's proper relationship to religion was to protect its free exercise rather than to dictate doctrine to the people.[271] But Tennent's philosophy was not one of total separation of church and state. He observed, "The state may do any thing for the support of religion, without partiality to particular societies, or imposition upon the rights of private judgment."[272] The problem with the South Carolina establishment was that it was rife with such partiality. It "makes a legal distinction between people of different denominations, equally inoffensive; it taxes all denominations, for the support of the religion of one; it only tolerates those that dissent from it" rather than firmly guaranteeing their rights.[273] The distinction made by the law between the established church and other denominations harms individuals and retards the work of the Dissenter churches in serving God and their members. In rolling cadences Tennent listed the grievances:

> I say it makes a legal and odious distinction between subjects equally good. The law knows and acknowledges the society of the one, as a Christian church, the law knows not the other churches. The law knows the Clergy of the one, as ministers of the gospel; the law knows not the Clergy of other Churches, nor will it give them a license to marry their own people. Under this reputedly free government, licenses for marriage are even now refused by the ordinary, to any but the established clergy. The law makes provision for the support of one Church,—it makes no provision for the others. The law builds superb Churches for the one,—it leaves the others to build their own churches: the law by incorporating the one Church, enables it to hold estates, and to sue for rights; the law does not enable the others to hold any religious property, not even the pittances which are bestowed by the hand of charity for their support. No dissenting Church can hold or sue for their own property at common law. They are obliged therefore to deposit it in the hands of trustees, to be held by them as their own private property, and to lie at their mercy. The consequence of this is, that too often their funds for the support of religious worship, get into bad hands, and become either alienated from their proper use, or must be recovered at the expense of a suit in chancery.[274]

The petitioners were incensed that the established church wielded political as well as spiritual power. Particularly irritating was the commitment of "the whole management of elections, that most inestimable of all rights of freemen! into the hands of Church officers exclusively."[275] No minority, whether religious or secular, should have the power to manipulate the elections even if the opportunity is never used. Assistance to the poor was run by Church of England officials even though the tax-paying public at large bore the expense.[276]

Tennent referred to the tax-paying burden on the Dissenters again and again. He complained that Protestant dissenters, a majority of the population shouldered a heavy burden in paying for a religion that was not their own. He estimated that from 1765 to 1775 the established church received 164,027 pounds and 16 shillings with about half of this being paid by Dissenters, who—after making such payments— were hard put to find money for their own religion.[277]

What Tennent sought was not tolerance, a boon that could be granted or withdrawn at the sovereign's fickle pleasure, but a firm right of free exercise of religion. Religion that was merely tolerated had to be exercised timidly or else the sovereign might be stirred to suppress it.[278] This distinction between tolerance and rights was not peculiar to Tennent. In the 1776 Virginia Constitutional convention, young James Madison successfully argued for the substitution of language guaranteeing religious liberty for wording that spoke of mere toleration.[279] Later George Washington also embraced the need for a guaranteed right of free exercise of religion rather than revocable tolerance. In a message to leaders of the Newport Hebrew Congregation in the fall of 1790, President Washington observed that we no longer speak of tolerating another's religion "as if it was by the indulgence of one class of people that another enjoyed the exercise of their inherent natural rights."[280]

In South Carolina the Reverend Tennent attacked temporizing measures that would have left remnants of the establishment in place. One halfway measure would have halted support of the Church of England from general tax funds but left it as the official church receiving ideological endorsement from the state. This was still unacceptable since Nonconformists must "bear the reproach of the law, as not being on a level with those that are Christians in its esteem."[281] To preserve for the Anglican Church the "mere empty name" of the official church would be to create "a bone of endless contention in the state."[282]

No better was the suggestion that government financial support of religion be continued but equally distributed among all Protestant denominations or on the basis of so much per member. This too would be a source of "everlasting strife" as the various denominations would fight over members or otherwise try to increase their share of the fiscal pie.[283] The best method of church finance in a religiously diverse community was to "Leave each Church to be supported by its own members, and let its real merit be all its pre-eminence."[284] His rallying cry was "Equality or Nothing."[285]

Pragmatism was often more effective than theoretical arguments on church-state relations. Tennent argued that the Dissenter majority would more fervently work for the success of the Revolutionary War if they had a fairer share in the liberty for which it was being waged. Maintaining the establishment would drive away settlers hoping to find religious freedom and destroy the sense of community in the state.[286] The future belonged to states casting their lot with religious freedom and equality among religions. He observed: "That state in America which adopts the freest and most liberal plan will be the most opulent and powerful and will deserve it."[287]

The assembly debated a range of options extending from complete disestablishment to the retention of significant elements of official recognition of the Church of England. One commentator has described the four leading options as: (1) that no church be established either by government fiscal support or official recognition of its doctrine; (2) that the Church of England continue to exercise two key elements of civil power: administering the government's program of assistance to the poor and superintending elections but that no taxes be collected from the followers of other faiths to finance its worship; (3) that all Protestant churches meeting broad belief standards receive equal financial support from the government; (4) that all Protestant denominations meeting certain broad doctrinal standards be established to the limited extent of receiving the ideological approval of the government and certain legal powers, such as the right to incorporate.[288] The fourth alternative— ideological establishment, but no tax support, of all Protestant churches that adhered to certain broadly defined doctrines—was the core of the compromise that became Article 38 of the Constitution of 1778 after being vetoed by President John Rutledge but signed by his successor.[289]

Article 38 was self-contradictory. It granted a large measure of religious freedom but retarded its exercise by entangling it in an intricate labyrinth of regulations. It advanced religious freedom by dismantling the Church of England establishment and replacing it with a general Protestant establishment. Under this new regime, established churches were endorsed, but not financially supported, by the state. This removed the tax burden that was the crux of William Tennent's Dissenter petition. Article 38 stated that "no Person shall, by Law, be obliged to pay towards the Maintenance and Support of a religious Worship that he does not freely join in, or has not voluntarily engaged to Support."[290] David Ramsay, a physician, historian, and public official in late eighteenth-and early nineteenth-century South Carolina, described the new fundamental law as one that "comprehended every denomination of Protestant Christians, giving to each of them equal rights and capacities, but withholding public pecuniary support from all."[291] Other Protestant churches could now do what only Anglican churches could do before: petition the legislature for incorporation and directly own their property rather than having it held by a trustee. But Article 38 empowered only churches "professing the Christian Protestant religion" to incorporate; Catholic churches and Jewish synagogues still could not do so. Even Protestant churches had to jump through ideological hoops in order to be honored with the label of established church and to qualify for incorporation. Each had to certify that it adhered to the following principles:

> First, That there is one eternal God, and a future State of Rewards and Punishments.
> Second, That God is publicly to be worshipped.
> Third, That the Christian Religion is the true Religion
> Fourth, That the Holy Scriptures of the Old and New Testament, are of Divine Inspiration, and are the Rule of Faith and Practice.
> Fifth, That it is lawful, and the Duty of every Man, being thereunto called by those that govern, to bear witness to Truth.[292]

Religious beliefs are subjective; personal spiritual journeys are often continuous and are not amenable to being frozen into a legal code. Codified religions may strike some as incomplete. The Independent, or Congregational, Church of Charleston certified that it adhered to the five doctrines specified in Article 38 but added that it also believed in others, such as the trinity, that were not found in the official list.[293] In addition to the beliefs that a church had to accept to become part of the establishment and be incorporated, its pastor had to subscribe to an even more detailed set of beliefs, the core of which was that he should base his teaching only on the holy scriptures. This Article 38 injunction to ministers of established churches, together with directives in that provision, that ministers and their families must be "wholesome examples and patterns to the flock of Christ" and that they must foster "quietness, peace and love among all Christian people," used language nearly identical to the provisions on the "Form and Manner of Ordering Priests" from the 1662 version of the Church of England's Book of Common Prayer.[294] Thus, even though the Church of England was no longer the sole established Church, its influence lingered.

Article 38 sought to assure congregational democracy by specifying that only ministers elected by the congregation or its delegates could serve established churches. As liberal as this seems at first glance, it dictated a form of church governance that those denominations preferring ministerial appointment by a hierarchical superior could have found hard to accept.

The religious freedom provisions of the article were generous, but even so liberty was surrounded by conditions. The article stated, "That all persons and religious Societies, who acknowledge that there is one God, and a future State of Rewards and Punishments, and that God is publicly to be worshipped, shall be freely tolerated."[295] This language evokes that of Article 86 [61] of the Fundamental Constitution of July 21, 1669, which said, "No man shall be permitted to be a Freeman of Carolina, or have any Estate or habitation within it, that does not acknowledge a God, and that God is publicly and Solemnly to be worshipped."[296] Both provisions speak of tolerance, a sovereign act of grace that can be withdrawn, rather than of a guaranteed right. Both are somewhat self-contradictory in that they grant religious freedom but only to those who entertain specified beliefs. Still, the overall tone of Article 38, signaled by the replacement of the Church of England as the official religion with a general Protestant establishment, was one of widening tolerance. If the tent were not as large as it could be, at least the overall movement was in the direction of considering religion more a matter of individual conscience than state dictation. This is seen in the provision regarding the oaths to be taken by witnesses, which does not condition the oath taking on adherence to a highly specific set of beliefs. It states, "That every Inhabitant of this State, when called to make an Appeal to God, as a witness to Truth, shall be permitted to do it in that Way which is most agreeable to the Dictates of his own Conscience."[297]

Participation in the political system under the Constitution of 1778 was more of a mixed bag; office holders were required to meet more specific religious standards than voters. Article 3 stipulated that the governor, lieutenant governor, and members of the Privy Council be "all of the Protestant Religion."[298] Article 12 mandated that "no Person shall be eligible to a Seat in the said Senate, unless he be of the Protestant Religion," and Article 13 declared that members of the House of Representatives be Protestant.[299] The standards for electors in Article 13 did not require membership in a particular sect but did have broad belief standards. It mandated that an elector must be one "who acknowledges the Being of a God, and believes in a future State of Rewards and Punishments." Catholics and Jews were not disenfranchised if they adhered to these broad standards. This standard, like the Article 38 standard defining which religions would be tolerated, harkened back to the approach of Article 86 [61] of the July 21, 1669, Fundamental Constitution stipulating that certain basic religious beliefs were essential for a civilized society.[300]

Article 21 forbade ministers of the gospel from serving as governor, lieutenant governor, or members of the House of Representatives, Senate, or Privy Council because they "ought not be diverted from the great duties of their Function."[301] The

Reverend William Tennent, who had been such an adamant advocate of dismantling the Anglican establishment, attacked this ministerial disqualification as designed to weaken politically those who espoused change even though the ostensible purpose of the provision was to prevent religious quarrels from infecting legislative deliberations.[302] The Reverend Richard Furman later opposed retaining the ministerial disqualification in the 1790 Constitution since it would deny the state the services of many talented men.[303]

However, the provision did not prevent Furman and the Reverend Doctor Henry Purcell from serving as delegates to the Constitutional Convention of 1790. The convention records also list other ministers as delegates.[304] Despite Furman's views, Article 1, section 23, of the 1790 Constitution retained a ministerial-disqualification provision similar to that in the 1778 fundamental law.

Even though the 1778 Constitution replaced the Church of England establishment with an endorsement of all Protestant churches meeting the broad belief standards stipulated by Article 38, there was no hint of vengeance against the dethroned official church. Article 38 continued the corporate status of Anglican churches and allowed them to retain their property.[305]

Now that non-Anglican Protestant churches that certified adherence to the belief standards set in Article 38 could be incorporated, a flood of special laws poured from the legislature granting this status. One of the first 1778 enactments granted corporate status to the Independent, or Congregational, Church in Charleston, the Reverend Oliver Hart's Baptist Church in Charleston, the Presbyterian Church of Bethel in St. Bartholomew's parish, the Presbyterian Church of Cainhoy in St. Thomas parish, and the Presbyterian Church of Salem in St. Mark's parish.[306] After stating that the petitioning churches had met the constitutional standards for incorporating, the act granted each of them the status of a body corporate and politic, empowered them to adopt a seal, hold property directly rather than through trustees, receive contributions, have perpetual succession as an entity, sue and be sued, make bylaws in accordance with standards set by the state, elect ministers, hire other employees, and set their compensation. No government funds were authorized for use by the churches. Instead they were authorized to pay their bills from corporate funds and pew rentals assessed against members.

A casual reading of an incorporation statute might lead to the mistaken impression that a church was receiving government funds. For example, a 1783 statute incorporating a Calvinist church of French Protestants recited that the petitioner's motive for seeking corporate status was to put its affairs on a "more solid and lasting foundation than they could be by their voluntary subscriptions."[307] But the financial system authorized by the statute did not involve funds involuntarily wrested by the government from the general tax-paying public but rather assessments made by the church as pew charges on those who chose to become its members. The assessment was not made by government officials but by vote of the church members. The state hand was not entirely missing from the transaction, however, since the statute made the pew assessments legally enforceable by the church.[308] And the state controlled church fiscal growth to an extent by placing a limit of 500 pounds on the amount it could receive in one year.[309]

Even though pew assessments were distinguishable from the taxes formerly imposed by the state, under some circumstances they could provoke the same resentment. This was especially true when the person assessed was a member who was not renting the pew but had purchased it outright and had completed the payments originally agreed on. On February 19, 1787, Samuel Beach, a member of St. Philip's Church in Charleston, presented a petition to the General Assembly complaining that the assessment power given to his church violated Article 38 when the assessment was against someone in his position who had purchased rather than rented the pew. He argued that he was now the complete owner of the pew and any further exactions on him were illegal. Article 38 protected citizens against involuntary support of religion, and any further assessments after he had paid the agreed-on amount for the purchase were involuntary. He contended that although the assessments were not imposed directly by the government, the state incorporation of churches, the labeling of them as established, and the grant to them of pew-assessment authority that could be legally enforced gave such assessments the same effect as a state-imposed tax for religion, which was no longer legal under Article 38. Beach found a further constitutional violation. Pointing out that Article 38 decreed equal treatment of all Protestant denominations meeting the criteria for establishment, he argued that this principle had been violated since some Protestant churches had been given pew-assessment authority and others had not.[310] The General Assembly committee reviewing the petition rejected this last argument when it concluded that so many churches had been given pew-assessment authority that this amounted to equal treatment. The committee never directly met Beach's contention that the system was coerced contribution to religion in violation of Article 38. It cynically observed that if Beach did not like the pew assessments, he could solve the problem by selling his pew.[311] The Beach petition was not granted, but one scholar who surveyed the church-incorporation records under the 1778 Constitution concluded that the petition may have influenced the legislature in passing later incorporation laws to require the church to choose between a system of selling or renting pews. If the former was selected, these laws permitted no further assessment after a complete and unconditional sale.[312]

The Constitution of 1778 not only benefited Dissenter congregations, it also gave greater freedom of action to congregations of the old establishment, who had lost government funding but also the close government monitoring that went with it. A 1785 statute, which incorporated St. Michael's and St. Philip's Churches in Charleston, gave them plenary power over their affairs.[313] Since government financial support would no longer be possible under the Constitution of 1778, those churches were given the pew-assessment authority that was exercised in the manner that so incensed Samuel Beach.[314]

The 1778 Constitution and its grant to non-Anglican Protestant churches of the power to incorporate also spurred the development of larger denominational organizations, sometimes with an ecumenical flavor, to administer the growing number of incorporated churches. In 1787–88 Lutheran and German Reformed churches came together to form an organization called the Corpus Evangelicum, or Unio Ecclesiastica, which was designed to work for the incorporation of German churches, the ordination of ministers, and the provision of an administrative umbrella for the churches.[315] Although this organization proved to be short lived because of fundamental disagreements among the parties, its creation is further evidence of the vigorous growth unleashed by constitutional change.

But despite the encouragement to religious growth made possible by the partial disestablishment of 1778, the journey to religious freedom was not over. Still ahead lay the question of complete disestablishment in the climate created by the federal Constitution and its First Amendment and the need for equal freedom for all religions including Catholics and Jews. The ground grew fertile for the adoption of the Constitution of 1790.

Notes

Portions of this chapter and the following one were published under this title in *South Carolina Law Review*, 54, no. 1 (Fall 2002): 111.

1. James Lowell Underwood, *The Constitution of South Carolina*, vol. 3: *Church and State, Morality and Free Expression* (Columbia: University of South Carolina Press, 1992), 1–18.

2. See ibid., 19–28.

3. See Article 8 of the South Carolina Constitution of 1790, in *Basic Documents of South Carolina History*, ed. J. M. Lesesne and J. H. Easterby (Columbia: Historical Commission of South Carolina, 1952), n. pag. Article 8, section 1, states that "the free exercise and enjoyment of religious profession and worship, without discrimination or preference, shall, forever hereafter, be allowed within this State to all mankind; provided that the liberty of conscience hereby declared shall not be so construed as to excuse acts of licentiousness, or justify practices inconsistent with the peace or safety of this state."

4. See John Miller, *Charles II* (London: Weidenfeld & Nicolson, 1991), 76–80, 99–100, discussing Charles II's predilection toward tolerance for Protestant dissenters and Catholics and the pressure to which he was subjected by the House of Commons to curb that tendency and enforce the 1662 Act of Uniformity to fortify the position of the Church of England and maintain public order. For the text of the Act of Uniformity, see Statutes at Large, 12 Chas. 2, c. 4, An Act for the uniformity of publick Prayers, and Administration of Sacraments, and other Rites and Ceremonies: and for Establishing the Form of Making, Ordaining and Consecrating Bishops, Priests and Deacons in the Church of England. Anthony Ashley Cooper, Earl of Shaftesbury, a leading Carolina proprietor under the Charter granted by Charles II in 1663 is described as being in favor of a tolerant approach (Miller, *Charles II*, 154). In light of such crosscurrents of pressure, it is not surprising that the Charters are not consistent in their recognition of religious freedom.

5. See Mattie Erma Edwards Parker, ed., *North Carolina Charters and Constitutions, 1578–1698* (Raleigh, N.C.: Carolina Charter Tercentenary Commission, 1963), 77. A similar provision in the Maryland Charter granted in 1632 to Baron Baltimore gave him power to license churches "according to the Ecclesiastical Laws of the Kingdom of England." See Francis Newton Thorpe, *The Federal and State Constitutions, Colonial Charters and Other Organic Laws of the States, Territories and Colonies Now or Heretofore Forming the United States of America,* vol. 3 (1909; reprint, Buffalo, N.Y.: William S. Hein, 1993), 1677, 1678–79.

6. Parker, ed., *North Carolina Charters and Constitutions,* 88–89.

7. Ibid. The religious tolerance permitted under the Charter soon became a cornerstone of the proprietors' attempts to recruit settlers to migrate to Carolina. See, for example, "A Brief Description of the Province of Carolina," written in 1666, in *Narratives of Early Carolina, 1650–1708,* ed. Alexander S. Salley Jr. (New York: Barnes & Noble, 1939), 71, listing first among the "chief privileges" of the colony: "There is full and free Liberty of Conscience granted to all, so that no man is to be molested or called in question for matters of Religious Concern; but every one to be obedient to the Civil Government, worshipping God after their own way."

8. Parker, ed., *North Carolina Charters and Constitutions,* 88. Yet, this broad discretion in the hands of the proprietors did not necessarily render religious liberties uncertain in the new colony. As William J. Rivers notes, the proprietors generally followed a "liberal interpretation" of the religious provisions of the charter such that religious freedom became well established in Carolina despite the "remarkable" fact that "in the charter, the civil rights granted to the colonists are secured to them by the king independently of the proprietors, while religious freedom was left subject to their will and restriction" (William J. Rivers, *A Sketch of the History of South Carolina to the Close of the Proprietary Government by the Revolution of 1719* [Charleston: McCarter, 1856; reprint, Spartanburg, S.C.: Reprint Company, 1972], 78). To Rivers, this "toleration [is all] the more to be admired when we consider the spirit of persecution which still warmly existed in all denominations of Christians in the mother country" (ibid.) See also John Oldmixon, "From The History of the British Empire in America," in *Narratives of Early Carolina,* ed. Salley, 324, noting that under the colonial charter's language of toleration the "Lords Proprietors [took] care, that Persons of all Professions in Religion should be protected and secur'd in the free Exercise of them."

9. Parker, ed., *North Carolina Charters and Constitutions,* 104 (religious freedom provisions of Second Charter), 88–89 (religious freedom provisions of First Charter, 1663). The Charter of Rhode Island and Providence Plantation granted by Charles II in 1663 (replacing a 1643 Charter) to Roger Williams and others who had fled religious oppression in Massachusetts contained a similar provision. It stated:

> That our royall will and pleasure is, that noe person within the sayd colonye, at any tyme hereafter, shall bee any wise molested, punished, disquieted, or called in question, for any differences in opinione in matters of religion, and doe not actually disturb the civill peace of our sayd colony; but that all and everye person and persons may, from tyme to tyme, and at all tymes hereafter, freelye and fullye have and enjoye his and theire owne judgments and consciences, in matters of religious concernments, throughout the tract of lande hereafter mentioned; they behaving themselves peaceablie and quietlie, and not useing this libertie to lycentiousnesse and profanenesse, nor to the civill injurye or outward

disturbeance of others; any law, statute, or clause, therein contayned, or to bee contayned, usage or custome of this realme to the contrary hereof, in any wise, notwithstanding. (Thorpe, *The Federal and State Constitutions,* 5:3213. See ibid., 3209, for 1643 land patent granted by Lords and Commons to Williams and others.)

In 1635 a Court banished Williams from Massachusetts for several offenses including questioning the powers of the king to grant land patents in America without negotiating purchases from the Indians. However, the main charge related to his questioning the authority of civil magistrates over religious matters. See Edwin S. Gaustad, *Liberty of Conscience, Roger Williams in America* (Grand Rapids, Mich.: Eerdmans, 1991), 39. Williams had earlier received a deed for the land from Indian leaders (ibid., 48).

10. Parker, ed., *North Carolina Charters and Constitutions,* 104.

11. Ibid., 114–15.

12. Ibid. Note not only item 8, containing a broad grant of religious freedom, but also the Lords Proprietors' power to abrogate it contained in item 7.

13. Ibid.

14. Ibid., 114.

15. Ibid., item 9 (concessions and agreement).

16. Ibid.

17. Ibid., 128–240. See also the discussion, note 25 infra, of the earliest draft of the Fundamental Constitutions, which is located at the South Carolina Department of Archives and History in Columbia.

18. One historian captured the troubled history of the Fundamental Constitutions and the persistent efforts of the proprietors to have the constitutions adopted by the people of Carolina by analogizing the constitutions to a "garment that did not fit the infant [but which] was still so beautiful to the parent's eye, that it was altered, and pieced, and patched, and again and again lovingly tried upon his limbs, even in the years of his robust manhood" (Rivers, *A Sketch of the History of South Carolina,* 165).

19. See Robert M. Weir, *Colonial South Carolina: A History* (Millwood, N.Y.: KTO Press, 1983), 55–73, and David Ramsay, *The History of South Carolina From Its First Settlement in 1670, to the Year 1808,* vol. 2 (Charleston: David Longworth, 1809), 122–24. See also Walter Edgar, *South Carolina: A History* (Columbia: University of South Carolina Press, 1998), 42–43, noting that since the colonists refused to ratify the constitutions, they did not become the "basic law" of Carolina but many provisions were implemented "de facto" and the religious freedom provisions became influential in attracting settlers "looking for a new beginning"; Mattie Erma E. Parker, "Legal Aspects of Culpeper's Rebellion," *North Carolina Historical Review* 45 (1968): 111–27, attributing the Albemarle uprising of 1677 to a "constitutional crisis" caused by the ambiguous authority of the Fundamental Constitutions and the directives the proprietors issued under those constitutions.

20. David Ramsay, *The History of South Carolina,* 1:122, notes the controversy over Locke's authorship. See also E. S. DeBeer, ed., *Correspondence of John Locke,* vol. 1 (Oxford: Clarendon Press, 1976), 395n2, noting that key ideas may have come from Locke's patron Lord Shaftesbury. In his examination of the issue, J. R. Milton concludes, "It is therefore probable, though by no means certain, that Locke was not the original author of the *Fundamental Constitutions of Carolina,* though he undoubtedly contributed significantly to the

final text as it emerged from successive stages of revision" (J. R. Milton, "John Locke and the Fundamental Constitutions of Carolina," *Locke Newsletter* 21 [1990]: 128–29).

21. John Locke, "A Letter Concerning Toleration," in *The Library of Liberal Arts*, no. 22, ed. Oskar Piest, second edition (New York: Liberal Arts Press, 1955).

22. Ibid., 56.

23. Ibid., 50–52.

24. This effort by the proprietors to guarantee a limited, yet attractive, amount of religious liberty in a constitutional document was paralleled in the proprietary colony of East New Jersey. See John E. Pomfret, *The Province of East New Jersey, 1609–1702: The Rebellious Proprietary* (Princeton, N.J.: Princeton University Press, 1962), 140–43. In a "Fundamental Constitution" proposed for that colony in 1683, the New Jersey proprietors provided that all persons "who confess and acknowledge the one Almighty and Eternal God . . . shall in no way be molested or prejudged for their religious perswasions and exercise in matters of faith and worship." Article 16 of "The Fundamental Constitutions for the Province of East New Jersey in America, Anno Domini 1683," in Thorpe, *The Federal and State Constitutions*, 5:2579–80. However, this grant of religious freedom did have its limits—holders of public office were required to be Christians, the advocating of atheism or irreligiousness was prohibited, and sinful activities such as drunkenness, swearing, and "indulging . . . in stage plays" were not to be excused under the guise of religious liberty (ibid). But, like Carolina's Fundamental Constitutions, these proposed constitutions were never adopted in New Jersey. See Pomfret, *The Province of East New Jersey, 1609–1702*, 140.

25. Parker, ed., *North Carolina Charters and Constitutions*, 148. Article 91 [66] made clear that not only were monotheistic beliefs required but church membership as well. It stipulated that "no person above [sixteen] seventeen years of Age shall have any benefit or protection of the law, or be capable of any place of profit or honor, who is not a member of Some church or profession, having his name recorded in Some one and but one Religious Record at once" (ibid., 149). The numbers and words found in brackets are from a text of the July 21, 1669, version of the Fundamental Constitutions found in the South Carolina Department of Archives and History in Columbia. This text, now considered to be the earliest, was the version given to the first governor and settlers and later was cited by the colonists against new versions offered by the proprietors. For this text, see Ruth S. Green, "The South Carolina Archives Copy of the Fundamental Constitution, Dated July 21, 1669," *South Carolina Historical Magazine* 71, no. 2 (April 1970): 86. Mattie Erma Edwards Parker discusses this document and the reasons for considering it the earliest in "The First Fundamental Constitution of South Carolina," *South Carolina Historical Magazine* 71, no. 2 (April 1970): 78. See especially page 84, describing the colonists' championing of this document against altered versions. The author is grateful to Dr. Charles Lesser of the South Carolina Department of Archives and History for the observation concerning the significance of his department's text of the July 21, 1669, version.

26. Parker, ed., *North Carolina Charters and Constitutions*, 149.

27. Pennsylvania Charter of 1681, in Thorpe, *The Federal and State Constitutions*, 5: 3043.

28. Ibid., VI: 3783–3813. See especially 3788 for charter quotation. See also A. E. Dick Howard, *Commentaries on the Constitution of Virginia*, 2 vols. (Charlottesville: University

Press of Virginia, 1974), 1:1, discussing the liberty guarantees in the charter, and 1:289 for statement that religious and political persecution did not cause Virginia's settlement.

29. Parker, ed., *North Carolina Charters and Constitutions*, 149, quoting Article 90 [65], which set beliefs that must be espoused by an organization wishing to be considered a church.

30. See Article 38, Constitution of 1778, in *Basic Documents of South Carolina History*, ed. Robert L. Meriwether and J. H. Easterby (Columbia: Historical Commission of South Carolina, 1953). But Article 38 required more specific Protestant Christian beliefs before a church could enjoy the benefits of legal incorporation.

31. Article 92 [67] specified, "The Religious Record of every church or profession shall be kept by the public Register of the Precinct where they reside" (Parker, ed., *North Carolina Charters and Constitutions*, 149).

32. Article 99 [74] of the Fundamental Constitution of July 21, 1669, in ibid., 150.

33. Article 93 [68] and 97 [72] of the Fundamental Constitution of July 21, 1669, in ibid. Article 100 [75] further provided: "No person whatsoever shall disturb, molest, or persecute another for his speculative opinions in Religion or his way of worship" (ibid). This established an affirmative duty of the government to protect freedom of worship.

34. Article 94 [69] of the Fundamental Constitution of July 21, 1669, in ibid.

35. Article 98 [73] of the Fundamental Constitution of July 21, 1669, in ibid.

36. Article 101 of the Fundamental Constitution of July 21, 1669, in ibid. This provision is not included in the earliest text of the July 21, 1669, version discussed in Green, op. cit.

37. See Nicholas Trott, *The Laws of the British Plantations in America Relating to the Church and Clergy, Religion and Learning Collected in One Volume* (London: Printed for B. Cowse, 1721), 74, part of an act entitled "An Act for the Better Ordering and Governing of Negroes and Slaves," June 7, 1712, para. 34. The full act is set forth as Act No. 314 of June 7, 1712, in 7 S.C. Statutes at Large 352 (McCord 1840).

38. Mortimer J. Adler, ed., *The Annals of America*, vol. 1 (Chicago: Encyclopedia Britannica, 1968), 88.

39. See Maryland Toleration Act, April 21, 1649, in *Colonial Origins of the American Constitution*, ed. Donald S. Lutz (Indianapolis: Liberty Fund, 1998), 309–13.

40. Ibid., 312.

41. Ibid., 310.

42. Ibid.

43. See *Attorney General v. Lumbrozo* (February 19, 1658), Archives of Maryland, vol. 41 (database on-line) 203.

44. See Abram Vossen Goodman, *American Overture: Jewish Rights in Colonial Times* (Philadelphia: Jewish Publication Society of America, 1947), 141–43. Goodman speculates that the defendant may have been released as part of an amnesty accompanying Richard Cromwell's installation as lord protector.

45. See Act No. 202 of May 6, 1703, 2 S.C. Statutes at Large 196–97 (Cooper 1837).

46. Ibid.

47. Article 96 of the Fundamental Constitution of March 1, 1670, in *North Carolina Charters and Constitutions*, ed. Parker, 181. One of the proprietors said that another proprietor inserted this provision contrary "to Mr. Locke's judgment." See Langdon Cheves, ed.,

The Shaftesbury Papers (Charleston: South Carolina Historical Society, 1897; reprint, Charleston: Tempus Publishing, 2000), 312n2.

48. Article 95 of the Fundamental Constitution of March 1, 1670, in *North Carolina Charters and Constitutions,* ed. Parker, 165.

49. John Wesley Brinsfield, *Religion and Politics in Colonial South Carolina* (Easley, S.C.: Southern Historical Press, 1983), 7–8.

50. See Article 94, Fundamental Constitution of January 12, 1682, in *North Carolina Charters and Constitutions,* ed. Parker, 202.

51. See Article 100 of the Fundamental Constitution of August 17, 1682, in ibid., 227.

52. The 1682 removal of the tax burden to support the established church from the shoulders of non-Anglicans was part of a largely successful campaign by the proprietors to recruit English, Scottish, and French dissenters to Carolina. See Rivers, *A Sketch of the History of South Carolina,* 142; M. Eugene Sirmans, "Politics in Colonial South Carolina: The Failure of Proprietary Reform, 1682–1694," *William and Mary Quarterly* third series 23 (1966); 35–36, Weir, *Colonial South Carolina,* 64. This recruitment campaign and the accompanying amendments to the Fundamental Constitutions interjected religion squarely into the debates over the ratification of the constitutions; newly arrived Dissenters favored adopting the constitutions and their guarantees of religious freedom, and established Anglican elites resisted the efforts of the proprietors to force the Fundamental Constitutions on the colony. See Sirmans, "Politics in Colonial South Carolina," 39–40.

53. Article 101 of the Fundamental Constitution of August 17, 1682, in *North Carolina Charters and Constitutions,* ed. Parker, 227–28.

54. Article 102 of the Fundamental Constitution of August 17, 1682, in ibid., 228.

55. Article 26 of the Fundamental Constitution of April 11, 1698, in ibid. The ban on ministers occupying civil offices that had been in Article 102 of the August 1682, version was not included in the 1698 document.

56. See Act No. 154 of 1696–97, 2 S.C. Statutes at Large 131, 133 (Cooper 1837). A similar provision, granting equal rights to settlers of non-English origins is found in the Charter of Rhode Island and Providence Plantation granted by Charles II in 1663. See Thorpe, *The Federal and State Constitutions,* VI: 3220. A similar, if somewhat less-expansive provision is included in the 1662 Charter for Connecticut. See ibid., 1:529, 533.

57. Act No. 154 of 1696–97.

58. Ibid.

59. Barnett A. Elzas, *The Jews of South Carolina From the Earliest Times to the Present Day* (Philadelphia: Lippincott, 1905; reprint, Spartanburg, S.C.: Reprint Co., 1972), 17–19. See also James William Hagy, *This Happy Land: The Jews of Colonial and Antebellum Charleston* (Tuscaloosa: University of Alabama Press, 1993), 1, noting that early Jewish settlers in South Carolina referred to it as "'the Happy Land,' it was their New Jerusalem, New Palestine—the Promised Land."

60. Milton Viorst, *The Great Documents of Western Civilization* (New York: Barnes & Noble, 1994), 106–8 (setting forth the Edict of Nantes), 146–47 (setting forth key provisions of the revocation). For an argument against revocation, see Samuel Pufendorf, *Of the Nature and Qualification of Religion in Reference to Civil Society* (1687; reprint, Indianapolis: Liberty Fund, 2002). See also Bertrand Van Ruymbeke, "Minority Survival: The Huguenot Paradigm in France and the Diaspora," in *Memory and Identity: The Huguenots in France*

and the Atlantic Diaspora, ed. Van Ruymbeke and Randy J. Sparks (Columbia: University of South Carolina Press, 2003), 3–4.

61. See Jon Butler, "The Huguenots and the American Immigrant Experience," in *Memory and Identity,* ed. Van Ruymbeke and Sparks, 197.

62. See Viorst, *Great Documents of Western Civilization,* 106–8, 144.

63. Ibid., 146–47.

64. See Walter Utt and Brian E. Strayer, *The Bellicose Dove: Claude Brousson, and Protestant Resistance to Louis XIV, 1647–1698* (Portland, Ore.: Sussex Academic Press, 2003), 11–12.

65. Bertrand Van Ruymbeke, "Escape from Babylon," *Christian History,* 20, issue 71 (August 2001): 38, available on-line at http://web 4. infotrac.galegroup.com/itw/infomark/540/584/40967699w4/purl=re1_EAIM_0 . . . (visited September 30, 2003).

66. Ibid., 38–40.

67. Ibid., 40.

68. Ibid.

69. Ibid., 38.

70. Arthur Henry Hirsch, *The Huguenots of Colonial South Carolina* (1928; reprint, London: Archon, 1962), 6. See also Bertrand Van Ruymbeke, "The Huguenots of Proprietary South Carolina, Patterns of Migration and Integration," in *Money, Trade and Power: The Evolution of Colonial South Carolina's Plantation Society,* ed. Jack P. Greene, Rosemary Brana-Shute, and Randy J. Sparks (Columbia: University of South Carolina Press, 2001), 28, which estimates that 642 Huguenots, including children, migrated to South Carolina between 1680 and 1710.

71. Jo Anne McCormick, "The Quakers of Colonial South Carolina 1670–1807," Ph.D. dissertation, University of South Carolina, Columbia, 1984, 12–20.

72. See Shaftesbury to Percivall, June 9, 1675, in *The Shaftesbury Papers* (1897; reprint, with a preface by Robert M. Weir, Charleston: South Carolina Historical Society, 2000) 464–65.

73. See James Bowden, *The History of the Society of Friends in America,* vol. 1 (1850; reprint, New York: Arno, 1972) 32–33.

74. Ibid., 46–47.

75. Ibid., 157–60.

76. Ibid., 160.

77. Ibid., 184, 201, 214–15.

78. Ibid., 184.

79. D. Elton Trueblood, *The People Called Quakers* (New York: Harper & Row, 1966), 3.

80. Article 90 [65] of the Fundamental Constitution of July 21, 1669, in *North Carolina Charters and Constitutions,* ed. Parker, 149. For a discussion by Quaker founder George Fox of their belief against swearing oaths, see Fox to Friends in Charlestown, Carolina, December 23, 1683, in Bowden, *The History of the Society of Friends in America,* 414. Quaker leader William Penn condemned oath requirements by saying that "they have often *ensnared a Good Man,* but never *caught one Knave yet,*" in "One Project for the Good of England That is, Our Civil Union is Our Civil Safety. Humbly Dedicated to the Great Council, The Parliament of England" (1679), in *Political Writings of William Penn,* ed. Andrew Murphy (Indianapolis: Liberty Fund, 2002), 131.

81. Robert Barclay, *An Apology for True Christian Divinity: Being an Explanation and Vindication of the Principles and Doctrine of the People Called Quakers* (1678; reprint, Philadelphia: Kimber Konrad, 1805), 27, available on microfilm in Special Collections, Thomas Cooper Library, University of South Carolina, Columbia (hereafter cited as Barclay, *Apology*). See also Isaac Penington, "A Brief Account of What the People Called Quakers Desire in Reference to Civil Government," in *The Works of the Long Mournful and Sorely Distressed Isaac Penington Whom the Lord in His Tender Mercy, At Length Visited and Relieved By the Ministry of That Despised People Called Quakers and In the Springing of That Light, Life and Holy Power in Him, Which They Had Truly and Faithfully Testified of, and Directed His Mind To Were These Things Written, and Are Now Published As a Thankful Testimony of the Goodness of the Lord Unto Him, and For The Benefit of Others*, vol. 2 (Glenside, Pa.: Quaker Heritage Press, 1996), available on-line at http://ccat.sas.upenn.edu/~Kuenning/penington/magistrate.html (visited December 7, 2003). Penington (1616–1679) concluded that the "true church" was content to leave the correction of the infraction of God's will to the spirit. Only the "false church" needed the "carnal weapons" of the civil magistrate to enforce its will (ibid., 8).

82. Ibid., 27–33.

83. For an explanation of the Quaker dedication to peace, see Trueblood, *People Called Quakers*, 187–207. Trueblood discusses the writings of early Quaker leaders Robert Barclay and Isaac Penington and concludes that they viewed peace as a firm goal, but under appropriate circumstances acts of self defense or third-party defense could be justified (ibid., 199–201). See Barclay, *Apology*, 571–75, discussing Christ's command that strife be resolved by patience, charity, and forbearance rather than violence.

84. Friends exception in the Militia Act entitled *An Act for the Better Settling and Regulating of the Militia*, John Archdale Papers 1690–1706, available on microfilm at the South Carolina Department of Archives and History, Columbia. The act is also set forth in *City of Charleston Yearbook* (Charleston: News & Courier Presses, 1883), 384. The text of the statute is found in handwritten form in Archdale papers as cited. Thomas Cooper gives the title and date as act no. 138 of March 16, 1695–96, 2 S.C. STATUTES AT LARGE 121 (Cooper 1837) but does not set forth the text. For another discussion of Quakers and militia acts, see also Stephen B. Weeks, *Southern Quakers and Slavery: An Institutional Study*, vol. 15 of *Johns Hopkins Studies in Historical and Political Science* (Baltimore: Johns Hopkins Press, 1946), 189.

85. Act No. 206 of 1703, 9 S.C. STATUTES AT LARGE 617, para. 1 (McCord 1841).

86. Ibid., 620, para. 10. See Weeks, *Southern Quakers and Slavery*, 189, pointing out that the wording of the exemption became "the clergy" in 1747. See also Act No. 748 of 1747, 9 S.C. STATUTES AT LARGE 649, para. 15 (McCord 1841). In 1778 the wording became "all licensed clergymen, belonging to any established church." Act No. 1076 of 1778, 9 S.C. STATUTES AT LARGE 673, para. 14 (McCord 1841).

87. For records of the Charleston Business Meeting containing the Kimberley account, see Mabel L. Webber, "Quaker Records," *South Carolina Historical and Genealogical Magazine* 28 (1927): 30.

88. Ibid. See also McCormick, "The Quakers of Colonial South Carolina 1670–1807," 63–64.

89. McCormick "The Quakers of Colonial South Carolina 1670–1807," 170–203. A key event in the souring of the relations between the Quakers and state authorities was the lack

of response to an antislavery memorial presented by the Bush River Quaker meeting to the legislature in 1786 (ibid., 187–88). See Men's Minutes of the Bush River Monthly Meeting Religious Society of Friends 1772–1820, First Month, 1785 at 29 (committee report on the difficulty of obtaining an antislavery law); and see Minutes, Fourth Month 1786, at 55–56 (memorial presented to legislature), available on microfilm at the South Carolina Department of Archives and History, Columbia.

90. Robert St. John, *Jews, Justice and Judaism* (Garden City, N.Y.: Doubleday, 1969), 62–63. See also the Fundamental Constitution of July 21, 1669, Article 90 [65] (setting belief standards for freemen), Article 91 [66] (requiring those above seventeen [sixteen] to select a church to be eligible for places of honor and profit), and Article 87 [62] (setting a policy of tolerance to persuade nonbelievers to accept Christianity because of its benign nature), in *North Carolina Charters and Constitutions,* ed. Parker, 148–49.

91. See Article 87 [62] of the Fundamental Constitution of July 21, 1669, in *North Carolina Charters and Constitutions,* ed. Parker, 148–49, setting the goal of converting "heathens, Jews, and other dissenters from the purity of the Christian Religion."

92. See the Charter of 1663 granted by Charles II to the Lords Proprietors, in ibid., 76.

93. Thorpe, *The Federal and State Constitutions,* VII: 3784.

94. Ibid., 3:1677.

95. 1681 Pennsylvania Charter in ibid., 5:3035–36.

96. Indeed, as early as 1705, Daniel Defoe appealed to the tradition of religious liberty embodied in the colonial charter and the Fundamental Constitutions in his successful pamphlet campaign against the 1704 exclusion act, which had limited membership in the South Carolina Assembly to those who had taken the sacraments in conformity with Church of England doctrine. See John W. Brinsfield, "Daniel Defoe: Writer, Statesman, and Advocate of Religious Liberty in South Carolina," *South Carolina Historical Magazine* 76 (1975): 107–11.

97. See Act No. 225 of 1704, 2 S.C. STATUTES AT LARGE 236–46 (Cooper 1837). This law was repealed by Act No. 255 of 1706, 2 S.C. STATUTES AT LARGE 281 (Cooper 1837). See Act No. 256 of 1706, 2 S.C. STATUTES AT LARGE 282 (Cooper 1837), which replaced Act No. 225. See *The Colonial Records of North Carolina,* vol. 1. (Raleigh, N.C.: Printed by P. M. Hale, 1886), 635–44, setting forth the House of Lords' message of March 12, 1705; objecting to the law; petition from Carolina to the House of Lords; opinion of the attorney general and solicitor general that the laws were contrary to reason and English law and the Queen's Order in Council issued June 10, 1706; declaring the law null and void. See also Joseph Henry Smith, *Appeals to the Privy Council from American Plantations* (New York: Octagon, 1965), 534–35. On March 6, 1705, the Lords Proprietors, apparently reacting to objection of the bishop of London, to portions of the law encroaching on ecclesiastical power sent instructions to the governor that the law was null and void and should not be enforced. See A. S. Salley, ed., *Records in the British Public Record Office Relating to South Carolina, 1701–1710* (Columbia: Historical Commission of South Carolina, 1947), 140–41, containing text of proprietors' instructions to governor; available at the South Carolina Department of Archives and History, Columbia. See also Charles H. Lesser, *South Carolina Begins: The Records of a Proprietary Colony, 1663–1721* (Columbia: South Carolina Department of Archives and History, 1995), 262, providing a synopsis of documentation concerning the law. Jon Butler illustrates the intricacy of the early South Carolina colonial laws relating to religion by comparing a page count of those laws with those of other colonies. He notes that "Rhode Island

took up only two pages. But Pennsylvania required sixteen, New York thirteen, Massachusetts thirty-seven, Virginia forty-eight and . . . South Carolina eighty-two" (Butler, *Awash in a Sea of Faith: Christianizing the American People* [Cambridge, Mass.: Harvard University Press, 1999], 106; citing Nicholas Trott, *The Laws of British Plantations in America Relating to the Church and the Clergy, Religion and Learning* [London: Printed for B. Cowse, 1721], available on microfilm at the University of North Carolina, Chapel Hill).

98. Act No. 225 of 1704, 2 S.C. STATUTES AT LARGE 236 (Cooper 1837). Robert Olwell in *Masters, Slaves, & Subjects: The Culture of Power in the South Carolina Low Country, 1740–1790* (Ithaca, N.Y.: Cornell University Press, 1998), 200, observed "their desire to uphold and celebrate social hierarchy and secular authority led ministers to preach a doctrine of civil obedience to their assembled congregations."

99. Act No. 225 of 1704, 2 S.C. STATUTES AT LARGE 236 (Cooper 1837).

100. Ibid., 236, para. 2.

101. Ibid., 240–41, para. 16.

102. Ibid., 239–40, paras. 14 and 15. The governor had veto power over the firing of ministers (ibid., 246, para. 35).

103. See George C. Rogers, *Church and State in Eighteenth-Century South Carolina* (Charleston: Dalcho Historical Society, 1959), 13–15. See also Frederick Dalcho, *An Historical Account of the Protestant Episcopal Church in South Carolina From the First Settlement of the Province to the War of Revolution* (Charleston: Published by E. Thayer, printed by Archibald E. Miller, 1820; reprint, New York: Arnot, 1970), 62. See also Sarah M. Montgomery, "Drawing the Line: The Civil Courts' Resolution of Church Property Disputes, The Established Church and All Saints' Episcopal Church, Waccamaw," *South Carolina Law Review* 54 (2002): 223–24, discussing the role of the commission.

104. Brinsfield, *Religion and Politics in Colonial South Carolina*, 21.

105. See Dalcho, *An Historical Account of the Protestant Episcopal Church in South Carolina*, 54–58 (House censure of Reverend Marston), 63 (lay-commission proceedings concerning Marston). See also John S. Green's Transcript of the Commons House Journal 1702–1706, no. 2, 259–261 and 271–275 (entries for October 10, 1704, October 18, 1704, and October 19, 1704), available at South Carolina Department of Archives and History, Columbia.

106. Ibid., 271–73 (entries for October 18–19, 1704), describing charges against Marston.

107. Alexander Garden, *Mr. Commissary Garden's Six Letters to the Rev. Mr. Whitefield. With Mr. Whitefield's Answer to the First Letter,* second edition (Boston: T. Fleet, 1740), 5–6, available at South Caroliniana Library, University of South Carolina, Columbia.

108. See Josiah Smith, *The Character, Preaching, &c of the Reverend Mr. George Whitefield Impartially Represented and Supported in a Sermon Preached in Charleston, South Carolina March 26th,* anno Domini 1740 by Josiah Smith, V.D.M. (Charleston: Printed by Peter Timothy, 1765), available at South Caroliniana Library, University of South Carolina, Columbia.

109. See Dalcho, *An Historical Account of the Protestant Episcopal Church in South Carolina*, 128–46; Albert Micajah Shipp, *History of Methodism in South Carolina* (Nashville: Southern Methodist Publishing House, 1884), 118–21. See also Albert Deems Betts, *History of South Carolina Methodism* (Columbia: South Carolina Advocate Press, 1952), 24–25, arguing that the charges against Whitefield were a ploy by the established church to enlist the power of the civil government against a rival. See the *South Carolina Gazette* (Charleston),

July 18, 1740, describing the key charge as "not using the Form of Common Prayer in Charleston meeting houses where he has preached" and noting that he questioned the jurisdiction and impartiality of the court; available in the South Caroliniana Library, University of South Carolina, Columbia.

110. *George Whitefield's Journals* (London: Banner of Truth Trust, 1960), 502–503. See also *South Carolina Gazette,* January 8–15, 1741, describing Whitefield's plans to leave for a temporary stay in England in the wake of the accusations that he edited Bryan's letter.

111. Benjamin Franklin, *The Autobiography of Benjamin Franklin* (New York: Barnes & Noble, 1994), 133.

112. Alan Gallay, *The Formation of a Planter Elite: Jonathan Bryan and the Southern Colonial Frontier* (Athens: University of Georgia Press, 1989), 30–47. See "Hugh Bryan to a Friend, 20 November 1740," postscript to the *South Carolina Gazette,* January 1–7, 1741, describing the perils that will be visited on an unrepentant colony. See also *South Carolina Gazette,* March 20–27, 1742, describing the grand-jury presentment condemning Hugh and Jonathan Bryan and others for assembling "great Bodies of Negroes" under the "Pretense of religious Worship, contrary to Law, and destructive to the peace and Safety of the Inhabitants of this Province." The presentment recommended that measures be taken to suppress these dangerous activities (ibid). See also Gallay, *The Formation of a Planter Elite,* 46. Eliza Lucas Pinckney described Hugh Bryan's impact on the slave-owning community: "People in general were very uneasey tho' convinced he was no prophet, but they dreaded the consiquence of such a thing being put in to the head of the slaves and the advantage they might take of us" (memorandum, March 11, 1741, in *The Letterbook of Eliza Lucas Pinckney 1739–1762,* ed. Elise Pinckney [Chapel Hill: University of North Carolina Press, 1972], 30).

113. Gallay, *The Formation of a Planter Elite,* 45–47.

114. Leigh Eric Schmidt, "'The Grand Prophet,' Hugh Bryan: Early Evangelicalism's Challenge to the Establishment and Slavery in Colonial South Carolina," *South Carolina Historical Magazine* 87 (1986): 238–50.

115. Ibid., 242.

116. Gallay, *The Formation of a Planter Elite,* 46–47; Schmidt, "'The Grand Prophet,' Hugh Bryan," 247–50.

117. Gallay, *The Formation of a Planter Elite,* 52.

118. Ibid., 47–54. Gallay points out that Whitefield eventually became a slave owner and an "apologist" for the institution and that he was instrumental in introducing it into Georgia. This approach was taken under the facile justification that owning slaves would give the master an opportunity to improve their lot and introduce them to Christianity (ibid., 49–50). A detailed account of Whitefield and the Bryans is found in this volume in Bernard Powers Jr., "Seeking the Promised Land: Afro-Carolinians and the Quest for Religious Freedom to 1830."

119. See Act No. 225 of 1704, 2 S.C. STATUTES AT LARGE 237, para. 6 (Cooper 1837).

120. Ibid., 238, para. 8. The supervisors of the church-building projects could draft skilled and unskilled labor for the project.

121. Ibid., 239, para. 13.

122. Ibid., 245, para. 31.

123. See Hirsch, *The Huguenots of Colonial South Carolina,* 94, 127.

124. Act No. 225 of 1704, 2 S.C. STATUTES AT LARGE 242, para. 21–23 (Cooper 1837).

125. Ibid., 242, para. 22. The vestrymen also had to be Church of England members and taxpayer/freeholders.

126. Ibid., 244, para. 30.

127. For examples of statutes that divided parishes and also had to provide for reallocation of legislative representation, see Act No. 795 of 1751, 7 S.C. STATUTES AT LARGE 83, para. 16 (McCord 1840). See also Act No. 567 of 1734, 3 S.C. STATUTES AT LARGE 374–75, para. 5 (Cooper 1838). Many statutes regulating established church activities were passed in the wake of the 1704 enactment. A 1706 law replaced the 1704 statute. See Act No. 256 of 1706, 2 S.C. STATUTES AT LARGE 282 (Cooper 1837). This law continued the establishment of the Anglican Church, the required use of the Book of Common prayer, and use of province-wide church commissioners, but it deleted commission authority concerning firing ministers, created new parishes, set the compensation for priests, and provided the procedure by which all parish residents could be taxed for needs of the established church. The 1706 law provided for the seizure of the property of those who balked at paying the tax. See Act No. 256 of 1706, para. 19. The procedure for the election of vestrymen was refined in Act No. 241 of 1704, para. 2, 2 S.C. STATUTES AT LARGE 260 (Cooper 1837). It also reserved the right of the ministers of Dissenting congregations to conduct christenings, marriages, and burials (Act No. 241 of 1704, para. 3). The creation of auxillary ministries, called chapels of ease, often required statutory permission. See Act No. 533 of 1731, 3 S.C. STATUTES AT LARGE 304 (Cooper 1838) and Act No. 505 of 1725, 3 S.C. STATUTES AT LARGE 252–53 (Cooper 1838). Church repairs received statutory attention. See Act No. 568 of 1734, 3 S.C. STATUTES AT LARGE 376 (Cooper 1838). The buying, selling, renting, and altering of the use of land required statutory permission. See Act No. 880 of 1759, 7 S.C. STATUTES AT LARGE 84 (McCord 1840), granting St. Michael's permission to acquire additional land for a parsonage, and Act No. 991 of 1770, 7 S.C. STATUTES AT LARGE 93, granting St. Philip's permission to divide glebe lands into rental lots. See also Act No. 904 of 1761, 4 S.C. STATUTES AT LARGE 152 (Cooper 1838), granting permission to St. Bartholomew's to sell glebe lands to raise funds to buy young female slaves for the rector.

128. See Act No. 241 of 1704, 2 S.C. STATUTES AT LARGE 259 (Cooper 1837). This law also attempted to preserve the power of ministers of Dissenter churches to conduct marriages, christenings, and burials (Act No. 241 of 1704, para. 3). But we shall see later in this chapter that the issue recurred as Dissenter ministers, such as Rev. William Tennent, used their inability to get licenses to marry their parishioners as one of the bases for disestablishing the Church of England. See Underwood, *The Constitution of South Carolina*, vol. 3: *Church and State, Morality and Free Expressions*, 61.

129. See Act No. 222 of 1704, 2 S.C. STATUTES AT LARGE 232 (Cooper 1837).

130. See *The Colonial Records of North Carolina*, 1:635–44, setting forth the House of Lords' message; petition from Carolina to the House of Lords; opinion of the attorney general and solicitor general that the laws were contrary to reason and English law, and the Queen's Order in Council. See also Joseph Henry Smith, *Appeals to the Privy Council From American Plantations* (New York: Octagon, 1965), 534–35.

131. See Act No. 256 of 1706, 2 S.C. STATUTES AT LARGE 282 (Cooper 1837). Section 15 of Act No. 224 of 1704, 2 S.C. STATUTES AT LARGE 240 (Cooper 1837) gives the offensively broad powers to the lay commissioners. See also S. Charles Bolton, *Southern Anglicanism:*

The Church of England in Colonial South Carolina (Westport, Conn.: Greenwood Press, 1983), 28, which discusses the objections to the broad powers given the lay commissioners.

132. Act No 256 of 1706, paras. 16–18, 2 S.C. STATUTES AT LARGE 286–287 (Cooper 1837) (rector's salaries); ibid. 283–84, para. 6 (money for building churches).

133. Ibid., 287, para. 19.

134. Ibid., 288, para. 22.

135. See Act No. 307 of 1712, 2 S.C. STATUTES AT LARGE 366 (Cooper 1837).

· 136. Ibid., 374–75, paras. 21–26 (library); ibid., 366–67, paras. 1–4 (power of commissioners); ibid., 368–69, para. 6 (vestry); ibid., 368, 372–73, paras. 5, 12, 15 (rectors' salaries).

137. Ibid. The statutes mentioned in this section are merely a sampling of the prolific set of laws defining and redefining church regulation. Additional laws are discussed in Underwood, *The Constitution of South Carolina,* vol. 3: *Church and State, Morality and Free Expression,* especially pages 19–28, et seq.

138. See Transcript of the Minute Book of the Church Commissioners, 1717–1742 (hereafter cited as Minute Book), available at the South Carolina Department of Archives and History, Columbia.

139. Ibid., 1.

140. See ibid., 62, election of Alexander Garden as commissioner on September 13, 1736.

141. Ibid., 2, Minutes of October 1, 1717, approving orders of forty pounds per year to defray expenses during 1713 and 1716 for the parish of Goose Creek. Similar orders to defray expenses were issued on November 17, 1722, to pay the expenses of St. James Goose Creek, St. Andrew's, Christ Church, St. John's, St. Paul's, St. James Santee and St. Philip's of Charleston (ibid., 7). Most of these orders were for 40 pounds per year for several years but the larger parish of St. Philip's received 55 pounds. St. Paul's received two grants, one for 80 and one for 15 pounds (ibid.).

142. See ibid., 40–42 (minutes of March 4, 1725).

143. See Act No. 394 of 1719, 3 S.C. STATUTES AT LARGE 51 (Cooper 1838) (parishes as election districts). For a discussion of the government functions of parishes, see James Lowell Underwood, *The Constitution of South Carolina,* vol. 2: *The Journey toward Local Self-Government* (Columbia: University of South Carolina Press, 1989), 16–20, 30. See also Underwood, "African American Founding Fathers, The Making of the Constitution of 1868," in *At Freedom's Door: African American Founding Fathers and Lawyers in South Carolina,* ed. Underwood and W. Lewis Burke (Columbia: University of South Carolina Press, 2000), 4, 183n34, discussing the demise of the parish electoral system by omission from the Constitution of 1865.

144. See Minute Book, minutes of June 1, 1739, 68–69. See also ibid., 70–74, for records of commission consideration of a boundary dispute between Prince George and Prince Frederick parishes.

145. See the discussion of the 1704 church law in this essay in the section entitled "The Established Church: Caught in a Regulatory Web."

146. The 1717–42 commission minutes do not reveal that body conducting clergy-removal proceedings. Dalcho describes an incident occurring in 1774, near the end of the commission's life, when members of St. Michael's Church, who opposed the firing of the assistant minister by the vestry for injecting politics into a sermon, requested the commission to intervene and grant redress. Lt. Gov. William Bull called a meeting of the commission to

consider the petition, but since no quorum appeared no action was taken, and the commission did not meet again. See Dalcho, *An Historical Account of the Protestant Episcopal Church in South Carolina,* 201–4.

147. Minute Book, 8–9.

148. Ibid., 9.

149. Ibid., 9–10.

150. Ibid.

151. Ibid., minutes for November 6, 1722, 17.

152. For examples of commission examination of credentials, see ibid., minutes of May 15, 1723, 22–24; ibid., minutes of May 18, 1723, 27, showing the examination of Rev. Alexander Garden's credentials by the commission.

153. Ibid., minutes of December 17, 1724, 36, showing that the election of Garden was "ratified and confirmed"; see also ibid., minutes of December 24, 1724, 37, showing the election of the Reverend Francis Varnod [?] by St. George's Parish was "approved, ratified and confirmed."

154. See *Lemon v. Kurtzman,* 403 U.S. 602, 612 (1971), describing the three evils caused by establishment, including ideological and financial sponsorship of religion by the state and active involvement by the state in religious activity; see also *Walz v. Tax Commission,* 397 U.S. 664, 668 (1970), same.

155. See Act No. 861 of 1757, 4 S.C. Statutes at Large 38–39, para. 2 (Cooper 1838).

156. Ibid.

157. See Act No. 977 of 1768, 4 S.C. Statutes at Large 303 (Cooper 1838).

158. Ibid.

159. See Underwood, *The Constitution of South Carolina,* vol. 3: *Church and State, Morality and Free Expression,* 24–25.

160. See B. James Ramage, "Local Government and Free Schools in South Carolina," *Johns Hopkins Studies in Historical and Political Science* 12 (1883): 13.

161. See Act No. 307 of 1712, 2 S.C. Statutes at Large 374–76, paras. 21–26 (Cooper 1837).

162. See Act No. 290 of 1710, 2 S.C. Statutes at Large 342, 345, paras. 10–11 (Cooper 1837). For a discussion of the early history of education in South Carolina, see Underwood, *The Constitution of South Carolina,* vol. 2: *The Journey toward Local Self-Government,* 27–32.

163. See Luke 14:13–14: "But when you give a banquet invite the poor, the crippled, the lame, and the blind. And you will be blessed, because they cannot repay you, for you will be repaid at the resurrection of the righteous"; Gal. 2:10: "They asked only one thing, that we remember the poor" (Bible, New Revised Standard Version).

164. See Act No. 325 of 1712, 2 S.C. Statutes at Large 593 (Cooper 1837).

165. Ibid., 594, para. 3.

166. See Act No. 256 of 1706, 2 S.C. Statutes at Large 290, para. 30 (Cooper 1837). See also *Vestry of St. Luke's Church v. Mathews,* 4 S.C. Eq. (4 Des.) 578 (1815). When sitting vestrymen attempted to impose a fifty-dollar poll tax on Episcopalians seeking to vote in an election that might replace the incumbents, the chancellor struck down the new-voter qualification and observed that under well-established tradition stretching back to the early eighteenth century, the electors have to be (1) inhabitants of the parish, (2) freeholders or those

who otherwise contributed to the public tax fund, and (3) adherents to the Church of England. Replacing the vestries as administrators of the government aid to the poor was a drawn-out process that was completed in Act No. 2388 of 1826, 6 S.C. STATUTES AT LARGE 283–84 (Cooper 1839), which granted secular commissioners of the poor any vestiges of authority over aid to the poor remaining in the church boards.

167. See Act No. 394 of 1719, 3 S.C. STATUTES AT LARGE 51 (Cooper 1838). See also "Sixteenth Assembly List," in *Biographical Directory of the South Carolina House of Representatives,* ed. Walter Edgar, vol. 1 (Columbia: University of South Carolina Press, 1974), 41. Several of the parishes were beginning to become election districts with the election of 1717. For a general discussion of the governmental functions of the parish see Underwood, *The Constitution of South Carolina,* vol. 2: *The Journey toward Local Self-Government,* 16–20, 30.

168. See Act No. 222 of 1704, 2 S.C. STATUTES AT LARGE 232 (Cooper 1837).

169. Ibid.

170. Ibid.

171. Ibid.

172. See Brinsfield, *Religion and Politics in South Carolina,* 14–37. Previously, Act No. 202 of 1703, 2 S.C. STATUTES AT LARGE 196–97 (Cooper 1837) had discouraged religious debate by disqualifying from "employments, ecclesiastical, civil or military" anyone who professed to be a Christian but denied the existence of the holy trinity or that there is only one God or that Christianity is the true religion and that the Bible is inspired by God.

173. See Brinsfield, *Religion and Politics in South Carolina,* 18–19; see also M. Eugene Sirmans, *Colonial South Carolina: A Political History 1663–1763* (Chapel Hill: University of North Carolina Press, 1966), 76–89.

174. Brinsfield, *Religion and Politics in South Carolina,* 19–24.

175. Daniel Defoe, *Case of the Protestant Dissenters in Carolina* (London, 1706), 3–4, available on microfilm at Emory University, Atlanta.

176. Ibid.

177. Ibid., 4.

178. Ibid., 8.

179. Ibid., 10.

180. Ibid., 11.

181. Ibid., 14–16, 26–27.

182. See ibid., 23–24. See also Act No. 225 of 1704, 2 S.C. STATUTES AT LARGE 240–41, para. 16 (Cooper 1837).

183. See Defoe, *Case of the Protestant Dissenters in Carolina,* 29–33. See also Fundamental Constitution of July 21, 1669, Article 87, containing generous provisions for organizing a church of "any Religion" in *North Carolina Charters and Constitutions,* ed. Parker, 148–49.

184. See Parker, ed., *North Carolina Charters and Constitutions,* 78–79, containing the legislative provisions of the Charter of March 24, 1663.

185. See Defoe, *Case of the Protestant Dissenters in Carolina,* 29–33. See also Parker, ed., *North Carolina Charters and Constitutions,* 88, containing provisions of the March 24, 1663, Charter encouraging the proprietors to grant indulgences and dispensations to those who do not conform to the Church of England so long as they do not disturb the peace.

186. The merchant's petition, the House of Lords address, and the queen's reply are available on microfilm in John Archdale Papers 1690–1706, at the South Carolina Department

of Archives and History, Columbia. See also Brinsfield, *Religion and Politics in Colonial South Carolina,* 22–32.

187. See *The Colonial Records of North Carolina,* 634–44, setting forth the order in council and the merchant's petition, House of Lords' message, and opinions of crown legal advisers.

188. Ibid. For a discussion of the official action with regard to the petition opposing the exclusion law see Smith, *Appeals to the Privy Council from American Plantations,* 534–35.

189. See Act No. 255 of 1706, 2 S.C. STATUTES AT LARGE 281 (Cooper 1837). See also Alexander S. Salley Jr., ed., *Commissions and Instructions from the Lords Proprietors of Carolina to Public Officials of Carolina, 1685–1715* (Columbia: Historical Commission of South Carolina, 1916), 188–94, containing ratification of the repealing statute by the proprietors, July 22, 1707, available on microfilm at the Thomas Cooper Library, University of South Carolina, Columbia. See also a June 13, 1706, notation on the records of the Commissioners for Trade and Plantations that the order of council and report of the attorney general and solicitor general recommending proceedings against the Charter were read to the commissioners, in *Records in the British Public Record Office Relating to South Carolina, 1701–1710,* ed. Salley, 160. For a synopsis of the orders relating to this law, see Lesser, *South Carolina Begins,* 262.

190. See Hirsch, *The Huguenots of Colonial South Carolina,* 103–30. The argument was that some Huguenots were not fully naturalized and lacked the right to vote. Hirsch criticized Defoe's account of the Protestant dissenter controversy as being one-sided in that it was based entirely on views of the Dissenters' supporters (ibid., 108).

191. Ibid., 121; see also Edgar, *South Carolina: A History,* 51–52.

192. Edgar, *South Carolina: A History,* 52. See also Act No. 154 of 1696–97, 2 S.C. STATUTES AT LARGE 131–33 (Cooper 1837). The assembly journals for 1702 show that opposition to Huguenot voting continued to some extent despite the 1696–97 law. See Alexander S. Salley Jr., ed., *Journals of the Commons House of Assembly For 1702* (Columbia: Historical Commission of South Carolina, 1932), 52–53, available at the South Carolina Department of Archives and History, Columbia. The *Journals* show that petitioners alleged voting by unqualified persons in a recent "Berkly" county election for members of the assembly. To resolve the dispute, the assembly ordered a group of voters, many of whom had French names, to appear before the Grand Committee to prove that they were qualified to vote. See also Hirsch, *The Huguenots of Colonial South Carolina,* 121, who says that the vote was by a "purely Dissenter-party Assembly" since the Church of England members had withdrawn.

193. Act No. 228 of 1704, 2 S.C. STATUTES AT LARGE 251, 253, paras. 5–6 (Cooper 1837); see also Act No. 446 of 1721, 3 S.C. STATUTES AT LARGE 135, 136, 137, paras. 3, 8 (Cooper 1837), specifying that voters must have been residents for a year prior to the election and assembly members must have been free born subjects or naturalized. See also Act No. 1025 of 1776, repealing the 1721 act and requiring Assembly members to be subjects of the state and to have been residents twelve months prior to the election (4 S.C. STATUTES AT LARGE 356 [Cooper 1838]).

194. Butler, "The Huguenots and the American Immigrant Experience," in *Memory and Identity,* ed. Van Ruymbeke and Sparks, 200.

195. See *Journals of the Commons House of Assembly of South Carolina for 1702,* ed, Salley, 52–53.

196. See Hirsch, *The Huguenots of Colonial South Carolina,* 121n68.

197. See the sessions for April 4 and May 13, 1702, in *Journals of the Commons House of Assembly of South Carolina For 1702,* ed. Salley, 50–60. See also Hirsch, *The Huguenots of Colonial South Carolina,* 121.

198. See Act No. 365 of 1716, 2 S.C. STATUTES AT LARGE 683, 688, para. 20. See ibid., 691, for a note on repeal by proprietors and replacement by 1721 act described below.

199. Ibid. See also Act No. 373 of 1717, 3 S.C. STATUTES AT LARGE 4, para. 5 (Cooper 1838). Before taking his seat, a legislator had to take an oath "on the holy evangelists or according to the form of his profession," which ended with the words "so help me God." This act was also repealed by the proprietors (ibid., 4). It was replaced by the 1721 act cited below. The Lords Proprietors gave as the reason for vetoing the 1716 and 1717 laws that they "tend to the entire alteration and subversion [?] of the Constitution of the Province of South Carolina and are contrary to the Laws and Customs of Parliament in Great Britain." This July 22, 1718, statement of the Lords Proprietors is found in *Records of the British Public Record Office Relating to South Carolina, 1717–1720,* ed. Salley, VII: 143–45. See also Act No. 394 of 1718–19, 3 S.C. STATUTES AT LARGE 52, para. 10 (Cooper 1838), oath on the holy evangelists or according to the form of his profession, and Act No. 446 of 1721, 3 S.C. STATUTES AT LARGE 137, para. 9 (Cooper 1838), oath on the holy evangelists. The 1721 law also required that voters be Christians. In *City Council of Charleston v. Benjamin,* 33 S.C.L. (2 Strob.) 508 (1846), Justice O'Neall described the traditional oath on the holy evangelists as having the following significance: "A Christian witness, having no religious scruples against placing his hand on the book, is sworn upon the holy Evangelists—the books of the New Testament, which testify of our Saviour's birth, life, death, and resurrection; this is so common a matter, that it is little thought of as an evidence of the part which Christianity has in the common law" (ibid., 523). Not only would the New Testament focus exclude Jews from taking the oath, its meaning as described by O'Neall gives it an aggressive proselytizing flavor.

200. See Act No. 446 of 1721, 3 S.C. STATUTES AT LARGE 136, para. 3; Ibid., 137, para. 9.

201. See Act No. 730 of 1745, 3 S.C. STATUTES AT LARGE 657, para. 3 (Cooper 1838), requiring legislators to swear on the "holy evangelist" that they were qualified.

202. See Act No. 746 of 1747, 3 S.C. STATUTES AT LARGE 692 (Cooper 1838).

203. Ibid., 693.

204. See Act No. 885 of 1759, 4 S.C. STATUTES AT LARGE 99, paras. 1–3 (Cooper 1838).

205. Ibid., para. 3.

206. See Journal of the General Assembly of South Carolina for the 26th day of December 1761, 274–75 (available in the South Carolina Department of Archives and History, Columbia), for the proclamation of royal disallowance of the 1759 law announced by Gov. Thomas Boone; available at the South Carolina Department of Archives and History, Columbia. On May 29, 1761, the Board of Trade sent a letter to the king recommending that the law be disallowed because it had been passed without a suspending clause that would have delayed effectiveness of the law until the king gave his assent. Thus the law may have been vetoed more because it was an affront to the king than because it discriminated on the basis of religion. See British Public Record Office Records (Board of Trade), vol. 29, South Carolina, containing a May 29, 1761, letter from Board of Trade to the king; available at the South Carolina Department of Archives and History, Columbia. See also Frances Haskell Porcher, "Royal Review of South Carolina Law," Master's thesis, University of South Carolina,

Columbia, 1962, 66–76, ascribing similar reasons for the disallowance of several election laws during that period; available at the South Carolina Department of Archives and History, Columbia.

207. See Journal of the General Assembly of South Carolina, supra. note 206, at 275.

208. See Act No. 885 of 1759, 4 S.C. STATUTES AT LARGE 101 (Cooper 1838), showing the act completed all local phases of the legislative process.

209. George Fox to friends in Charleston, Carolina, December 23, 1683, Bowden, *The History of the Society of Friends in America,* 414. See also McCormick, "The Quakers of Colonial South Carolina 1670–1807," 44.

210. Matt. 5:33–35, Bible (Authorized Version). See also William F. Medlin, *Quaker Families of South Carolina & Georgia* (Columbia: Ben Franklin Press, 1982), 5.

211. Underwood, *The Constitution of South Carolina,* vol. 3: *Church and State, Morality and Free Expression,* 38–39.

212. See Journals of the Commons House of Assembly 1766, 50 (available at the South Carolina Department of Archives and History, Columbia), entry for Saturday, January 25, 1766.

213. Ibid. See also Charles Woodmason, *Carolina Backcountry on the Eve of the Revolution,* ed. Richard J. Hooker (Chapel Hill: University of North Carolina Press, 1953), 7n7. William Roy Smith notes that the 1745 and 1747 [48] laws and other election reform laws were disallowed by the king, with the result that the 1721 law remained in force for the most part until the Revolution. See William Roy Smith, *South Carolina as a Royal Province, 1719–1776* (1903; reprint, Freeport, N.Y.: Books for Libraries Press, 1970). The older law, Act No. 446 of 1721, 3 S.C. STATUTES AT LARGE 137, para. 9, required an oath on the holy evangelists. A 1776 Revolutionary era law contained no reference to an oath on the holy evangelists or any other religious standard for most officials, but the oath for president (governor) required that he swear to "defend the laws of God and the Protestant religion." See Act No. 1012 of 1776, 4 S.C. STATUTES AT LARGE 338, para. 1 (officers in general) and para. 2 (president) (Cooper 1838). Another act, passed later in 1776, required that a member of the General Assembly be one "professing the Protestant religion." Act No. 1026 of 1776, 4 S.C. STATUTES 356 para. 2 (Cooper 1838). This act repealed the 1721 law.

214. See STATUTES AT LARGE, 30 Car. 2, c. 2.

215. *Biographical Directory of the South Carolina House of Representatives,* ed. Edgar, 3:632.

216. Ibid.

217. Ibid. Earlier sources were less precise than the *Biographical Directory of the South Carolina House of Representatives* about the time of Salvador's legislative service and how much of it was in the Provincial (Revolutionary) Assembly and how much in the first State Assembly. See Irving J. Sloan, *The Jews in America 1621–1970,* (Dobbs Ferry, N.Y.: Oceana, 1971), 3–4; St. John, *Jews, Justice and Judaism,* 75; I. Goldberg [Rufus Learsi], *The Jews in America: A History* (Cleveland: World, 1954), 33–34; Lee J. Levinger, *A History of Jews in the United States* (Cincinnati: Union of American Hebrew Congregations, 1944), 94; Elzas, *The Jews of South Carolina From the Earliest Times to the Present,* 84n21; and Charles Reznikoff, *The Jews of Charleston* (Philadelphia: Jewish Publication Society of America, 1950), 34–40.

218. *South Carolina Gazette,* September 26, 1762, available in the South Caroliniana Library, University of South Carolina, Columbia. See also Hagy, *This Happy Land,* supra n. 59 at 44.

219. See Max Farrand, *Records of the Federal Convention of 1787,* vol. 2 (New Haven: Yale University Press, 1911), 342.

220. Ibid., 468. It could be argued that Pinckney's revised language is broader than the original in that it prohibits any religious qualifications for federal office and not just the recitation of religious oaths on assuming office.

221. Article 6, section 3, of the U.S. Constitution states in part "but no religious test shall ever be required as a qualification to any office or public trust under the United States." Even though this language can be interpreted to apply only to prohibit religious qualifications for federal offices, it was used by the Supreme Court of South Carolina, along with the federal constitution's First Amendment protection of free exercise of religion and prohibition of government establishment of religion, as authority for a 1997 decision striking down a provision of the South Carolina Constitution stating that "no person who denies the existence of the Supreme Being shall hold any office under this constitution." See *Silverman v. Campbell,* 486 S.E. 2d 1 (S.C. 1997), invalidating Art. 6, sec. 2, and Art. 17, sec. 4, of the Constitution of South Carolina in a suit brought by an applicant for notary public who claimed a violation of his religious freedom as an atheist to hold public office. Even though the court did not explain its invocation of Article 6, section 3, of the U.S. Constitution in a case involving a state office, the most likely explanation is that the court considered state offices to be "under the United States." See also *Torcaso v. Watkins,* 367 U.S. 488 (1961), invalidating on First Amendment grounds a Maryland law requiring belief in God as a prerequisite for holding public office. In reaching its decision in *Torcaso,* the U.S. Supreme Court did not reach the question of whether the Maryland law violated Article 6, section 3.

222. The Sunday Observance Act, 1677, *Halsbury's Statutes of England,* 29 Car. 2, c. 7, p. 23 (hereafter cited as Sunday Observance Act 1677).

223. Sunday Observance Act 1677. Those who engaged in worldly work on Sunday were subject to a fine of five shillings, and those who sold goods on Sunday forfeited the merchandise.

224. Ibid., 24.

225. Ibid., 25.

226. Ibid.

227. Ibid., 24–25.

228. See Act No. 74 of 1691, 2 S.C. STATUTES AT LARGE 68 (Cooper 1837). It is difficult to identify the first South Carolina Sunday laws because of the scarcity of records. A 1685 law reinstates a 1682 law but does not describe its contents, and the text of the 1682 statute has not otherwise survived. See Act No. 28 of 1685, 2 S.C. STATUTES AT LARGE 13 (Cooper 1837). For an argument that a 1670 law enacted to curb "grand abuses, practiced by the people to the great dishonor of God almighty" was the first Sunday law, see Lesser, *South Carolina Begins,* 231.

229. See Act No. 74 of 1691, 2 S.C. STATUTES AT LARGE 68–69 (Cooper 1837).

230. Ibid., 69.

231. Ibid. The prohibition on travel reflected the circumstances of the New World by forbidding travel by canoe as well as by more conventional modes.

232. Ibid.

233. Ibid.

234. Ibid.

235. See Act No. 74 of 1691, 2 S.C. STATUTES AT LARGE 70 (Cooper 1837).

236. Ibid.

237. Act No. 320 of 1712, 2 S.C. STATUTES AT LARGE 396, para. 1 (Cooper 1837).

238. See Article 86 [61] of the Fundamental Constitution of July 21, 1669, in *North Carolina Charters and Constitutions,* ed. Parker, 148.

239. Act No. 320 of 1712, 2 S.C. STATUTES AT LARGE 396, para. 1 (Cooper 1837).

240. Ibid., 397, para. 4

241. Ibid.

242. Ibid., 397, para. 5.

243. Ibid., 397, paras. 6 and 7.

244. Woodmason, *Carolina Backcountry on the Eve of the Revolution,* 47.

245. "Journal of Josiah Quincy," *Massachusetts Historical Society Proceedings* 49 (1915–16): 424, 455.

246. Woodmason, *Carolina Backcountry on the Eve of the Revolution,* 96–97.

247. See Brinsfield, *Religion and Politics in Colonial South Carolina,* 71. See also the South Carolina Constitution of 1778, Article 38, in *Basic Documents of South Carolina History* (1953).

248. George Rogers, *Charleston in the Age of the Pinckneys* (Columbia: University of South Carolina Press, 1969), 21–22.

249. Woodmason, *Carolina Backcountry on the Eve of the Revolution,* 57.

250. Ibid., 57n48.

251. Ibid., 90.

252. Ibid., 43.

253. Ibid., 27–28, 72, 86.

254. Ibid., 86.

255. Quebec Act, 14 Geo. 3, c. 83.

256. Ibid., para. 5.

257. Ibid., para. 6.

258. From the Preamble to the South Carolina Constitution of 1776, in *Basic Documents of South Carolina History.*

259. Richard Furman, Address on Liberty, 1775, 5, in the Richard Furman Collection, Furman University, Greenville, South Carolina.

260. See John Drayton, *Memoirs of the American Revolution,* 2 vols. (Charleston: Printed by A. E. Miller, 1821; reprint, New York: Arno Press, 1969), 1:136; ibid., 2:186–87. See also Brinsfield, *Religion and Politics in Colonial South Carolina,* 81.

261. Brinsfield, *Religion and Politics in Colonial South Carolina,* 64.

262. *South Carolina and American General Gazette,* December 5–12, 1776, 129, col. 3, available at the South Caroliniana Library, University of South Carolina, Columbia.

263. Ibid.

264. Woodmason, *Carolina Backcountry on the Eve of the Revolution,* 15.

265. *Rodgers v. Herron,* 85 S.E.2d 104, 113 (S.C. 1959), discussing the difficulties of proving a common-law marriage. See the annotation by Professor William G. Hammond in William Blackstone, *Commentaries on the Laws of England,* book 1, ed. William Carey Jones (Baton Rouge: Bancroft-Whitney, 1915; reprint, Baton Rouge: Claitor's Publishing Division,

1976), 617. Hammond noted that "cohabitation and reputation of being husband and wife" both had to exist before a presumption of marriage would apply. Wallace observed that the attempts by Anglican ministers to get the government to give them exclusive authority to perform licensed marriages failed repeatedly but finally succeeded at some unascertained time between 1760 and 1777. See David Duncan Wallace, *The History of South Carolina*, vol. 1 (New York: American Historical Society, 1934), 417. However, he determined that marriages performed without licenses could still have been valid. If he was relying on the concept of common-law marriage for this statement, the validity of the marriage would probably have depended on meeting the elements described in the above annotation although it is hard to ascertain the exact status of South Carolina law at that time.

266. Tennent's speech is reproduced as an appendix to David Ramsay, *The History of the Independent or Congregational Church in Charleston, South Carolina, From Its Origin Till The Year 1814* (Philadelphia: Maxwell, 1815), 53–71 (hereafter cited as Ramsay, *Independent History*.)

267. Ibid., 53–54, 65.

268. Ibid., 54.

269. Ibid., 54–55.

270. Ibid., 54.

271. Ibid., 54–55.

272. Ibid., 55.

273. Ibid., 57–58.

274. Ibid.

275. Ibid., 58.

276. Ibid.

277. Ibid., 59.

278. Ibid., 60.

279. Ralph Ketcham, *James Madison: A Biography* (Charlottesville: University Press of Virginia, 1971), 72–73.

280. See Willard Sterne Randall, *George Washington: A Life* (New York: Holt, 1997), 465. For the full text, see Mark A. Mastromarino, ed., *Papers of George Washington*, Presidential Series, vol. 6, July–November 1790 (Charlottesville: University Press of Virginia, 1996), 284.

281. Ramsay, *Independent History*, 60–61.

282. Ibid., 61.

283. Ibid., 62.

284. Ibid.

285. Ibid.

286. Ibid., 63–64.

287. Ibid., 63.

288. Brinsfield, *Religion and Politics in Colonial South Carolina*, 120–23. See also Harvey T. Cook, *A Biography of Richard Furman* (Greenville, S.C.: Baptist Courier Job Rooms, 1913), 55, based on notes by Wood Furman. Charles Cotesworth Pinckney is sometimes credited with fashioning the fourth option, a compromise that significantly influenced the final outcome. See Brinsfield, 120. The second alternative, which would have kept the Church of England's authority to superintend elections and administer assistance to the poor but with

no tax support for worship, was defeated in a close vote. See Edward McCrady, *The History of South Carolina in the Revolution 1775–1780*, (New York: Russell & Russell, 1969), 212–13; Brinsfield, 120.

289. Ibid., 126. See Article 38 in the South Carolina Constitution of 1778, in *Basic Documents of South Carolina History* (1953).

290. Article 38, South Carolina Constitution of 1778.

291. Ramsay, *Independent History,* 33.

292. Article 38, South Carolina Constitution of 1778.

293. Ramsay, *Independent History,* 33–34. Apparently the church was concerned that the incompleteness of the doctrines listed in Article 38 would leave an opening for nonbiblical beliefs to be attributed to the church. See George Howe, *History of the Presbyterian Church in South Carolina,* vol. 2 (Columbia: Duffie & Chapman, 1883), 22.

294. See "Form and Manner for Ordering Priest," in Church of England, *Book of Common Prayer and Administration of the Sacraments, and Other Rites and Ceremonies of the Church of England Together With Psalter or Psalms of David Pointed As They Are to Be Sung or Said in Churches and the Forms and Manner of Making Ordaining, and Consecrating Bishops, Priests, and Deacons* (Cambridge, England: University of Cambridge, Printed by John Field, 1662), n. pag.; or see http://www.eskimo.com/~1howell/bcp1662/ordinal/priests.html (visited November 27, 2004.) There are some minor differences between the hard-copy and on-line versions. The author would like to thank Dr. Herbert Johnson for calling to his attention the similarity in the wording of the ministerial qualifications portions of the Book of Common Prayer and the 1778 Constitution.

295. Article 38, South Carolina Constitution of 1778.

296. Article 86 [61], Fundamental Constitution of July 21, 1669, in *North Carolina Charters and Constitutions,* ed. Parker, 148.

297. Article 38, South Carolina Constitution of 1778.

298. Article 3, South Carolina Constitution of 1778.

299. Articles 12 and 13, South Carolina Constitution of 1778.

300. Underwood, *The Constitution of South Carolina,* vol. 3: *Church and State, Morality and Free Expression,* 8.

301. See Article 21 of the South Carolina Constitution of 1778 in *Basic Documents of South Carolina History* (1953). The U.S. Supreme Court struck down similar ministerial disqualifications as violating the First Amendment right of pastors to exercise their religion freely in the 1978 case of *McDaniel v. Paty,* 435 U.S. 618 (1978). The case involved a Tennessee provision that had been used to block a Baptist minister from serving in the state constitutional convention. The court concluded that the provision invalidly punished the minister for engaging in his religion.

302. Brinsfield, *Religion and Politics in Colonial South Carolina,* 113–14.

303. See James A. Rogers, *Richard Furman, Life and Legacy* (Macon: Mercer University Press, 1985), 70; see also Harvey T. Cook, *A Biography of Richard Furman,* 21.

304. *Journal of the Constitutional Convention of South Carolina May 10, 1790–June 3, 1790* (Columbia: Historical Commission of South Carolina, 1946), 1–6. The 1778 constitutional revisions are described in Arthur H. Shaffer, *To Be An American: David Ramsay and the Making of the American Consciousness* (Columbia: University of South Carolina Press 1991), 45–46.

305. Article 38, South Carolina Constitution of 1778.

306. Act No. 1102 of 1778, 8 S.C. STATUTES AT LARGE 119 (McCord 1840).

307. Act No. 1166 of 1783, 8 S.C. STATUTES AT LARGE 122 (McCord 1840).

308. Ibid., 123–24, para. 9.

309. Ibid., 122–23, para. 4.

310. See Petition of Samuel Beach with Regard to Pew Assessments for St. Philip's and St. Michael's Churches to the General Assembly, February 19, 1787, South Carolina Department of Archives and History, Columbia. See also Act No. 1278 of 1785, 8 S.C. STATUTES AT LARGE 131, para. 4 (McCord 1840), incorporating St. Michael's and St. Philip's in Charleston and granting the vestries the right "annually to rate and assess each and every of the pews in the said churches, at such sum or sums of money as they, or a majority of them, shall think proper" and if a member fails to make the payment, empowering the churches "to let to hire the said pew or pews."

311. See Reports of the Committee to Review the Petition of Samuel Beach on Pew Assessments at St. Philip's and St. Michael's Churches, February 24 and 26, 1787, South Carolina Department of Archives and History, Columbia. See also Marion Chandler, "Church Incorporations in South Carolina under the Constitution of 1778," M.A. thesis, University of South Carolina, 1969, 56–58, discussing the committee's reasons for rejecting the petition. Chandler questions the committee's conclusion that equal assessment authority had been given to the various Protestant churches since one of the "laws" on which this conclusion was based had never been passed.

312. See Chandler, "Church Incorporations in South Carolina under the Constitution of 1778," 58–59. But see Act No. 1415 of 1788, 8 S.C. STATUTES AT LARGE 145, 147, para. 4 (McCord 1840).

313. See Act No. 1278 of 1785, 8 S.C. STATUTES AT LARGE 130 (McCord 1840).

314. Ibid., 131, para. 4. The transition of the Episcopal churches from government financial support to membership support is depicted in Act No. 1289 of 1785, 4 S.C. STATUTES AT LARGE 703–04 (Cooper 1838). See also Dalcho, *An Historical Account of the Protestant Episcopal Church in South Carolina*, 206–7, describing a church-finance system involving "rents and assessments of Pews, the rent of Glebe lands, Interest on Stock, Burial Fees" and "annual subscriptions." The minutes of the parishes of St. Philip's and St. Michael's reveal that these churches on December 7, 1778, adopted a voluntary subscription system since the new constitution meant that government funds would no longer be available. See Mrs. C. G. Howe and Mrs. Charles F. Middleton, eds., *The Minutes of St. Michael's Church of Charleston, S.C. from 1758–1797* (Charleston: Historical Activities Committee of the South Carolina Society of Colonial Dames of America, n.d.), entry no. 155, 137.

315. See G. D. Berheim, *History of the German Settlements and of the Lutheran Church in North Carolina* (Philadelphia: Lutheran Bookstore, 1872). See also S. T. Hallman, *History of the Evangelical Lutheran Synod of South Carolina* (Columbia: Farrell Printing, 1924), 22–23.

"Without discrimination or preference"

Equality for Catholics and Jews under
the South Carolina Constitution of 1790

James Lowell Underwood

It took only twelve years for the rising tide of reform to submerge the Constitution of 1778, which signaled the coming of the Constitution of 1790. Although it achieved disestablishment of the Church of England in favor of a general Protestant establishment, as a charter of religious freedom the 1778 Constitution was incomplete. Catholic churches and Jewish synagogues still could not incorporate and had to own their property through trustees who might abuse their power. Legislators and key executive officials had to be Protestants.[1] Looking back over South Carolina constitutional history in a scholarly argument before the South Carolina Court of Appeals in 1834, Thomas Smith Grimké, a distinguished constitutional lawyer, lamented those provisions in the Constitution of 1778: "Shocked and indignant, as we are, at the catalogue of European bigotry, has it not had its rival even in America? We look with astonishment on the persecutions of the Quakers and Baptists in New England, and of the Puritans in Virginia. We behold with surprise and gratitude the tolerant institutions of Lord Baltimore, the Catholic; and of Wm. Penn, the Quaker. We regard with mortification our own Constitution of 1778, establishing the Protestant as the religion of the State, and rejecting the Catholic and Jew as political outlaws."[2]

A forceful new advocate for equal treatment of Catholics trained his rhetorical guns on unfair state constitutions by going straight to the top with a stinging complaint. An early 1790 letter to President George Washington from John Carroll, who was on the cusp of becoming the first Catholic bishop in the United States, genuflected to Washington with patriotic sentiments but vehemently complained about states that did not extend the *"equal rights of citizenship"* to Catholics despite their having paid the *"price of [their] blood spilt under your eyes."*[3] This dramatic language alluded to the injustice of denying equal rights to those who had earnestly served the Revolutionary cause. Washington's March 1790 reply said that all *"worthy members of the community,* ARE EQUALLY ENTITLED TO THE PROTECTION OF CIVIL GOVERNMENT," and he lauded *"the patriotic part which you took in the accomplishment of [the] Revolution."*[4] He noted that a Catholic nation (France) had contributed greatly to the colonists' victory in the Revolutionary War. He predicted that society would grow more liberal and their fellow citizens would recognize the contributions of Catholics to building the nation and extend greater rights.[5] Sentiments such as those expressed by the president, just as South Carolina was preparing to meet in convention to rewrite its constitution, helped create an atmosphere for reform.

The Constitution of 1778 sagged under the weight of its convoluted, busybody nature. Like a stern patriarch lecturing his children, it laid down religious and moral precepts. Even the Protestant churches that could incorporate had to certify adherence to constitutionally stipulated belief requirements.[6] The Constitution was laden with detailed instructions of how ministers of established churches were to comport themselves.[7] Broad standards of religious tolerance were included in the Constitution, but even these were hedged about with traditional conditions of belief in God and that God was publicly to be worshiped.[8] The Church of England was no longer the favored religion. The government no longer levied taxes to support religion, but some, such as Samuel Beach, viewed legally enforceable pew assessments as having the same impact.[9] The net of tolerance was more broadly cast, but church and state were still entwined. The fatal flaw of the Constitution of 1778 was its self-contradictory nature; it sought to grant broad religious freedom but at the same time it attempted to regulate it intensely through the codelike Article 38. And it spoke of tolerance rather than guaranteed rights. It remained for the Constitution of 1790 to advance beyond the halfway measures of 1778.

Distrust of the unfamiliar still retarded the expansion of the rights of Catholics and Jews. The unreasonable fear that the Quebec Act of 1774 meant a Catholic establishment in a major part of Canada and the apprehension that a Catholic army would be dispatched across the border by Britain to control malcontents in the lower colonies probably lingered in 1778.[10] These fears revived earlier concerns that had arisen in 1749 as rumors spread that Jesuits were plotting with French agents in Mobile to launch an attack against South Carolina.[11] A 1775 edict of the Committee of Public Safety of the Provincial Congress directed the disarmament of Catholics, Negroes, and Indians.[12] At the core of these fears was the suspicion that Catholics owed allegiance to foreign powers, whether the papal state, or the British or French. Charles Woodmason, Anglican missionary to the backcountry in the 1760s, reported that the suspicion was so pervasive that some Catholics took the precaution of disguising themselves as followers of religions that were regarded as less threatening. In a 1768 passage in his journal, he observed, "Among these Quakers and Presbyterians are many concealed Papists—They are not tolerated in this Government—And in the Shape of New Light Preachers, I've met with many Jesuits."[13]

Even after the ratification of the First Amendment to the U.S. Constitution in 1791, with its strong protection of free exercise of religion, and adoption of the South Carolina Constitution of 1790, with its safeguard of freedom of worship "without discrimination or preference," Catholic leaders had to fight questions about their loyalty.[14] As late as 1826, Bishop John England of Charleston had to combat such distrust in a speech in the hall of the House of Representatives. He rebutted not only charges that the primary loyalty of Catholics was to the papal state but also contentions that the hierarchical nature of their church governance would undermine their allegiance to democracy.[15] But Catholics had already proved their loyalty in the Revolutionary War, and this helped create a climate for the extension of greater constitutional protection to them in 1790. A contemporary observer, David Ramsay, noted: "The orderly conduct and active co-operation of its [Catholic Church] members in all measures for the defence and good government of the country, proves that the apologies offered in justification of the restrictions imposed on them by the protestant governments of Europe are without foundation, or do not apply to the state of things in Carolina."[16]

The Revolutionary War fueled the growth of religious liberty by furnishing an incentive to replace the Anglican establishment with a general Protestant establishment to cement Dissenter support of the Revolution. It also furnished a chance for Catholics and Jews to prove their loyalty and thus their entitlement to greater religious freedom. With regard to conciliating non-Anglican Protestants, Ramsay observed, "The dissenters felt their weight, and though zealous in the cause of independence, could not brook the idea of risking their lives and fortunes for anything short of equal rights.... The prize contended for being made equally interesting to all, equal exertions were made by all for obtaining it."[17]

Jewish citizens had a generous measure of freedom, but their rights were not fully equal to others. Robert St. John notes, "In Charleston, Jews had the right to worship as they pleased and to work at any occupation they chose, or to conduct any type of business, or to engage in any form of trade, without restriction. This was the sort of freedom that persecution-weary Old World Jews were seeking."[18]

But since the Constitution of 1778 permitted incorporation only by Protestant churches, even venerable congregations such as Charleston's Beth Elohim, one of America's oldest synagogues, with its earliest surviving records dating back to 1750, still could not take advantage of the more efficient corporate form of operation.[19] But in addition to holding property through trustees, Catholics and Jews could incorporate charitable organizations that were not churches per se.[20] For example, in 1778 the Catholic Society was incorporated to operate a school.[21] Despite their not-quite-equal legal status, David Ramsay described the South Carolina Jews: "Equally interested in the welfare of the country, they are equally zealous for its defence and good government."[22] This patriotism is seen in the political and military career of Francis Salvador, who was a member of the Revolutionary legislative assembly that declared independence.[23] Further evidence of commitment to the American cause is found in the Revolutionary War service of a military unit informally known as the Jewish Company, but a scholarly dispute has emerged over whether it was completely, predominantly, or only fractionally, composed of Jews.[24] Those who participated in the struggle for freedom wanted to share equally in its fruits.[25]

Events on the national scene created an atmosphere ripe for expansion of religious freedom. The Northwest Ordinance was passed by Congress on July 13, 1787, to provide standards for governing the territories. Article 1 ensured, "No person demeaning himself in a peaceable and orderly manner shall ever be molested on account of his mode of worship or religious sentiments in the said territory."[26] National and local leadership passed into the hands of persons with a deep interest in freedom of religion and reducing the entwining of church and state. Charles Pinckney was both governor and constitutional convention president in 1790.[27] As a federal constitutional convention delegate in 1787, Pinckney offered a scheme of government with a strong civil rights component. The sixth article stated: "The Legislature of the United States shall pass no Law on the subject of Religion, nor touching or abridging the Liberty of the Press nor shall the Privilege of the Writ of Habeas Corpus ever be suspended except in case of Rebellion or Invasion."[28] In the federal convention, Pinckney was a relentless foe of religious test oaths for federal offices.[29] Along with James Madison, he proposed to the federal convention that Congress be given the power "to establish an University, in which no preferences or distinctions should be allowed on account of religion."[30] The proposal was not successful, but it anticipated the provision against religious discrimination that was the keystone of the religious freedom article in the South Carolina Constitution of 1790. Further evidence of Pinckney's interest in eliminating religious discrimination is seen in an address he delivered on May 14, 1788, to the South Carolina Convention for ratifying the federal constitution. In his speech he criticized Great Britain's unequal treatment of its subjects because of their religion, stating that "even the government I have alluded to [Great Britain] withholds from a part of its subjects the equal enjoyment of their religious liberties. How many thousands of the subjects of Great Britain at this moment labor under civil disabilities, merely on account of their religious persuasion!"[31] He regretted the poor record of European countries on religious freedom.[32] America and South Carolina must do better. Pinckney would preside over finishing the task of disestablishment and provide the link between federal and state constitutional reform.

Disestablishment and Religious Liberty for "all Mankind"

Federal constitutional reform spurred state constitutional reform. The religious clauses of the federal First Amendment and the strong freedom of conscience provisions of Article 8 of the South Carolina Constitution of 1790 were part of the same wave of revisions. The First Amendment, along with the rest of the Bill of Rights, cleared Congress on September 25, 1789.[33] It provided that "Congress shall make no law respecting an establishment of religion, or prohibiting the free exercise thereof; or abridging the freedom of speech, or of the press, or the right of the people peaceably to assemble, and to petition the government for a redress of grievances." These rules applied to Congress and left the states unaffected. James Madison had attempted to persuade the House of Representatives to adopt a measure forbidding the states, not just the national government, to impinge on fundamental rights such as the "right of conscience."[34] Madison observed that some state constitutions guaranteed basic rights and others did not. Federal civil rights protection that is binding on the states was needed to provide a "double security."[35] Madison's proposal failed to pass. State constitutional change was needed to shore up the protection of basic civil liberties.

South Carolina's adoption of a new constitution followed close on the heels of its ratification of the Bill of Rights, with its First Amendment religious freedom provision. Congress received presidential notice of South Carolina's ratification of the Bill of Rights on April 3, 1790, and on May 10, 1790, the state's constitutional convention began.[36] After the South Carolina convention, commentators described the influence of federal constitutional revision in creating a climate for change in South Carolina. Judge Joseph Brevard noted, "The delegates of the people met in general convention at Columbia, in June 1790, established a constitution for the government of the state, conformably to the principles of the constitution of the United States."[37] David Ramsay, physician, historian, and political leader, made comparable observations but with more direct references to the clauses on freedom of conscience, when he said that the new constitution was crafted by a convention called to frame a new fundamental law "adapted to the new order of things" spawned by the new federal Constitution.[38] The need for a new state constitution more in line with the new federal one also pervaded a letter written by a visiting observer, John Brown Cutting, to John Rutledge Jr. It described the South Carolina political scene in 1789 as the legislature debated calling the convention: "A committee of both houses is appointed to take into consideration the propriety of calling a convention this year to alter and amend the constitution. It is proposed, I find, to lessen the enormous representation which now prevails, and in a word to diminish the expense of the civil list and establish a constitution for South Carolina more conformable to that of the Union than the present."[39]

Cutting's remark about the "enormous representation" probably referred to the crowded House of Representatives, which had 208 members and was considered to be too costly and unwieldily.[40] Issues of power allocation and government efficiency —such as the location of the capital, the consolidation of executive power, and the balance of legislative representation between lowcountry and backcountry—fueled much of the demand for constitutional revision and occupied much of the convention's time.[41]

Although only twelve years old, the Constitution of 1778—with its complex, weblike regulation of religion—already seemed an anachronism. This view was expressed in a letter to the *City Gazette, or The Daily Advertiser* of Charleston, published on May 11, 1790, just as the convention was getting underway. It was signed simply "Freeman." He was relieved that reform was on its way: "I am happy to find a great number of gentlemen of acknowledged abilities employed in the arduous task, not doubting but their outmost abilities will be exerted to compose a just and permanent code, whereby not only our civil and religious liberties will be secured, but our political interest attended to, that we may rise from obloquy."[42]

The 1790 Constitution completed disestablishment. The 1778 Constitution moved from a Church of England establishment to a general Protestant establishment. The

1790 Constitution made no reference to any form of establishment. However, the 1790 Constitution was not born in an atmosphere of complete separation of church and state. This is seen in the calling and conduct of the convention. The legislative resolution calling for the election of delegates designated church wardens as election managers in those areas still using parishes as units of political representation and required the managers to take an oath ending with the words "so help me God."[43]

Early in the convention, during the organizational phase, John Drayton suggested that clergymen members of the convention lead it in thanking God and asking for his leadership in drafting the Constitution. Col. John Lewis Gervais stated that he had no objection to such proceedings but suggested that they be held on Sunday.[44] From then on, convention members regularly met on Sundays, at least sometimes in the State House, to hear a discourse or sermon by a clergyman who was a delegate to the convention. These included the Reverend Richard Furman and the Reverend Dr. Henry Purcell.[45] Thus the convention whose hallmark was disestablishment and the broadening of the beneficiaries of religious freedom met for worship as a group at official premises. The content of these sermons was not recorded, and we cannot precisely ascribe later remarks of a speaker in another context to an earlier address, but a letter written a few years later by Furman to Oliver Hart is at least suggestive of the views of one leading religious freedom advocate who was a delegate. Furman's advocacy of dismantling the Church of England establishment is described in the previous essay. The following passage reflects his belief that political principles cannot be entirely divorced from religion. Criticizing the excesses of the French Revolution, he wrote in a 1793 letter to Hart that the zealots of reform would "lay aside Religion altogether, and have nothing but a little Morality taught to the Youth, and this Morality to be founded on Political Principles; which even exclude the Idea of God's Providence if not of his Existence from the Mind."[46] His approach appears to have been one of broad acceptance of God's leadership in government as well as in the other affairs of life but with no preference given to any denomination.[47] In addition to the group worship services, such as those addressed by Furman and Purcell, the members of the 1790 Convention incorporated religion into one of their final acts. In a May 31, 1790, address to George Washington congratulating him on his election as president and thanking him for his leadership during the Revolutionary War, the delegates told him that they were "offering up our prayers to the great Father of the universe that he may be pleased to shed his influence over all Your councils."[48] Thus the delegates's behavior seemed to connote that such broad, nondenominational civic religious ceremonies did not violate their concept of the relationship of church and state.

Members of the Jewish community followed the constitutional revision process closely. In his essay "The Jewish Congregation of Charleston," Nathaniel Levin noted that "as none of our brethren were delegates at that convention, they determined to support such persons as were of known sterling integrity, and liberal sentiments, who were favourably disposed to the interests and privileges which our nation should enjoy, and who would faithfully discharge their duty to their country."[49] He observed that "undivided support was given to Gen. Gadsden, Charles Cotesworth Pinckney, Edward Rutledge, Thomas Heyward Jr., John F. Grimke, David Ramsay, William Drayton, John J. Pringle, Daniel Desassure, Elihu H. Bay, and others, men who will always be associated with the honour and character of our state, and who adorned and dignified the several exalted states they occupied."[50]

During the months immediately prior to the convention, South Carolina newspapers printed documents from other states that espoused a constitutional philosophy of broad religious freedom without establishment. One was a provision suggested by a Rhode Island convention for inclusion in the Bill of Rights. It stated, in part, that "therefore all men have an equal, natural and unalienable right to the free exercise of religion, according to the dictates of conscience;—and that no particular religious sect, or society, ought to be favored or established by law, in preference to others."[51] A copy of the new Pennsylvania Constitution of 1790 was also printed. It stated that "no human authority can controul or interfere with the rights of conscience in any case whatever, nor shall any preference ever be given, by law, to any religious establishments or modes of worship."[52] There is no record of these provisions having been discussed at the South Carolina Convention, but the South Carolina Constitution took a similar approach of guaranteeing freedom of conscience without giving special privileges to any denomination.

The report of a fourteen-member committee charged with making a digest of key proposals suggested strong religious freedom guarantees. With respect to religion it recommended that "all mankind are to enjoy equal liberty in matters of religion, and the rights of conscience to be defended. Civil officers to be appointed to manage elections throughout the state, and the name of parish exchanged for district."[53] The provision finally adopted was Article 8 of the Constitution of 1790, which stated:

> Sec. 1. The free exercise and enjoyment of religious profession and worship, without discrimination or preference, shall, forever hereafter, be allowed within this State to all mankind; provided that the liberty of conscience hereby declared shall not be so construed as to excuse acts of licentiousness, or justify practices inconsistent with the peace or safety of this State.
>
> Sec. 2. The rights, privileges, immunities, and estates of both civil and religious societies and of corporate bodies shall remain as if the constitution of this State had not been altered or amended.[54]

Article 1 retained religious names for many lowcountry election districts.[55]

The chief legacy of the 1790 document's religious freedom article was that there were no longer second-class citizens relegated to a diluted brand of religious freedom. In a July 15, 1790, letter to President Washington, commemorating his contributions to liberty, Jacob Cohen, president of Beth Elohim, praised the Revolution and the new federal and state constitutions for replacing the "political degradation and grievous oppression" that had beset Jews in "almost every other part of the world" with "equal participation" and enjoyment of freedom.[56] In a June 19, 1790, letter to Washington, Charles Cotesworth Pinckney, a leading delegate, noted that the new state constitution was not perfect but "by it the poor will be protected in their freedoms, & the rich in their property."[57] Not everyone was impressed. In a July 4, 1790, letter to Edward Rutledge, who had been a leading member of the South Carolina Convention, Congressman William Smith grumbled that the "constitution-mongers" in the nation's capital (then New York), including James Madison, had poured contempt on some parts of the new South Carolina Constitution including "the want of power in the Executive" and the unusual provision for "Two Treasuries, [one in Columbia and one in Charleston] without one Treasure."[58] The religious freedom article was not a target of their ire.

The religious freedom provisions became a point of pride. The venerable Henry Laurens was able to report in a July 25, 1790, letter to his friend Bishop John Ettwein of the Moravian Church of North America, which was searching for a new location, that the state constitution posed no barrier to his group. No religious test would block service of its members in the legislature, and an affirmation could be substituted for an oath by those elected.[59]

One religious disqualification remained. "Ministers of the gospel" of "any religious persuasion" were barred from serving as governor, lieutenant governor, or member of the House or Senate so that they would not be "diverted from the great duties of their function."[60] In a 1796 comparison of the South Carolina Constitution with those of other states and the federal government, William Smith criticized the ministerial disqualification by noting that "When the *laity* undertake to exclude the clergy by constitutional regulations, the exclusion savours rather too much of political *intolerance*" and deprives the people of representation by a profession whose members often possess "those excellent qualities of the mind, which would be productive, in legislative bodies, of order, moderation, justice and public rectitude."[61] The provision created a paradox: ministers were politically penalized because they were so religious that they became ministers, but the purpose of the provision appears to have been to encourage their ministry by limiting diversions. An argument for such a provision might be that it is possible some ministers might turn legislative service into a partisan instrument for their religion, but it would be better to wait until such problems appear and deal with them in the election process rather than enact a sweeping prohibition on office holding by ministers. Ironically, read literally, the provision contains a double-edged prejudice. The exclusion barred only "ministers of the gospel." Thus it could have been argued that it would ban Christian ministers from serving but not Jewish rabbis or others who did not espouse the "gospel." Surely, such an effect was not intended, but, if implemented, it could have been prejudicial against not only the Christian ministers who were excluded from office but also the non-Christian clerics whose work was not considered worth protecting from diversion. Many years later, in 1978, the U.S. Supreme Court in *McDaniel v. Paty* struck down a similar Tennessee provision on the ground that it violated the First Amendment free exercise of religion rights of ministers.[62]

Aside from the odd ministerial disqualification, the new South Carolina Constitution set an enlightened standard for the treatment of religious minorities. It proved especially liberating for Catholics and Jews.

A More Secure Religious Freedom
for Catholics and Jews

The new religious freedom provision eliminated all references to establishment of religion whether of a particular denomination or Protestantism in general and explicitly prohibited preferring one religion over another. Gone were the provisions of Article 38 of the 1778 Constitution, which reserved the right to incorporate to Protestant churches that subscribed to certain beliefs.[63] This freed the historic Charleston synagogue of Beth Elohim to petition the legislature on January 12, 1791, for incorporation.[64] This congregation had been formed in 1749 or 1750.[65] The petition stated, "Humbly Sheweth, That the said Congregation conceive that it will be conducive to the decent and regular exercise of their religion, and public worship of the great Jehovah and Almighty ruler of the Universe, to the proper maintenance of the poor, & to the support and education of the orphans, of their Society, as well as other pious purposes, to have their said Congregation legally incorporated, and with privileges and powers similar to those, which have been heretofore granted by the legislature, to other religious Sects."

The petition cited Article 8, section 1, of "our excellent new constitution" as providing authority for the petition. The petition then continued: "They therefore humbly pray this honorable house, to grant that they may be legally incorporated, with privileges and powers as abovementioned, and they hope, that their religious and political conduct, will tend to exemplify the true wisdom, genuine charity, and sound policy of the said Article of the Constitution, which entitles them, as they presume, to that equal participation of religious freedom and immunities."

Jacob Rader Marcus, noted historian of American Jews, said of the petition: "The tone certainly seems apologetic, but the concept of Jewish integration into an overwhelmingly Gentile society was, after all, something very new and precarious in 1791."[66] Marcus speculated that one reason why minority religions such as Catholics and Jews were making progress in achieving equality in the late eighteenth century was that separation of church and state and abolition of discrimination helped avoid the "confessional strife" [bitter doctrinal disputes] that preference would have created in an increasingly diverse country.[67]

The legislature granted the incorporation.[68] The statute conferring incorporation began by noting that Article 8, section 1, bestowed freedom of "religion without discrimination or preference." The law awarded typical corporate powers to the congregation, including the power to hold property up to five thousand pounds in value.[69] The statute gave a key role in property management to the elders of the congregation and granted the synagogue the right to hire and fire rabbis.[70]

At the time of its incorporation, Beth Elohim had more than four hundred members composing fifty-three families.[71] The new constitution with its grant of equal religious freedom, including the power to incorporate, helped release the congregation's pent-up energy for growth. The cornerstones were laid in 1792 for a new synagogue, which was completed in 1794.[72] The dedication of the beautiful new building was treated by the *South Carolina State-Gazette* as an occasion for celebration in the city at large, not just in the Jewish community. In describing the dedication ceremony the paper stated:

> The ceremony was attended by a numerous concourse of ladies and gentlemen; from which circumstance, as well as from the style of the building and the splendor of its ornaments, we can perceive those little prejudices and weaknesses that have for ages, disgraced the human character, to be wearing off and safely pronounce, that injured people, in the blessed climes of America, to have realized their promised [*sic*] land. The shackles of religious distinctions are now no more; the oppressive and cramping capitation tax, that has for ages scattered them upon the face of the earth, is here unknown; they are here admitted to the full privileges of citizenship, and bid fair to flourish and be happy.[73]

To the Congregation of Beth Elohim, the ability to incorporate was no arcane legal technicality. It was a mark of freedom and acceptance by the community. In his 1843–44 history of Beth Elohim Nathan Levin noted that, when writing Jewish leaders in London in 1805 for assistance in obtaining a new hazan (reader of scriptures), the congregation cited the generous religious freedom in South Carolina, including the right to incorporate, as an inducement to settle in Charleston. The letter stated: "In a free and independent country like America, where civil and religious freedom go hand in hand, where no distinctions exist between the clergy of different denominations, where we are incorporated and known in law; freely tolerated; where, in short, we enjoy all the blessings of freedom in common with our fellow-citizens, you may readily conceive we pride ourselves under the happy situation which makes us feel that we are men, susceptible of that dignity which belongs to human nature."[74]

As important as the 1790 Constitution proved to Beth Elohim, the congregation did not compromise its high ethical standards during the period in which adoption was being debated. The 1790 Constitution was the first of the state's fundamental laws to be adopted by a separately elected convention rather than by the legislature assuming the role of a constituent assembly. Apparently members of the congregation had worked for the election of a candidate, Christopher Knight. After the election he offered a contribution to the congregation that was turned down by its president, Jacob Cohen, who responded that while the offer was probably well intended, acceptance of it would create the impression that the congregation could be bought.[75]

In her 1812 *History of the Jews,* Hannah Adams included a letter from Philip Cohen, a Charleston merchant. Cohen emphasized that the religious freedom provisions facilitated integration of the Jewish community into the community at large without destroying its identity. He observed that "Hebrews in this city pay their hearty homage to the laws, which guarantee their rights, and consolidate them into the mass of a free people."[76] He noted that educational as well as political and commercial opportunities were open to the Jewish community, who preferred a broad classical education rather than one focusing only on religion.[77] Cohen celebrated the acceptance of religious minorities as part of the larger community under the enlightened laws guaranteeing religious freedom, observing that the Jews "have built an elegant synagogue; and what strongly exhibits the liberality of the city is, that the Roman Catholick church is directly opposite to it."[78] He further offered an example of the esteem with which the synagogue services were viewed, pointing out that "the seats in a Jewish synagogue are often crowded with visitors of every denomination."[79]

On the same day of the Beth Elohim incorporation, an act was passed incorporating the Catholic church in Charleston.[80] It gave the church the typical corporate powers to adopt a seal, "sue and be sued," to "have perpetual succession of officers and members," to adopt bylaws so long as they were in conformity with the "laws of the land," to hire ministers, and to buy, sell, and hold property of up to five thousand pounds in value.[81] Giving Catholic and Jewish congregations equal power to incorporate represented major progress in religious liberty, but one distinguished commentator saw dangers in any religious body having corporate powers. On February 21, 1811, President James Madison vetoed a bill by which Congress incorporated the Protestant Episcopal Church of Alexandria in the District of Columbia. In his veto message Madison criticized the bill as giving churches "a legal agency in carrying into effect a public and civil duty," including responsibilities such as the education and support of the poor, which he viewed as belonging more on the secular rather than the religious side of the line separating church and state.[82] In an 1819 memorandum, the retired James Madison spoke against the "evil" from "the indefinite accumulation of property from the capacity of holding it in perpetuity by ecclesiastical corporations."[83] Apparently, he was concerned that religious corporations would acquire such vast resources that they would dominate civil as well as spiritual affairs. Therefore he recommended limits on the life of such corporations and the funds that they could acquire.[84]

Progress and Challenges for Catholics

The favorable legislative climate for Catholics signified by the incorporation act for the church in Charleston is also seen in a 1799 law facilitating a bequest to that church. Joseph Mincon had declared a wish to leave property to the church, but before this wish was formalized he died and the property escheated to the state. The statute carried out Mincon's intention by transferring the property from the state to the church.[85] The Catholic Church had come a long way from the time of Revolutionary War era suspicion about members' loyalty to the American cause.

There are other instances in which legislation facilitated Catholic Church support of its own institutions without crossing the line separating church and state by directly financing, controlling, or endorsing the institutions. For example, legislation passed in the late 1820s several times authorized or expanded the authority of the Roman Catholic church in Columbia to hold a lottery.[86] But such legislative assistance did not always come easily. Flash points arose. In 1835 Bishop John England succeeded in getting the legislature to incorporate two Catholic religious orders for women, the Sisters of Our Lady of Mercy of Charleston and the Ladies of the Ursuline Community of Charleston, who were engaged in a variety of good works, especially conducting schools and running an orphanage.[87] England initially encountered stiff opposition. Such religious orders were sometimes viewed with suspicion, but England found the major reason for the opposition was his appointment as a papal representative to Haiti. The fear arose that this might be a prelude to abolitionist activity. The bishop obtained an invitation to address the State Senate, which was joined in that session by many members of the House of Representatives. In a two-hour address the bishop recounted the history of prejudice against Catholics, refuted erroneous conceptions of the Catholic Church, explained its mode of governance, its dedication to education in the arts and sciences, the role of the orders he sought to incorporate, and their rights under the state constitution. The opposition evaporated, and the measures passed.[88] Less successful was Bishop England's attempt to operate a school for free black children. The school opened in early 1835, but the bishop was soon pressured into closing it when it was swept up into a controversy about abolitionist literature mailed to the Charleston post office. Even though it educated only free blacks, the school was viewed as a threat to the slavery system. England held firm when anti-abolitionist rioters gathered at the Catholic seminary, but, when what he called a "very respectable body of our fellow citizens" requested the school's closing, he complied, blaming the controversy on what he described as "unwarrantable interference of strangers [northern abolitionists] with our peculiar institutions [slavery]."[89] England's views on slavery are discussed in this volume in Peter Clarke and James Underwood's essay about him.

In addition to enhancing Catholic Church organizational powers, such as the ability to incorporate and create social-welfare organizations including the orders of nuns, the 1790 Constitution made open celebration of the Mass feasible.[90] In his history of the Catholic diocese of Charleston, the Right Reverend John England observed that during the Revolutionary War period there were few Catholics in the diocese, and those who were there were often unwilling to identify themselves as such either to their fellow Catholics or to others.[91] In England's view, they kept their religion secret because their presence was still resented by Huguenots, whose ancestors had suffered persecution at the hands of Catholic clergy in France, and by Scotch-Irish settlers, whose ancestors had occupied land in Northern Ireland that had been confiscated from Catholics.[92] He cited one 1775 incident in which distrust went beyond mere resentment. Two Catholics, who were said to be in favor of arming Catholics, Negroes, and Indians, were alleged to have threatened a citizen and were cited in a petition to the Committee of Public Safety.[93] The petitioner, Michael Hubart, complained to the committee that the two Catholics, James Dealey and Laughlin Martin, had not only advocated arming Catholics, Negroes, and Indians, threatened him with a knife, and cursed the committee but were also working against "the Protestant interest."[94] The committee transferred the matter to a "secret committee of five," who ordered Dealey and Martin to be stripped, tarred, and feathered, and "carted through the streets of Charlestown."[95] This distrust of Catholics began early and lingered long. Bishop England cited a 1696 South Carolina statute that granted a wide latitude of religious freedom to all Christians except "Papists."[96] Remnants of this distrust survived into the Revolutionary War era. Bishop England observed that although state constitutions of that period still excluded Catholics from positions of trust, they were soon succeeded by amendments or new constitutions (such as the South Carolina Constitution of 1790) that removed these impediments.[97] But, he argued, that despite these legal changes, "the strong current of popular opinion" was still "set strongly against him [the Catholic]."[98]

The Constitution of 1790 was real progress, but the prejudice that inspired the events just described was deep enough that it still had to be fought from time to time. The progress of minority religions in entering the political process was mixed. Levi Myers, a young physician of the Jewish religion, was elected to represent the Winyah District soon after the adoption of the 1790 Constitution.[99] Myers was a South Carolina native who was born near Jacksonborough. He studied medicine under South Carolina doctors, including David Ramsay, and enrolled in the medical schools at Edinburgh and Glasgow, from which he received his medical degree in 1787.[100] His service is a realization of the philosophy of Charles Pinckney, governor and president of the 1790 Constitutional Convention, who had been a leading opponent of religious test oaths in the Federal Constitutional Convention.[101] But removing disqualifications does not always usher the previously disqualified group into powerful positions. Bishop John England complained in a letter to his friend Dr. Paul Cullen that, when he made his 1835 address to the legislature in support of incorporation of the orders of nuns, no member of either house was a Catholic.[102]

In Bishop England's view, the best way for Catholics to gain the respect of their fellow citizens was for them to exercise the franchise in an ethical and responsible manner. In an 1831 letter to the Catholic citizens of Charleston, written during a time of bitter factionalism concerning whether the state could nullify federal tariff laws, Bishop England stated that he had no infallible insight to guide their voting choices. He carefully avoided expressing his personal preferences but advised them that their vote should be cast according to what was best for South Carolina and the country and not pursuant to partisanship, political intrigue, bribery, promise of office, or any other selfish motive.[103] He counseled those who were, as he was, Irish immigrants, to vote based on the merits of the candidates and to not let any politician sway their votes by appealing to them as fellow Irishmen.[104]

A strong influence on England's philosophy of the separation of church and state was the Reverend Arthur O'Leary, an Irish priest and a staunch advocate for Catholic equality in late eighteenth-century Ireland. England had begun working on a biography of O'Leary prior to leaving Ireland to assume the Charleston bishopric. When he was unable to write the work prior to his departure, he turned the task over to his brother Thomas, also a priest. The volume Thomas England produced described the doctrine of the separation of church and state as not only not contrary to the teachings of Christ but flowing from them. The book states that "the spirit of Christ abhors the intrusion of temporal powers into the sanctuary of religion. *They who take the sword* for the advancement of the Christian creed, shall perish with the sword; and they who invoke the vengeance of heaven on their erroneous brethren *know not of what spirit they are.*[105] In his "Essay on Toleration" (1781), O'Leary warned that the Kingdom of Jesus Christ is not of this world and should not be "interwoven with civil and political institutions" and thus the church should convert people by "persuasion, prayer and good example" rather than by invoking civil power.[106] John England embodied this philosophy in the constitution he issued for the diocese of Charleston. That document says that Jesus did not give temporal governments authority over spiritual concerns or church rulers authority over civil matters.[107]

To England the separation of church and state protected each side of the equation from undue interference by the other. An example of his application of this philosophy is seen in a September 26, 1830, letter he wrote to President Andrew Jackson, complaining that the earlier administration of President John Quincy Adams had permitted state department functionaries to seek Vatican reconsideration of Pope Leo XII's order that two priests be reassigned from Philadelphia to Cincinnati. England denounced this interference by the civil authorities in ecclesiastical affairs as an attempt to intimidate the religious authorities.[108]

In view of his strong dedication to the doctrine of the separation of church and state, it must have been worrisome to England to accept state financial assistance in rebuilding the Catholic church in Charleston destroyed by the great fire of 1838. Even though private contributions were solicited throughout the diocese and country, a state loan was also needed to finance rebuilding.[109] Because of the great devastation caused by the fire over a wide area in Charleston, the legislature authorized a state loan program.[110] The law empowered the state to issue bonds backed by its faith and credit. Proceeds of the bond sales were to be deposited with the State Bank of South Carolina, which would then loan money for rebuilding to those whose property was destroyed by the fire. The loans were to be made at a rate just sufficient to enable the state to repay the bonds. The law did not favor or exclude any class of loan applicants. In exchange for the loan, the bank received a mortgage and an insurance policy as collateral. If the borrower defaulted, the bank could sell the property. The City of Charleston was to provide further guarantee against loss by the state.[111] The new church was dedicated by Bishop England on June 9, 1839.[112] In a November 1839 address to a diocese convention, he said that the church still owed a big debt to the state under the fire-rebuilding loan program but the debt was not "oppressive."[113]

Did the use of state funds in the fire-recovery program violate the spirit of the 1790 Constitution under which regular government support of religious institutions was discontinued? Did it engage in the religious discrimination or preference that the 1790 fundamental law forbade? This incident went close to the borderline marking excessive mingling of church and state, but it did not cross it. The law did not favor or disfavor any particular religious organizations or religious organizations in general. They were merely beneficiaries along with a broad and diverse class defined only by the requirements that they had suffered damage in the fire and were intent on rebuilding property that was of sufficient value to support the loan. The program did not provide continuing support for religious or other organizations but funded only the rebuilding projects needed after a specific disaster. The state was not given supervisory powers over the beneficiary organizations as the government had over the old established church. Indeed, Bishop England said the loan was not "oppressive," which would not have been the case if the bishop's decisions were being monitored by the state. True, the mortgagee had the power to sell the covered property, but this right applied only on default and could not be used as an effective wedge to gain state control.[114] The intent of the program was not maintaining religion but the civic goal of rebuilding the city. Indeed, it could be argued that failing to include minority churches in the class of beneficiaries of an otherwise generally available loan program would have violated the Constitution of 1790's admonition that the state treat religions "without discrimination or preference."[115]

Perhaps the most important consequences of the fire-loan program's availability to minority religions were that it demonstrated acceptance by the larger community and the realization by those religions that they were entitled to equal treatment. Indeed, the program assisted Beth Elohim, as well as St. Mary's, after the 1838 fire. Beth Elohim had raised money to rebuild its synagogue through insurance and solicitation of individuals locally and in Jewish communities throughout the United States. But when the amount obtained through these efforts was insufficient to cover the rebuilding cost, the board of trustees authorized the president to seek a state loan.[116] Although the receipt of state funds by religious organizations runs the risk of making those organizations dependent on or controlled by the state, this program's limitation to the narrow purpose of rebuilding reduced that risk and helped maintain religious diversity by aiding the survival of minority religions.

Jews under the Constitution of 1790

The Constitution of 1790 created a new climate for religion. Was religion handicapped after it lost first the financial support and then the ideological endorsement of the government as the law shifted from granting fiscal aid to the Church of England establishment to a legal and ideological support of Protestantism in general in the 1778 Constitution, and finally to no establishment at all in the 1790 Constitution? Would it wither away without the government crutch? One observer of the state-constitutional status of religious freedom in the late eighteenth century argued that instead the result would be a reenergizing of religion. In 1791 John Leland, a Baptist minister and advocate of the separation of church and state, said: "Here, let me add, that in the southern states, where there has been the greatest freedom from religious oppression, where liberty of conscious is entirely enjoyed, there has been the greatest revival of religion; which is another proof that true religion can and will prevail best where it is left entirely to Christ."[117]

Richard Furman credited disestablishment with spurring the growth of the Baptist religion. In a February 12, 1791, letter to a Reverend Pearce, he observed that "the interest of our Churches appear on the whole to be advancing. Our liberty, religious as well as civil is unrestrained, and those who have ability and worth of every denomination are eligible to places of civil trust which makes a considerable difference between our Temporal Situation and that of our Brethren in Britain, where a partial Establishment prevails."[118]

Jews shared in this energizing impact of the Constitution of 1790 as they emerged from the cloud cast by the earlier Protestant Christian preference. But the dramatic departure of the Constitution of 1790 from the tradition of religious preference could be limited by narrow interpretations. One such interpretation is found in the annotation made by Dr. J. Adams, president of the College of Charleston, to a sermon he delivered to the Episcopal diocese of South Carolina in 1833. His view was that, although the Constitution of 1790, still then in force, forbade a legal preference for Protestantism over other forms of Christianity, it still embraced Christianity in general as the favored religion.[119] One might argue that Adams's view is supported by Article 8, section 2, which states that "the rights, privileges, immunities, and estates of both civil and religious societies and corporate bodies shall remain as if the Constitution of this state had not been altered or amended." The argument would be that this language does more than preserve to the Anglican Church property it acquired by government fiscal support during the establishment and does more than make it unnecessary for churches incorporated under the 1778 constitution to do so again, that it somehow preserves a favored position for Christianity in general while prohibiting discrimination among Christian denominations. But the section 1 provisions prohibiting preference or discrimination do not mention Christianity or any other particular religion. The language is neutral in the style of the U.S. Constitution's First Amendment but with different wording. The provision does not restrict the scope of the antipreference language to prohibit only government preference of one Christian denomination over another. Adams's interpretation also clashed with that of the General Assembly when it granted Beth Elohim's petition for incorporation in 1791 even though it was not a Christian organization. But Adams argued that contemporary legislation, such as Sunday closing laws, showed a proper legislative interpretation of Article 8 as permitting government encouragement of Christian worship.[120] Adams was not alone in this view.

A similar approach is found in an 1846 decision by the South Carolina appellate court. In *City Council of Charleston v. Benjamin* the court upheld a conviction of a Jewish merchant who had been charged with violating the laws forbidding worldly work and the sale of goods on Sunday.[121] When the defendant pleaded that the Sunday closing law violated his religious freedom under the Constitution of 1790, the court upheld the law. In an opinion by Judge John Belton O'Neall, the court gave Article 8, section 1, a "Christian construction."[122] To O'Neall, religious freedom was less a matter of guaranteed rights and more a matter of tolerance expressed by Christians toward practitioners of other faiths, and this tolerance flowed from Christ's teaching his followers to love their enemies.[123] Constitutional and common law were grounded not in the beliefs of any particular denomination but on the doctrines of Christianity in general.[124] But then, after having gone to considerable trouble to provide a religious basis for Article 8, section 1, O'Neall shifted his ground. He concluded that the Sunday closing laws were not designed to serve a religious purpose but to provide everyone with a day of rest.[125] The law was not a direct interference with the Jewish merchant's free exercise of religion because he was still free to observe his own Sabbath on another day and he was not required to engage in any Christian rituals on Sunday. Of course this ignored the economic plight that could befall the faithful adherent to Jewish doctrine, who must close his store one day because of his religion and again on another day because of the civil law. However, the result was similar to that reached many years later by the U.S. Supreme Court, which in *Braunfeld v. Brown* (1961) upheld Sunday-closing laws as providing a secular day of rest that did not directly interfere with Jewish free exercise of religion.[126] But the U.S. Supreme Court opinion had none of the Christian rhetoric found in the earlier South Carolina decision. The jaundiced interpretations of Dr. Adams and the *Benjamin* case seem to minimize the language of Article 8, section 1, which extended religious freedom "to all mankind" and "without discrimination or preference." O'Neall unconvincingly made the argument that there was no discrimination because adherents of all faiths had to give equal compliance to the Sunday closing laws.[127] He failed to note that there is a differential impact of a Sunday-closing law since that day is the preferred religious day of rest for one group but not the other. One might just as well argue under O'Neall's logic that a law requiring everyone to recite a Buddhist chant was not discriminatory since Buddhist and non-Buddhist must recite the same chant.

The *Benjamin* case was influenced by *Ex parte Duke,* an 1833 decision upholding the Columbia Sunday closing ordinance against a challenge by two merchants, one of whom was Jewish.[128] In *Duke,* Judge William D. Martin sustained the Columbia ordinance against an attack under the First Amendment to the U.S. Constitution because the amendment did not apply to states at that time.[129] He also rejected challenges under Article 8, section 1, of the South Carolina Constitution of 1790, concluding that there was no preference for Christianity as a favored religion or discrimination against Judaism because the law treated everyone equally by requiring all to close their stores on Sunday. Like the *Benjamin* court thirteen years later, he gave no weight to the unique burden on Jews who had to close on Saturday because of their religion and on Sunday because of the ordinance, thus creating an economic crisis for them not shared by others. Crucial to the decision was the judge's conclusion, foreshadowing *Benjamin,* that the law did not coerce Jews since they were not compelled to worship on Sunday or forbidden to worship on Saturday. But the dilemma created by the law for Jewish merchants, who had to choose between the principles of their religion and their economic well being, could have been considered a species of coercion and a form of discrimination because others were not placed in this quandary. But the judge did not so hold.[130]

O'Neall's approach in *Benjamin* provoked protest from Jewish commentators. One denounced O'Neall as "unquestionably a fanatic" and an "unsafe judge on all questions bearing on his own bigoted notions."[131] To the commentator this ruling marginalized Jews in the political community. The commentator further observed,

"The Judge, throughout, treats Jews as though they were not his equals—his fellow citizens. . . . I protest against these terms, '*you*,' '*us*,' '*our laws*.' Such language is unworthy of an American judge."[132] Others decried O'Neall's argument that only Christianity could form a sound basis for morality. In terms that seemed to fortify that criticism, O'Neall asked, "How I, *not born a Jew*, could say otherwise than that Christianity was the only standard *known* to me of good morals is hard to conceive."[133] But O'Neall did have his supporters among Jewish commentators. One described the *Benjamin* case as "a very able opinion" with which he was in total accord.[134] That observer called the Sunday laws reasonable measures that did not intrude on Jewish worship and merely insured a tranquil day for Christian worshipers.[135]

It would be a mistake, however, to focus with monocular intensity on the *Benjamin* and *Duke* cases and conclude that the antebellum courts entertained antipathy toward Jews. The cases were the product more of the deeply entrenched nature of Sunday closing than animus. In an 1846 case, *State ex rel. Ottolengui v. Ancker*,[136] the South Carolina court showed the greatest respect to the Jewish religion by the manner in which it created the legal framework for resolving a dispute within the historic Beth Elohim synagogue without intruding on its free exercise of religion. The synagogue was rocked by disputes over the mode of worship, specifically whether an organ could be used in services, and by a theological dispute over the nature of the Messiah, specifically whether this term referred to a physical presence that would interact with the world or to an idealized concept. These religious questions lay in the background of a case brought by a majority of the members of the synagogue corporation against dissidents to resolve a dispute over the allocation of power within the congregation. The dispute involved the issues of who was a member, who could vote, and what was a properly called meeting. The court refused to decide the religious issues, concluding that if it did so it would intrude on the religious freedom of the congregation and depart from the neutral position it should have in sectarian controversies. In disdaining intervention in the religious issues, the court observed, "If the court can be called on to settle by its decisions such disputes, it would be bound to require parties to conform to its standard of faith—a judicial standard for theological orthodoxy!"[137] The court avoided this theological quicksand and instead resolved the power-allocation dispute under neutral civil law principles for interpreting contracts and similar documents, such as the congregation's articles of incorporation and bylaws. Thus the court sought to assist a respected segment of the community in resolving a rancorous dispute without dictating religion to it.

At the opposite pole from the narrow, retrograde interpretation given to the religious freedom provisions of the 1790 Constitution in the *Benjamin* and *Duke* cases was the expansive reading it was given by the renowned collector of early South Carolina law, Thomas Cooper. In 1831 he defended himself against charges that he had taught heretical doctrines as president of the South Carolina College. He argued that the Article 8, section 1, language, mandating that the state conduct itself "without discrimination or preference" concerning religion, forbade any state action that even touched on the subject of religion because such action would inevitably result in some kind of preference.[138] Therefore the state could not force orthodoxy on him as a teacher. But in his more objective role as collector of laws, Cooper conceded that the 1790 religious clauses did not forbid the incorporation of religious groups to achieve civil goals and did not prohibit the passage of laws declaring Sunday to be a secular day of rest.[139]

Mere constitutional language is no guarantee against religious discrimination. Much depends on the attitude of those in official positions. This is illustrated by comparing the disparate manner in which two governors treated Jewish citizens with regard to Thanksgiving proclamations. Gov. James H. Hammond of South Carolina issued a Thanksgiving Day proclamation in 1844 in which he stated that the United States was a Christian nation and exhorted "our citizens of all denominations to assemble at their respective places of worship, to offer up their devotions to God their Creator, and his Son Jesus Christ, the Redeemer of the World."[140] Charleston Jews objected to the exclusively Christian orientation of the proclamation. When private attempts to obtain an apology from the governor were ignored, a meeting of the Jewish community produced a formal complaint signed by more than one hundred of its members.[141] The signatories argued that by excluding them from the proclamation and by giving a specific Christian cast to the call to worship rather than inviting everyone to give thanks according to his own beliefs, the document violated Article 8, section 1, of the Constitution of 1790, which required the government to afford freedom of worship "without discrimination or preference."[142] The complainants displayed their reverence for this provision of the constitution when they said, "It would seem . . . as if the finger of Providence had penned that section of the constitution, in prophetic anticipation of the case in point."[143] Hammond offered no apology and responded: "I have always thought it a settled matter that I lived in a Christian land! And that I was the temporary chief magistrate of a Christian people. That in such a country and among such a people I should be, publicly, called to an account, reprimanded and required to make amends for acknowledging Jesus Christ as the Redeemer of the world, I would not have believed possible, if it had not come to pass."[144]

Hammond intimated that the complainants had inherited "the same scorn for Jesus Christ which instigated their ancestors to crucify him."[145] A committee of the Jewish community framed a response that characterized the governor's remarks as "tending to excite the prejudices of eighteen hundred years against a small portion of his constituents."[146] That Hammond's action was not an inadvertent omission is seen in later diary entries in which he excoriated his successor as governor, William Aiken, for not making a "point" to the Jews by giving a similarly Christian cast to his Thanksgiving Day proclamations.[147] This incident continued to be notorious and was cited by U.S. Supreme Court Justice Harry Blackmun in his lead opinion in the 1989 case of *County of Allegheny v. ACLU* [148] as an example of hostile government action that makes a religious minority feel it is not a valued member of the political community.[149] Blackmun stated that such proclamations "demonstrate an official *preference* for Christianity and a corresponding official *discrimination* against all non-Christians, amounting to an exclusion of a portion of the political community."[150]

Hammond's anti-Semitism was not limited to Thanksgiving proclamations. In an 1842 diary entry, he complained about a nominee to be a director of the Columbia branch of the Bank of the State of South Carolina on the grounds that he was "a miserable Jew" but that the appointment was made anyway because the candidate's brother, Moses Cohen Mordecai, was an influential financier.[151]

The Jews were not the only minority religion to provoke Hammond's ire. On an 1836 European tour that included visits to renowned Catholic cathedrals, he described those buildings as decaying anachronisms rather than the stately antiquities he expected. He referred to Catholicism as "neither more nor less than pure idolatry."[152] These views did not mellow with time. When a friend converted to Catholicism, Hammond described him in an 1845 diary entry as "prostrated by bigotry" with "his mind . . . perfectly closed to reason and common sense" and with "nothing . . . too silly or too wicked for belief."[153]

Hammond's actions stand in stark contrast to those of an earlier governor, Henry Middleton, even though they were both operating under the same constitutional language. In an 1812 Thanksgiving proclamation, Middleton inadvertently omitted Jews from those who were invited to be celebrants. When he learned of this mistake, he sent an apology to Beth Elohim synagogue.[154] The Hammond episode was significant, but it should not be considered in isolation. James William Hagy found that the Jews of Charleston participated on an equal basis in a wide variety of public-spirited activities in the late eighteenth century and antebellum periods.[155] For example, in 1825 Jewish religious leaders, along with representatives from other beliefs, served on a welcoming committee for Marie Joseph du Motier, Marquis de Lafayette, when he visited Charleston on a grand tour of America, and in 1791 the Jewish community enthusiastically participated in raising funds for an orphanage.[156] In recounting the Lafayette visit to Charleston, his secretary, A. Levasseur, noted that the varied sects represented on the welcoming committee were so convivial as to appear to belong to "one communion" and praised the American approach to the separation of church and state, which forced the clergy, since they could not rely on the government for financial support, into "conciliating public esteem by the practice of real virtues."[157] On August 28, 1840, only four years before the Hammond incident, Mayor Henry Pinckney and an ecumenical group of Charleston religious leaders and officials joined with the Jewish community to protest a notorious incident in which thirteen Jews in Damascus had been incarcerated, tortured, and killed on the basis of absurd rumors that they had killed a French priest to obtain blood for a Passover ritual.[158] In 1847, only three years after the Hammond incident, members of a variety of denominations participated in a ball and other fund-raising activities of the Hebrew Benevolent Society.[159]

Jews blended into the larger community without compromising their beliefs. Writing early in the nineteenth century, David Ramsay observed, "Their dress and habits do not distinguish them from the other citizens."[160] Jews served in important government positions. For example, Lyon Levy's long career of public service culminated in his selection as state treasurer in 1817, an office he held until 1822.[161]

Mordecai C. Cohen served in the General Assembly in 1845–46 and the State Senate from 1855 to 1858.[162] In Columbia, Dr. Mordecai Hendricks DeLeon, a physician, became intendant (mayor) in 1833 and served three consecutive terms; he was followed by a second antebellum Jewish mayor, the affable Henry Lyons, in 1850.[163] Four Jews served as delegates to the nullification convention of 1832, in which the state considered whether it could nullify federal laws that it considered unconstitutional. Charles Reznikoff and James William Hagy found that two of these delegates, Philip Phillips and Chapman Levy, voted against nullification while Philip Cohen and Myer Jacobs voted for it.[164] The convention declared the tariffs of 1828 and 1832 to be invalid.[165] This record of office holding shows that Jews were not admitted only to the fringes of civic and political life but earned the public trust that resulted in their being given positions central to government. Jews also participated in the mundane duties of citizenship, such as jury service, usually without incident, but there was occasional tension between religious and civic duties. On October 9, 1829, Abraham Ottolengui, wrote Judge Elihu H. Bay a polite letter pointing out that service as a juror in the case for which he had been called would probably "infringe on my Sabbath, a thing I have never done in all my life—moreover it is not impossible, it may last till Monday next which is a Holy day among our Nation and they being at present without a regular Minister, that duty is performed by me."[166]

It was not only in civic affairs that the Jewish community produced eminent people. Isaac Harby (1788–1828) was a distinguished playwright and critic in the early nineteenth century. He was also a leader in the movement to reform the Jewish worship service. In his *Anniversary Oration Before the "Reformed Society of Israelites"* (1825) he called for the introduction of sermons from the pulpit as a means of giving more moral guidance. He also urged that readings in Hebrew be followed by English translations. He argued that this would make the services more meaningful to young people and thus work to preserve the faith against Protestant attempts to convert congregation members.[167] The Reform Society's efforts to persuade Beth Elohim to change its services initially failed, and the society wound down its operations from 1833 to 1836, but on July 10, 1839, the board of trustees of Beth Elohim petitioned the hazan, Rev. Gustavus Poznanski, to introduce English into the service, and he replied "that he would consider the subject and endeavor to comply with the wishes of the Board as much as possible."[168]

Harby took up the cudgels for religious freedom of his fellow Jews. When Mordecai Manual Noah, the U.S. consul to Tunis, was dismissed by Secretary of State James Monroe, Harby wrote Monroe inquiring about rumors that the reason for the dismissal was Noah's religion rather than his performance.[169] Gary Phillip Zola, in his biography of Harby, concluded that Harby appeared to be satisfied with Monroe's explanation that the dismissal did not result from American opposition to Jews in official positions but from objections to him on the part of Muslims and Moors with whom he was negotiating.[170] Of course, such a rationale raises additional issues of whether it is proper for the American government to acquiesce in the prejudice of others even where delicate negotiations are at stake. But Harby did not press the matter in public since he did "not wish to be seen as a narrow promoter of Jewish issues."[171] Like others in the Jewish community, Harby was also interested in broader civic affairs.

The approach of the Jewish community was to participate as citizens of the larger community rather than as a special interest group.[172] Evidence of this is seen in an 1832 message sent by "Eighty-four Israelites" to the *Southern Patriot* in Charleston in response to rumors that Jews wanted to be represented in the legislature only by Jews and that they had prepared a list of favored candidates.[173] The message refuted such an approach and stated, "That we wholly disclaim any wish or intention to be represented as a peculiar community, and that we discountenance the idea of selecting any individual for office, either of profit or honor, upon the ground that such individual belongs to a particular sect, with the view of securing or of influencing the suffrages of such sect."[174]

From Fickle Tolerance to Guaranteed Religious Rights and Disestablishment

Even though an unsympathetic administrator such as Governor Hammond could erode the quality of religious freedom from time to time, and even though court rhetoric such as that in the *Benjamin* case could create an aura of preference for Christianity, in general, if not for a particular denomination, the climate produced by the Constitution of 1790 was far more conducive to religious freedom than under the old system of Church of England establishment, during which tax money from the population at large was used to support the buildings, priests, and social programs of the official church. Freed of this burden by the partial reform brought by the Constitution of 1778, dissenting Protestant denominations could devote their energies to their own growth rather than having it siphoned off to another church whose beliefs were not their own. So long as they supported the broad belief requirements stipulated in Article 38, Protestant churches of all varieties were allowed to incorporate and hold their property directly rather than risk its misuse by trustees. The 1778 Constitution also freed congregations of the old established church from much of the paralyzing regulation of their internal affairs by the government. The price they paid in the loss of financial support under the 1778 Constitution was made worthwhile by this increased freedom for Anglican congregations.[175]

But the general Protestant establishment of the Constitution of 1778, though it benefited and energized dissenting Protestant denominations, was still an incomplete victory for religious freedom. The intricate weblike regulations of Article 38 were at war with themselves—at once trying to grant religious freedom and precisely regulate it by applying belief standards to Protestant congregations seeking incorporation, and even presuming to tell ministers their duties and how to perform them. Articles 3, 12, and 13 continued to insist that key officers be Protestant. Most important, the 1778 Constitution wrought an incomplete victory for religious freedom because the message of ideological support for Protestantism that it conveyed still seemed to exclude Catholics and Jews from the inner circle of the political community. Even though the Charters and Fundamental Constitutions had sent signals of tolerance and welcome to all who embraced the broad idea that there was a God and that he was publicly to be worshiped and even though generous provisions for forming congregations with a variety of beliefs were found in the Fundamental Constitutions, the inability of Jewish and Catholic congregations to incorporate and own property directly was a serious handicap that continued under the 1778 document. It took the Constitution of 1790 to eliminate this handicap and complete the evolution from Church of England establishment to general Protestant establishment to complete disestablishment and religious freedom "without discrimination or preference . . . to all mankind."[176]

A fundamental flaw of the Charters and pre-1790 Constitutions was that they embodied a belief that a pervasive establishment and a vigorous religious freedom could coexist. They cannot. The government and the established religion will always be disposed to scrutinize intensely other religions and participants in the political process to guard against encroachment on the prerogatives of the established church. A pervasive establishment was particularly troublesome in a society such as colonial South Carolina, which relied on attracting a varied population of immigrants for its growth. An establishment is an homogenizing force; immigration is a diversifying force. The clash between these incompatible forces accounts for much of the on-again off-again quality of religious freedom in colonial South Carolina, as in the imposition, revocation, reimposition, and revocation again of religious qualifications for participation in the political process. The 1790 Constitution ended the attempt to have it both ways (a pervasive establishment coexisting with vigorous religious freedoms) by coming down squarely on the side of freedom. The Charters and Fundamental Constitutions had exuded the invigorating aroma of tolerance. But tolerance is a shifting quicksand upon which to erect freedom. Freedom that is merely tolerated can be taken away or narrowed at the whim of the sovereign. Such freedoms can expand or contract as political fortunes shift from faction to faction.

The Constitution of 1790 moved from this uncertain foundation to the firm ground of a guaranteed right to "free exercise and enjoyment of religious profession and worship."[177] This did not mean that there was a right that would forever be immune from official encroachment. Much depends on the attitudes of administrators. The battle for religious freedom is never permanently won, but the Constitution of 1790 gave firm textual roots to religious freedom that fostered its hardy growth. James Madison argued, "Religion flourishes in greater purity, without than with the aid of Govt."[178] Religion departs from such "purity" when it tailors its programs to the agenda of the government grant maker rather than the needs of its parishioners. Disestablishment removes this temptation. In addition, disestablishment removes the pressure on nonadherents of the official religion to feign acceptance of the beliefs of the established church. Freeing people to be sincere in their religious profession, disestablishment releases the energy that invigorates religion.[179] It is establishment, not disestablishment, that is hostile to religion. An unarticulated assumption underlying an establishment is that God is satisfied with humankind's interpretation of his revelations, that God has ceased to be active in worldly events and therefore no further divine revelations will be forthcoming.[180] Thus, religion can be frozen into the form acceptable to the establishment. Disestablishment and a guarantee of religious freedom, by their avoidance of pressuring society in a religious direction, not only free government from domination by religion, they free individuals to either ignore religion or to conduct their own search for God's message rather than having to make do with a prefabricated watered-down version. Furthermore, an establishment, by combining civil and spiritual authority in the same hands, brings about a dangerous concentration of power that inspires such overconfidence in officials that they believe that they can ignore the needs of their constituents.[181] The disestablishment achieved by the Constitution of 1790 signified an appreciation of the dangers of such concentrations of religious and secular power in a society of varied beliefs and guarded against them by a generous grant of religious freedom.

Notes

The title of this essay, "Without discrimination or preference," is from S.C. CONST. of 1790, art. 8, sec. 1, which states that "free exercise and enjoyment of religious profession and worship, without discrimination or preference, shall, forever hereafter, be allowed within this State to all mankind; provided that the liberty of conscience hereby declared shall not be so construed as to excuse acts of licentiousness, or justify practices inconsistent with the peace or safety of this state." See *Basic Documents of South Carolina History,* ed. J. M. Lesesne and J. H. Easterby (Columbia: Historical Commission of South Carolina, 1952).

    1. Articles 3, 12, and 13, S.C. CONST. of 1778, in *Basic Documents of South Carolina History,* ed. Robert L. Meriweather and J. H. Easterby (Columbia Historical Commission of South Carolina, 1953).

    2. *State ex rel. M'Cready v. Hunt,* 20 S.C.L. (2 Hill) 1, 66 (S.C. Ct. App. 1834). This case struck down as violating the federal and state constitutions an oath required of state militia officers during the nullification controversy. Grimké argued that the requirement was a political test oath that intruded on freedom of conscience as much as the old religious test oath. For biographical material on Grimké see John Belton O'Neall, *Biographical Sketches of the Bench and Bar of South Carolina,* vol. 2 (Charleston: S. G. Courtenay, 1859), 378–89, and George C. Rogers, *Generations of Lawyers: A History of the South Carolina Bar* (Columbia: South Carolina Bar Foundation, 1992), 16–35.

    3. John Carroll et al, "Address of the Roman Catholics to George Washington, President of the United States," *United States Catholic Miscellany* (Charleston), August 11, 1822, p. 83. The appointment of John Carroll as the first Catholic bishop in the United States was an important step in advancing the Catholic Church in America, where the church had been rent by schism and disorganization. The circumstances leading to Carroll's appointment are discussed in Annabelle M. Melville, *John Carroll of Baltimore: Founder of the American Catholic Hierarchy* (New York: Scribners, 1955), 103–9. Melville discusses the correspondence with Washington at 110–12. John Carroll had been appointed bishop by Pope Pius VI on November 6, 1789, but was not consecrated until August 15, 1790 (New Advent, *Catholic Encyclopedia:* "John Carroll," available on-line at www.newadvent.org/Cathen/

0338lb.htm (visited April 9, 2004). See also Peter Guilday, *The Life and Times of John Carroll: Archbishop of Baltimore, 1735–1815* (New York: Encyclopedia Press, 1922), 363–68.

4. George Washington, "Answer to the Roman Catholics in the United States of America," *United States Catholic Miscellany*, August 11, 1822, pp. 83–84.

5. Ibid. The *United States Catholic Miscellany* was one of Bishop John England's instruments for refuting arguments that Catholicism was incompatible with American-style republicanism. The *Miscellany* used Washington's reply to Carroll as evidence that the Catholics were good citizens of the United States, thus proving that Catholicism and republicanism blended well. For example, see "Review of the Strictures Upon the Letters of Right Rev. Dr. England and the Rev. J. McEnroe," *United States Catholic Miscellany*, January 21, 1824, pp. 34–37, and January 28, 1824, pp. 50–55. The correspondence between Carroll and Washington on religious equality is also found in Dorothy Twohig ed., *The Papers of George Washington*, Presidential Series, vol. 5, January–June 1790 (Charlottesville: University of Virginia Press, 1996), 299–301, and in *The John Carroll Papers*, ed. Thomas O'Brien Hanley, vol. 1: 1755–1791 (Notre Dame, Ind.: University of Notre Dame Press, 1976), 410–11.

6. S.C. CONST. of 1778, art. 38.

7. Ibid.

8. Ibid.

9. Marion Cecil Chandler Jr., "Church Incorporation in South Carolina Under the Constitution of 1778 (1778–1790)," Master's thesis, University of South Carolina, 1966, 56–58, discussing the Beach complaint and its rejection by a legislative committee.

10. Quebec Act, 14 George 3, C83, paras. V and VI, providing for a dual Protestant/Catholic establishment but giving rise to fears of Catholic dominance. See also Preamble to the Constitution of 1776 in *Basic Documents of South Carolina History*, giving voice to those fears as a complaint against British authorities.

11. John Wesley Brinsfield, *Religion and Politics in Colonial South Carolina* (Easley, S.C.: Southern Historical Press, 1983), 47.

12. Ibid., 47, 90. See also John Drayton, *Memoirs of the American Revolution*, vol. 1 (Charleston: Printed by A. E. Miller, 1821; reprint, New York: Arno Press, 1969), 300–302.

13. Charles Woodmason, *Carolina Backcountry on the Eve of the Revolution*, ed. Richard J. Hooker (Chapel Hill: University of North Carolina Press, 1953), 42.

14. U.S. CONST. amend. 1; S.C. CONST. of 1790, art. 8. The religious clauses of the U.S. Constitution state "congress shall make no law respecting an establishment of religion, or prohibiting the free exercise thereof."

15. John England, *The Substance of a Discourse Preached in the Hall of the House of Representatives of the Congress of the United States, in the City of Washington, on Sunday, January 8, 1826* (Baltimore, Md.: F. Lucas Jr., 1826), 32–35, available at South Caroliniana Library, University of South Carolina, Columbia. In 1835 Alexis de Tocqueville concluded that the religion of American Catholics was most compatible with democracy because the same doctrinal standards applied to all members, and the priests, unlike some in Europe, were not active in politics. See Alexis de Tocqueville, *Democracy in America*, trans. Harvey C. Mansfield and Delba Winthrop (Chicago: University of Chicago Press, 2000), 275–76.

16. David Ramsay, *The History of South Carolina From Its First Settlement in 1670 to the Year 1808*, vol. 2 (Charleston: David Longworth, 1809), 37–38.

17. Ibid., 17–18.

18. Robert St. John, *Jews, Justice and Judaism* (Garden City, N.Y.: Doubleday, 1969), 63.

19. S.C. CONST. of 1778, art. 38, granted "equal religious and civil Privileges" to "all Denominations of Christian Protestants" who conduct "themselves peaceably and faithfully." It also limited the right of incorporation to groups "professing the Christian Protestant Religion"; "The Congregation 'Beth Elohim,' Charleston, S.C.," in *City of Charleston Year Book, 1883* (Charleston: News and Courier Book Presses, 1883), 301, available at South Caroliniana Library, University of South Carolina, Columbia. See also Lee J. Levinger, *A History of the Jews in the United States* (Cincinnati: Union of American Hebrew Congregations, 1952), 93, which concludes that Beth Elohim is the third oldest Jewish congregation in the United States following congregations in New York and Newport, with Savannah, Philadelphia, and Richmond having the fourth, fifth, and sixth oldest.

20. Chandler, "Church Incorporation," 3. An interesting discussion of the role the organ played is found in [Jacob De La Motta?], "The Congregations of Charleston," *Occident and American Jewish Advocate* 1, no. 12 (March 1844), available on-line at http://www.jewish-history.com/Occident/volume1/mar1844/charleston.html.

21. Act No. 1066 of 1778, 8 S.C. STATUTES AT LARGE 115–116 (McCord 1840). In *State ex rel. Ottolengui v. Ancker*, 31 S.C.L. (2 Rich.) 245, 247 (S.C. 1846), the trial judge concluded that Beth Elohim probably existed prior to its 1791 incorporation as a synagogue as an "incorporated society." Since Article 38 of the 1778 Constitution limited incorporation as churches to Protestant Christian organizations that could sign a book attesting to specifically Christian beliefs—including the divinity of Jesus and that the New and Old Testaments were both inspired by God—perhaps the trial judge referred to incorporation of a charitable society for which records have been lost. No statutory or other records concerning a pre-1791 incorporation can be found. A compilation of pleadings and evidence in this case by an anonymous member of the bar shows both sides using 1791 as the incorporation date. No evidence was adduced to indicate an earlier time. See *The State Ex Rel. A. Ottolengui et al. v. G.V. Ancker, Report of the Evidence and Arguments of Counsel by a Member of the Charleston Bar* (Charleston: Samuel Hart, 1844), 3, 39, 59, appendix, available at the South Caroliniana Library, University of South Carolina, Columbia. The 1791 incorporation date is used by a noted Jewish historian. See Jacob Rader Marcus, *United States Jewry 1776–1985*, vol. 1 (Detroit: Wayne State University Press, 1989), 234.

22. Ramsay, *History of South Carolina*, 2:40.

23. Irving J. Sloan, *The Jews in America 1621–1977* (Dobbs Ferry, N.Y.: Oceana, 1978), 4; St. John, *Jews, Justice and Judaism*, 75; Goldberg, *The Jews in America, a History*, 33–34; Levinger, *A History of the Jews in the United States*, 94; *Elzas v. Huhner*, reprinted from the *Charleston News and Courier*, February 1903, p. 2, available at South Caroliniana Library, University of South Carolina, Columbia; and Charles Reznikoff, *The Jews of Charleston* (Philadelphia: Jewish Publication Society of America 1950), 34–40, 7–8.

24. St. John, *Jews, Justice and Judaism*, 75, concluding that roughly 50 percent of the company were Jews. See also Leon Huhner, *Some Additional Notes on the History of Jews in South Carolina*, Publication of the American Jewish Historical Society, no. 19 (1910), available in the South Caroliniana Library, University of South Carolina, Columbia. But Rabbi Dr. Barnett Elzas concluded that the company, which was commanded by Captain Richard Lushington, was not made up completely or even largely of Jews (Elzas, *Elzas v. Huhner*, 3).

25. Goldberg, *The Jews in America*, 48.

26. "The Northwest Ordinance," in *The Annals of America,* vol. 3 (Chicago: Encyclopedia Britannica, 1976), 194, 196.

27. Francis M. Hutson, ed., *Journal of the Constitutional Convention of South Carolina, May 10, 1790–June 3, 1790* (Columbia: Historical Commission of South Carolina, 1946), 11.

28. S. Sidney Ulmer, "James Madison and The Pinckney Plan," *South Carolina Law Quarterly* 9, no. 3 (Spring 1957): 415, 442.

29. See Max Farrand, ed., *The Records of the Federal Convention of 1787,* vol.2 (New Haven, Conn.: Yale University Press, 1911), 342, describing Charles Pinckney's introduction on August 20, 1787, of a provision that provided: "No religious test or qualification shall ever be annexed to any oath of office under the authority of the U.S." This was an influential precursor of the test oath ban eventually adopted as U.S. Const. art. 6, sec. 3.

30. See Marty D. Matthews, *Forgotten Founder: The Life and Times of Charles Pinckney* (Columbia: University of South Carolina Press, 2004), 45; see also the entry for September 14, 1787, in *The Records of the Federal Convention of 1787,* ed, Farrand, vol. 2, revised edition (New Haven: Yale University Press, 1911), 616.

31. Jonathan Elliot, ed., *The Debates in the Several State Conventions on the Adoption of Federal Constitution as Recommended by the General Convention at Philadelphia,* vol. 4 (Philadelphia: Lippincott, 1907), 319.

32. Ibid.

33. Joseph Gales Sr., ed., *Annals of the Congress of the United States, First Congress,* vol. 1 (Washington, D.C.: Gales & Seaton, 1834), 915–16. The printer seems to have mislabeled the date as February 25 even though the passage is found in the September sequence.

34. Ibid., 440–41.

35. Ibid.

36. Ibid., 961. See also Hutson, ed., *Constitutional Convention of South Carolina.*

37. Judge Brevard's Observations on the Legislative History of South Carolina, 1 S.C. Statutes at Large 436 (Cooper 1836).

38. Ramsay, *History of South Carolina,* 2:139.

39. John Brown Cutting to John Rutledge Jr., Charleston, February 21, 1789, in *The Documentary History of the First Federal Elections, 1788–1790,* vol. 1., ed. Merrill Jensen and Robert A. Becker (Madison: University of Wisconsin Press, 1976.), 213–14.

40. See James Haw, *John & Edward Rutledge of South Carolina* (Athens.: University of Georgia Press, 1997), 219. The size of the House was later reduced to 124 members. See Article 1, section 3, of the Constitution of 1790 in *Basic Documents of South Carolina History* (1952). See also Haw, 219–20.

41. Ibid., 188–89, 219–20. See also Marvin R. Zahniser, *Charles Cotesworth Pinckney: Founding Father* (Chapel Hill: University of North Carolina Press, 1967), 106–10, discussing the dominance of allocation of power issues such as the legislative apportionment dispute between the lowcountry and backcountry and the controversy over the location of the capital in the 1790 convention debates. See also David R. Chesnutt and C. James Taylor, eds., *The Papers of Henry Laurens,* volume 16: September 1, 1782–December 17, 1792 (Columbia: University of South Carolina Press for the South Carolina Historical Society, 2003), 541 n.6, discussing 1785 petitions by backcountry residents for more representation in the legislature.

42. *Charleston City Gazette, or the Daily Advertiser,* May 11, 1790. All copies of the *City Gazette* cited herein are available at the Charleston Library Society, Charleston, South Carolina.

43. The resolution authorizing the election of convention delegates was widely published in newspapers. For example, see the *Charleston Columbian Herald, or the Independent Courier of North America,* March 26, 1789, reprinting legislative resolutions of March 6 and March 13, 1789, recommending to voters that they elect delegates to "a state convention, for the purpose of revising, altering, or forming a new constitution of this state," setting the election for the "26th and 27th days of October, 1789," and naming election managers, including church-wardens, in areas still using parishes as election units. See also the convention resolution of March 6, 1789, in Michael E. Stevens and Christine M. Allen, eds., *The State Records of South Carolina: Journals of the House of Representatives, 1789–1790* (Columbia: University of South Carolina Press, 1984), 229–34.

44. *Charleston City Gazette, or the Daily Advertiser,* May 18, 1790.

45. Ibid., May 26, 1790, reporting that on Monday, May 17, 1790, the convention thanked Reverend Furman for his discourse the previous Sunday and asked Rev. Henry Purcell to give one the next Sunday. In his diaries, the Reverend Evan Pugh, a delegate, noted that he attended three such sermons—on May 16, May 23, and May 30. As to the last of these, he explicitly mentioned that it took place in the "State House." See Evan Pugh, *The Diaries of Evan Pugh (1762–1801),* ed. Horace Fraser Rudisill (Florence, S.C.: St. David's Society, 1993), 300–301.

46. Furman to Oliver Hart, Charleston, September 23, 1793, Richard Furman Correspondence, 1777–1825, Special Collections Library, Furman University, Greenville, South Carolina; also available on microfilm at Livingston Library, Shorter College, Rome, Georgia. Oddly enough, this letter appears to have been begun in 1793, interrupted, and then resumed in 1795. The portion quoted above is from 1793.

47. See James A. Rogers, *Richard Furman: Life and Legacy,* (Macon, Ga.: Mercer University Press, 1985), 70. In his "Address to the Residents Between the Broad and Saluda Rivers (address On Liberty)," issued in November 1775, Richard Furman referred to the "liberty of Conscience" as "that precious jewel of the constitution"; address available at Furman University.

48. See Mark A. Mastromarino, ed., *The Papers of George Washington,* Presidential Series, vol. 6, July-November 1790 (Charlottesville: University Press of Virginia, 1996), 19.

49. Nathaniel Levin, "The Jewish Congregation of Charleston," *Occident and American Jewish Advocate* 1, no. 7 (October 1843): 339 [29], available on-line at http://www.jewish-history.com/Occident/volume1/oct1843/charleston.html.

50. Ibid.

51. "The Bill of Rights and Amendments to the Constitution of the United States as Agreed to by the Convention of the State of Rhode Island and Providence Plantation at South Kensington, in the County of Washington on the First Day of March A.D. 1790," *Charleston City Gazette, or the Daily Advertiser,* April 22, 1790.

52. The Pennsylvania Constitution of 1790 was printed in the *Charleston City Gazette, or the Daily Advertiser,* February 16, 1790. See especially art. 9, para. 4.

53. "Extract of a letter from Columbia, May 31," *Charleston City Gazette, or the Daily Advertiser,* June 5, 1790.

54. S.C. Const. of 1790, art. 8.

55. Ibid., art. 1.

56. Jacob Cohen to George Washington, Charleston, S.C., July 15, 1790, quoted in Barnett A. Elzas, *The Jews of South Carolina: From the Earliest Time to the Present Day* (Philadelphia: Lippincott, 1905; reprint, Spartanburg, S.C.: Reprint Co., 1972), 123. Washington's gracious reply (found in Elzas, 125) stated "May the same temporal and eternal blessings which you implore for me, rest upon your congregation." Charles Pinckney must also have been pleased with the religious clauses produced by the 1790 convention since he did not list them among the deficient provisions, such as that giving the governor too short a term, that he complained about in a letter to James Madison written shortly after the close of the convention. See Matthews, *Forgotten Founder,* 71. See Charles Pinckney to James Madison, Charleston. June 14, 1790, in *The Papers of James Madison,* vol. 13: January 20, 1790–March 31, 1791, ed. Charles F. Hobson and Robert A. Rutland (Charlottesville: University Press of Virginia 1981), 242–43. In a letter to George Washington, also dated, Charleston, June 14, 1790, Charles Pinckney seemed most pleased with the work done by the convention to bring about the "the Unity of the Executive," which had theretofore been dispersed among many officers. See Mark A. Mastromarino, ed., *The Papers of George Washington,* Presidential Series, VI: 32n2. Neither letter mentions the religious clauses. Delegate Christopher Gadsden gave lukewarm praise to the emerging constitution as the convention neared its end when he said, "The outline of the Constitution as far as agreed upon, I am far from thinking a bad one" (Christopher Gadsden, Columbia, May 30, 1790, to Thomas Morris, available at South Carolina Historical Society, Charleston).

57. See Charles Cotesworth Pinckney to George Washington, June 19, 1790, Twohig, ed., *The Papers of George Washington,* Presidential Series, vol. 5, January-June 1790 (Charlottesville: University Press of Virginia, 1996), 537. See also Haw, *John & Edward Rutledge of South Carolina,* 332.

58. William Smith to Edward Rutledge, New York, July 4, 1790, in George C. Rogers Jr., "The Letters of William Loughton Smith to Edward Rutledge, June 6, 1789 to April 28, 1794," *South Carolina Historical Magazine* 69, no. 2 (1968): 121. Article 2 of the South Carolina Constitution of 1790 created a weak governor since that official was elected by the legislature and thus had no independent power base. He served for only two years and was not eligible for reelection until after the expiration of four years. The governor had no veto power. Article 10, section 1, provided for two treasurers, one in Charleston and one in Columbia.

59. See Laurens to Ettwein, Mepkin, S.C., July 25, 1790, in *The Papers of Henry Laurens,* XVI: 761. See also Ettwein to Laurens, Bethlehem, Pa., August 21, 1787, ibid., 731–32, noting that the rules of his church stipulated that an inquiry be made into the "laws and Situation of Church & State" in the area to which a move was being considered. Ettwein had also inquired whether his group could be exempted from military service during war, but Laurens told him that was a matter for federal law (ibid., 761). See also S.C. Const. of 1790, art. 4, providing for oath or affirmation by officeholders (in *Basic Documents of South Carolina History* [1952]).

60. S.C. Const. of 1790, art. 1, sec. 23.

61. William Smith, *A Comparative View of the Constitutions of the Several States With Each Other and With That of the United States* (Philadelphia: Printed by John Thompson, 1796), 24–25, available at South Carolina Historical Society, Charleston. Smith listed New

York, Maryland, Kentucky, North and South Carolina, Georgia, and Tennessee as having such a disqualification (ibid., 23).

62. *McDaniel v. Paty,* 435 U.S. 618 (1978).

63. See S.C. CONST. of 1778, art. 38.

64. Stevens and Allen, eds., *The State Records of South Carolina: Journals of the House of Representatives, 1791* (Columbia.: University of South Carolina Press, 1985), 16.

65. Reznikoff, *The Jews of Charleston,* 17.

66. Marcus, *United States Jewry 1776–1985,* 1:234.

67. Ibid., 117.

68. Act No. 1516 of 1791, 8 S.C. STATUTES AT LARGE 162–163 (McCord 1840). This statute spells the name of the synagogue as Beth Eloihim.

69. Ibid.

70. Ibid.

71. Reznikoff, *The Jews of Charleston,* 54.

72. Ibid.

73. *South Carolina State-Gazette,* September 20, 1794.

74. Levin, "The Jewish Congregation of Charleston," 390. Levin concurs in the view that 1791 is the incorporation date (ibid., 384–85).

75. Reznikoff, *The Jews of Charleston,* 59–60; Elzas, *The Jews of South Carolina,* 126–27. These accounts imply that Knight's candidacy was successful, but his name is not found on the convention roster. However, the list may be incomplete. See Hutson, ed., *Constitutional Convention of South Carolina,* 3–6.

76. Hannah Adams, *History of the Jews from the Destruction of Jerusalem to the Nineteenth Century,* vol. 2 (Boston: John Eliot Jr., 1812), 218.

77. Ibid., 218–19.

78. Ibid., 219.

79. Ibid., 218.

80. Act No. 1515 of 1791, 8 S.C. STATUTES AT LARGE 161–162 (McCord 1840).

81. Ibid.

82. "House of Representatives, Returned Bill 21, 23 Feb. 1811," in *The Founders' Constitution,* vol. 5, ed. Philip B. Kurland and Ralph Lerner (Chicago: University of Chicago Press, 1987), 99, containing Madison's veto of church incorporation.

83. James Madison, Detached Memoranda, *Writings,* ed. Jack N. Rakove (New York: Library of America, 1999), 761.

84. Ibid., 761–62. Madison wanted similar limits on other types of corporations as well.

85. Act No. 1723 of 1799, 5 S.C. STATUTES AT LARGE 357 (Cooper 1839).

86. Act No. 2451 of 1828, 8 S.C. STATUTES AT LARGE 365, para. 5 (McCord 1840). See also Act No. 2516 of 1830, 8 S.C. STATUTES AT LARGE 369, para. 6 (McCord 1840).

87. Act No. 2669 of 1835, 6 S.C. STATUTES AT LARGE 534, para. 19, (McCord 1839). See also Richard C. Madden, *Catholics in South Carolina: A Record* (Lanham, Md.: University Press of America, 1985), 46, describing the work of the Ursulines in higher education for girls and of the Sisters of Mercy in educating black children. See also Jeremiah J. O'Connell, *Catholicity in the Carolinas and Georgia: Leaves of Its History* (1879; reprint, Spartanburg, S.C.: Reprint Co., 1979), 64–69, describing the organization and work of the Charleston nuns. The most detailed biography of John England is Peter Guilday, *The Life and Times of*

John England, First Bishop of Charleston 1786–1842 (New York: America Press, 1922). In-depth treatment is also found in Peter Clarke, *A Free Church in a Free Society: The Ecclesiology of John England, Bishop of Charleston, 1820–1842: A Nineteenth Century Missionary Bishop in the Southern United States* (Hartsville, S.C.: Center for John England Studies, 1982). A useful shorter work focusing more on the development of England's political philosophy than events in his life is Patrick Carey, *An Immigrant Bishop: John England's Adaptation of Irish Catholicism to American Republicanism* (Yonkers, N.Y.: U.S. Catholic Historical Society, 1982). See also Madden, *Catholics in South Carolina*, 31–49. Collections of England's writings include Sebastian G. Messmer, ed., *The Works of the Right Reverend John England, First Bishop of Charleston*, 7 vols. (Cleveland, Ohio: Arthur H. Clark, 1908), and Ignatius Aloysius Reynolds, ed., *The Works of the Right Rev. John England, First Bishop of Charleston*, 5 vols. (Baltimore, Md.: John Murphy, 1849). Reynolds was England's successor as bishop in Charleston.

88. Letter from Bishop John England to Dr. Cullen, February 23, 1836, *Records of the American Catholic Historical Society* (ACHS), vol. 8 (Philadelphia, 1897), 222–24. See also Clarke, *A Free Church in a Free Society*, 364–66. Madden, *Catholics in South Carolina*, 46, describes the trouble the Haitian mission caused England by distracting him from his work in Charleston and causing him to be linked with abolition in southern public opinion.

89. *Works of John England*, ed. Messmer, VII: 151, address to an 1835 church convention in which England describes the circumstances leading up to the school's closure. See also Letter of Bishop John England to Dr. Paul Cullen, February 1836, in *Records of the American Catholic Historical Society* (ACHS), VIII: 219–21.

90. Brinsfield, *Religion and Politics in Colonial South Carolina*, 47, concludes that the first legal mass was celebrated in Charleston in 1790. One commentator concluded that masses had been performed beginning in 1788 by a Father Ryan sent to Charleston by Bishop John Carroll. See Guilday, *The Life and Times of John Carroll*, 736.

91. John England, "The Early History of the Diocese of Charleston," in *Works of John England*, ed. Messmer, IV, pt. 3: 300–302.

92. Ibid., 300.

93. John England, "The Republic in Danger," in *Works of John England*, ed. Messmer, IV, pt.4: 436–37, citing John Drayton, *Memoirs of the American Revolution*, 1:273, 300. For another account of this incident see William M. Dabney and Marion Dargan, *William Henry Drayton & the American Revolution* (Albuquerque: University of New Mexico Press 1962), 82–83.

94. England, "The Republic in Danger," 436–37.

95. Ibid.

96. Ibid., 433. The statute to which England referred is Act No. 154 of 1696–97, 2 S.C. Statutes at Large 132–33, para. 6 (Cooper 1837).

97. England, "The Republic in Danger," 433.

98. England, "The Early History of the Diocese of Charleston," 303.

99. Stevens and Allen, eds., *The State Records of South Carolina: Journals of the House of Representatives, 1791*, ix–x.

100. N. Louise Bailey, *Biographical Directory of the South Carolina House of Representatives*, vol. 4: 1791–1815 (Columbia: University of South Carolina Press, 1984), 420.

101. Farrand, ed., *Records of the Federal Convention of 1787* (New Haven: Yale University Press, 1911), 2:342, 468, Charles Pinckney introducing measures against religious test oaths.

102. Letter from Bishop John England to Dr. Cullen, February 23, 1836, *Records of the American Catholic Historical Society* (ACHS), VIII: 222–24; Clarke, *A Free Church in a Free Society,* 365. In an 1835 convention address England gave "special acknowledgment" to the South Carolina legislature for passing the act incorporating the orders of nuns even though none of the legislators was Catholic and the debate took place during a time of prejudice against convents, such as that displayed by the burning of a convent in Massachusetts (*Works of John England,* ed. Messmer, VII: 165).

103. John England, "Letter on Civic and Political Duties to the Roman Catholic Citizens of Charleston," in *Works of John England,* ed. Messmer, VI, pt. 5: 352–63. See also the account of the nullification controversy and the bitter election contests produced by it in Walter Edgar, *South Carolina: A History* (Columbia: University of South Carolina Press, 1998), 330–37.

104. England, "Letter on Civic and Political Duties," 370.

105. Thomas R. England, *The Life of the Reverend Arthur O'Leary, including Historical Anecdotes, Memoirs, and Many Hitherto Unpublished Documents, Illustrative of the Condition of the Irish Catholics, During the Eighteenth Century* (London: Longman, Hurst, Rees, Orme & Brown / Keeting, Brown & Co., 1822), 96, available at Pitts Theology Library, Emory University, Atlanta, Georgia. The author cautions the reader that the arrangement of the book is such that it is difficult to tell whether the quoted words are O'Leary's or those of Thomas England describing O'Leary's views.

106. Arthur O'Leary, *Miscellaneous Tracts,* second edition (Dublin: John Chambers, 1781), 345, available at Pitts Theology Library, Emory University, Atlanta, Georgia. For a discussion of England's involvement in the reform of the condition of Catholics in Ireland, see Carey, *Immigrant Bishop,* 8, 46–54, 80.

107. John England, *The Constitution of the Roman Catholic Churches of the States of North-Carolina, South-Carolina, and Georgia; Which are Comprised in the Diocess of Charleston; and Province of Baltimore* (Charleston: Office of the Seminary, 1826), 6. This document was adopted on September 25, 1822, and then sent to the Vatican for a determination of its compatibility with doctrine of the universal church. The spelling "Diocess" (for Diocese) is in the original.

108. John England to Andrew Jackson, Georgetown, D.C., September 26, 1830, in *Works of John England,* ed. Reynolds, VI: 227–28.

109. Madden, *Catholics in South Carolina,* 47.

110. Act No. 2744 of 1838, 7 S.C. STATUTES AT LARGE 156–160 (McCord 1840). See also Act No. 2769 of 1838, 7 S.C. STATUTES AT LARGE 161 (McCord 1840).

111. Act No. 2744 of 1838, 7 S.C. STATUTES AT LARGE 156–160 (McCord 1840).

112. Clarke, *A Free Church in a Free Society,* 367.

113. *Works of John England,* ed. Messmer, VII: 263, Clarke, *A Free Church in a Free Society,* 367–68.

114. Clarke, *A Free Church in a Free Society,* 367–68; Act No. 2744 of 1838, 7 S.C. STATUTES AT LARGE 156–160 (McCord 1840).

115. S.C. CONST. of 1790, art. 8, sec. 1.

116. Minutes of the Board of Trustees of Beth Elohim (hereafter referred to as Beth Elohim Minutes), September 1, 1839, p. 59, resolution authorizing the president of the congregation to seek a loan from the state; available at College of Charleston, Special Collections.
See also Beth Elohim Minutes, September 13, 1839, p. 66, in which the president reports
that he has applied for the state loan pursuant to the resolution of September 1, 1839; see
also Beth Elohim Minutes, October 27, 1839, in which president reports that first install-
ment of $8,250 on state loan has arrived and that he gave the state bank a mortgage dated
October 16, 1839, as security. Charles Reznikoff describes the fund-raising efforts that preceded the loan application in *The Jews of Charleston*, 137, 294. He notes that appeals to European congregations were unsuccessful for the most part, but American Jewish communities
were more forthcoming. See also Hagy, *This Happy Land*, 238–39; Gene Waddell, "An Architectural History of Kahal Kadosh Beth Elohim, Charleston," *South Carolina Historical Magazine* 98 (January 1997): 1, 21–35, discusses the architectural plan for the new building and
refers to the fire-bond loan.

117. John Leland, *The Rights of Conscience Inalienable, and Therefore Religious Opinions
Not Cognizable by Law, or the High-flying Church-man Stript of His Legal Robe, Appears a
Yaho* (New London, Conn.: T. Green & Son, 1791); John Leland, *The Connecticut Dissenter's
Strong Box: No. 1* (New London, Conn.: Charles Holt, 1802), 22.

118. Furman to Reverend Pearce, Charleston, February 12, 1791, Richard Furman Correspondence, 1777–1825, Special Collections Library, Furman University, Greenville, South
Carolina; also available on microfilm at Livingston Library, Shorter College, Rome, Georgia.

119. J. Adams, *The Relation of Christianity to Civil Government in the United States: A Sermon, Preached in St. Michael's Church, Charleston, February 13th, 1833, Before the Convention of the Protestant Episcopal Church of the Diocese of South Carolina* (Charleston: A. E.
Miller, 1833), 38–44, available at South Caroliniana Library, University of South Carolina,
Columbia.

120. Ibid.

121. *City Council of Charleston v. Benjamin*, 33 S.C. L. (2 Strob.) 508 (S.C. Ct. App. 1846).

122. Ibid., 522.

123. Ibid.

124. Ibid., 524–25. The issue of whether the common law is rooted in Christianity at-
tracted the attention of Thomas Jefferson, who argued that it was not since many basic prin-
ciples of the common law were already framed prior to the introduction of Christianity into
England. See Letter from Thomas Jefferson to Dr. Thomas Cooper, February 10, 1814,
"Christianity and the Common Law," in *Jefferson Writings*, ed. Merrill D. Peterson (New
York: Library of America, 1984), 1321, 1324–25.

125. *City Council of Charleston v. Benjamin*, 33 S.C.L. at 529.

126. *Braunfeld v. Brown*, 366 U.S. 599 (1961), which concluded that Pennsylvania Sunday
law did not violate Equal Protection, Establishment, and Free Exercise Clauses. In *McGowan
v. Maryland*, 366 U.S. 420 (1961) the U.S. Supreme Court rejected an argument that Sunday closing laws violated the Establishment Clause of the First Amendment; the original
religious purpose of such laws had been replaced by the secular one of providing a uniform
day of rest. For similar results see *Two Guys from Harrison-Allentown v. McGinley*, 366 U.S.
582 (1961), which concluded that Pennsylvania Sunday law did not violate the Establishment Clause, and *Gallagher v. Crown Kosher Super Market*, 366 U.S. 617 (1961), concluding

that the Massachusetts Sunday closing law does not violate Equal Protection, Free Exercise, or Establishment Clauses. See also *State v. Solomon,* 245 S.C. 550, 141 S.E.2d 818 (S.C. 1965), upholding Sunday closing laws.

127. S.C. Const. of 1790, art. 8, sec. 1; *City Council of Charleston v. Benjamin,* 529–30. The *Benjamin* analytical approach sometimes adumbrates that which the U.S. Supreme Court took in late twentieth-century free-exercise cases: government laws of general applicability that do not target religion, but only incidentally harm it, will not be subject to strict scrutiny by the court (*Employment Division v. Smith,* 494 U.S. 872 [1990]).

128. See *Ex Parte Duke,* 33 S.C. L. (2 Strob.) 530 (1833), appended to *Benjamin.*

129. See *Barron v. Baltimore,* 32 U.S. (7 Pet.) 243, 250–51 (1833), holding that the Bill of Rights applies to the federal but not the state governments—as does *Livingston's Lessee v. Moore,* 32 US (7 Pet.) 469, 551–52 (1833). Joseph Story concluded that the purpose of the First Amendment religious clauses was "to exclude all rivalry among Christian sects, and to prevent any national ecclesiastical establishment, which would give to a hierarchy the exclusive patronage of the national government" (Joseph Story, *Commentaries on the Constitution of the United States,* vol. 2, third edition (Boston: Little, Brown, 1858), 664, sec. 1877. For a twentieth-century application of the First Amendment religious clauses to the states through incorporation by the Due Process Clause of the Fourteenth Amendment see *Cantwell v. Connecticut,* 310 U.S. 296, 303 (1940); *Hamilton v. Board of Regents,* 293 U.S. 245, 262 (1934); *Everson v. Board of Education,* 330 U.S. 1, 3, 7, 8 (1947); and *Illinois ex rel. McCollum v. Board of Education,* 333 U.S. 203 (1948).

130. *Ex Parte Duke,* 530–36.

131. Morton Borden, *Jews, Turks and Infidels* (Chapel Hill: University of North Carolina Press, 1984), 114.

132. Ibid.

133. Ibid., 115.

134. Ibid.

135. Ibid.

136. *State ex rel. Ottolengui v. Ancker,* 31 S.C.L. (2 Rich.) 245 (S.C. 1846).

137. Ibid., 269.

138. Thomas Cooper, *The Case of Thomas Cooper, M.D., President of the South Carolina College, Submitted to the Legislature and the People of South Carolina, December 1831,* second edition (Columbia: Times & Gazette, 1832), 3–6, available at South Caroliniana Library, University of South Carolina, Columbia.

139. See 2 S.C. Statutes at Large 707 (Cooper 1837).

140. Borden, *Jews, Turks and Infidels,* 142n2.

141. Jonathan D. Sarna and David G. Dalin, *Religion and State in the American Jewish Experience* (Notre Dame, Ind.: University of Notre Dame Press, 1997), 113–15.

142. Ibid., 114.

143. Ibid., 114–15.

144. Borden, *Jews, Turks and Infidels,* 142n2. In 1797 and 1805, the United States concluded two treaties with Tripoli. The first of these stated that "the United States is not, in any sense, founded on the Christian religion." This wording was dropped from the 1805 treaty. See Anson Phelps Stokes and Leo Pfeffer, *Church and State in the United States* (1964; reprint, Westport, Conn.: Greenwood Press, 1975), 89.

145. Sarna and Dalin, *Religion and State in the American Jewish Experience*, 115–118 (setting forth Hammond's reply to the Jewish community), 117.

146. Ibid., 120.

147. James Henry Hammond, *Secret and Sacred: The Diaries of James Henry Hammond, a Southern Slaveholder*, ed. Carol Bleser (New York: Oxford University Press, 1988), 137–38, 142, 125–26. Drew Gilpin Faust, *James Henry Hammond and the Old South: A Design for Mastery* (Baton Rouge: Louisiana State University Press 1982), 249, 253–54.

148. *County of Allegheny v. ACLU*, 492 U.S. 573 (1989), ruling that a stand-alone creche display in courthouse was an illegal establishment of religion, but a varied display of religious and secular items in a county office building was valid.

149. Ibid., 604n53.

150. Ibid. Blackmun was interpreting the federal First Amendment in a modern case rather than the South Carolina Constitution of 1790, but his views on the meaning of discrimination are still useful in understanding the impact of the earlier events in South Carolina.

151. James Henry Hammond, diary entry for June 10, 1842, in *Secret and Sacred*, ed. Bleser, 94–95.

152. Faust, *James Henry Hammond and the Old South*, 193. The quotation is from a letter from Hammond, Rome, Italy, to John Fox, December 18, 1836, James Henry Hammond Papers, South Caroliniana Library, University of South Carolina, Columbia.

153. Hammond, diary entry for July 18, 1845, in *Secret and Sacred*, ed. Bleser, 151–52.

154. Both the Hammond and Middleton incidents are discussed in Reznikoff, *The Jews of Charleston*, 111–12.

155. James William Hagy, *This Happy Land: The Jews of Colonial and Antebellum Charleston* (Tuscaloosa: University of Alabama Press, 1993), 42–43.

156. Ibid., 42. See also Reznikoff, *The Jews of Charleston*, 91; A. Levasseur, *Lafayette in America, in 1824 and 1825; or, Journal of Travels, in the United States*, vol. 2 (New York: Clayton & Van Norden, 1829), 54, 57, 62.

157. Levasseur, *Lafayette in America*, 2:57.

158. Hagy, *This Happy Land*, 86–87.

159. Ibid., 44.

160. David Ramsay, *Universal History Americanised; or, An Historical View of the World, From the Earliest Records to the Year 1808. With a Particular Reference to the State of Society, Literature, Religion, and Form of Government, in the United States of America*, vol. 1 (Philadelphia: M. Carey & Son, 1819), 389.

161. Hagy, *This Happy Land*, 45.

162. Ibid.

163. See Belinda Gergel and Richard Gergel, *In Pursuit of the Tree of Life: A History of the Early Jews of Columbia, South Carolina, and the Tree of Life Congregation* (Columbia: Tree of Life Congregation, 1996), 8, 22.

164. Reznikoff, *The Jews of Charleston*, 100–101; Hagy, *This Happy Land*, 104.

165. Hagy, *This Happy Land*, 104.

166. Abraham Ottolengui to Judge Bay, October 9, 1829, Manuscripts Division, South Caroliniana Library, University of South Carolina, Columbia. The outcome of this dispute is not known.

167. See Abraham Moise "A Memoir of His Life," in *A Selection From the Miscellaneous Writing of Isaac Harby, Esq.,* ed. Henry L. Pinckney and Abraham Moise (Charleston: Printed by James S. Burgess, 1829), 28–34; see also Isaac Harby, *A Discourse Delivered in Charleston (S.C.) On the 21st of Nov. 1825 Before the Reformed Society of Israelites for Promoting True Principles of Judaism According to Its Purity and Spirit on This First Anniversary* (Charleston: Printed by A. E. Miller, 1825), 5–6; see also Gary Phillip Zola, *Isaac Harby of Charleston, 1788–1828: Jewish Reformer and Intellectual,* (Tuscaloosa: University of Alabama Press, 1994), 12–149, discussing Harby's reform efforts; see also Max J. Kohler, "Issac Harby, Jewish Religious Leader and Reformer," *Publications of the American Jewish Historical Society,* vol. 32 (Baltimore: Lord Baltimore Press, 1931), 35–53; see also L. C. Moise, *Biography of Isaac Harby With An Account of The Reformed Society of Israelites of Charleston, S.C. 1824–1833* (N.p., 1931), 32–45, containing an interesting discussion of the spirit and rationale behind the Charleston reform movement. Hagy, *This Happy Land,* 145–52, discusses Harby's role in the reform movement.

168. Hagy, *This Happy Land,* 158–59 (decline of Reform Society); Beth Elohim Minutes, July 10, 1839 (board petition to Poznanski), July 24, 1839 (Poznanski's reply). See also Reznikoff, *The Jews of Charleston,* 296n181.

169. Zola, *Isaac Harby,* 62–63, 208–09.

170. Ibid., 208–9n48.

171. Ibid., 63.

172. See Zola, *Isaac Harby of Charleston,* 62–63, 208–9.

173. Reznikoff, *The Jews of Charleston,* 101–2.

174. *Charleston Southern Patriot,* October 1, 1832. See also Congregation Beth Elohim, *Constitution of the Hebrew Congregation of Kaal Kadosh Beth Elohim, or House of God* (1820; reprint, Charleston: Daggett Printing, 1904), available at South Caroliniana Library, University of South Carolina, Columbia. The Constitution sought to maintain solidarity in the Jewish community by refusing to approve the building of any other synagogue within five miles of Charleston (p. 9). The Constitution also attempted to require any "Israelites" who had resided in Charleston one year to subscribe to the synagogue and provide seats for themselves and their wives (p. 11). For more information regarding the Constitution's provisions, see Reznikoff, *The Jews of Charleston,* 116–19.

175. See Arthur Henry Hirsch, *The Huguenots of Colonial South Carolina* (1928; reprint, London: Archon, 1962), 94, 127.

176. S.C. Const. of 1790, art. 8, section 1.

177. Ibid.

178. James Madison to Edward Livingston, 10 July 1822, in *The Founders' Constitution,* vol. 5, ed. Philip B. Kurland and Ralph Lerner (Chicago: University of Chicago Press, 1987), 105–6.

179. Garry Wills, *James Madison* (New York: Times Books, 2002), 18, commenting on Madison's view that freedom of religion leads to "sincerity of religious practice" that energizes religion.

180. See William Penn, "The Great Case of Liberty of Conscience," in *The Political Writings of William Penn,* ed. Andrew R. Murphy (Indianapolis: Liberty Fund, 2002), 88–89, arguing that government sanctions that invade liberty of conscience "overturn the Christian Religion" by discouraging new "discoveries" of God's will.

181. One powerful religious figure, Pope Galasius I, expressed misgivings about permitting the two swords of authority, political and spiritual, to be wielded by the same set of fallible human hands. See Robert Warrand Carlyle and Alexander James Carlyle, *A History of Mediaeval Political Theory in the West,* third edition, vol. 1 (Edinburgh: Blackwood, 1928).

190. See also *Larkin v. Grendel's Den,* 459 U.S. 116 (1982), in which the Supreme Court noted the importance of avoiding a unification of secular and sectarian power in an opinion striking down a law granting churches a role in licensing decisions concerning saloons that would operate near them.

"A bright era now dawns upon us"

Jewish Economic Opportunities, Religious Freedom,
and Political Rights in Colonial and
Antebellum South Carolina

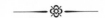

Richard and Belinda Gergel

BY THE DAWN OF THE AMERICAN REPUBLIC, in the year 1800, Jews had settled up and down the eastern seaboard, with significant Jewish communities in the major northeastern cities of Philadelphia and New York. But the largest, most sophisticated, and probably most affluent Jewish community in the United States resided in Charleston, South Carolina. A number of Jews had also settled at that time in the port city of Georgetown, South Carolina, and in the early decades of the nineteenth century small Jewish communities were established in such inland South Carolina towns as Columbia, Sumter, and Camden. Prior to the Civil War, Jews were elected mayors of Georgetown three times and Columbia twice, and Jewish state senators and state representatives represented Charleston, Sumter, Chesterfield, and Kershaw counties. This chapter explores the remarkable origins of the Carolina colony as a haven of tolerance and opportunity for its early Jewish settlers and the subsequent development within South Carolina of one of America's most significant and politically active antebellum Jewish communities.

The "Darkness" of Old Europe

One cannot appreciate the Jewish attraction to the New World without understanding the extraordinary burdens and disabilities that Jews suffered in most European countries during the seventeenth and eighteenth centuries. A broad array of official and officially sanctioned discrimination and harassment against Jews was part of the fabric of European life. In Spain and Portugal, Jews faced the choice of exile, conversion, or death in the notorious Inquisitions of the late 1400s and early 1500s. Many Jews lived in those countries as supposed converts to Christianity. Known as Marranos, these "secret Jews" practiced their religion by stealth with the sure knowledge that, if discovered, they could face terrible punishment, including death. Jews in Italy were mostly confined involuntarily to ghettos and lived under the wrath of the

Catholic Church's unabashed anti-Semitism. In April 1775, two weeks after the beginning of the American Revolution, Pope Pius VI issued an edict prohibiting any Jew of Rome to be outside the Jewish ghetto for even one night. This same edict forbade any Jew to engage in any form of business or commerce outside the ghetto.[1]

Jewish life in Germany was also dismal. As late as the eighteenth century, Jews in Frankfurt were confined to the ghetto, and the gates were locked each evening and on Sundays and holidays. Jews were forbidden to be members of any guild or to work as merchants. A special "body tax" was placed on all goods, animals, and Jews passing through the ghetto gates of Dresden in 1776. As a result, the celebrated philosopher Moses Mendelssohn, on a visit to the city, was taxed as if he were "a Polish ox." Jews in Austria were required until 1781 to wear a badge identifying themselves as Jews. Moreover, Austria required synagogues to allow Christian missionaries at will to proselytize during Jewish religious services. When one synagogue on Yom Kippur Eve, the holiest day of the Jewish year, threw a minister out of its sanctuary, the Austrian authorities responded by destroying the synagogue and branding and exiling its leaders.[2]

England and Holland provided a measure of tolerance for their Jewish citizens and allowed Jews to engage in a broad range of business and commerce. But even in these countries, bastions of religious liberty in an otherwise hostile Europe, Jews were viewed as aliens and mostly lived in sections of town separated from their Christian neighbors. Indeed, Jews were not allowed to be citizens of England until 1740. Many Jews came to London during this era from other parts of Europe, acquired a command of English, and set sail for the English colonies in the West Indies as well as the new American colonies. The hope of these Jewish immigrants, as well as the other immigrant religious dissenters of this era, was to escape the intolerance and narrow-mindedness of Old Europe, particularly the dominating and unceasingly hostile role of the established churches against nonbelievers.[3]

An Island of Religious Tolerance

In 1663 King Charles II of England granted to eight English noblemen a massive tract of land lying between the Virginia colony and the Spanish settlement in Florida. This land grant, known as the Charter of Carolina, was in appreciation for the role these men, now known as the Lords Proprietors, had played in Charles II's ascendency to the throne in 1660, following the execution of his father, Charles I, during the Commonwealth period of British history. From the beginning the Lords Proprietors viewed the colony as a business proposition, and there was little of the religious fervor and mission that was associated with the establishment of many of the other colonies, such as the Massachusetts Bay Colony. The key question for the Lord Proprietors was how to persuade residents of Europe or the early colonies of the New World to set sail for the vast and undeveloped wilderness of Carolina. An obvious and promising source of potential settlers was religious dissenters, who often found themselves in unending battles with the established churches of their home countries.[4]

This pragmatic need and desire to lure Dissenters to the Carolina colony coincided with the selection of Anthony Ashley Cooper, Lord Ashley (later Earl of Shaftesbury), as the leader of the Carolina colony enterprise. Ashley, one of the most skilled and thoughtful public figures of his day, employed his close friend and confidant, John Locke, to serve as chief secretary of the Carolina colony project. Locke was one of the most brilliant and original political philosophers of his time and, along with Lord Ashley, a champion of religious tolerance. Driven by the pragmatic desire to recruit new settlers to the wilderness of Carolina and by the idealism of the Enlightenment, Locke participated in drafting the Fundamental Constitution of the Government of Carolina in 1669. In a world of seemingly unremitting religious strife, the Fundamental Constitutions reflected an extraordinary sentiment of inclusiveness and tolerance essentially unknown at that time.[5]

The Fundamental Constitution of July 21, 1669, provided that any seven or more persons "agreeing in any Religion, shall constitute a church or profession." This straightforward grant of the right to organize any religion was accompanied by prohibitions against the disturbing of "any Religious Assembly" and the "use of any reproachful, Reviling, or abusive language" against any religion. Leaving no ambiguity regarding their target audience, the Lords Proprietors expressly provided these protections to "heathens, Jews, and other dissenters from the purity of Christian Religion."

These remarkable provisions were justified on two separate and independent grounds. First, there was the practical problem that settlers from different places would "unavoidably be of different opinions concerning matters of religion," and tolerance was necessary so that "civil peace may be maintained amidst diversity of opinion." Second, the drafters expressed the hope that these Dissenters "from the purity of Christian Religion" might come to Carolina and have "an opportunity of acquainting themselves with the truth and reasonableness of its doctrines." This seeming openness to Jews and dissenting Protestant groups did not extend, however, to Catholics, who faced significant social and legal adversities in early colonial South Carolina.[6]

The striking and explicit reference in the Fundamental Constitutions to Jews and the protection of their right to worship has caused some scholars to speculate that these provisions were a not-so-subtle effort to recruit to the Carolina colony members of the Barbados Jewish community, who by this time were thought to monopolize the very lucrative trade on the island. Jews then constituted 54 of the 404 households on Barbados and obviously possessed skills and knowledge in establishing international trade and commerce that would have been invaluable to a new colony in Carolina. Whether Barbadian Jews actually came to Carolina in the early days of the settlement is not known, but clearly immigrants from Barbados were a part of the colony's early population.[7]

The Fundamental Constitutions did not lead to a rush of immigration to Carolina. Charleston, the colony's first town, was founded only a year after the first

Fundamental Constitution was drafted, and its initial development was not rapid. But events across Europe in the late seventeenth century had led many Dissenters to explore New World settlement, and the word that Carolina was open and accepting to Dissenters spread widely. Indeed, after King Louis XIV of France revoked the Edict of Nantes in 1685, effectively eliminating freedom of religion for the French Huguenots, significant numbers of them immigrated to the Carolina colony.[8]

Although the Fundamental Constitutions were never formally adopted by the colonists, their significance to the colony's development was substantial. Jacob Rader Marcus, the preeminent twentieth-century scholar of American Jewish history, referred to the Fundamental Constitutions as "a document without counterpart elsewhere in the North American colonies, which provided specifically—and liberally —for Jews." Rabbi Barnet Elzas, in his early *Jews of South Carolina* (1905), described the Fundamental Constitutions as a "veritable Magna Charter of liberty and tolerance." More recently, James Hagy, in his definitive history of Charleston's early Jewish community, noted that while the colonists never ratified the Fundamental Constitutions, the document provided the basic law of the colony for thirteen years and "set the tone for religious interactions in Carolina." James Underwood, in his exhaustive four-volume history of South Carolina's constitutions, notes that the Fundamental Constitutions struck a "tolerant note" and "encouraged a climate of tolerance." Simply stated, the Fundamental Constitutions represented the first time in human history that religious liberty was made a constitutional right.[9]

By the 1690s, Dissenters, particularly French Huguenots and Jews, were present and actively engaged in the life of the Carolina colony. The first documented presence of a Jew in South Carolina was a translator for then Gov. John Archdale, presumably a Sepharidic Jew (one of Spanish or Portugese origin), who assisted the governor in 1695 in communicating with Indians from the Spanish colony of Florida. Legal developments, both in the English Parliament and in the colonial legislature, provided further assurances of broad economic opportunities for religious minorities. In 1696 a proposal came before Parliament to exclude all non-British-born subjects from trade within the colonies. For Jews and Huguenots, then becoming among the leading traders and merchants in Charleston, this was a potentially devastating blow. A group of London-based Jews and Huguenots intervened with parliamentary leaders, and the proposal quickly died.[10]

Perhaps recognizing the fragility of their legal position, sixty Huguenots and four Jews jointly petitioned the governor of the Carolina colony the following year, 1697, for citizenship rights. Gov. Joseph Blake endorsed the petition and recommended adoption in an address to the colonial legislature. The legislature responded by adopting legislation granting citizenship rights to all aliens, their wives, and children, regardless of their nation of origin. The legislation noted that a number of Dissenters petitioning for citizenship had come to the colony for religious freedom. Shortly thereafter, colonial records reflect that two Charleston Jews, Simon Valentine and Abraham Avila, were issued citizenship papers. It is notable that citizenship rights for

Jews in the Carolina colony were granted more than forty years before such rights were given to Jews residing in England.[11]

Establishment of the Church of England and Limitations on the Franchise and Office Holding

In the early 1700s, significant tensions arose between the Anglicans and other Protestant denominations over the standing and prerogatives of the Anglican Church. After a particularly vituperative 1703 election, in which certain Dissenter groups complained of electoral fraud and misconduct by the Anglicans, the colony's legislature was convened on short notice by Gov. Nathaniel Johnson in May 1704 to consider legislation that required members of the legislature to take the sacrament of communion in accord with the rites of the Anglican Church. Since the nature of communion was a major point of contention between Anglicans and dissenting Protestant groups, this legislation was designed to exclude Christian Dissenters from the colonial legislature. The legislation passed 12 to 11, with seven members absent. The battle soon crossed the Atlantic, with the House of Lords requesting that the queen veto the bill. Eventually, the queen referred the matter to the Board of Trade, which declared the act null and void.[12]

The Anglicans, now holding a majority of the seats in the colonial legislature, moved in November 1704 to make the Church of England the established church of the colony. The same act had no religious qualification for voting but prohibited aliens from voting or holding office. Since a significant number of the Dissenters—and many of the Jews—were not British subjects, this legislation effectively eliminated their right to vote or hold office. The legislation reaffirmed the right, however, of aliens to own property and engage in commerce. Subsequent electoral legislation in 1716, 1721, 1745, and 1759 required all voters and officeholders to be professing Christians.[13]

What significance did these eighteenth-century legislative acts limiting the right of franchise and the holding of public office have on the lives and opportunities of the Jews of South Carolina? While the electoral limitations seem strikingly out of character with earlier constitutional and legislative provisions, the fact of the matter is that they had minimal impact on the colony's Jewish citizens. At the time of the adoption of the first of the offensive election-law changes in 1704 (and until South Carolina elected its first Jewish officeholder in 1774), no Jew in human history had been elected to public office anywhere. The real issue for South Carolina's early Jewish community—and its potentially future Jewish immigrants—was economic opportunity, and at no time were Jews denied the right to own property, engage fully in commerce, or make contracts. South Carolina was and remained a place Jews could do business. Furthermore, despite the Anglican Church's effort to obtain establishment status, Jews were never harassed or prevented from organizing religious services, practicing their customs, or operating synagogues. Indeed, despite these electoral-law restrictions on Jewish suffrage and office holding, Charleston's Jewish population grew steadily throughout the eighteenth century, making the city by the year 1800 the largest and most vibrant center of Jewish life in North America.

Charleston as a Major Center of Jewish Life

In the first half of the eighteenth century, Charleston was transformed from a small port town on the edge of a wilderness into a bustling and growing city with great economic opportunities. For Jews seeking a welcoming location for immigration, there were, practically speaking, few options at that time. As Jacob Rader Marcus noted, "south of New York, in effect, there was no place which appealed to Jews until Charleston rose and opened her doors to them."[14] Jews initially arrived in small numbers and engaged primarily in trade and commerce. It is, therefore, not surprising that the four Jews who petitioned for citizenship in 1697 were merchants. By 1715 Jewish merchants were engaged in shipping kosher beef out of Charleston Harbor to Jewish settlers in other communities. The pace of Jewish immigration quickened in the 1730s and 1740s, as Charleston grew into the South's largest city, with upwards of seven thousand residents.[15]

As the South Carolina colony grew and thrived, Jews in London associated with the city's major synagogue, Bevis Marks, began to explore the possibility of creating a Jewish settlement in Carolina. Beginning in the 1730s and continuing in fits and starts for the next two decades, these efforts never led to the establishment of a distinct Jewish settlement. However, these Bevis Marks colonization activities apparently did result in the arrival of a group of London Jews in Charleston during the 1730s under the leadership of Moses Cohen (who played a leadership role in the next two decades in establishing the colony's first synagogue) and the purchase of one hundred thousand acres of land by London merchant Joseph Salvador in the Ninety-Six District of South Carolina. This land, known popularly as the "Jews Land of South Carolina" and lying near the modern-day town of Greenwood, never was used as a Jewish colony, although Joseph Salvador himself moved onto the land in an apparent effort to settle this vast area of inland South Carolina. As an interesting historic footnote, Joseph Salvador's nephew, Francis Salvador, was elected from the Ninety-Six District as a member of South Carolina's First Provincial Congress in 1774, marking the first time a Jew was elected to public office.[16]

The growth of Charleston's Jewish community, totaling perhaps twelve households in 1749, created sufficient numbers for the minyan of ten adult males necessary to conduct Jewish religious services. In or around 1749 (the precise date being somewhat in dispute), the Jewish community of Charleston formed a congregation, which was to become known as Kahal Kadosh Beth Elohim ("The Holy Congregation of the House of God"). The congregation met in its early years in a small wooden home near Queen Street in downtown Charleston and followed the strictly orthodox protocol for services of the Minghag Sephardim, a prayer book generally followed by Spanish and Portuguese Jews. The Charleston synagogue, from its inception, was closely aligned with the Bevis Marks Synagogue of London, then one of the major centers of Jewish learning in the world. Bevis Marks provided much of the prayer liturgy and order of service (conducted primarily in Spanish and Hebrew) and later arranged for the congregation's early prayer leaders. In fact, the influence of Bevis Marks on the early days of Beth Elohim was so profound that, when the congregation finally constructed its first synagogue in 1794 on Hasell Street, it built a nearly exact replica of the Bevis Marks London sanctuary.[17]

Charleston's port expanded rapidly during the 1750s and 1760s, becoming one of the busiest ports in the New World. By the 1770s, the city's population had grown to ten thousand, and signs of great wealth were emerging. One visitor to Charleston during this time observed that "in general . . . the grandeur, splendor of buildings, decorations, equipages, numbers of commerce, shipping, and indeed in almost everything, it far surpasses all I ever say or ever expect to see in America." Charleston's Jewish community also grew during this period, totaling by the time of the American Revolution perhaps two hundred persons and forty to fifty households. Jewish merchants were actively engaged in shipping and trade; some had ties to trade in Curaçao, the British West Indies, Barbados, and Havana. Other merchants began expanding up the Carolina coast and into the backcountry. In 1761 two Charleston Jews, Phillip Hart and Samuel Isaacs, sailed into Winyah Bay and opened a business in Georgetown.[18]

Charleston's Jews began organizing more substantial communal organizations, reflecting the growing size and affluence of the community. The initial prayer leader of the congregation was Moses Cohen, who apparently had some religious training and ties to Bevis Marks. Cohen was an unpaid volunteer who made his living as a shopkeeper. Cohen served the congregation until his death in 1762 and was succeeded by another volunteer reader and businessman, Isaac Da Costa. When Da Costa resigned his position in 1764 over some internal quarrel within the congregation, the synagogue's leaders turned to Bevis Marks for a professional replacement. In August 1766, Abraham Alexander, the son of the Bevis Marks rabbi, arrived in Charleston. Alexander was the Congregation of Beth Elohim's first salaried prayer leader and was titled its hazan, which was roughly equivalent to the present-day role of the rabbi. Alexander served the congregation until 1784. According to Jacob Rader Marcus, with the selection of Alexander as hazan, "the congregation had acquired a full complement of officials, both honorary and paid; it had emerged a fully developed community in every sense of the word."[19]

Charleston's Jewish community developed other organizations to support communal life. In 1754 Isaac Da Costa established a Jewish cemetery. This was followed in 1784 by the creation of the Hebrew Benevolent Society, which was the first Jewish charitable organization of its kind in America. According to James Hagy, the establishment of the Hebrew Benevolent Society told the greater community "that the Jews intended to take care of their own people." The society would later play a significant role in various public disasters, most notably several yellow-fever epidemics in the antebellum era. In 1801 Charleston Jews formed the Hebrew Orphan Society, which had a long and noble history of helping orphans and needy children within the Jewish community. The Orphan Society's aid was reportedly extended to the near-destitute Charleston shopkeeper's son Judah Benjamin, who would later attend Yale University and serve as a U.S. senator from Louisiana and secretary of state of the Confederacy.[20]

By the early 1790s, Charleston Jews were ready finally to build their own synagogue, befitting what was fast emerging as one of the New World's premier Jewish communities. Designed as a near model of the legendary Bevis Marks Synagogue of London, the striking building was located on Hasell Street, right off bustling King Street. The cornerstone of the building was laid in 1792, and the synagogue was consecrated in 1794 to great fanfare that included various civil, religious, and political figures of Charleston. The interior of the sanctuary contained a centrally located reading desk, traditional with Sephardic worship, and balconies for women to separate the sexes in accord with orthodox religious practices. The synagogue served the community until 1838, when the notable structure burned to the ground.[21]

By 1800 Charleston had the largest Jewish population of any city in America, with perhaps as many as six hundred Jewish residents. Charleston maintained its status as having the largest Jewish population in America for at least two decades, with one scholar noting that one-third of all Jews in America in 1818 lived in the lowcountry of South Carolina. For all practical purposes, Charleston at the turn of the nineteenth century had become the unofficial "Jewish capital of America," with one historian describing the city's Jewish community as "the largest, most prosperous, and probably most sophisticated Jewish community in the New World." This prosperity, both in Charleston generally and in the Jewish community, declined after 1830 as the development of the steamship made Charleston less critical in the world of international shipping.[22]

As the Charleston Jewish community grew and prospered, with many of its members now native-born Americans, questions arose regarding the strict Sephardic prayer service followed at Beth Elohim, all of which was in two foreign tongues, Spanish and Hebrew. In December 1824, a group of forty-seven Charleston Jews petitioned the leadership of Beth Elohim regarding the need to reform the traditional religious service. In particular, the group advocated the use of English to promote a "more rational means of worshiping." The group, headed by playwright and intellectual Isaac Harby, was obviously influenced by reform movements being advanced in major European Jewish communities of Holland, Germany, and Prussia. When the Beth Elohim leadership was dismissive of the petition and refused even to respond to it, the group left the congregation en masse and formed the Reformed Society of Israelites in 1825.[23]

The Reformed Society began conducting religious services that departed dramatically from the traditional Sephardic rituals. Services were predominately in English and included a sermon, then unknown in Jewish practice. The religious service included a choir, hymns, and musical instruments, and reportedly the men did not wear head covers. The Reformed Society continued for approximately a decade, with the group dissolving and its members returning to Beth Elohim, where they effectively took over the congregation with constitutional changes adopted in 1836. With the ascendency of the reformers within the Congregation of Beth Elohim in 1836, Charleston became the first Reform synagogue in America, predating the establishment of Reform congregations in Baltimore and New York by nearly a decade. Many of the modes of worship and liturgical styles first introduced in Charleston by the Reformed Society soon swept other parts of the country and provided the foundation of the first genuinely American Jewish movement, Reform Judaism, which today is the largest denomination of Judaism in the United States.[24]

Participation in the Political Process

As the American Revolution approached, Jews in South Carolina had realized an unprecedented level of financial success and social acceptance, yet they remained subject to colonial statutes limiting the right to vote and hold office to Protestants. Some scholars have suggested that it is likely these restrictions were frequently ignored since it would be difficult to believe that some of the state's most successful and respected businessmen were barred from the polls. They note, quite accurately, that when Francis Salvador was elected to the First Provincial Congress in 1774, and reelected the following year to another term, he was allowed to take office without incident, despite the statutory requirement that all officeholders be of the Protestant faith.[25]

The persistence of religious qualifications for voting and holding office became even more indefensible when members of the Jewish community enthusiastically responded to the call of arms of the colonists against the British in the Revolutionary War. Jews of South Carolina, in proportion to their numbers, had more officers in the revolutionary cause than their fellow Jews of the twelve other states. One company had so many Jewish volunteers that, although the majority of solders were Christians, it was dubbed the "Jew Company." Most prominent of the Jewish patriots for the revolutionary cause was State Representative Francis Salvador, who in addition to being the first Jew in human history to be elected to public office, was also a member of his local militia. While riding on an expedition battling Indians aligned with the British, Salvador was shot three times and then scalped while still alive. His death on July 31, 1776, made him another "first"—the first Jew to die in the cause of American independence. One Jewish veteran of the Revolutionary War later observed that the "conduct of the Hebrews during the late revolution" with "their steady adherence to the American cause" was "substantial proof of their patriotism and attachment."[26]

Even with the enthusiastic support of the Jewish community for the cause of American independence, religious qualifications persisted following the Declaration of Independence. In 1776 South Carolina's first Constitution as an independent state maintained existing requirements that voters and officeholders be members of the Protestant faith. The religious test for voting was eliminated two years later in the Constitution of 1778 and was replaced by a requirement that the voter believe in God and own at least fifty acres of land. The religious test for public office holding persisted, however, both in postrevolutionary South Carolina and in all twelve other states.[27]

The striking durability of the religious oath requirement for public officeholders finally succumbed to the idealism surrounding the federal constitutional convention of 1787. Charles Pinckney of South Carolina proposed to the convention what was to become Article 6, section 3. His proposal, which varied slightly from the version finally adopted, provided that "no religious test or qualification shall ever be annexed to any oath of office under the authority of the United States." Pinckney explained to the delegates that the abolition of religious tests is "a provision the world will expect from you, in the establishment of a System founded on Republican Principles, and in an age so liberal and enlightened as the present." The section was adopted by the convention by a large margin and, while vigorously debated in some states' ratification conventions, did not ultimately interfere with the formal adoption of the Constitution.[28]

A new state constitutional convention, convened in 1790, was obviously influenced by the vigorous advocacy of Pinckney, who was by then governor, against all forms of religious tests or oaths. The new state Constitution of 1790 eliminated all religious tests or requirements for voting and holding office and guaranteed that "the free exercise and enjoyment of religious profession and worship, without discrimination or preference shall forever hereafter be allowed within this State to all mankind." The 1790 Constitution further authorized the incorporation of religious groups. Shortly after its adoption, Beth Elohim petitioned for and was granted incorporation status. With the adoption of the 1790 Constitution, South Carolina eliminated the last vestiges of electoral disabilities of non-Protestant voters and office seekers.[29]

Although the removal of the religious oath requirements for office holding did not result in the immediate election of Jewish public officials, there is no question that Charleston's substantial and sophisticated Jewish community was becoming increasingly assimilated and accepted by the larger Christian community. Moreover, as inland South Carolina began developing in earnest during the early decades of the nineteenth century, Jewish businessmen were often among the early and active leaders of these communities. When the state legislature established Columbia as the new state capital and authorized an auction of the new town's lots in 1786, seven Charleston Jews were among the purchasers. Jewish businessmen were an integral part of the early business activities of Columbia, and the new state capital became very rapidly a second center of Jewish life in South Carolina. By 1830 Columbia had the highest concentration of Jews to the total population of any city in the United States and had a number of Jewish physicians practicing within the town. Jews had long been part of the life of the pre-Revolutionary War port town of Georgetown and were by the turn of the nineteenth century prominent members of the town's business and civic community. Jewish attorneys had also migrated to Sumter and Camden by the 1820s and were respected voices in the public affairs of those inland communities.[30]

With this widespread tolerance and acceptance of Jewish businessmen and professionals across South Carolina in the early nineteenth century, it, at first, seems hardly surprising that Jews soon began seeking and being elected to public office. It is notable, however, that except for South Carolina, none of the original thirteen states experienced any widespread election of Jews to public office during the antebellum era. Moreover, in the only other state with any significant number of Jewish elected officials before the Civil War, Louisiana, many of the most prominent Jewish office-holders were natives of South Carolina.[31]

In 1810 Myer Moses, a prominent Charleston businessman, banker, and major in the militia, was elected to the South Carolina House of Representatives. Moses was an active member of the Jewish community of Charleston and an outspoken advo-cate of Jewish immigration to South Carolina. His son, Franklin Moses Sr., an attor-ney, established his law practice in Sumter during the 1820s and in 1842 was elected to the South Carolina State Senate from Sumter County, where he would serve for two decades as one of the state's most powerful public officials. Franklin Moses Sr. later was elected a circuit judge and in 1868 became the first Jewish chief justice of any state supreme court.[32]

Franklin Moses Sr. was by no means the only Jewish South Carolina state senator elected during the antebellum era. Chapman Levy, an attorney, businessman, and veteran of the War of 1812, was elected to the South Carolina House from Kershaw County in 1829 and was thereafter elected to represent the county in the State Senate in 1836. Levy was an unapologetic Unionist and vigorously defended the Union dur-ing the Nullification Crisis of the 1830s. Levy was also active in nearby Columbia, where he owned a substantial brick business, headed the local masons' lodge, and participated in the founding of Columbia's Jewish burial society in 1822. In fact, the burial place of Levy's first wife, Flora, is the oldest recorded grave in Columbia's his-toric Hebrew Benevolent Society Cemetery.[33]

Moses Cohen Mordecai of Charleston followed Levy's path to State office, serv-ing first in the House and later winning election to the State Senate. Mordecai was a businessman, international trader, and shipowner. His election as Charleston's sena-tor is particularly notable because in that era political power rested in the General Assembly. (The governor was elected by the General Assembly and had no veto power.) Furthermore, each county had but one senator. Charleston was then by far the state's largest and wealthiest city, and the office of Charleston County senator was a position of great power and prestige. When the city of Columbia (the hometown of Mordecai's wife, Isabella) was burned following Gen. William Tecumseh Sher-man's capture of the state capital in February 1865, Mordecai was summoned to assist in directing the city's relief efforts.[34]

Another sign of early acceptance of Jewish public officials was the 1817 election by the General Assembly of Lyon Levy as the state treasurer, a post he held for five years. Levy, a native of England and a member of the board (*adjunta*) of Kahal Kadosh Beth Elohim Synagogue, was a longtime employee of the Treasurer's Office, where he started as a lowly clerk in 1806. Obviously Levy's election as state treasurer was a source of great honor for him and his family, as reflected by the reference on his tombstone that his election was "a reward for his integrity."[35]

Philip Phillips, a native of Charleston, began his law practice in Chesterfield County, a rural area near the North Carolina border. Phillips was elected in 1834 to the South Carolina House representing Chesterfield County and served one term. He thereafter moved to Mobile, Alabama, where he was elected to the U.S. Congress. Described by Elzas, as "perhaps the greatest native-born American Jew," Phillips subsequently remained in Washington following his service in Congress (except during the Civil War) and became one of the premier appellate-court lawyers in America, handling more than four hundred cases before the U.S. Supreme Court. On his death, the U.S. Supreme Court Bar paid tribute to Phillips, noting that he was "by common consent, one of the greatest" and "the personification of the ideal of a great lawyer."[36]

Although Jews served in the General Assembly throughout the antebellum era, representing counties from Charleston to the most inland, isolated communities, it is arguable that their greatest impact was at the local level, where Jewish members of local governments became a relatively common feature of South Carolina political life. Georgetown, the second oldest Jewish community in South Carolina, elected its first Jewish mayor, Solomon Cohen, in 1818. This was followed by the election of Abram Myers in 1826 and Aaron Lopez in 1836. Columbia elected a local merchant, Judah Barrett, to city council in 1827, and Dr. Mordecai Hendricks DeLeon was elected to the first of two terms as mayor in 1833. Dr. DeLeon, one of the city's most respected physicians, reportedly had Columbia's finest personal library and was a protégé and confidant of South Carolina College's brilliant and outspoken president Thomas Cooper. Nearly twenty years after Dr. DeLeon's election, in 1850, Columbia elected a second Jewish mayor, Columbia businessman Henry Lyons. Additionally, in nearby Camden, a pre–Revolutionary War town, Hayman Levy was elected mayor in 1843.[37]

The widespread electoral success and social acceptance of Jews in South Carolina in the pre–Civil War era, while impressive, cannot obscure the presence of some discriminatory attitudes and intolerance toward Jews during this time period. Some of this can be seen in the credit reports prepared during this era by the R. G. Dun Company. Local correspondents collected these reports with the presumption that they were confidential. Jewish merchants were routinely identified by their religion and a number of the reports contained disparaging stereotypes. One report characterized a business as "a little Jew shop," and another observed "as you know, Jews are sometimes slippery." A report concerning a successful Columbia merchant, Lipman Levin, referred to him as "a sharp, keen, shrewd Jew . . . just as sharp as a razor" but concluded that "if he were not a Jew, I should be willing to trust him."[38] These attitudes did not, however, significantly impair the ability of the Jewish businessmen to succeed in, and in many instances dominate, areas of the mercantile trade in Charleston, Columbia, and on the main streets of numerous South Carolina small towns.

One area of considerable sensitivity to Jewish merchants was the Sunday closing laws, which were designed to require the cessation of all business and trade on the Christian Sabbath. Many of the Jewish merchants of this era closed their stores on Saturday, the Jewish Sabbath, and found the requirement to be closed on Sunday as well an unjust economic burden in violation of the state constitutional guarantee of the "free exercise and enjoyment of religious profession and worship, without discrimination or preference." The Sunday-closing laws were adopted from the earliest days of the colony, an interesting fact in light of the colony's tradition of religious tolerance. In fact, Law Number One, adopted by the South Carolina legislature in 1682, required the observance of the Sabbath on Sundays. This act was ratified and expanded in 1685 and 1712.

Suffice it to say, this was an issue that Jewish merchants and their Christian neighbors saw in fundamentally different ways.[39] From a formal legal standpoint, the issue arose with some intensity first in Columbia, in 1833, when city council adopted an ordinance requiring the closing of businesses on Sunday and prohibiting trade with persons of color on that day. Jewish merchants loudly objected to the proposed ordinance, and then many ignored its closing requirements. This led to the arrest of three businessmen, two of whom were Jewish. A trial was conducted by city council, and all three were convicted. Among those charged and convicted was Alexander Marks, a prosperous merchant and brother of a prominent Columbia physician and educator, Dr. Elias Marks.

Marks challenged his conviction in court, asserting that it violated his guarantee of freedom of religion and freedom from religious discrimination found in Article 8 of the South Carolina Constitution. The court rejected Marks's argument and upheld the Sabbath closing law on the dubious basis that the prohibition or all labor and commerce on Sunday was unrelated to the Christian Sabbath.[40] The Sunday Sabbath prosecutions reverberated through Columbia's next municipal election, in which a competing slate of candidates included two Jewish businessmen for council seats. One of the protest candidates, Henry Lyons, won his council seat. This began Lyons's longtime service as an elected city official, ultimately culminating in his election as Columbia's second Jewish mayor in 1850.[41]

The issue of Sunday closing laws surfaced again in Charleston in 1845, when an Orthodox Jew, Solomon Benjamin, operating a business on East Bay Street, was arrested for selling a pair of gloves to a customer on Sunday. There was also the allegation that he showed the customer other merchandise, including pantaloons. The matter was tried before a Charleston city recorder, who concluded that the city did not have the authority under the 1790 State Constitution to adopt a broad ban on business activity on the Christian Sabbath. The city appealed the decision to the South Carolina Court of Appeals, which reversed the court decision on what the appellate court itself described as a "Christian construction" of the State Constitution. The Court of Appeals ultimately concluded, like the earlier court in the Columbia case, that there was no discrimination because all religions were compelled to close on Sunday. The Sunday closing laws, also known as "blue laws," continued essentially unchanged in South Carolina until they were relaxed in 1983.[42]

While many even today differ on whether enforcement of Sunday closing laws constitutes an act of intolerance toward Jews or a show of respect toward the Christian majority, the conduct of Gov. James Hammond following the issuance of the governor's 1844 Thanksgiving Day proclamation unquestionably constituted a disturbing episode of virulent anti-Semitism inconsistent with the normal civil discourse of that era on such matters. At that time there was no set day to celebrate Thanksgiving. Instead, in South Carolina, the governor would annually issue a proclamation urging the citizens to participate in a particular day of prayer and thanksgiving. When Gov. Henry Middleton issued a proclamation in 1812 urging all Christian ministers to have religious services honoring a day of thanksgiving, leaders of Beth Elohim in Charleston wrote the governor complaining that their omission was an insult to the Jewish community. Governor Middleton respectfully responded that the wording of his proclamation had been an "oversight" and he requested that the Congregation of Beth Elohim join other religious groups in a setting aside the day of prayer and thanksgiving. The congregation accepted the governor's explanation and conducted religious services on the specified day of thanksgiving as requested.

Thirty-two years later, in 1844, Gov. James Hammond issued a Thanksgiving Day proclamation asking all citizens to set aside a day to "offer up their devotions to God the Creator, and his son Jesus Christ, Redeemer of the World." Leaders of the Charleston Jewish community initially attempted to approach Governor Hammond informally about the proclamation, but he ignored their efforts. Finally the community prepared and publicly issued a statement attacking Hammond's proclamation for its insensitivity and lack of appreciation of the state's traditions of religious tolerance. The statement concluded by observing that it was a good thing that his days in office were "about to expire."[43] In fact, as this controversy over the proclamation simmered, Hammond found himself in a extraordinary personal and political crisis over an allegation by his late wife's family, the Hamptons, that he had sexually abused his four teenage nieces. As his term as governor ended, Hammond was under threat from the father of his nieces, none other than Wade Hampton II, one of America's wealthiest men, and Hampton's sons, who warned they intended to "horsewhip" him if they found him in Columbia, because of the shame he had inflicted on the Hampton girls and their family.[44]

In Hammond's last days in office, he responded to the public statement of the Charleston Jewish community by claiming that their goal was to remove the name of Jesus Christ from the official communications of the government. Hammond stated that the Jews should understand they lived in a "Christian land" and that he was the "chief magistrate of a Christian people." He then accused his Jewish critics of having "the same scorn for Jesus Christ which instigated their ancestors to crucify him." A stunned Charleston Jewish community convened a public meeting and issued another statement expressing their "pain" over the governor's response.[45]

It is instructive that a few weeks after Hammond's vituperative statement to the Jewish community of Charleston, a new governor, William Aiken, assumed office. Aiken, a resident of Charleston, was a member of the state's landed gentry and closely aligned with the politically influential Jewish business community of Charleston. Within weeks of his inauguration, Aiken issued a new Thanksgiving Day proclamation, this one urging "all denominations of Christians, and all other persons of whatever sect or persuasion" to set aside the day for prayer and devotion to "offer up thanks to the Almighty God."[46] With this subtle show of tolerance and sensitivity, far more typical of the era than Hammond's statement, the Aiken proclamation brought the controversy to an end.

"This city our Jerusalem, this happy land our Palestine"

When attempting to evaluate attitudes and opportunities from an era in the distant past, particularly one that begins at the very dawn of the European settlement of North America, it is often difficult to capture truly the tone and sense of that time. Indeed, it is easy to see the past through the prism of modern sensibilities and developments and impose our twentieth- and twenty-first-century biases onto seventeenth-, eighteenth-, and nineteenth-century worlds. When looking at the story of the early Jewish experience of South Carolina, a fair question to ask is whether the colony and young state were best characterized by the guarantees of religious freedom in the Fundamental Constitutions and the widespread election of Jewish public officials, or whether the true nature of South Carolina was more accurately reflected by the establishment of the Anglican Church in the early colonial era and the blatantly anti-Semitic comments of Gov. James Hammond?

The greater weight of the historic records supports the conclusion that South Carolina was a special and, at times, an extraordinary place for its Jewish citizens during the colonial and antebellum eras. A few nondebatable historic facts bolster that conclusion. First, South Carolina was the first government anywhere to make religious freedom a constitutional right. Second, more Jews immigrated to South Carolina in the colonial and early antebellum eras than to any other state or colony in North America. In other words, Jews voted their endorsement of South Carolina as a land of tolerance and opportunity with their feet. Third, Jews were able to build an extraordinary infrastructure of businesses in the early development of the state that was, perhaps with the exception of the later creation of Louisiana, unrivaled on the American continent. Fourth, Jews built upon that tremendous early economic base as the foundation for the future remarkable electoral successes, which were so widespread that it is difficult to describe them as some type of historic fluke. This electoral success included many "firsts," but perhaps none more significant than Francis Salvador's election in 1774 as the first Jew in human history elected to public office. The simple truth is that Jews enjoyed tremendous tolerance and acceptance in early South Carolina and used their native talents and passion to build one of America's great original centers of Jewish life.

In many ways, South Carolina became early America's incubator for religious freedom and expression. The Fundamental Constitution (1669) signaled the world's dissenter communities that they were welcome in South Carolina, which then begat Charleston's vibrant and prosperous early Jewish community. This community developed America's first genuinely American Jewish movement, Reform Judaism, which thereafter profoundly influenced the direction of American Judaism. Moreover, South Carolina's tolerance and acceptance of its Jewish citizens inspired widespread Jewish civic and political involvement, leading ultimately to the most significant

number of Jewish elected officials in any of the original states during the antebellum era. Finally, out of this incubator of religious freedom came South Carolinian Charles Pinckney, who successfully led the adoption in the U.S. Constitutional Convention of the provision prohibiting religious oaths or tests for holding public office.

Another validation of the conclusion that early South Carolina afforded its Jewish citizens an unparalleled level of acceptance and tolerance are the statements made contemporaneously by Jewish leaders. In 1816 Charleston intellectual Isaac Harby, who later founded the Reform Jewish movement in America, wrote Secretary of State James Monroe expressing his distress about Monoroe's removal of an American consul, who was Jewish, as representative to Tunis because of his religion. Harby, speaking from his special perch in Charleston, explained to Monroe that Jews "are by no means to be considered a religious sect, tolerated by the government; they constitute *a portion of the people.* . . . Quakers and Catholics, Episcopalians and Presbyterians, Baptists and Jews, all constitute *one great political family*" (emphasis added).[47]

This sense of inclusion, of being part of the fabric of the society, is echoed in many statements of South Carolina Jewish leaders and ordinary citizens of that era. At the dedication of the new Beth Elohim sanctuary in 1844, the congregation's rabbi, Gustavus Poznanski, told the assemblage of the state's political, religious, and civic leaders the profound attachment that Jews had for Charleston and South Carolina: "This synagogue is our temple, this city our Jerusalem, this happy land our Palestine."[48] In another community address, delivered in Columbia in the year 1849, Henry S. Cohen perhaps best summarized this extraordinary, almost spiritual feeling that Jews felt toward South Carolina, sobered by the reality of how their fellow Jews still suffered across the world: "A bright era now dawns upon us, rendered brighter in contrast with the darkness by which we have heretofore been surrounded. . . . In contemplating, as Israelites, our position in this land, to us truly a 'land of milk and honey,' we may justly exclaim, with Israel of old, 'the Lord hath brought us forth out of Egypt with a mighty hand and an outstretched arm, He hath brought us into this place, and hath given us this land.'"[49]

Notes

1. Jacob Rader Marcus, *The Colonial American Jew, 1492–1776*, 3 vols. (Detroit: Wayne State University Press 1970), 1:10–12; James William Hagy, *This Happy Land: The Jews of Colonial and Antebellum Charleston* (Tuscaloosa: University of Alabama Press, 1993), 29.

2. Marcus, *The Colonial American Jew*, 1:13; Daniel Lazare, "Estranged Brothers: Reconsidering Jewish History," *Harper's* (April 2003).

3. Marcus, *The Colonial American Jew*, 1:14–31; Hagy, *This Happy Land*, 29.

4. James Lowell Underwood, *The Constitution of South Carolina*, vol. 3: *Church and State, Morality and Free Expression* (Columbia: University of South Carolina Press 1992), 3–9; Abram Vossen Goodman, "South Carolina from Shaftesbury to Salvador," in *Jews in the South*, ed. Leonard Dinnerstein and Mary Dale Palsson (Baton Rouge: Louisiana State Press, 1973), 29–30.

5. Goodman, "South Carolina from Shaftesbury to Salvador," 30; Hagy, *This Happy Land*, 30; Barnett Elzas, *The Jews of South Carolina* (Philadelphia: Lippincott, 1905), 17–18; Marcus, *The Colonial American Jew*, 1:343.

6. Underwood, *The Constitution of South Carolina*, vol. 3: *Church and State, Morality and Free Expression*, 10–11; Marcus, *The Colonial American Jew*, 1:464, 466. The full version of the Fundamental Constitutions (1669) can be found on-line at www.yale.edu/lawweb/avalon/states/nco5.htm.

7. Marcus, *The Colonial American Jew*, 1:343, 464, 466; Hagy, *This Happy Land*, 6, 31.

8. Elzas, *The Jews of South Carolina*, 20; Goodman, "South Carolina from Shaftesbury to Salvador," 32–33; Hagy, *This Happy Land*, 30.

9. Marcus, *The Colonial American Jew*, 1:343; Elzas, *The Jews of South Carolina*, 17–18; Underwood, *The Constitution of South Carolina*, vol. 3: *Church and State, Morality and Free Expression*, 15; Hagy, *This Happy Land*, 30.

10. Elzas, *The Jews of South Carolina*, 19; Hagy, *This Happy Land*, 31.

11. Hagy, *This Happy Land*, 30–32; Goodman, "South Carolina from Shaftesbury to Salvador," 33–34; Elzas, *The Jews of South Carolina*, 20–23.

12. Marcus, *The Colonial American Jew*, 1:464–66; Hagy, *This Happy Land*, 32–33. See Act No. 222 S.C. STATUTES AT LARGE 232 (Cooper 1837), the law excluding Protestant dissenters. The queen's order declaring the law null and void is discussed in this book in the essay by James Lowell Underwood entitled "The Dawn of Religious Freedom in South Carolina: The Journey From Limited Tolerance to Constitutional Right."

13. Hagy, *This Happy Land*, 33; Marcus, *The Colonial American Jew*, 1:466. The electoral statutes are discussed in James Lowell Underwood's "The Dawn of Religious Freedom in South Carolina" in this volume.

14. Marcus, *The Colonial American Jew*, 1:344.

15. Ibid., 1:345–46; 2:549, 593.

16. Goodman, "South Carolina from Shaftesbury to Salvador," 41; Hagy, *This Happy Land*, 10–11; Elzas, *The Jews of South Carolina*, 68–74, 117–18.

17. Charles Reznikoff, *The Jews of Charleston: A History an American Jewish Community* (Philadelphia: Jewish Publication Society of America 1950), 17–18; Elzas, *The Jews of South Carolina*, 30–34; Marcus, *The Colonial American Jew*, 1:345, 2:885; Hagy, *This Happy Land*, 58–60.

18. Marcus, *The Colonial American Jew*, 1:346–47, 2:618.

19. Reznikoff, *The Jews of Charleston*, 13, 15–18; Elzas, *This Happy Land*, 34–37, 43; Marcus, *The Colonial American Jew*, 2:885–86.

20. Hagy, *The Jews of South Carolina*, 63, 68–73; Elzas, *The Jews of South Carolina*, 282–87; Reznikoff and Engleman, *The Jews of Charleston*, 154–57.

21. Hagy, *This Happy Land*, 73–78; Elzas, *The Jews of South Carolina*, 121–22.

22. Alfred O. Hero Jr., "Southern Jews," in *Jews in the South*, ed. Dinnerstein and Palsson, 232; Hagy, *This Happy Land*, 14–16; Elzas, *The Jews of South Carolina*, 241–59. Belinda Gergel and Richard Gergel, *In Pursuit of the Tree of Life: A History of the Early Jews of Columbia, South Carolina, and the Tree of Life Congregation* (Columbia: Tree of Life, 1996), 1.

23. Gary Phillip Zola, *Isaac Harby of Charleston, 1788–1828: Jewish Reformer and Intellectual* (Tuscaloosa: University of Alabama Press, 1994), 112–27; Elzas, *The Jews of South Carolina*, 147–65; Hagy, *This Happy Land*, 128–32.

24. Jacob Rader Marcus, *United States Jewry, 1776–1985*, 4 vols. (Detroit: Wayne State University Press 1991), 1:622–37; Zola, *Isaac Harby of Charleston*, 135–41, 146–47; Hagy, *This Happy Land*, 154–56.

25. Marcus, *The Colonial American Jew*, 1:510; Underwood, *The Constitution of South Carolina*, vol. 3: *Church and State, Morality and Free Expression*, 35–39; Hagy, *This Happy Land*, 33–36.

26. Elzas, *The Jews of South Carolina*, 74–77; Hagy, *This Happy Land*, 36; Marcus, *The Colonial American Jew*, 3:1304–1306.

27. Marcus, *The Colonial American Jew*, 1:467–68; Underwood, *The Constitution of South Carolina*, vol. 3: *Church and State, Morality and Free Expression*, 42; Hagy, *This Happy Land*, 36.

28. Stephen A. Smith, "The Ordeal of the Religious Test Oaths in Pennsylvania," *Free Speech Yearbook* 30, no. 1 (1992): 3; available on-line at www.uark.edu/depts/comminfo/www/oath.html.; Max Farrand, ed. *The Records of the Federal Convention of 1787* (New Haven: Yale University Press, 1911), 11:342, 468; Underwood, *The Constitution of South Carolina*, vol. 3: *Church and State, Morality and Free Expression*, 39. As finally, adopted Article 6, section 3, states "but no religious test shall ever be required as a qualification to any office or public trust under the United States."

29. Hagy, *This Happy Land*, 37; Underwood, *The Constitution of South Carolina*, vol. 3: *Church and State, Morality and Free Expression*, 42–43.

30. Gergel and Gergel, *In Pursuit of the Tree of Life*, 2–11; Malcolm Stern, "A New Look at the Founding Fathers of Columbia, S.C.," *Southern Jewish Historical Newsletter* (October 1990): 3, 5; Elzas, *The Jews of South Carolina*, 241–53.

31. Marcus, *United States Jewry*, 2:68. U.S. Sen. Judah Benjamin (Louisiana), Lt. Gov. Henry Michael Hyams, and Speaker of the House Edwin Warren Moise were all natives of Charleston.

32. Elzas, *The Jews of South Carolina*, 140, 198–99; Belinda Gergel and Richard Gergel, "Palmetto Jews," *Sandlapper* (Autumn 2002): 22. Franklin Moses Jr., the notorious "robber" governor of South Carolina (1872–1874), was the son of South Carolina Chief Justice Franklin Moses Sr. and the grandson of State Representative Myer Moses. South Carolina Jews have long attempted to disassociate themselves from Governor Moses, as reflected by Elzas's statement that Governor Moses "was not brought up as a Jew, nor were his affiliations Jewish in any way" (*The Jews of South Carolina*, 199). Some Moses relatives actually changed their last names because of the stain on the family cast by Governor Moses. Although much of the controversy over Moses was caught up in the high-pressure racial politics of Reconstruction, there is no doubt that Moses was one of the most corrupt officials ever to hold high public office in America. See Robert H. Woody, "Franklin J. Moses, Jr., Scalawag Governor of South Carolina, 1872–1874," *North Carolina Historic Review* 10 (April 1953): 111–23; Eric Foner. *Reconstruction: America's Unfinished Revolution, 1863–1877* (Baton Rouge: Louisiana State University Press 1988), 542, 544; Robert N. Rosen, *The Jewish Confederates* (Columbia: University of South Carolina Press 2000), 393 n.124.

33. Gergel and Gergel, *In Pursuit of the Tree of Life*, 6–7.

34. Hagy, *This Happy Land*, 194–95; Gergel and Gergel, *In Pursuit of the Tree of Life*, 42–43.

35. Reznikoff, *The Jews of Charleston*, 285 n.109; Hagy, *This Happy Land*, 45.

36. Robert N. Rosen, *The Jewish Confederates*, 285, 369; Elzas, *The Jews of South Carolina*, 202–3.

37. Elzas, *The Jews of South Carolina*, 243, 245; Gergel and Gergel, *In Pursuit of the Tree of Life*, 8–11, 24.

38. "South Carolina," vol. 1, 10, 52, 53, R. G. Dun & Co. Collection, Baker Library, Harvard University Graduate School of Business Administration; Gergel and Gergel, *In Pursuit of the Tree of Life*, 23.

39. Underwood, *The Constitution of South Carolina*, vol. 3: *Church and State, Morality and Free Expression*, 90–98; Hagy, *This Happy Land*, 37–39.

40. *Town Council of Columbia v. C.O. Duke and Alexander Marks,* which is an exhibit to the opinion in the later case of *City Council of Charleston v. Benjamin*, 33 S.C.L. (2 Strob) 508 (1846), and is reprinted in Joseph L. Blau and Salo W. Baron, *The Jews of the United States, 1790–1840: A Documentary History*, vol. 3 (New York: Columbia University Press 1963), 24–26; Underwood, *The Constitution of South Carolina*, vol. 3: *Church and State, Morality and Free Expression*, 96–98; Gergel and Gergel, *In Pursuit of the Tree of Life*, 24. Shortly after his conviction, Marks—presumably angered by his criminal prosecution—left Columbia for New Orleans. Marks built with his brother-in-law a thriving mercantile business in New Orleans, and by his children's generation the Marks family was one of the wealthiest and most prominent Jewish families in Louisiana. In recounting the Alexander Marks story and the great loss of talent on the family's departure from Columbia, historian Jacob Rader Marcus commented, "oh, the price of intolerance." Bertram Wallace Korn, *The Early Jews of New Orleans* (Waltham, Mass.: American Jewish Historical Society, 1969), 103; Elliott Ashkenazi, *The Business of Jews in Louisiana 1840–1875* (Tuscaloosa: University of Alabama Press 1988), 115; authors' interview with Jacob Rader Marcus, April 1994.

41. Gergel and Gergel, *In Pursuit of the Tree of Life*, 24.

42. *City Council of Charleston v. Benjamin*, supra note 40 at 522; Underwood, *The Constitution of South Carolina*, vol. 3: *Church and State, Morality and Free Expression*, 98–102.

43. Hagy, *This Happy Land*, 40–41; Gergel and Gergel, *In Pursuit of the Tree of Life*, 25–26. The "Christian Construction" statement is found at 33 S.C.L. (2 Strob.) at 522.

44. Carol Bleser, *The Hammonds of Redcliffe* (New York: Oxford University Press, 1981), 9–10. The four Hampton daughters, aged thirteen to seventeen, were so scandalized by this incident in upper-class circles of South Carolina that none ever married.

45. Gergel and Gergel, *In Pursuit of the Tree of Life*, 25; *Occident* 2 (December 1844): 496–510; Hagy, *This Happy Land*, 40–41; Leo Shpall, "Anti-Semitic Incidents in South Carolina," *Jewish Forum* (February 1947): 43–44, 66, 88, 104.

46. *South Carolinian*, January 16, 1844; Gergel and Gergel, *In Pursuit of the Tree of Life*, 26.

47. Zola , *Isaac Harby of Charleston*, 63.

48. Hagy, *This Happy Land*, 236.

49. Henry S. Cohen, "Extracts from an Address," *Occident* 7 (July 1849): 216–17.

Public Politics and Private Faith

Huguenot Political Acculturation
in South Carolina, 1687–1707

Alexander Moore

FRENCH CALVINISTS, CALLED HUGUENOTS, suffered persecution in their native land throughout the sixteenth and seventeenth centuries. The Protestant Reformation and the political and social revolutions that it precipitated had given rise to Roman Catholic opposition throughout those nations where Protestantism had taken root. France was one of those nations where the battles were outright, violent, and long lasting. The English Reformation had taken a different course, and, because it had begun with King Henry VIII, at the apex of the nation's political culture, its eventual success was more assured than on the European continent. A precarious truce to the French wars of religion, called the Edict of Nantes, kept peace between Protestants and Catholics from 1598 until 1685. During that time of comparative leniency toward them, many Huguenots immigrated to England, the Low Countries, and the new English colony of Carolina. When Louis XIV revoked the edict in 1685 and began a new round of persecutions, a flood of Huguenots entered England and the British colonies in the New World.[1]

This essay springs from an investigation of the political culture of South Carolina prior to 1720. An important question to the early Carolinians and to students of colonial politics is: where did the Huguenots fit in? The Fundamental Constitutions of Carolina offered a degree of religious toleration remarkable for the time. Protestants of all denominations, Jews, and other non-Christians technically could find homes in Carolina and a breadth of toleration for all their creeds. Those were the conditions under which Huguenots in England and on the Continent were encouraged to immigrate to Carolina. Once they arrived at Charleston, the metropolis of the Carolina colony, the ways in which they assimilated into the colony and, indeed, the ways in which they were able to exercise the religious liberty promised in the Fundamental Constitutions, were not through appeals to the terms of the Constitutions or to lofty principles of toleration; their rights were secured in a rough-and-tumble fight between two rival political factions in Carolina that used religion as one of many weapons against their opponents. For nearly two decades, an Anglican Tory antiproprietary party battled a Nonconformist Whig proproprietary party for political mastery in Carolina. Some of the sources of the rivalry were borrowed from England and transplanted, along with the settlers, into early Carolina, but others—especially those involving patronage, control of the Commons House of Assembly, and monopoly of economic advantages—were homegrown in the province or were the products of specific proprietary policies.

One way that rivalry was contested was in denominational terms. Anglicans and Dissenters, planters and merchants, new and old arrivals fought among themselves in Carolina and often battled the Lords Proprietors at home in England and among them in the New World for the political and economic spoils of a province that had no more than four thousand settlers, free and enslaved, prior to 1710. The ferocity of the battles seemingly belied the value of the prize.

Louis XIV's revocation of the Edict of Nantes in 1685 provoked a crisis in the Huguenot communities of France and in those countries—England, Holland, and the colonial New World—that took in floods of French Protestant refugees. In England the arrival of large numbers of French aliens, subjects of a foreign prince who was often at war with England, raised pressing legal, political, and religious questions. Among the most immediate were the nature of allegiance of a subject to his king; civil liberty versus national security; the powers of the Anglican Church; and, finally, the character of party warfare between Dissenter Whigs and Anglican Tories.[2]

Proprietary Carolina wrestled with the Huguenot question in all its religious, legal, and constitutional ramifications. And the Carolina version of the Huguenot question had a special political character that thrust it squarely into nearly every political controversy between 1687 and 1707. These critical decades in the life of Carolina shaped the political culture of the province, arguably until the American Civil War. The important constitutional questions of naturalization, allegiance, and religious liberty were worked out within a context of bitter factional warfare.[3]

A key element of Carolina's Huguenot question was the Lords Proprietors' unwavering insistence that Huguenots—and, indeed, all Protestant immigrants in 1685— be guaranteed the same rights as English Carolinians to vote, hold office, and sit in the Commons House of Assembly.[4] The proprietors encouraged Protestant refugees to immigrate to Carolina. In order to attract settlers they made liberal concessions to prospective immigrants, including aliens, regarding religious liberty, property rights, and political privileges. In addition they engaged in promotional campaigns directed toward French, Swiss, and German religious refugees.

The proprietors had placed much emphasis on religious toleration in their Fundamental Constitutions of Carolina, written largely by Anthony Ashley Cooper, Lord Ashley (later Earl of Shaftesbury), and first promulgated in 1669. The Constitutions were both an inducement for prospective immigrants and a plan of government that reflected contemporaneous political thought.[5] Without the proprietors' oversight, it is likely that both the Anglicans and Dissenters in Carolina might have oppressed the French minority simply because of their non-Englishness. But, as it was, the

Huguenots arrived in Carolina with this constitutional protection—-one they soon perceived and used to their advantage.

Huguenots settled largely in Craven County, north of Berkeley County around the Santee River. Although few in number, they were a considerable majority in Craven County.[6] The proprietors had decreed that representation in the Commons House of Assembly was to be apportioned according to geography, not population. Each of the three large counties—Berkeley, Craven, and Colleton—had ten delegates, making a total of thirty delegates in the Commons House. This gave to the Huguenots the same number of delegates as Berkeley and Colleton counties. This was a version of the old-style political culture in which the winner of a local election took all. With a monopoly of the Craven County seats, the Huguenots had political strength disproportionate to their numbers in the province.[7]

Carolina Huguenots first flexed their political leverage in alliance with the Berkeley County Anglican political leaders, loosely called the Goose Creek Men. In 1682 a Berkeley-Craven County political alliance refused to ratify a new version of the Fundamental Constitutions, ironically because it contained political and religious concessions to another group of aliens, Scottish Presbyterians or Covenanters, who had settled at Stuart Town on the Port Royal Sound.[8] The reason the Berkeley County Anglicans opposed ratification was obvious: to increase the number of Dissenters in Carolina and to offer them a degree of political autonomy from the government at Charleston would diminish the Anglicans' prospects of hegemony.

One of the mysteries of early Carolina politics is why the Huguenots joined in opposition to the 1682 version of the Constitutions. The choice was highly ironic and proved of lasting consequence. The alliance of Anglicans and Huguenots persisted through the proprietary era, but it did not materially improve the Huguenots' situation. They seem to have acted with temporary expediency that hardened into a disadvantageous alliance. Their Dissenter opponents claimed that the Huguenots, uncertain of the language and too trusting of their nearby neighbors in Berkeley County, had been duped by the Goose Creek Men into taking a position disadvantageous to themselves. This Anglican-French alliance was directed against the Nonconformist-dominated government of Gov. James Colleton and also against the proprietors' policy of increasing Dissenter immigration. At any rate, this was the first of a series of political alliances against the Dissenters. Aided by the Huguenots, the Goose Creek Men enhanced their control over provincial politics with each succeeding battle. By virtue of the political alliances, each subsequent battle strengthened Huguenot-Anglican bonds and deepened Huguenot-Dissenter enmity.

In *From Babylon to New Eden: A History of the Huguenots in Seventeenth-Century France and Colonial South Carolina, 1660–1740* (2005) Bertrand Van Ruymbeke wisely yoked the religious liberty issue to the one that seemed to be more pressing to the Carolina Huguenots: the issue of naturalization. In the early versions of their Fundamental Constitutions, the proprietors had offered generous terms of naturalization and denization much in the spirit of their commitment to religious liberty.

Aliens could become naturalized by the simple procedure of subscribing their names to a roll kept by the proprietary secretary in Charleston.[9]

Naturalization gave the Huguenots and any other non-English subjects full rights of an English subject, including voting privileges, rights of inheritance, and, of course, whatever degree of religious liberty that the Constitutions and—after the battles were over—the General Assembly could provide. The rights to register valid marriages and to bequeath property to heirs were of overriding concern to the Huguenots, and they hewed to whatever course of political action that would ensure those aims.

The unexpected arrival at Charleston in 1690 of Seth Sothell, one of the Lords Proprietors, gave the Berkeley-Craven alliance an opportunity to overthrow Gov. James Colleton and the Dissenter party. Berkeley County men and Huguenots petitioned Sothell to assume the governorship according to his prerogative as a proprietor. Sothell seized the moment, dismissed Colleton, and took over as governor.[10] He then rewarded the Craven County Huguenots and Goose Creek Men for their support. One of Sothell's first laws was a naturalization act, passed in May 1691, that granted to all Huguenots in Carolina full naturalization and made them as free "as if they and every [one?] had been and were borne within that part of this province." Because the act was limited to those Frenchmen already in Carolina and did not extend to immigrants, it had every appearance of a political payoff.[11]

Gov. Philip Ludwell ousted the renegade Proprietor Sothell in April 1692 and, on the proprietors' instructions, annulled all the acts of his regime, including the Huguenot naturalization act. Ludwell's actions provoked a political crisis that blocked all action in the Commons House and probably gave the Huguenots considerable apprehension about the future.[12] If the proprietors could make such a poor decision as to annul the naturalization act and if the Dissenters could rejoice so much at Sothell's downfall, what might the future hold in a Dissenter-dominated province?

In 1693 the proprietors informed Ludwell and his council that they had received complaints from Huguenot leaders of harassment by Carolina Dissenters. The proprietors forbade any kind of religious discrimination and pledged that, although the Huguenots were technically aliens and their lands subject to escheat by English law (reversion to the proprietors on a landowner's death), the proprietors would never exercise that right against them.[13] The proprietors made the same pledges in private correspondence to Huguenot leaders but pointedly observed to them that the Huguenots had brought their problems upon themselves. By cooperating with the Goose Creek Men to defeat ratification of the 1682 Fundamental Constitutions, they had undermined their own political positions. Had they voted to adopt the Constitutions, their rights would have been guaranteed under its provisions.[14]

John Archdale, owner of a proprietor's share in Carolina, came to Charleston in August 1685 in hopes that a proprietor-governor could resolve the political chaos there. The Huguenot question dominated his term. Himself a Quaker (one of the most persecuted of Dissenters) Archdale was predisposed, if not to favor the Carolina Dissenters, at least not to indulge the High Church Anglicans. Immediately on his arrival "about an hundred of the Englishman," most of whom were Colleton County Dissenters, petitioned him that Englishmen only be allowed to sit in the Commons House and vote for its members. Despite pressure from the Berkeley-Craven group and some personal misgivings, Archdale sided with those who wished to exclude the French from the franchise and from Commons House membership. He issued writs of election for a new Assembly to the sheriffs of Berkeley and Colleton counties but excluded Craven altogether. He then defended his action to the Lords Proprietors as the only way he could secure a working assembly.[15] Unfortunately this Second Assembly proved completely intractable. Without the Craven members it had only twenty delegates, ten from Berkeley and ten from Colleton. It deadlocked ten to ten on every issue. After a month of wrangling, Archdale dissolved the Assembly and issued writs for a new election, this time apportioning twenty members for Berkeley and Craven together as a single district and ten for Colleton.[16]

In their recent instructions from England the proprietors refused to sanction any restrictions on the Huguenots' civil or religious liberties. They ordered Archdale to dissolve the Second Assembly (already done) and to issue writs of election to Craven County.[17] In this case slow obedience proved to be no obedience. By the time Archdale received the instructions, he had already dissolved the Assembly and reapportioned it. He reported to the proprietors that he had unofficially prevailed on the Huguenots to refrain "temporarily" from exercising their rights of membership and suffrage. He claimed that if he had not done this, "the ruining of this part of the Province had very probably followed."[18] Anti-French feeling subsided briefly after the Third Assembly met.

The proprietors' steadfast commitment to religious toleration kept pressure on the Dissenters. They suggested to Joseph Blake, Archdale's successor and a leading Dissenter, that he propose a naturalization act to extend to Huguenots the rights of Englishmen but make those rights subject to Commons House authority. That way, the Huguenots' rights would be hostage to good order in the Assembly.[19]

One of the most vehement Dissenters in the province, Governor Blake adopted a variation of the proprietors' plan. He linked a new Commons House apportionment bill to a naturalization bill and steered both to enactment. The naturalization bill was introduced in the Commons House on February 26, 1697, and passed its first reading on March 3. On that day a Commons House member introduced a "Bill to Regulate the Ellections of the members of Assembly." The two proceeded rapidly to enactment and were signed into law on March 10, 1697.[20]

"An Act for Making aliens free of this part of the Province and for granting Liberty of Conscience to all Protestants" provided that "all aliens, male and female, of what nation soever" could be naturalized by taking an oath of allegiance to William III, King of England, and registering their names with the secretary of the province. The act guaranteed to Huguenots the rights of native-born Englishmen with respect to property ownership, inheritance, and religious liberty but failed to mention the political rights of suffrage and Commons House membership. These significant omissions were clearer in the provisions of the election act passed the same day. That act barred aliens and naturalized Englishmen from Commons House membership, thus making statutory the "voluntary" exclusion that Archdale had reported to the proprietors in 1695. It also fixed the apportionment of the Commons House in the ratio of twenty members for Berkeley-Craven and ten for Colleton County.[21] Governor Blake explained to the proprietors the relationship between the naturalization and election acts: "The act for naturalizing the Aliens is as ample as wee could prevaile with the Commons to pass it and Satisfactory to the French as they say but wee could not possibly have gott this till wee promised the Commons to unqualifie all aliens for assembly men which is done in the act for regulation Ellection of members of Assembly." Blake reported to the proprietors that at present the French enjoyed all the rights of Englishmen "except being of the Assembly here, which the Act for their naturalization hath not given them, and their being Jurymen."[22]

The Sixth Assembly (1702–1703) was a climax in the Anglican versus Dissenter struggle—and the Huguenots were prominently in the middle of it. John Ash of Colleton County emerged as the Dissenter party's leader and he led them into a political wilderness. The 1697 law—the one that gave Berkeley and Craven together twenty seats—tipped the balance in favor of the Anglicans. Instead of voting with their Nonconformist coreligionists, the Huguenots supported their neighbors, the Berkeley County Anglicans. By 1702 the Anglicans not only had one of their own, James Moore, as governor but also had majorities in the Commons House and Council. Ash and his party had lost the battle but they caused considerable disruption in defeat. In a desperate measure Ash tried to seize power by altering the composition of the Commons House. On February 13, 1703, he introduced a naturalization bill of his own "making all aliens & foreigners . . . free." The bill passed its first reading and was sent to the governor and Council on the same day. It died when Ash and his followers walked out of the Assembly on February 24.[23]

The provisions of Ash's bill are not known. It was not passed into law or debated sufficiently to suggest its contents. Eugene Sirmans has suggested that the bill was designed to increase political disabilities of the Huguenots, perhaps even to deny them suffrage by making it more difficult to obtain citizenship. His interpretation was consistent with Dissenter antipathy and with the political realities of the situation.[24] By negating the Huguenots' political power, Colleton County Dissenters could compete evenly with the Berkeley County Anglicans. Sirmans's interpretation is also consistent with a remonstrance of Colleton County assemblymen and inhabitants in June 1703 protesting the actions of the Sixth Assembly. The petitioners stated that Ash's bill was "for granting as much freedom to the French and other Aliens, as could be granted by the Assembly, or the French reasonably expect."[25] Ash's actions may have been a last-ditch xenophobic appeal to "Englishmen" of all denominations to unite against foreign "Frenchmen," with whom Great Britain was presently at war.

The Seventh Assembly was the zenith of Anglican party domination and the nadir of the Dissenters. The Anglicans used their absolute majority in the Assembly to enact legislation to perpetuate their control. In May 1704 they passed an act "Requiring all Persons Chosen to Be Members of the Commons House of Assembly . . . to

Conform to the Religious Worship in This Province According to the Church of England," often called the exclusion act, and in November they passed the "Act for the Establishment of Religious Worship . . . according to the Church of England," the first Carolina establishment act. These two statutes consolidated power in the hands of the Anglicans and their Huguenot allies by making Anglican communion a requirement for House membership. The establishment of the Church of England in South Carolina was a far cry from the religious liberty promised by the proprietors in their Fundamental Constitutions, but by then the configuration of the Proprietary Board had changed. High Church Anglican proprietors, led by Palatine (chief proprietor) Lord John Granville, cared little for the Carolina Dissenters and had no difficulty supporting Anglican domination.[26]

The two Carolina acts proved to be so blatantly partisan and contrary to the laws of England, that the Queen in Council struck down the acts. A High Church partisan herself, Queen Anne saw the disruption that would be caused in Carolina by the two acts. She and her advisers struck down the establishment act, not for its religious partisanship but because it contained provisions for lay control of the local church that conflicted with British usages and diminished the power of church authorities in England. She vetoed them herself and instructed the proprietors to better mind the political liberties of their Protestant settlers, no matter what denomination. These vetoes were promulgated in royal orders in council on June 10, 1706.[27]

Thwarted at the farthest reach of their power grab, the Carolina High Churchmen revised their local acts less to provide more latitude to their Dissenter foes but to avoid having their new statutes struck down. While Parliament and the queen were investigating the 1704 acts, Gov. Nathaniel Johnson, who succeeded Moore in 1703, and his Anglican majority enacted statutes to amend some of the most offensive provisions of the acts. The revised acts recognized the legitimacy of Nonconformist clergy to conduct valid baptisms, marriages, and funerals as long as the ceremonies were recorded in Anglican parish records. The acts also amended procedures for elections of Anglican vestrymen and church wardens. None of these modifications went to the heart of the establishment and exclusion acts of 1704 and, therefore, did not alter the political hegemony of the Anglicans and Huguenots over the Dissenters.[28]

Johnson and the Anglican majority returned to the drawing board when the Eighth Assembly convened on November 20, 1706. They quickly enacted a new establishment act that superseded the invalid act of May 1704 and its amendments and conformed to the commands of the Queen in Council. The church act of November 30, 1706, was the milestone of Anglican establishment in Carolina. It organized the province into parishes, created lay vestries, and apportioned the Commons House according to parish lines.[29] It eliminated the Anglican communion requirement for House membership and reduced the power of the lay church commissions but those were the sole concessions to the queen's veto. Until the American Revolution, the Church of England in South Carolina was a quasigovernmental agency, receiving funds from general taxes and serving local communities in a number of English ways.

The Assembly specifically created an Anglican parish in Berkeley County, St. James Santee Parish, to serve the political and spiritual needs of the Huguenots. Anglican ministers there had reported that the continued growth of the Church of England among the Huguenots was threatened by a lack of maintenance and that some Huguenot converts were returning to their Calvinist practices.[30] Any ebb of enthusiasm for the Church of England threatened the Anglican-Huguenot political alliance at its most important point. By subsidizing the Anglican Church at St. James Santee, the Commons House guaranteed that it would always have an active presence in that region to encourage conversion. The statute also provided that the Anglican liturgy could be conducted in French, a gesture that further encouraged adherence to the Church of England.[31] A second "Huguenot" parish, St. Dennis, was created in the Orange Quarter region of Berkeley County. This provided the opportunity for the Huguenots—faithful and converts—to increase the number of their own representatives in the Commons House.[32] And the fact that this increased participation had come at the hands of the Anglican majority helped to consolidate power in the hands of the Anglican-Huguenot party. The Dissenters were increasingly outnumbered and isolated.

For good measure, the Assembly also enacted the "Act for Making Aliens Free of this part of the Province." Gov. Nathaniel Johnson was a militant supporter of the Church of England. In his opening address to the Commons House he called for a new naturalization act. Ralph Izard, one of his High Church allies, wrote the bill. This new act was for all practical purposes a restatement of the 1697 act. It continued to exclude aliens and naturalized Carolinians from Commons House membership, but it affirmed, as the earlier act had not, their right to vote.[33]

This new naturalization act was not much of an improvement over the old one, but it had a clear political message. With its passage Huguenots were made amply aware just who were their political benefactors and who were their enemies. Gov. Joseph Blake and his Dissenter party had passed the first naturalization act, but they had no part in drafting, managing, or passage of the new act. Consequently they were tarred with the brush of being anti-Huguenot while the High Churchmen, by virtue of their sponsorship of the new act, claimed the mantle of guarantors of Huguenot rights in the province. The new act had an obvious political advantage: it cemented the alliance between Berkeley and Craven counties and gave strong evidence that Huguenot rights depended on the continued rule of the Anglicans.

The ostensibly pro-Huguenot statutes of November 1706 certainly recognized that the Huguenot-Anglican political alliance had held firm even in the face of royal disapproval, and the acts were likely rewards by Johnson and the Anglicans for Huguenot loyalty. But, there was other evidence of Huguenot loyalty not only to the Anglicans but also to the whole province. Until the summer of 1706, Queen Anne's War had not reached the soil of Carolina. The province had undertaken ill-fated expeditions against the Spanish at St. Augustine in 1702 and 1704, and by 1706 the Spanish and their French allies at Martinique had determined to retaliate. At the end of August a combined force of French and Spanish sailors and soldiers, commanded by the French admiral LeFevre made landings north and south of Charleston. French troops landed on James Island on August 29 and at Allen's Plantation on Seewee Bay on September 1. The French at Seewee Bay may have hoped to be welcomed by their countrymen, the Huguenot settlers of Craven County. But that was not the case. The local militia defeated the invaders, killing and capturing many of them. Little considered as an aspect of Huguenot acculturation, the fact that the Huguenots of the French Quarter had stood with the Carolinians in battle against French troops, who were Catholic, demonstrated a high level of Huguenot loyalty. Governor Johnson and Captain William Rhett commanded forces that soundly defeated the invaders.[34] The creation of two "French" Anglican parishes north of the Cooper River, St. James Santee and St. Dennis, soon after the 1706 establishment act has always been perceived as a reward for Huguenot political loyalty, but there may have been an element of recognition of the French Carolinians loyalty in war as well.

This examination of early politics in Carolina suggests that Dissenters squandered early opportunities for alliance while they were a majority in the 1680s and by 1702—when they were a minority in the government—it was too late. The Huguenot-Anglican political alliance had been forged and tested in the Commons House. It held strong in politics and was a harbinger of further communication between the two faiths. Anglicans labored to keep vital the Huguenot political alliance. They also sought to assimilate Huguenots into the English-dominated society of South Carolina.

The 1706 church act and subsequent legislation made provisions for the appointment and maintenance of French-speaking Anglican ministers and the creation of St. Thomas and St. Dennis Parish in 1706 and apportionments such as the 1716 act assured that some members in the Commons House would be of Huguenot origin. French-language translations of the Book of Common Prayer and financial support from the Carolina government and the English Society for the Propagation of the Gospel in Foreign Parts (SPG) assisted acculturation. Intermarriage between Huguenots and Anglicans became commonplace, and Huguenot political, business, and religious leaders entered enthusiastically into the life of the province.

The proprietors' vision of religious liberty as articulated in the Fundamental Constitutions attracted Huguenot refugees to their Carolina colony and laid the groundwork for the creation of a generally diverse population. Dissenters of all stripes—including Quakers, Scots Covenanters, and New England Congregationalists—believed that they had found a place in the New World where they could practice their faiths in an atmosphere of toleration. The real situation in Carolina proved otherwise. Local political rivals and an entrenched antiproprietary faction in Carolina used religion as one weapon among many in their quest for hegemony. The Anglican Goose Creek faction ultimately won out when they enlisted the Huguenots as allies against the Huguenots' fellow Dissenters. Religious toleration of the Huguenots became a reality in Carolina as an aspect of party warfare, not through idealism. Carolina certainly proved a refuge for the Huguenots, but that refuge came at the price of political accommodation and eventual assimilation into the dominant Anglican English society.

Notes

1. E. Armstrong, *The French Wars of Religion, their Political Aspects* (New York: Russell & Russell, 1904), passim; Henry M. Baird, *The Huguenots and the Revocation of the Edict of Nantes*, vol. 2 (New York: Scribners, 1895), 92–93; Samuel Smiles, *The Huguenots: Their Settlements, Churches, and Industries in England and Ireland*, third edition (London: John Murray, 1869), chapter 7: "Early Walloon and French Churches in England"; Jon Butler, *The Huguenots in America: A Refugee People in New World Society*, Harvard University Monographs, volume 72 (Cambridge, Mass.: Harvard University Press, 1983), passim. See also Arthur M. Hirsch, *The Huguenots of Colonial South Carolina* (1928; reprint, Columbia: University of South Carolina Press, 2001), passim; Bertrand Van Ruymbeke, introduction to *Memory and Identity: The Huguenots in France and the Atlantic Diaspora*, ed. Van Ruymbeke and Randy J. Sparks (Columbia: University of South Carolina Press, 2003), 1–25.

2. William A. Shaw, ed., *Letters of Denization and Acts of Naturalization for Aliens in England and Ireland, 1603–1700*, in Publications of the Huguenots Society of London 18 (1911), vi, ix; James H. Kettner, prologue to *The Development of American Citizenship, 1608–1870* (Chapel Hill: University of North Carolina Press, 1978).

3. Arthur Hirsch, "Some Phases of the Huguenot-Anglican Rivalries in South Carolina before 1730," *Journal of the Presbyterian Historical Society* 13 (March 1928): 2–28, describes the political assimilation of Huguenots into Carolina's English society. See also Robert Kingdon, "Why did the Huguenot Refugees in the American Colonies become Episcopalian?" *Historical Magazine of the Protestant Episcopal Church* 49 (December 1980): 330–35, and Amy Ellen Friedlander, "Carolina Huguenots: A Study in Cultural Pluralism in the Low Country, 1679–1768," Ph.D. dissertation, Emory University, 1979, chapter 3: "The Political Establishment."

4. John Alexander Moore, "Royalizing South Carolina: The Revolution of 1719 and the Evolution of Early South Carolina Government," Ph.D. dissertation, University of South Carolina, 1991, 33.

5. E. E. Rich, "The First Earl of Shaftesbury's Colonial Policy," *Transactions of the Royal Historical Society*, fifth series 7 (1957): 47–70. Versions of the Fundamental Constitutions are found in *North Carolina Charters and Constitutions, 1578–1698*, ed. Mattie Erma Edwards Parker (Raleigh, N.C.: Carolina Charter Tercentenary Commission, 1963), passim; Friedlander, "Carolina Huguenots," 51–55; William S. Powell, "Carolina in the Seventeenth Century: An Annotated Bibliography of Contemporary Publications," *North Carolina Historical Magazine* 41 (1964): 76–104.

6. Hirsch, *The Huguenots of Colonial South Carolina*, 107–8; Frederick A. Porcher, "Historical and Social Sketch of Craven County, South Carolina," in *A Contribution to the History of the Huguenots of South Carolina Consisting of Pamphlets by Samuel Dubose and Frederick A. Porcher* (New York: Knickerbocker Press, 1887; reprint, Columbia: R. L. Bryan, 1972), 87–176.

7. John Archdale reported to the proprietors that Craven County had fewer than forty freeholders; Archdale to Proprietors, August 28, 1696, Commissions and Instructions from the Lords Proprietors of Carolina to Public Officials of South Carolina, 1685–1715, manuscript volume at the South Carolina Department of Archives and History, Columbia, 128–29; Friedlander, "Carolina Huguenots," 153–54.

8. M. Eugene Sirmans, *Colonial South Carolina: A Political History, 1663–1763* (Chapel Hill: University of North Carolina Press, 1966), 45–46; Proprietors to M. Trouillard and others, April 12, 1693, Colonial Office Records, Class 5: America and West Indies, Great Britain Public Record Office, London, 5: 288, p. 236, available on microfilm at the South Carolina Department of Archives and History, Columbia. George Insh, *Scottish Colonial Schemes, 1620–1686* (Glasgow: Maclehose, Jackson, 1922), 194.

9. Bertrand Van Ruymbeke, *From Babylon to New Eden: A History of the Huguenots of Seventeenth-Century France and Colonial South Carolina, 1660–1740* (Columbia: University of South Carolina Press, 2005), 295.

10. Petition to Seth Sothell, ca. 1691, in William J. Rivers, *A Sketch of the History of South Carolina to the Close of the Proprietary Government by the Revolution of 1719. With An Appendix containing many valuable Records hitherto unpublished* (Charleston: McCarter, 1856), appendix, 418–30.

11. Act No. 65 of 1691, 2 S.C. Statutes at Large 59 (Cooper 1837).

12. Commons House Journals of the South Carolina General Assembly, 1692–1721, (hereafter Commons House Journals), 21 manuscript volumes, South Carolina Department of Archives and History, Columbia, I (fair copy): 47–49.

13. Proprietary Proclamation, April 12, 1693, Colonial Office Records 5: 288, p. 222; Proprietors to Deputies and Council, April 10, 1693, Colonial Office Records, 5: 288, pp. 232–34.

14. Proprietors to M. Trouillard and others, April 12, 1693, Colonial Office Records, 5: 288, p. 236.

15. Archdale and Council to Proprietors, August 20, 1695, and October 2, 1695, Commissions and Instructions, 115, 120.

16. Results of the Berkeley-Craven election were reported by Robert Gibbes, sheriff of Berkeley County, to Archdale and the Council on December 19, 1695. Commissions and Instructions, 125.

17. Proprietors to Archdale, January 29, 1696, Colonial Office Records, 5: 289, p. 30.

18. Archdale and Council to Proprietors, August 28, 1696, Commissions and Instructions, 128–29; Archdale to M. Buretell and others, October 19, 1695, John Archdale Papers, Library of Congress, Washington, D.C.

19. Proprietors to Archdale, September 10, 1696, Colonial Office Records, 5: 289, p. 33.

20. Commons House Journals, I (fair copy): 192, 194, 199; Act No. 152 of 1696–1697, 2 S.C. Statutes 130 (Cooper 1837). Act No. 154 of 1696–1697, ibid., 131.

21. Ibid., 2: no. 152.

22. Joseph Blake and Council to Proprietors, March 24, 1697, Commissions and Instructions, 136.

23. Commons House Journals III (fair copy): 170, 186–87, 194.

24. Sirmans, supra note 8 at 86.

25. "Representation and Address of the Inhabitants of Colleton County, June 26, 1703," in Daniel Defoe, *Party-Tyranny; Or An Occasional Bill in Miniature, As now Practised in Carolina. Humbly offered to Both Houses of Parliament* (London, 1705), 12–17.

26. Act No. 222 of 1704, 2 S.C. Statutes at Large 232 (Cooper 1837) (exclusion act); Act No. 225 of 1704, ibid. at 236 (church establishment act).

27. See William E. Saunders, ed., *The Colonial Records of North Carolina*, volume 1 (Raleigh, N.C.: P. M. Hale, 1886), 635–44, for the text of Queen Anne's veto and documents pertaining to the episode.

28. Moore, "Royalizing Carolina," 246–47.

29. Act No. 256 of 1706, 2 S.C. Statutes at Large 282 (Cooper 1837).

30. Hirsch, *The Huguenots of Colonial South Carolina*, 86. See Act No. 248 of 1706, 2. S.C. Statutes at Large 268 (Cooper 1837), creating St. James Santee.

31. Act No. 248 of 1706, 2 S.C. Statutes at Large 269 (Cooper 1837).

32. Act No. 256 of 1706, 2 S.C. Statutes at Large 282-83, para. 3 (Cooper 1837), creating St. Dennis and St. Thomas. See also Act No. 280 of 1708, 2 S.C. Statutes at Large 329, discussing St. Thomas and St. Dennis. See also Act No. 365 of 1716, 2 S.C. Statutes at Large 685 para. 7, making them more French, superceded by Act No. 446 of 1721, 3 S.C. Statutes at Large 137, para. 7.

33. Commons House Journals (Green copy), 2: 249–54; Act No. 228 of 1704, 2 S.C. Statutes at Large 251–53, para. 6 (Cooper 1837).

34. Kenneth R. Jones, "A 'Full and Particular Account' of the Assault on Charleston in 1706," *South Carolina Historical Magazine* 83 (January 1982): 1–11, republishes a contemporary report of the assault and includes supplemental historical and bibliographical information on the events.

Seeking the Promised Land

Afro-Carolinians and the Quest
for Religious Freedom to 1830

Bernard E. Powers Jr.

THE ATMOSPHERE OF RELIGIOUS TOLERATION created by the first Fundamental Constitution was the earliest example of Carolina's uniqueness. Completed in 1669, the year before the first settlers arrived, this document promised that, with the exception of Roman Catholics, all who believed in God were welcome to practice their faith unmolested. The result was a religious climate more tolerant than any other mainland colony south of Rhode Island.[1] Paradoxically, Carolina's toleration for the religious diversity of Europeans had adverse consequences for Africans. As a Restoration-era colony, Carolina had a different relationship to slavery than its Chesapeake neighbors to the north. In Virginia the practice of slavery preceded its statutory recognition by several decades. As Virginians became more sophisticated in the complexity of slavery law, they eliminated some of the legal loopholes in the system. For example, until the Virginia Act of 1667 slaves had sometimes successfully sued for their freedom on the basis of conversion to Christianity. Carolina benefited from Virginia's legal experience with slavery. Even before its first settlers landed, the Fundamental Constitution of July 1669 provided that "Every Freeman of Carolina shall have absolute power and authority over Negro slaves, of what opinion or Religion soever."[2] There were multiple versions of the Fundamental Constitution, but none ever became law in Carolina. The Fundamental Constitutions are nevertheless important for the sentiments and values they reveal. At an early date there was obvious concern over the consequences of the slaves' exposure to Christianity. The purpose of this essay is twofold. First it seeks to examine how white Carolinians conceived of the problem of Christianizing the slave population in the face of their need to maintain racial hegemony. Second, it examines the way that black Carolinians actively engaged Christianity in their attempt to create psychic and sometimes physical living space by which to challenge Christian slaveholders.

In 1737 a Swiss immigrant to South Carolina was struck by one of its most characteristic demographic features, when he observed that "Carolina . . . looks more like a Negro country than like a country settled by white people." After several false starts, by the final years of the seventeenth century Carolinians had successfully experimented with rice cultivation, and exportation of this crop formed the basis of the colony's economy. Later, in the 1740s, indigo production became an important adjunct to the rice-based economy.[3] Rice was among the most labor-intensive crops produced in the New World and required a large labor force. The rice plantations were routinely the largest productive units in mainland North America. As one of the principal slave-trading nations of the eighteenth century, Great Britain was readily able to supply the labor needs of the Carolina colonists. Their labor demands were so great that, as early as 1708, slaves composed the majority of the colony's population. In the lowcountry parishes they were not a slight majority but two-thirds of the total population. The colony's racial disparities, dramatic enough, were sometimes exaggerated by impressionable visitors. During a 1742 trip through the lowcountry, Rev. Henry Muhlenberg concluded, "slaves are so numerous here that it is estimated that there are fifteen for every white man."[4]

From an early date colonial authorities expressed concerns about the potentially bloody consequences of their minority status. They took legal steps to improve their security and reduce the possibility of slave insurrection by passing legislation in 1698 and 1716 requiring planters to import a certain number of white indentured servants to offset the burgeoning slave population.[5] Nevertheless South Carolina's substantial racial imbalances persisted in the early nineteenth century. In 1830 blacks outnumbered whites 3:1 in Charleston District, 5:1 in Beaufort District, and 8:1 in Georgetown District. These disparities varied seasonally. During the sickly season between May and November, planters with large landholdings deserted their properties, seeking higher, more healthful ground. Many ventured to Charleston or went into the upstate, while others left the South entirely during the period. Movement westward from the coast inland created a different demographic, with Richland, Lexington, and Edgefield, all midlands districts, showing a black to white ratio of 1.5:1. To the extreme northwest—in Greenville, Spartanburg, and York counties—whites outnumbered blacks 3:1.[6]

The size of South Carolina's black population was not its only distinctive characteristic. Throughout the eighteenth century the colony had an unusually high percentage of native-born Africans in its enslaved population. In 1740 Africans numbered 66 percent of South Carolina slaves, almost double the percentage of Africans found in Virginia in that same year. The persistent African presence in South Carolina was further bolstered in the early nineteenth century because South Carolina was the final state to end the foreign slave trade.[7] The high percentage of slaves in South Carolina's population and the profound African presence were part of this place's distinctive demographic profile and shaped many aspects of the society and its religious experience.

The Society for the Propagation of the Gospel in Foreign Parts (SPG) was founded in 1701 to supervise the missionary efforts of the Church of England in North America, and by 1703 it had established its presence among South Carolina's Native

American and slave populations.[8] Proselytizing among the slaves was difficult and frustrating work for the early missionaries, in part because of planter opposition. Questions had arisen in the seventeenth century as to whether a slave who became a Christian had to be emancipated. The Fundamental Constitutions, which addressed the problem by granting masters complete control over their slaves, "of what opinion or Religion soever," never became law in South Carolina, and the first slave law, the act of 1690, stating there was no conflict between conversion and slavery, was disallowed by the Lords Proprietors.[9] So by the early eighteenth century, there was still some uncertainty on this matter. For this reason, when Rev. Francis Le Jau undertook missionary work among the slaves in Goose Creek parish in 1708, he encountered immediate planter opposition. It became so bad, that in the attempt to allay slaveholder apprehension and stifle slave hopes, Le Jau required each candidate for baptism to swear that they were not attempting to use the rite as a ruse to escape from slavery. The controversy was finally resolved definitively in 1712, when the Assembly recognized that legal uncertainties surrounding slave conversion had caused some slaveholders to "neglect to baptize their negroes or slaves, or suffer them to be baptized, for fear that thereby they should be manumitted." As a remedy, the act of 1712 unequivocally stated that "such slave or slaves [who] shall receive and profess the christian [sic] religion, and be baptized , he or they shall not thereby be manumitted or . . . his or their owner, . . . lose his or their civil right, property and authority over such slave or slaves."[10]

Even after the elimination of the legal uncertainties, there remained other objections to Christian education. Some planters believed religious instruction was wasted on African people, whom they considered just a step above brutes in the scale of civilization. Others led morally lax lives themselves or were too preoccupied with their pecuniary interests to be concerned with slaves' spiritual needs. In 1712 Francis Le Jau reported that, although he urged slave masters to take care of their slaves' souls, "some submit to my exhortations (few indeed) and all Generally seem to be more concerned for the loss of their money." To reduce their overhead costs, many lowcountry planters allowed slaves to maintain plots on which they cultivated foodstuffs for their own subsistence. Sundays were devoted to household chores and to working these plots, often leaving little time for formal Christian instruction.[11]

Other masters opposed religious education for fear that literacy would result and that slaves would thereby become more difficult to manage. In a Georgia case one literate slave convert frequently observed his master inside the house, reading the Bible and praying at the height of the work day. It was reported, "The Negro began to do the same thing and wanted to spend half the day in the shade over his devotions; and when the master instructed him from God's Word that one must work if one would eat, he made a wry mouth and declared that that kind of Christianity was not becoming or suitable to him, etc." In another case a slave was certain that the various Christian denominations offered different prescriptions on labor. In assessing two of them he concluded that "he would rather belong to the Moravian Brethren than to the High Church because the latter was always preaching about work and labor, whereas the former preached faith without works, and he was tired of working."[12]

There was also a fear that, left to their own devices, literate slaves would entertain unorthodox and even dangerous interpretations of the scriptures. Such was the case during the early eighteenth century in Goose Creek parish, from which Reverend Le Jau reported, "The best Scholar of all the Negroes in my Parish and a very sober and honest Liver, thro' his Learning . . . Create[d] some Confusion among all the Negroes." After reading a book that detailed God's judgments against men for their sins, the slave predicted to his master that "there wou'd be a dismal time and the Moon wou'd be turned into Blood, and there wou'd be a dearth of darkness and went away." The Anglican cleric admonished the man but not before rumors circulated about his special metaphysical abilities, including the capacity to hear the voices of spirits and to communicate with angels. Reverend Le Jau feared that all too often "those Men [Negroes and Indians] have not judgment enough to make good use of their Learning" and therefore ought not to be taught indiscriminately to read. Along similar lines Rev. Henry Muhlenberg observed that slavery was so harsh in South Carolina and black women in particular were so brutally exploited that "no one dares to say anything to the blacks concerning the true religion." Many "so-called Christians" objected that with an understanding of Christian tenets and the judgment entailed upon sinners, "the blacks would kill them all, and make themselves masters of Carolina."[13]

Given the array of reservations about Christian instruction and its implications, when Anglican ministers and missionaries convinced masters to permit it, the slaveholders strictly limited access to their slaves. Allowing selective conversions and baptisms and even some literacy, the master class used access to the Christian community as an important means of reinforcing its hegemony. Simultaneously masters hoped that this select group of black Anglicans would see their interests connected to the slaveholding regime, rather than to the mass of slaves. By one estimate only about 3–5 percent of South Carolina's slaves were baptized into the Anglican Church in the eighteenth century. Of these one-fifth were mulattoes, more than five times the estimated proportion of mulattoes in the South Carolina slave population during the mid to late eighteenth century. Such figures suggest a disproportionate number of the Christian converts were the progeny of the master class and as such would have been expected to identify with its interests.[14]

Even without the Christian instruction that many planters believed could engender dissatisfaction among slaves, Carolina bondsmen made every effort to slip their chains. The leading eighteenth-century newspaper of the colony, the *South Carolina Gazette*, is replete with notices of fugitive slaves. Others committed acts of arson or assault, and some even poisoned their owners.[15] On a few occasions Africans and Afro-Carolinians even plotted collective acts of rebellion to secure their freedom. Sometimes these efforts had important international dimensions.

The Spanish presence in Florida to the south posed a perennial military and economic problem for the Carolina settlement because of the longstanding imperial and religious rivalry between Spain and Great Britain. South Carolinians frequently complained about raiding parties dispatched from St. Augustine against their lower coast or southern frontier. For example, in 1688 Gov. James Colleton protested against Spanish raids in 1686 against his territory, which resulted in loss of life, the kidnaping of English citizens, property destruction, and the theft of eleven slaves. Attempting to avoid future acts of hostility, to obtain appropriate recompense, and to secure the return of the slaves, the governor dispatched a diplomatic mission to St. Augustine. While all the details of the negotiations are not entirely clear, the disposition of the slave property is certain. According to William Dunlop, the Carolina representative, "And whereas the Most Noble Governor of fflordia [sic] in consideration that these negroes are turned Roman Catholick Christians [he] hath desired that these negroes do stay still in this province." The agreement also provided compensation to the owners for their capital losses. Even so, such provisions could not be depended on, nor was there assurance that slaves' market value assigned by the Spanish would be acceptable to their erstwhile English owners.[16] Given the frequency of the escapes, the financial losses to slave owners could be considerable. In November 1738 alone, one master lost nineteen slaves to St. Augustine while several others lost a total of at least fifty slaves to the Spanish province. Sometimes escape to Florida was part of a larger plan for rebellion, organized by slaves desirous of reaching a destination entirely beyond English authority. For example, in May 1720, the so-called Primus Plot was formulated by approximately fourteen slaves from various locations on the Ashley River north of Charleston. These rebels intended to burn their plantations and others nearby, arm neighborhood slaves, and then march on the city of Charleston. When the plot was discovered, several participants fled toward St. Augustine, but at least four were captured near the Savannah River and returned to Charleston, where they were executed.[17]

The most threatening challenge to slavery in eighteenth-century South Carolina had religion at its core, but it may have had less to do with what slaves learned in the New World and more to do with what Africans brought from their homeland. On Sunday September 9, 1739, a cadre of twenty primarily Angolan slaves, gathered about twenty miles southwest of Charleston on the Stono River and started an insurrection. With this uprising, these men became the latest to set their sights on St. Augustine as a destination. Undoubtedly their bold bid for freedom was encouraged by a 1733 Spanish royal edict, published with great fanfare, awarding freedom to all English fugitive slaves who reached the St. Augustine. The Spanish may also have made efforts to spread the word clandestinely that freedom could be had in St. Augustine.

A Georgia legislative report on the Stono Rebellion indicated, "Several Spaniards upon diverse Pretences have for some time past been strolling about Carolina, two of them, who will give no account of themselves have been taken up and committed to Jayl [sic] in Georgia. . . . [Thus] The good reception of the Negroes at Augustine was spread about." The same report and a South Carolina legislative report both suggested sinister motives on the part of a Spanish military official, who went as far north as Charleston under the guise of delivering a message to Gen. James Oglethorpe of

Georgia. The South Carolina Assembly report, which provided greater detail on this episode, noted that during his return trip this man was observed to stop and tarry at all the inlets along the coast. The most damning evidence in the report was the following: "And in the very Month in which the above Insurrection was made the General acquainted our Lieutenant Governour by Letter that the Magistrates of Georgia had seized a Spaniard whom he took to be a Priest, and that they thought from what they had discovered that he was employed by the Spaniards to procure a general Insurrection of the negroes."[18]

With the Angolans as their nucleus, the rebels ransacked a local warehouse, arming themselves with guns and ammunition and beginning to march southward, attacking homesteads and killing whites they encountered along the way. As they advanced through the countryside, other slaves joined them until the rebels numbered somewhere between sixty and one hundred.[19]

The coast and the immediate interior of contemporary Angola, in south-central Africa, was one of the most important sources of captives for South Carolina's colonial slave communities. During the eighteenth century approximately 40 percent of the African imports to the colony originated there, and for the years 1735–40 the figure reached 70 percent.[20] Modern scholarship suggests that the Stono rebels probably originated in the Bantu kingdom of Kongo, an interior nation in south-central Africa. Kongo royals embraced Christianity brought by the Portuguese, beginning in 1491. The state maintained diplomatic relations with Rome, and by the seventeenth century each provincial capital maintained its own school. By this time the kingdom had a catechism written in KiKongo, and Portuguese became its official language. More important, creole Portuguese was used extensively by traders, ensuring some degree of knowledge of the language outside strictly elite circles.[21]

Understanding the Portuguese and Catholic heritage of this part of Africa is essential to comprehending what may have been essential aspects of the Stono Rebellion. The evidence of both these elements among eighteenth-century Carolina slave communities is clear. In 1711 Reverend Le Jau referred to the presence of several "Portuguese Slaves" in the St. James Goose Creek parish, some of whom desired to receive communion. When, however, Le Jau's investigation revealed that they were familiar with "Popish tenets," he required them to renounce such beliefs forever, especially praying to saints, before he agreed to administer the sacrament. Likewise, a Georgia legislative account of the Stono Rebellion reported, "Amongst the Negroe Slaves there [in South Carolina] are a people brought from the Kingdom of Angola in Africa, many of these speak Portuguese, [which Language is as near Spanish as Scotch is to English], by reason that the Portuguese have considerable Settlement, and the Jesuits have a Mission and School in that Kingdom and many Thousands of the Negroes there profess the Roman Catholic Religion."[22] So, with a bit of adaptation, some Carolina slaves were probably able to understand Spanish appeals and enticements even if they were not articulated in English. In addition, the fact that Florida was a Catholic settlement may have made the offers of freedom and life there even more compelling.

According to accounts, as the rebel band grew "they calling out Liberty, marched on with Colors displayed, and two Drums beating" until reaching the vicinity of Jacksonburough Ferry, where they "halted in a field, and set to dancing, Singing and beating Drums, to draw more Negroes to them, thinking they were now victorious over the whole Province." Although our knowledge of the rebellion remains fragmentary, certain details are highly suggestive of deeper meanings and are worthy of further comment. For example, to Africans dance can be a much more complex behavior than is the case in modern Western civilization. The cultural historian Sterling Stuckey explains that Africans engaged in sacred dance, which was primarily devotional and had a function similar to prayer. Such dances were a means of summoning and engaging ancestral spirits or deities. In traditional African societies, dance was also performed to encourage warriors near or far away to greater effort, to increase their strength, or to express victory in battle. Drums often served the same purposes; that is, to summon the spirits, to articulate their message, and then to return them to their habitat.[23]

The Stono Rebellion was doomed to failure. At one point the lieutenant governor of South Carolina almost fell into the hands of the insurrectionists, but he managed to escape. Soon the colonial militia was assembled, and, although the rebels fought valiantly, after a week most were captured. Many were shot on the spot.[24] Physical freedom was their goal, but the prospect of uniting with their Catholic coreligionists might have been a special encouragement to insurrection or some of the participants. Some of the behavior of the Stono rebels was also highly suggestive of powerful African spiritual forces. In rare combination, these Catholic and African religious elements were in part responsible for producing the most formidable slave insurrection ever faced in any eighteenth-century British mainland colony.

In late September 1739, new security measures already passed before Stono Rebellion went into effect, requiring white men to bring firearms to church on Sundays.[25] The most sweeping legislative attempt to prevent another insurrection was enacted in the form of the Negro act of 1740. This was the most comprehensive and draconian law for regulating slave behavior ever passed to that date. Based on Caribbean slave codes, it reinforced older strictures while instituting new policies that would govern slave life in broad outline until the Civil War era. Among its myriad features, were provisions prohibiting slaves from ever striking white persons, from holding "public meetings," and from learning to write. (Reading was not mentioned.) Slave hiring was strictly regulated, as was the keeping of canoes and trafficking in goods, to prevent theft and, more important, to reduce the opportunity "to plot and confederate together, and form conspiracies dangerous to the peace and safety of the whole province." The law also banned "wooden swords, and other mischievous and dangerous weapons or using or keeping drums or horns or other loud instruments which may call together, or give sign or notice to one another of their wicked designs or purpose." Equating musical instruments with dangerous weapons reveals the extent of masters' fears. Finally, to ensure that visual symbols of the slaves' subordination were ever present, this law even limited the kind of apparel they could legally wear.[26]

The increased need to ensure the slaveholders' hegemony had a direct impact on Carolina slaves' religious lives. The series of religious revivals that swept through the colonies beginning in the 1730s and continuing until the Revolutionary era were known collectively as the Great Awakening. While the effects of this upsurge in religious enthusiasm sometimes disrupted communities, its impact in South Carolina was muted because of white apprehensions about the slave population. The Great Awakening arrived in South Carolina in January 1740 with the controversial firebrand George Whitefield, an Anglican minister from England and follower of John Wesley known for his fire-and-brimstone sermons, which he delivered in an unforgettably evangelical style. The young preacher almost immediately got into trouble with Commissary Alexander Garden, representative of the bishop of London and rector of St. Philip's Church. In calling for spiritual revival, Whitefield was highly critical of the worldly preoccupations and often lavish lifestyles of the planters and Charleston's monied elite. Nor was the clergy spared from Whitefield's criticism. He observed that, while there were many ministers in South Carolina, they like Commissary Garden were preoccupied with "the outward discipline of the Church." When it came to rejuvenating men's souls, the essence of the Great Awakening, Whitefield lamented, "I hear of no stirring among the dry bones." Garden rebuked Whitefield for attacking rank and status distinctions, for misinterpreting scriptures, and for violating church policies, especially deviating from the Book of Common Prayer during services. The relationship between the two men deteriorated further, and in 1740 Garden had Whitefield charged for his errant ways and brought before an ecclesiastical court, which convicted him. Whitefield engendered further animosity when he criticized planters for the unnecessary brutality of lowcountry slavery and upbraided them for neglecting the spiritual lives of their slaves. The reforms he urged included Christian instruction to elevate the quality of slave life. Unlike most other Anglican clerics, Whitefield argued for the spiritual equality of the races, and his emphasis on proselytizing among the slaves marked the substantial beginning of the Protestant evangelical missionary effort among them.[27]

Whitefield's preaching generated support as well as opposition, and brothers Jonathan and Hugh Bryan, members of the gentry from St. Helena were among his earliest and most ardent supporters. Under Whitefield's instruction they realized the inadequacy of their previous religious lives, and both men underwent a profound spiritual transformation. As Whitefield's protégés, these men echoed their teacher's criticism of their society. Hugh Bryan criticized Carolinians for delighting in the pleasures of the world at the expense of their spiritual lives. The Anglican clergy was no better because its members preached false doctrines, tolerated the people's sin, and lulled them into spiritual complacency. Jonathan Bryan was so disturbed by the spiritual abominations he observed in Charleston, that he predicted a fate similar to that of Sodom and Gomorrah for the city unless its citizens made dramatic and soul-rending changes. Finally, the Bryan brothers saw the need for Christian education among slaves, and they promised Whitefield that they would establish schools for this purpose on their plantations.[28]

When he began holding religious services for large numbers of slaves on his property, Hugh Bryan's activities incurred the opprobrium of his neighbors and the attention of legal authorities. In early 1742 the legislature informed Lt. Gov. William Bull about what it called "frequent Meetings of great Numbers of Slaves in the Parish of Saint Helena, to the Terror of the Inhabitants, [which] had been countenanced and encouraged by some white Persons, residing in those Parts."[29] Hugh Bryan may have used some of his own writings in addition to the Bible for instructional purposes, and this also became a cause of public concern. The previous year in an open letter to the *South Carolina Gazette,* Bryan contended that the woeful state of spiritual decline in the colony had provoked God's wrath, which explained the several calamities suffered by the colony in recent years. In late 1740 Charleston had experienced a devastating fire that did considerable property damage; in recent years there had been disease epidemics in the city. A 1740 attempt to invade St. Augustine ended in humiliating failure. For the larger community, the most disturbing of Hugh Bryan's contentions must have been that even the Stono Rebellion was part of God's plan to chastise South Carolina.[30] Desiring all to know that only immediate repentance could prevent God's apocalyptic judgment, Hugh Bryan sent some of his writings to the Assembly, where they proved deeply unsettling. Bryan's works were described as containing "sundry enthusiastic Prophecies of the Destruction of Charles Town and Deliverance of the Negroes from their Servitude." The Assembly recommended that the writings be brought to the attention of a civil magistrate because they "might prove of dangerous Consequence to be published amongst the People." Recounting this episode in a letter, Eliza Lucas Pinckney reported, "People in general were uneasy" but not because they placed credence in the prophesy. Most "dreaded the consiquence [*sic*] of such a thing being put in to the head of the slaves and the advantage they might take of us." The fact that England and Spain had been at war since 1739 added to the general malaise and made Hugh Bryan's predictions especially chilling. Although the focus of such conflicts centered in Europe, the lower South Carolina coast was always vulnerable, as demonstrated by the 1742 Spanish invasion of Georgia and French maritime threats in 1744.[31]

After some disconcerting personal religious experiences, Hugh Bryan suddenly renounced his earlier prophecies and publicly attributed his behavior to the delusions of Satan. Nonetheless, a grand jury indicted him in March 1742 for his inflammatory writings and for his assembling slaves under the auspices of religious services in violation of the law and in ways destructive of peace and public safety. Given Bryan's disavowal and the colony's heritage of religious toleration, the charges against him were subsequently dropped.[32] The experiences of George Whitefield and Hugh Bryan are important because they reveal the potential difficulties of Christian instruction for the slaves. The Anglicans were suspicious of "religious enthusiasm" in general because they believed it relied on feeling and emotions rather than on a systematic and rational approach to worship.[33] In a slaveholding society such as South Carolina, errors in imparting God's word, such as those committed by Hugh Bryan, were fraught with dire consequences and had to be guarded against at all costs. So the Great Awakening, which might have been an important avenue by which Afro-Carolinians were integrated more fully into the Christian community, had only minimal effects. Writing on the subject of slave conversion only a month after Hugh Bryan's indictment, Josiah Smith, pastor of the Independent Church in Charleston and a vocal supporter of George Whitefield, reported to the *South Carolina Gazette* that "the Bishop of London was seriously affected to find, when the Numbers are so prodigiously great, 'how small progress has been made, in a Christian Country toward the delivering those poor Creatures from the Pagan darkness and Superstition, in which They were [illegible], and the making Them Partakers of the Light of the Gospel, and of the Blessings and Benefits belonging to it.' And particularly laments, 'That all *Attempts* towards it have been by too many industriously discouraged and hindered.'" Smith expressed support for these sentiments and vowed to encourage his parishioners to fulfill their religious responsibilities. Finally, Smith chided civil and Anglican authorities in South Carolina: "We humbly Submit to the Wisdom of our *Superiors*, whether, and how far, ATTEMPTS of this Nature may be thought to deserve Their Publick protection, countenance, and sanction."[34]

Reverend Smith did not to have the final word because another reader requested clarification. With unmistakable sarcasm the writer asked:

> Do they mean, that under PRETENCE OF ATTEMPTS *of this Nature,* every idle or designing Person that pleases, shall be at Liberty to pursue ATTEMPTS not *of this,* but *another* and most dangerous *Nature,* viz. Gathering *Cabals* of *Negro's* [*sic*] about him, without public Authority, at unseasonable Times, and to the Disturbance of a Neighbourhood; and instead of teaching them the *Principles* of *Christianity,* filling their Heads with a Parcel of *Cant-Phrases, Trances, Dreams, Visions, and Revelations,* and fomenting still *worse,* and which Prudence forbids to name?

The need for careful limitations on Christian education among the slaves continued in the mid–eighteenth century. The willingness of Hugh Bryan and those who came after him to conform their proselytizing efforts to the needs of slaveholding society allowed evangelical Christianity to spread widely in the South.[35]

The Church of England possessed the advantages of its official establishment in South Carolina, but Afro-Carolinian church leadership first emerged among the Baptists. In the era of the American Revolution, David George, a slave at Silver Bluff in Edgefield District, was influenced by the missionary teachings of George Liele, a Georgia slave who preached in Savannah and along the Savannah River. During the years 1773–75, when David George's master allowed a white Baptist missionary to minister on his plantation, George was converted and became an elder over the other Baptist slaves on the premises. When the movement of itinerants were curtailed during the war for security purposes, George became the main preacher for this fledgling congregation, which seems to have been the first black Baptist organization in the South, certainly in South Carolina. This case reveals how quickly Afro-Carolinians could seize on the church's potential for political activism. When the British occupied Savannah in 1778, George led approximately fifty members of his congregation to that city to seek freedom and protection under British auspices. When the British Navy evacuated Savannah, George and his congregants accompanied it, first to Charleston and from there to Halifax, Nova Scotia, where he established the congregation's second Baptist church. A somewhat restless spirit, George eventually left Canada for Sierra Leone, West Africa.[36] All the members of David George's church did not follow him to the British, and by 1793 the remnant of the congregation in South Carolina had apparently moved twelve miles away to Augusta, Georgia, where they reorganized, becoming the First African Baptist Church of Augusta. By doing so they eliminated the only black congregation in South Carolina.[37]

The short-lived, yet volatile, activities of David Margate, the only black British missionary dispatched to the South in the late eighteenth century, provide another example of how black clerics tried to use the church to subvert the existing racial hierarchy. Shortly after Margate's arrival in Charleston in January 1775, he began to proclaim himself a kind of Moses, who was responsible for delivering his people from bondage. Despite admonitions from white ministers to refrain from such unorthodox and incendiary statements, David Margate would not allow his tongue to be bridled. One observer who heard Margate's exhortations stated that he "not only severely reflected against the Laws of the Province respect[ing] slaves but even against the thing [slavery] itself: he also compared their state to that of the Israelites during their Egyptian Bondade [sic]." White Carolinians were outraged and fearful that such imprudent remarks could lead to insurrections or mass poisonings. When word reached his supervisor of a plan to kidnap and murder Margate, he was quickly spirited away to the relative safety of Great Britain.[38]

The rise of Methodism produced its own controversial leadership, which included whites as well as blacks. While the earlier ministries of evangelical Anglicans such as George Whitefield, laid the groundwork for Methodism, the Methodist Episcopal Church, created in 1784 as a national denomination in America, grew out of the American Revolution. Charleston was considered the center of the denomination for the state; the first ministerial appointment was made for 1785; and Cumberland Street Church was organized as the first Methodist congregation.[39] From its inception the Methodist denomination was popular with Afro-Carolinians. For instance, in Charleston during 1787 the black membership increased by 53 while whites showed no increase, and by 1815 black Methodists numbered 3,793 compared to only 282 whites.[40]

In its earliest years the racial disparity in membership was at least in part due to the ardently antislavery posture adopted by the Methodist Church. In the denomination's first discipline, published in 1785, slavery was condemned as "contrary to the Golden Law of God . . . and the unalienable Rights of Mankind, as well as every Principle of the [American] Revolution." At the general conference of 1800 several antislavery resolutions were introduced, requiring Methodist slaveholders to emancipate their human chattel and to bar slaveholders from future membership. These measures failed to pass, but the conference again condemned slavery as anathema to the spirit of the American Revolution, the natural rights of man, and the Christian faith. The conference also directed the annual conferences to petition their state leg-islatures to initiate gradual emancipation, where it had not already been done.[41]

Many whites were naturally offended by the Methodists' antislavery stance and refused to support a church staffed by ministers they considered to be nothing more than roving abolitionists. No wonder many of the early ministers were castigated and sometimes even physically assaulted. The first anti-Methodist mobs assembled in Charleston in winter 1801, after the city intendant (mayor) verified the allegation that a Methodist minister had received antislavery literature. Even though the materials were destroyed, a mob assembled, seized another cleric, and carried him through the streets until the city police intervened. But the ruffians were not deterred so easily, and the next night, after Rev. George Dougherty led a racially integrated prayer meeting, a mob grabbed him and held him under a pump nearly drowning him in the water before passersby forcibly freed him.[42] The deep suspicion and hostility encountered by many Methodists impeded the denomination's growth, and forced the national church to reach an accommodation with slavery in the opening years of the nine-teenth century. After 1804 the discipline used in the South no longer criticized human bondage.[43] Even so it is likely that some slaves learned of Methodism's early antislavery sentiments and were attracted to the denomination for this reason.

The fact that Methodism allowed black Carolinians to participate as leaders in the church was another factor that made the denomination especially attractive to them. As the church began to extend its influence among Afro-Carolinians, it relied heavily on the missionary labors of black lay preachers, or exhorters. In recounting the early days of the church, Bishop William Capers had high praise for the quality of free black leaders found among Charleston's congregations. These he described as "extraordinary colored men" and as "men of intelligence and piety who read the Scriptures and understood them, and were zealous for religion among the negroes." Their influence was not limited to the city. They were known on the upper Cooper River and the Wando, in Goose Creek and St. Paul's parish. Capers recalled that there were areas from which white Methodist ministers were excluded simply because of their denomination, but Richard Holloway and Amos Baxter, both black lay preach-ers, were granted access. Rural missionary work was especially arduous, but in Bishop Capers's judgment these early black leaders were often "the only persons who for Christ's sake were zealous enough to undertake such a service"—and who also had the approval of rural masters. In fact, these early free black leaders were given extra-ordinary responsibilities. Even though it was a violation of church regulations as set forth in the discipline, they were authorized to "admit and exclude members" as nec-essary and simply to report their actions to officials in Charleston.[44]

In Charleston's Methodist churches, black members and leaders exercised a con-siderable amount of independence. Until 1815 they maintained their own quarterly conferences and even disbursed their own funds. They also convened and presided over church trials. In 1815 the arrival of Rev. Anthony Senter as the new supervising minister and complaints that some of the funds raised by black class leaders were being diverted from poor relief prompted an investigation. The results showed that, indeed, some of the monies had been used to purchase and emancipate slaves. To prevent future "improprieties," regulations governing the black membership were made more stringent; white stewards supervised the use of their funds and church trials could be held only when a white minister was present.[45]

Black Methodists refused to abide the new restrictions passively. They sent Morris Brown, a black lay preacher from Charleston, along with another delegate, to Philadelphia, where they were ordained in the newly formed African Methodist Episcopal Church. The first African American religious denomination, this church was formed by blacks who rejected the practice of racial discrimination in the Philadelphia church. Led by Richard Allen, a former slave and antislavery activist, they formed Bethel Church, which was joined by others in 1816 to create a national organization.[46] In 1818, informed by the knowledge of the Philadelphia precedent, Morris Brown led 4,367 blacks from the white Methodist churches in Charleston and founded the new African Methodist Episcopal Church in that city. This was an amazing feat of leadership; between two-thirds and three-quarters of all Charleston's black Methodists elected to follow Brown. Recalling the event, a white minister lamented, "The galleries, hitherto crowded, were almost completely deserted, and it was a vacancy that could be felt."[47]

The road ahead was fraught with severe difficulties because of the exigencies of life within a slaveholding society. When black church leaders approached the legislature for permission to hold services in the northern suburbs of Charleston, they tried to forestall any opposition by providing reassurances. The conditions set forth in their petition included:

> that the door of the church remain open always, and that all white ministers of the Gospel of every denomination shall be respectfully invited to officiate in the said Church, whenever disposed so to do, and that separate seats shall be provided for such citizens as may honor the congregation with their presence, either for religious instruction or to inspect their morals and deportment. That no minister of color who does not reside in this State shall officiate for the said congregation, nor shall any slave be admitted a member thereof without the approbation of his or her owner. . . . That every exertion will be used . . . to preserve the utmost order and decorum.[48]

Even with these pledges, Charleston members of the State House called for rejection of the petition because "the petitioners would be better instructed by well educated and pious Divines in the Churches in that city than by ignorant and fanatical preachers of their own color."[49]

Their official detractors notwithstanding, black Methodists were undeterred and continued to meet regularly. The series of acts that unfolded in response to the organizational changes of 1815, and culminated in the formation of an independent African American denomination in Charleston, were events of almost unparalleled audacity and boldness. Amplifying this point, historian and theologian Vincent Harding concluded that "organized rebellion on another level had already been built deeply into the structure of black church life in Charleston." The significance of what had occurred was not lost on city officials, who harassed members of the new church. For example, on one occasion in mid 1818 one hundred forty free black and slave members of the congregation were arrested for holding worship services in violation of city and state law. Most were released with a warning but several of the ministers were fined or given the choice of leaving the state or being incarcerated for a month. Morris Brown chose imprisonment so he could remain in his home and continue his ministry. The will of these black Methodists could not be broken, and the new church continued to bedevil white Charlestonians, who recognized the threat it posed.[50]

In 1822 white Carolinians' worst fears were realized with the discovery of the Denmark Vesey slave conspiracy.[51] Vesey was a free black who had formerly been owned by a ship's captain and merchant who had traveled throughout the Caribbean before settling in Charleston following the American Revolution. In 1799, after winning a local lottery, Vesey purchased his freedom and began making his living as a carpenter. But although Vesey was now free, he was disenchanted with the restrictions on free black life in the early years of the nineteenth century and the indignities free persons of color routinely suffered in a slaveholding society. One of his greatest frustrations was that he was unable to purchase his wife and children from slavery. Another source of embitterment was Charleston officials' persecution of the A.M.E. church, where Vesey was not only a member but also a class leader.[52]

It seems that the attacks on black churchmen and churchwomen were the catalyst for Vesey to take the fateful step of conspiring physically to assault the slave system. He was a studious man who conscientiously read and contemplated his Bible, and despite the teachings of white ministers Vesey concluded that slavery and Christian ethics were incompatible. As a class leader he frequently met with members and other church officials, and whenever possible he conveyed this lesson to them. Vesey did not limit his remarks about the injustice of slavery to black church members though; he sometimes boldly made the same assertions to whites. In one white-owned shop near his home Vesey frequently complained about racial injustice. One white observer recalled that "he would speak of the creation of the world in which he would say all men had equal rights, blacks, as well as whites and all his religious remarks were mingled with Slavery."[53] Vesey was not satisfied with mere talk, nor was he willing to pray and wait on God's deliverance. Vesey considered any who would counsel such a course foolish and asserted that "if we did not put our hand to the work & deliver ourselves, we would never come out of Slavery." Armed with his knowledge of the Bible, especially the Old Testament, which emphasized God's avenging justice and power of deliverance, as seen in Exodus, Vesey urged God's people to rise up and strike for freedom.[54]

Christian doctrines were not the only spiritual influences on Vesey's supporters. Because Charleston was a major seaport, thousands of Africans entered the city and were dispersed throughout the lowcountry and the interior of the South. In fact South Carolina was the only state to reopen the foreign slave trade in 1803 and maintained it through 1807. Approximately forty thousand Africans entered South

Carolina during these years, and the supply of new slaves was only ended officially in 1808 by federal law. The ongoing operation of the slave trade ensured that the Charleston area had many African slaves, and many of them were members of the A.M.E. Church. Gullah Jack from Angola was one of the most important of such persons. A member of the church, he was also a powerful African priest who was both feared and respected by many Africans and Afro-Carolinians. He used his special metaphysical talents to cast protective spells and to convince men who retained more-traditional African spiritual ideas to join with Vesey, no doubt assuring them of victory.[55]

Vesey's plan was to seize the arsenals in Charleston on July 14, and to arm the slaves there as well as those who came into town from the countryside. Once armed, they would plunder the banks, set the town on fire, and kill whites; then as many of the rebels as possible would flee the country, perhaps heading to Haiti. For all the careful preparations that went into this effort, the conspiracy never matured into an insurrection because informants notified the authorities, who moved quickly to arrest and interrogate the accused ring leaders. In the resulting trials, thirty-five of those convicted of conspiracy were executed, including Vesey, and thirty-seven others were banished from the state. For good measure, city officials ordered the destruction of the African Methodist church. Resisting white hegemony, even to seek religious liberty in early nineteenth century South Carolina was indeed a dangerous and deadly business.[56]

For Afro-Carolinians religion and freedom had an important symbiotic relationship. They often used religion and the church to create psychological living space. That space could expand dramatically if Christian instruction provided access to literacy, as it sometimes did. Christian doctrine became a yardstick by which the behavior of the master class could be judged and condemned. Correspondingly—when measured against that same moral standard—the oppressed could build their self-esteem. The evangelical denominations were especially important, particularly the Baptists and Methodists, as their worship styles and more democratic ethos were particularly appealing. These denominations also gave black Carolinians greater opportunity to exercise leadership roles than in other churches.

From the beginning of their exposure to Christianity, there were those Afro-Carolinians who recognized the revolutionary potential contained in the faith. The entreaties Catholic authorities in Florida made toward Protestant slaves in South Carolina may have been an attempt to capitalize on that potential. There were those such as Denmark Vesey who hoped to use church structure and theology to obtain physical freedom and were even willing to embraced insurrection to achieve this end. Sometimes important Christian tenets were joined with African spiritual notions, as the actions of the Stono rebels suggest and those of Gullah Jack clearly reveal. These examples suggest strongly that, while African people were becoming Christianized, the brand of Christianity they practiced could probably best be described as Afro-Christianity because it contained substantial traditional African elements.[57] The adaptation of Christianity to an African cultural framework was another means by which Afro-Carolinians attempted to assert control over their own psychological world. By the early 1820s, however, the majority of black southerners were still without regular access to Christian instruction and were still outside the framework of the institutional church. New more extensive efforts were undertaken in the 1830s to evangelize the slaves but their artfulness in turning the Christian message to their own purposes remained a source of serious concern.[58]

After the insurrectionary scare of 1822, heightened fears led to a host of new restrictions on free black life. As both the African Methodist church and the Vesey plot were predicated on their leaders' contacts with the North or the Caribbean, one of the new security measures was designed to reduce the potential for these and other such dangerous associations. In December 1822, South Carolina became the first state to pass a Negro seaman act; over time similar laws became widespread throughout the coastal southern states. South Carolina's law required that free blacks employed on out-of-state and foreign vessels be incarcerated in the local jail while their ships remained in port. The costs of the imprisonment were to be borne by the ship captain and, if they were not paid, a detainee could be sold as a slave. African American seamen were imprisoned immediately, and state courts were unsympathetic. In 1823, when a federal circuit court judged the law unconstitutional as a violation of the commerce clause and in contravention of at least one commercial convention, South Carolina officials ignored the decision and continued to enforce the measure.[59]

The Negro seaman act raised the ire of northern states, but the stakes were even higher when foreign nationals were arrested. On several occasions during the antebellum years, Britain lodged diplomatic complaints with American secretaries of state against the incarceration of its black citizens in South Carolina, but to no avail. When in 1824 Secretary of State John Quincy Adams personally urged South Carolina governor John Wilson to abide by the recent federal-court decision, the governor refused. His rationale was "if an appeal to . . . the right of self-government be disregarded . . . there would be more glory in forming a rampart with our bodies . . . than to be the victims of a successful rebellion, or the slaves of a great consolidated Government." Likewise, the state Senate resolved that the right of protection against slave insurrections was "paramount to all Laws, all Treaties, [and] all Constitutions."[60] These portentous words would be echoed throughout the antebellum years and ultimately led the South to secede from the Union, with South Carolina in the lead. Their genesis can in part be found in the dogged Afro-Carolinian quest for religious freedom. The greatest achievement of that long and arduous struggle was the decision made by black Methodists in Charleston to create a New Zion where they could worship. In the early nineteenth century the results were temporary and limited, but they nevertheless contributed to the onset of a four-year civil war that brought Afro-Carolinians both spiritual and physical emancipation.

Notes

1. Walter Edgar, *South Carolina: A History* (Columbia: University of South Carolina Press, 1998), 43.

2. A. Leon Higginbotham Jr., *In the Matter of Color: Race & the American Legal Process, The Colonial Period* (New York: Oxford University Press, 1978), 36–37, 163.

3. Quoted in Peter Wood, *Black Majority: Negroes in Colonial South Carolina from 1670 through the Stono Rebellion* (New York: Knopf, 1974), 75, 132;

4. Philip Curtin, *The Atlantic Slave Trade: A Census* (Madison: University of Wisconsin Press, 1969), 219; Philip Morgan, *Slave Counterpoint : Black Culture in the Eighteenth-Century Chesapeake & Lowcountry* (Chapel Hill: University of North Carolina Press, 1998), 39–40, 42; Wood, *Black Majority*, 149; Henry Melchior Muhlenberg, *The Journals of Henry Melchior Muhlenberg*, 3 vols. (Philadelphia: Evangelical Lutheran Ministerium and Muhlenberg Press, 1942), 1:58.

5. Higginbotham, *In the Matter of Color*, 159–60.

6. William W. Freehling, *Prelude to Civil War: The Nullification Controversy in South Carolina, 1816–1836* (New York: Harper Torchbooks, 1966), 11–12, 18.

7. Morgan, *Slave Counterpoint*, 61; Freehling, *Prelude to Civil War*, 11.

8. Faith Vibert, "The Society for the Propagation of the Gospel in Foreign Parts: Its Work for the Negroes in North America Before 1783," *Journal of Negro History* 25 (April 1933): 171, 173.

9. David J. McCord, *The Statutes At Large of South Carolina*, vol. 7 (Columbia: A. S. Johnston, 1840), 343; Higginbotham, *In the Matter of Color*, 169.

10. Sylvia Frey and Betty Wood, *Come Shouting to Zion: African American Protestantism in the American South and British Caribbean to 1830* (Chapel Hill: University of North Carolina Press, 1998), 65–66; McCord, *The Statutes at Large of South Carolina*, VII: 364–65.

11. Frank J. Klingberg, ed., *The Carolina Chronicle of Dr. Francis Le Jau 1706–1717* (Berkeley: University of California Press, 1956), 105; Klingberg, *Carolina Chronicle: The Papers of Commissary Gideon Johnston 1707–1716* (Berkeley: University of California Press, 1946), 11.

12. Klingberg, ed., *Chronicle of Dr. Francis Le Jau*, 10; Muhlenberg, *Journals of Henry Melchior Muhlenberg*, 2:638.

13. Klingberg, ed., *Chronicle of Dr. Francis Le Jau*, 70; Muhlenberg, *Journals of Henry Melchior Muhlenberg*, 1:58.

14. Robert Olwell, *Masters, Slaves and Subjects: the Culture of Power in the South Carolina Low Country 1740–1790* (Ithaca, N.Y.: Cornell University, 1998), 117–19, 125.

15. Wood, *Black Majority*, chapters 9 and 11.

16. J. H. Easterby, ed., *Journal of the Commons House of Assembly March 26, 1741–December 1, 1741* (Columbia: Historical Commission of South Carolina, 1953), 80–82; "William Dunlop's Mission to St. Augustine in 1688," *South Carolina Historical and Genealogical Magazine* 34 (January 1933): 2, 22, 24–27.

17. J. H. Easterby, ed., *Journal of the Commons House of Assembly November 10, 1736–June 7, 1739* (Columbia: Historical Commission of South Carolina, 1951), 1:596; Edgar, *A History of South Carolina*, 73.

18. Wood, *Black Majority*, 314–25; Allen D. Candler, comp., *The Colonial Records of the State of Georgia: Original Papers, Correspondence, Trustees, General Oglethorpe and Others 1737–1740* (Atlanta: Charles Byrd, State Printer, 1913), XXII, pt. 2: 233–34; J. H. Easterby, ed., *Journal of the Commons House of Assembly March 26, 1741–December 1, 1741* (Columbia: Historical Commission of South Carolina, 1953), 83–84.

19. Candler, comp., *The Colonial Records of the State of Georgia*, XXII, pt. 2: 233–34.

20. Daniel Littlefield, *Rice and Slaves: Ethnicity and the Slave Trade in Colonial South Carolina* (Urbana: University of Illinois Press, 1991), 113; Wood, *Black Majority*, 340–41.

21. John K. Thornton, "African Dimensions of the Stono Rebellion," *American Historical Review* 96 (October 1991): 1103–1108.

22. Klingberg, ed., *Chronicle of Dr. Francis Le Jau*, 77;

23. Candler, comp., *The Colonial Records of the State of Georgia*, XXII, pt. 2: 233–35; Wood, *Black Majority*, 316; Sterling Stuckey, *Slave Culture: Nationalist Theory & the Foundations of Black America* (New York: Oxford University Press, 1987), 20, 365.

24. Candler, comp., *The Colonial Records of the State of Georgia*, XXII, pt. 2: 234–35; Wood, *Black Majority*, 318; Edgar, *South Carolina: A History*, 75.

25. One of the reasons Peter Wood contends that Sunday, September 9, was chosen to begin the Stono Rebellion, is because it was a date before the planters would become better armed as required by the new law. Mark Smith has shown the pertinence of the African background for understanding the timing of the revolt. In Catholic-influenced Kongo, Saturdays were dedicated to St. Mary and Saturday, September 8, was specifically "the day of Nativity of the Virgin Mary" in the Catholic world. Thus, according to Smith, the choice of that particular weekend was designed to imbue the rebels' cause with Mary's special protective power. See Wood, *Black Majority*, 312–14, and Mark Smith, "Remembering Mary, Shaping Revolt: Reconsidering the Stono Rebellion," *Journal of Southern History* 67 (August 2001): 521–28.

26. Wood, *Black Majority*, 313; Edgar, *South Carolina: A History*, 76; Joseph Brevard, *An Alphabetical Digest of the Public Statute Law of South Carolina*, 3 vols. (Charleston: John Hoff, 1814), 2:229–44; Deena Epstein, *Sinful Tunes and Spirituals: Black Folk Music to the Civil War* (Urbana: University of Illinois Press, 1977), 59.

27. Robert M. Weir, *Colonial South Carolina: A History* (Millwood, N.Y.: KTO Press. 1983), 220–21; David T. Morgan, "The Great Awakening in South Carolina 1740–1775," *South Atlantic Quarterly* 70 (Autumn 1971): 596–97, 601; George Whitefield, *George Whitefield's Journals (1737–1741) To Which Is Prefixed His "Short Account" (1746) and "Further Account" (1747)* (London, 1756; reprint, Gainesville: Scholars' Facsimiles and Reprints, 1969), 387; Harvey H. Jackson, "Hugh Bryan and the Evangelical Movement in Colonial South Carolina," *William and Mary Quarterly* third series 43 (October 1986): 600, 605; Frey and Wood, *Come Shouting to Zion*, 88–90.

28. Alan Gallay, *The Formation of a Planter Elite: Jonathan Bryan and the Southern Colonial* Frontier (Athens: University of Georgia Press, 1989), 33–35; George F. Jones, "John Martin Boltzius' Trip to Charleston, October 1742," *South Carolina Historical Magazine* 82 (April 1981): 102; *South Carolina Gazette*, January 1–8, 1741; *Living Christianity Delineated, in the Diaries and Letters of Two Eminently Pious Persons lately deceased; Viz. Mr. Hugh Bryan, and Mrs. Mary Hutson, Both of South-Carolina* (London: J. Buckland, 1760), 38; Jackson, "Hugh Bryan," 605.

29. Easterby, ed., *Journal of the Commons House of Assembly May 18, 1741–July 10, 1742*, 3:388.

30. *South Carolina Gazette*, January 1–8, 1741; Jackson, "Hugh Bryan," 598–99.

31. *Living Christianity Delineated*, 38, 54; Easterby, ed., *Journal of the Commons House of Assembly May 18, 1742–July 10, 1742* (Columbia: Historical Commission of South Carolina,

1953), 3:388, 405–7; Elise Pinckney, ed., *The Letterbook of Eliza Lucas Pinckney 1739–1762* (Chapel Hill: University of North Carolina Press, 1972), 30; Gallay, *Formation of a Planter Elite*, 39, 55.

32. *South Carolina Gazette,* postscript to February 27–March 6, 1741; *South Carolina Gazette,* March 20–27, 1742; Jackson, "Hugh Ryan," 610.

33. Weir, *Colonial South Carolina,* 238.

34. *South Carolina Gazette,* April 10–17, 1742;

35. *South Carolina Gazette,* April 17–24, 1742; Gallay, *Formation of a Planter Elite,* 164.

36. Margaret W. Creel, *"A Peculiar People": Slave Religion and Community-Culture Among the Gullahs* (New York: New York University Press, 1988), 133–35; Janet Cornelius, *Slave Missions and the Black Church in the Antebellum South* (Columbia: University of South Carolina Press, 1999), 26; Frey and Wood, *Come Shouting to Zion,* 116–17.

37. Creel, *Peculiar People,* 134.

38. Frey and Wood, *Come Shouting to Zion,* 112–13.

39. Dee E. Andrews, *The Methodists and Revolutionary America, 1760–1800: The Shaping of an Evangelical Culture* (Princeton, N.J.: Princeton University Press, 2000), 62–67; A. M. Chreitzberg, *Early Methodism in the Carolinas* (Nashville: Publishing House of the Methodist Episcopal Church South, 1897), 39; *The Churches of Charleston and the Lowcountry* (Columbia: University of South Carolina Press, 1994), 6.

40. Marina Wikramanayake, *A World in Shadow: the Free Black in Antebellum South Carolina* (Columbia: University of South Carolina Press, 1973), 117.

41. Quoted in Andrews, *Methodists and Revolutionary America,* 125–27.

42. W. P. Harrison, *The Gospel Among the Slaves: A Short Account of Missionary Operations Among The African Slaves of the Southern States* (Nashville: Publishing House of the Methodist Episcopal Church South, 1893), 142; Chreitzberg, *Early Methodism,* 78.

43. Within six months the 1785 discipline's antislavery section was suspended and the dispensation of slavery was left to quarterly and annual conferences. The 1804 general conference retracted the earlier directive to petition state legislatures for gradual emancipation laws. Now the Methodist Episcopal Church took the extraordinary step of publishing two disciplines. The one was for Virginia and the northern states contained a section on slavery, and the one for the other southern states excluded the offensive section (Andrews, *Methodists and Revolutionary America,* 126–27).

44. Willliam M. Wightman, *The Life of William Capers D.D.* (Nashville: Publishing House of the Methodist Episcopal Church South, 1896), 138–40.

45. Peter Hinks, *To Awaken My Afflicted Brethren: David Walker and the Problem of Antebellum Slave Resistance* (University Park: Pennsylvania State University Press, 1997), 25–26; Albert D. Betts, *History of South Carolina Methodism* (Columbia: Advocate, 1952), 237–38.

46. Bernard E. Powers Jr., *Black Charlestonians: A Social History, 1822–1885* (Fayetteville: University of Arkansas Press, 1994), 21; Carol V. R. George, *Segregated Sabbaths: Richard Allen and the Rise of Independent Black Churches, 1760–1840* (New York: Oxford University Press, 1973), 55, 86.

47. Betts, *History of South Carolina Methodism,* 237–38; F. A. Mood, *Methodism in Charleston* (Nashville: E. Stevenson & J. E. Evans, 1856), 131–32;

48. Wikramanayake, *World in Shadow,* 124–25.

49. Ibid., 125.

50. Vincent Harding, "Religion and Resistance Among Antebellum Negroes, 1800–1860," in *The Making of Black America: Essays in Negro Life and History*, 2 vols., ed. August Meier and Elliott Rudwick (New York: Atheneum, 1969), 1:184–85; *Charleston Courier*, June 9, 1818; Powers, *Black Charlestonians*, 21.

51. In recent years there has been considerable scholarly attention devoted to the Vesey conspiracy, resulting in the publication of the following books: Douglas R. Egerton, *He Shall Go Out Free: The Lives of Denmark Vesey* (Madison, Wis.: Madison House, 1999); Edward A. Pearson, *Designs Against Charleston: the Trial Record of the Denmark Vesey Slave Conspiracy of 1822* (Chapel Hill: University of North Carolina Press, 1999); and David Robertson, *Denmark Vesey: The Buried History of America's Largest Slave Rebellion and The Man Who Led It* (New York: Knopf, 1999). All these works accept the existence of a conspiracy of slaves to foment rebellion, but in 2001 Michael Johnson touched off an intense scholarly debate when his controversial reinterpretation of the trial record denied the existence of a slave conspiracy. To the contrary, he asserts the only conspiracy that existed was among court officials, who coerced witnesses and falsified the trial record to portray themselves as the most ardent defenders of white supremacy and to quash the criticism of their detractors. See Michael P. Johnson, "Denmark Vesey and His Co-Conspirators" *William and Mary Quarterly*, third series, 58 (October 2001): 915–976. A series of historians respond to the Johnson thesis in a forum published in the *William and Mary Quarterly*, third series, 59 (January 2002): 135–202.

52. Egerton, *He Shall Go Out Free*, 15–26, 68, 77, 82, 98, 112, 124.

53. Ibid., 124; Documents Relative to the Denmark Vesey Insurrection, Document B, South Carolina Department of Archives and History, Columbia.

54. Documents Relative to the Denmark Vesey Insurrection, Document B; Egerton, *He Shall Go Out Free*, 124.

55. Freehling, *Prelude to Civil War*, 11; Documents Relative to the Denmark Vesey Insurrection, Document B.

56. James Hamilton Jr., *An Account of the Late Intended Insurrection Among a Portion of the Blacks of this City Published by the Authority of the Corporation of Charleston*, (Charleston: A. E. Miller. 1822), 17; Documents Relative to the Denmark Vesey Insurrection, Document B; Egerton, *He Shall Go Out Free*, 136, 154.

57. For a significant treatment of the creolized features of antebellum African American spirituality see Sterling Stuckey, *Slave Culture*, chapter 1, and Charles Joyner, *Down by the Riverside: A South Carolina Slave Community* (Urbana: University of Illinois Press, 1884), chapter 5.

58. Albert Raboteau, *Slave Religion: The "Invisible Institution" in the Antebellum South* (New York: Oxford University Press, 1980), 149–50; Cornelius, *Slave Missions and the Black Church*, 91–96.

59. Powers, *Black Charlestonians*, 32. The Vesey leaders attempted to communicate with the Haitian government through sailors en route to that destination. See Documents Relative to the Denmark Vesey Insurrection, Document B, and Philip M. Hamer, "Great Britain, the United States, and the Negro Seamen Acts, 1822–1848," *Journal of Southern History* 1 (February 1935): 3–6.

60. Hamer, "Great Britain, the United States, and the Negro Seamen Acts," 7–12.

Religious Tolerance and the Growth of the Evangelical Ethos in South Carolina

Orville Vernon Burton and David Herr

BRITISH INTEREST IN THE CAROLINA COLONY began as a strategic matter. Thomas Lowndes, when writing to the Lords of Trade about the Carolinas' potential for the Crown, called attention to their value, "South Carolina is situate between the French on the Messissippi and the Spaniards in Florida and in the Neighbourhood of Cuba, a very strong Spanish settlement and in case of a Rupture with France or Spain and an Invasion from either must in the Condition it was in by the Disunion of the Proprietors and the Animosities between the Proprietors and Inhabitants have inevitably faln a prey, unless the British Nation had at very great expense rescued the Colony, which the immediate Protection of the Crown may in a great measure be made able to defend itself upon all Occasions and of eminent use not only to all the British settlements in America, but to the Mother-Country."[1]

Wanting to attract loyal English settlers, Anthony Ashley Cooper, Lord Ashley (later Earl of Shaftesbury), and his personal secretary, John Locke, drafted five versions of the Fundamental Constitutions of Carolina. The document emerged from the utopian influences of the time, such as James Harrington's *Oceana* (1656). While Carolina settlers ultimately rejected the Constitutions, certain ideas in them made their way into colonial law. One important carryover West Indian slaveholders found attractive was the provision granting the property owner "absolute power and authority over his negro slaves."[2] Ashley and Locke recognized the colony's offering of available land and secure slavery would prove appealing.

Another portion of the Fundamental Constitutions the colony adopted was religious freedom. Although the Lords Proprietors made the Church of England the official church of the colony, they emphasized tolerance of other religious expression. On one occasion the South Carolina Commons House of Assembly sought the ouster of religious Dissenters from its ranks before calmer thinking encouraged them to repeal the measure. The coexistence among the Anglican majority and other religions could create tension, but colonial leaders recognized the concession aided the colony's growth and prosperity.

South Carolina law provided religious freedom to almost everyone who believed in God in some general sense. Any seven individuals could organize a church and expect protection from harassment in the practice of their faith: "No person whatsoever shall disturb, molest, or persecute another for his speculative opinions in Religion, or his way of worship." The promise of religious toleration attracted a wide variety of Anglican Dissenters, Calvinists from New England, Ireland, and Scotland, and French Huguenots in the years following Louis XIV's Protestant suppression. Jews were welcome, but not Roman Catholics, in keeping with English political sentiment.[3] With no constitutional requirement of an oath in legal matters—simply an affirmation—Quakers felt welcome and settled in Kershaw, Laurens, Newberry, and Union counties. An early South Carolina governor, John Archdale (1695), was Quaker. By 1710 Quakers comprised 2.5 percent of those South Carolinians identified by religious belief.[4]

The western region of the state proved attractive to Germans and Scotch Irish. The diminishment of the Native American population created affordable land in the upcountry. Migration from the crowded Northeast fueled western growth, with Pennsylvania and New England immigrants arriving in both North and South Carolina. Protestants, particularly Presbyterians, Methodists, and Baptists, settled the rural countryside. While Baptists chose preachers from their congregants and eschewed formal training, Methodists and Presbyterians required educated clergy and found that their relative isolation frequently precluded a permanent minister. Even though all three denominations competed for congregants, the members of different rural churches often united and welcomed itinerant ministers regardless of their affiliation. With the exception of urban areas, the need for an official religious presence persisted throughout the state during the eighteenth century. Although the Church of England desired to maintain its majority standing in the colonies, its colonial emissaries did not capitalize on the need for rural ministers. The church often worked against its own interests when it sent English pastors on temporary assignments to minister across huge territories with no aid.

Rev. John Boyd witnessed weak support for the Anglican Church. When touring the backcountry, Boyd wrote that with the lack of regular clergy "many of the people are drawn away by Presbyterian anabaptists or other Dissenting Teachers, many of their children unbaptised & the administration of the Sacrament of the Lords Supper wholly neglected."[5] Another Anglican minister in the Carolinas remarked, "I think myself conscience bound to declare my mind that any Clergyman that has a mind to come thither . . . will find a lawless people, a scattered people, no glebe, no parsonage to receive him."[6]

Alexander Garden was responsible for managing the Anglican effort in the Carolinas. Assigned by the bishop of London, Garden was commissary for the Carolinas, a station created to compensate for the lack of a colonial episcopate. His ministers came from the Society for the Propagation of the Gospel in Foreign Parts; many of them appeared singularly ill suited for their responsibilities. One of Garden's concerns in the early fall of 1737 was the Reverend Boyd, who appeared to be at war with his local congregation. Boyd sought order and unquestioning support. The laity desired conformity from the outsider and provided financial support grudgingly. Congregants tormented Boyd by withholding pay or paying in barter. On one occasion Boyd claimed they provided him with spoiled rice. They protested his decisions and refused to cooperate with his plans for the church. Boyd responded in kind, exerting a minimal effort while complaining regularly. More appalling to Garden than the disagreements was Boyd's drinking problem. In his condemnation of Boyd to the bishop of London, Garden wrote, "This very missionary is one of the vilest and most scandalous persons in government. I gave you some hints of his Idleness and inclination to drunkeness . . . but since that time . . . on a Sunday, this spring, at noon day he was seen by many persons lying dead drunk (& fast asleep) on the great road to Virginia, with his horses bridle tied to his leg."[7]

Such poor behavior was not limited to the Anglicans. Colonial religious sentiment appeared in serious decline to ministers of different denominations. This changed with George Whitefield's arrival and the Great Awakening. This religious revival of 1739–41, largely inspired in South Carolina by Whitefield, helped the birth of an evangelical ethos in the American colonies, South and North. Whitefield called for individual conversion through a personal relationship with God. When Whitefield visited the colonies in 1738 and again in 1740, he attracted fervent and devoted followers, particularly in Charleston.[8] His preaching style included dramatic gestures and gruesome depictions of hell fire and damnation. Many in the staid Church of England did not approve, however, and on Whitefield's second visit to Charleston, the Anglican Church, through Alexander Garden, banned this sought-after revivalist from its pulpits. He then preached at non-Anglican churches and outdoors in tents.[9]

While some, such as Hugh Bryan, sought rapprochement between Whitefield and the Church of England, the evangelical tenets Whitefield espoused threatened the provincial gentry.[10] Official Anglican rejection of this new, emotional approach meant that people who were unwilling to press for internal change had to consider other denominations for their newly "awakened" religious feelings. The Church of England no longer met their needs. The Anglicans' failure to harness evangelicalism sealed their marginalization in South Carolina, particularly in the backcountry. Anglican doctrine and religious ritual faired poorly in frontier conditions. A religious ethos, however, permeated the culture as Baptists, Methodists, and Presbyterians settled. These evangelical Protestant denominations, especially the Baptists, attracted people needing spiritual rejuvenation and emotional religious experiences.

Evangelicalism emphasizes the authority of the Gospels and the doctrine that salvation comes from faith and grace rather than good works alone. In a cultural context it involves zealous testimony and a pious lifestyle as part of everyday life. According to Robert Calhoon, as evangelicalism in the new United States struggled with issues of freedom, community, and truth, it brought into religious thought a consciousness and an individualism that has affected Western civilization.[11] This essay addresses the growth of the evangelical ethos in South Carolina and the struggle it precipitated between the freedom to worship without harassment versus the freedom to own slaves without fear of community discord.

The conversion experience brought believers together in fellowship before God. Conversion also brought a desire for more converts. The evangelical ethos grew as camp meetings and revivals brought in new adherents, and circuit-riding itinerant preachers spread the message to the hinterlands. The preachers' hard work leading scores of small awakenings was the most effective religious force in the state.[12] Yet this growth required more structure and formalization—and compromise. From separation as a sect, evangelical Protestantism became more acceptable to the dominant culture. Significant hurdles to such change included the politically sensitive issues of slavery and gender. One of the first impulses in evangelical outreach was converting enslaved African Americans. Slaves embraced evangelicalism, and the creation of missions to South Carolina's black majority helped to spread the evangelical ethos. This, however, happened well within the realm of proslavery. With its stance on slavery and patriarchy eventually placed safely within the limits of genteel society, evangelicalism gained respectability in the dominant culture.

The evangelical experience began with conversion. Conversion marked a leap into the abyss, but, when successful, the convert found the everlasting support of God through a personal relationship. A person undergoing conversion engaged in a battle to relinquish free will, replacing it with submission and trust in the will of God. The physical manifestation of those battles was the hallmark of evangelical revivals. People cried uncontrollably or rolled about the floor, shaking. One person recollected a two-week meeting at which "most of the congregation were affected to tears, from very old men to young men and boys. From 20 to 30 or 40 left their seats at the close of each days service and went to the ministrating brethren, requesting them to pray for their salvation."[13] Outward displays reflected passionate internal struggles. For some evangelicals an easy conversion was no conversion at all. Converts had to break down personal identity and allow God to reconstitute them as divine vessels.

Much of evangelicalism was peculiar to those used to Anglican formalism. Conversion, emotional outcries, full immersion for baptism, and the laying on of hands were disturbing, strange behaviors to outsiders. Also disturbing was belief in the equality of the conversion experience. Conversion placed the individual in God's care, and this protection came before any other. Neither gender nor servitude changed this protection. Historian Susan Juster has studied conversion narratives and found them to be "a cultural mirror" or social commentary. She argues that male and female approaches to personal revelation were different but that the result invariably was gender neutral, a leveling of moral agency and spiritual potency.[14] Such equality fit poorly in slave society. Conversion could provide women an escape from male oppression. White and black women (as well as male slaves) spoke out about their liberating religious experiences, sometimes even in church; white women also confided their thoughts to diaries and prayer books.

The wider society looked askance at these ideas and practices. Evangelicals seemed "on the fringes of polite society as disturbers of accepted norms of religious decorum."[15] Hard work by evangelical clergy, combined with the fierce dedication of converts, helped such practices survive. Camp meetings and revivals took up Whitefield's outdoor tradition and institutionalized it. Suffering from a minister shortage, South Carolinians embraced these large gatherings, where a great deal of religious experience was packed into the engagements. As revival waves washed over nineteenth-century South Carolina, evangelical denominations grew. During the early republic years after 1776, evangelicalism spread to the upcountry. The Christian message of redemption in combination with a combative anti-authoritarianism appealed to rugged frontier people. Moreover, in the rough upcountry, where death was always close, people were hungry for spiritual meaning.

Religious work in the rural regions of South Carolina was challenging. John Wesley, an associate of Whitefield's, and Bishop Francis Asbury originated the idea of the itinerant preacher as Methodist circuit riders. Itinerants filled a clerical void and encouraged lay leaders to hold the community together in faith between ministerial visits. Both Methodists and Baptists tapped young white males to lead their call into the wilderness. Youth were attracted to the energy of evangelicalism. Methodist minister Philip Gatch recalled that three of his grandsons liked to sing and pray along the lines of a revival, mimicking the movements and rhythms of the preaching style. Although some had misgivings about their young converts, it became a mark of evangelicals to identify earnest young talent among congregations. Methodist preacher and South Carolinian James Jenkins boasted about bringing many children to their conversion, none of whom was "more than fourteen years old." Actively seeking youth, Jenkins recognized the infectious ability of young men and women to bring their friends into the church. At one point he targeted a leader among the boys, "sort of the captain among them," planning that, "if we could catch him, we should get all the company." Although there were young women who stood out through their religious devotion, young men were the focus because they could accept the mantle of an itinerant.[16] A "boy preacher" was a sensation, drawing a crowd to a religious gathering. Young preachers selected from their congregations and sent where there was a call, strenuously sought to represent well their home churches. The itinerants projected uncompromising zeal and steadfast faith. As members of the most privileged gender and race they went a long way toward making the evangelical ethos an integral part of South Carolina culture.

Evangelical itinerants ventured into the vast rural hinterland and preached a "warm, uncomplicated, optimistic theology"; the people responded with "an outpouring of allegiance."[17] Itinerants appreciated the laity, and the combination of lay desire and ministerial enthusiasm made Methodists the largest South Carolina denomination. In the upcountry, Methodists and Baptists shared the top spot. Itinerant preachers encouraged denominational tolerance because they were too few and rural populations too dispersed for demanding strict allegiances. Another indication of this tolerance was the "Fifth Sunday Union Meeting." In any month in which a fifth Sunday occurred, members of various congregations met together in worship and in meetings to discuss religious and secular issues. While congregants and ministers had occasions to compete, the broader religious community sought accord.[18]

Tolerance among white denominations was one thing; converting enslaved African Americans was quite another. Yet, just as the growth of the evangelical ethos in South Carolina and the South in general relied on new converts, it especially relied on the enslaved population of African Americans. Evangelicals wanted to reach out to slaves and free blacks in the competition for souls, but planters opposed these efforts, fearing instability. When in 1809 the South Carolina Methodist Episcopal Church commissioned James Mallard and James Glenn to convert the state's African Americans, planter resistance likely led the men to resign their commissions shortly after beginning. Francis Asbury wrote, "We are defrauded of great numbers by the pains that are taken to keep the blacks from us. . . . their masters are afraid of the influence of our principles."[19]

Evangelical theology's egalitarian leanings threatened wealthy planters as converts struggled with the inconsistency of slavery and Christianity in the same community. Some Presbyterian clergymen spoke out against slavery, and early Separatist Baptists definitely gave slave owners reason to fear. Daniel Marshall, a Separate minister, encouraged members of the Horn's Creek and Stevens Creek churches in Edgefield District to manumit their slaves. One slave owner, who became the minister at Stevens Creek, tried as late as 1815 to free his slaves. Another, Benjamin Ryan, petitioned the legislature repeatedly during the late eighteenth century for permission to free his slaves, and his brother John Ryan, continued the failed effort into the 1820s.[20] Methodist leaders such as Francis Asbury were adamant in their opposition to slavery, and Methodist clergy were not to own slaves. The Methodists had declared in 1784 that slave ownership was a serious offense, that "LIBERTY is the birthright of mankind."[21] Slave owners and enslaved knew the Methodist reputation for antislavery principles. Gabriel Prosser ordered Methodists spared during the 1800 Virginia uprising, and Denmark Vesey suggested a connection between insurrection and Methodists in his 1822 plans. Early Methodist antislavery convictions would erode, but so did proslavery resistance to allowing religion among slaves.

Wanting to avoid conflict with the ruling slaveholders, yet wanting more Christian converts, Presbyterian minister and slave owner Charles Colcock Jones proposed slave owners use Christianity to preach submission. Renowned Baptist minister Richard Furman was also careful to suggest that proper religious instruction for slaves would pose no threat to white South Carolinians. With such reassurances as Furman's and to refute growing northern abolitionist sentiments, slave owners eventually acceded to mission work among their slaves. One slave owner strove to maintain (but could not always manage), "Their religious training must be of the moderate sort, avoiding all excitements." In 1829 two South Carolina planters (Episcopalians) requested a full-time Methodist preacher be assigned the religious care of their slaves. When Charles Cotesworth Pinckney addressed the South Carolina Agricultural Society, he announced, "Every denomination of Christian teachers are willing and ready to send *white Southern* Missionaries to the plantations." In the 1830s and 1840s white Christians petitioned the General Assembly for permission to teach their slaves how to read the Bible.[22] By 1845 South Carolina had the largest missionary effort to the slaves, the Methodists boasting twenty-two missionaries assigned to slaves and more than eight thousand black members.[23] All denominations created, if they had not already, a special second-class status for black congregants. As slave missions grew, bondspeople grasped and expanded the evangelical outlook.

Religious fervor among African Americans in upcountry Edgefield had a tradition dating back to the colonial period. The first independent black church, Silver Bluff Baptist Church, was founded on George Galphin's plantation in the old Edgefield District. This church lasted until the Revolution, when Galphin fled the area and many slaves left for freedom in Sierra Leone and later Jamaica. After the Revolutionary War local black preachers continued to manage congregations in the area. Iveson Brookes used the example of these independent churches as a point of pride when writing in defense of slavery.[24]

Whites in South Carolina were determined that religion be used to keep the enslaved in their place without complaint. Certainly enslaved people did not miss the none-too-subtle white effort to bend religion into a form of social control. Former slave Joe McCormick remembered how white ministers were always preaching that slaves should "be good Negroes and mind their master." Another former slave from the upcountry recalled, "I 'member his tex'—'Obey! Be subdued to yo' marster and yo' Misses.'"[25] Yet, the effectiveness of the message was dubious. Even as whites tried to maintain control over the religious message, the listeners "overtly, covertly, and even intuitively fought to shape it themselves."[26]

Slave conversion to Christianity had multidimensional aspects. Christianity involved much more than submission; the Bible also had revolutionary aspects, a favorite was the story of Moses and his demand of freedom for God's people enslaved in Egypt. Evangelical emphasis on personal salvation and the Christian theology of equality before God were also appealing. Moreover, when Africans came to Christianity, they brought with them African religious beliefs. Historians Sylvia Frey and Betty Wood argue evangelicalism's ethos of equality and integration were consonant with African values.[27] Evangelical emphasis on oral communication with the supernatural strongly aligned with African traditions. Throughout slavery African Americans developed a unique Christianity from a variety of sources, embracing what they found beneficial and rejecting what they did not. Many slaves created syncretic religions, merging their traditions with new choices and forging an African American religious culture.

While African American evangelicalism emphasized creative expression, white evangelicals did not. They also rejected frivolous amusement, avoiding dances, races, and other social activities common among Southerners. They saw their gatherings as a refuge from a sinful world and advocated separation from worldly society. The Separate Baptists in upcountry Edgefield serve as an example. Like most of the South in the nineteenth century, South Carolina was a land of farms and plantations, and within this rural area the village of Edgefield was the seat of power. In the complex and variegated lives of antebellum South Carolinians, Edgefield was a political, social, judicial, and religious junction. Settled in the 1740s, made the county seat in 1791, and incorporated in 1830, Edgefield village by the 1850s had grocery stores, a druggist, some manufacturing, hotels, "four preachers, twelve lawyers . . . four doctors, one dentist, four teachers," as well as other features of a robust nineteenth-century county seat. The courthouse stood at the highest point in the town, a visible sign of legal authority, and served as one side of the town square, emphasizing its primacy in communal affairs. The building was truly a civic center, holding religious services, Masonic meetings, and music recitals, along with political meetings and court proceedings. Below the town square, Trinity Episcopal Church looked down on Village Baptist Church, signifying the position of Trinity as the church of the elite, the church where financially successful Baptists would migrate, often holding dual memberships. Symbols of spiritual authority, these two churches held the religious seats of power and influence.[28]

Edgefield's Separate Baptists grew out of George Whitefield's evangelism and, more directly, from a congregation in North Carolina, that of Shubal Stearns's Sandy Creek Meeting. Separate Baptists favored an emotional, unsophisticated outlook. More open to women in positions of responsibility and more skeptical of slavery, they were unenthusiastic about formally trained clergy. Believing that a person walked behind the plow for six days and that God inspired his sermon on the Sabbath, these early Separate Baptists saw no need for either a regular or a trained clergy. Sometimes the thoughts "sent by God," however, ran counter to the interest of the planter class. Episcopalians and Regular Baptists (who did not fully embrace the Great Awakening and the doctrine of new birth) were wont to find that the Separates were "a disorderly sect . . . permitting every ignorant man to preach that chose, and that they encouraged noise and confusion in their meetings."[29]

Disorder and disturbing the peace became an important cause for concern in a society heavily dependent on strict social order to enforce slavery. As cotton cultivation grew after the perfection of the cotton gin in 1793, so did slavery. In 1790 the African American population in upcountry Edgefield County was 3,684; in 1820 it was 12,255. Ten years later African Americans outnumbered whites. Slave society had spread to the upcountry, and a society based on slavery could not tolerate religious theology that questioned bondage. It became paramount that religion not question authority and promote peace and safety. Insurrection by Denmark Vesey in Charleston, the rise of cotton, and the growing attacks of northern abolitionists all but ended any outward discussion of the slavery question in the South. No hindrance to slavery was allowed. The forces supporting slavery feared unrest and opposed religious theology that advocated the end of slavery. The Nullification Crisis of 1832 further hardened the proslavery position of the South Carolina elite. Stephanie McCurry found that the South Carolina lowcountry experienced a major revival during the

Nullification Crisis, with many elite planters embracing evangelicalism.[30] This was also true in the upcountry. With elite support, the evangelicalism of the yeomen and poor reached a broader segment of the society and moved from margin to center of southern culture, but not without significant change.

The Nullification period revivals reveal how proslavery ideology and evangelicalism merged. White religious leaders advocated a firm proslavery stance, a "holier-than-thou" counterattack against abolitionist condemnation, and less tolerance for groups opposed to slavery.[31] Already by the early 1800s, the Methodist denomination had withdrawn its official denunciation of slavery, and staunchly antislavery clergymen had moved north. By this time also many Quakers had left the state because they could not tolerate South Carolina's support of slavery. Quakers had done little to encourage outreach or new converts, so their numbers had not grown in the state. By 1822 the very few remaining Quakers in Newberry no longer held meetings.[32] Even the old Anglican prohibition against Catholics was overlooked as long as they did not oppose slavery. When Catholic bishop John England came to Charleston in 1820, he passed muster with slaveholders by accepting, if not really approving, slavery, noting that many of his Irish congregants were treated worse than slaves. By the 1860s in upcountry Edgefield, Catholics, though few in number, were part of the community. When they needed help building a Catholic church, people of all denominations chipped in. Father Bermingham commented in his diary that the construction was "truly a community project," and he thanked "all classes and religious denominations."[33]

During the 1820s, Richard Furman published what many considered the definitive proslavery position. One reason for the 1826 founding of Furman Academy, later Furman University, was to indoctrinate the Separate Baptists in "right" religious thinking, and that included the now sanctioned status of slavery.[34]

Evangelicalism, however, did not simply abandon principles of antislavery. The complexity of southern religious life juxtaposed conflicting sentiments from the start of the South Carolina colony, and the struggle continued throughout its antebellum history. Religious leaders throughout the South and the North faced a similar theological contradiction. Evangelical leaders in South Carolina who opposed slavery, especially the Methodists, concluded that a fight to abolish slavery was fruitless, while mission work among slaves and slaveholders was an attainable goal. Although proslavery ideology dominated antebellum culture, South Carolina never wholly eradicated evangelical abolitionist thinking.[35]

Evangelical change was present from the beginning; proselytizing demanded it. Clergy wanted converts, and, as nineteenth-century revivalism brought thousands of new converts into churches, congregations altered things. Protestant evangelicalism began with an emphasis on personal conversion, and congregations served as refuge from a sinful world. The success of revivals and camp meetings, however, moved the evangelical focus to increasing membership. Churches strengthened their organizational structure, partly to maintain control over the dramatic emotional overtone conversion could involve and to accommodate a more diverse membership. Increased rosters brought more money. Bible organizations and reading groups, Sunday schools, class meetings, religious almanacs and other publications, temperance societies, and missionary work all grew from increased fiscal strength.

With independence from England, South Carolina removed the Anglican Church as the official church of the state. After a close but unsuccessful attempt to have a limited sort of established church, "the question of disestablishment passed unanimously."[36] Now the state, still requiring moral virtue among its citizens, turned to evangelical denominations. The churches saw this as their opportunity to seek converts and to infuse society with piety and discipline. Evangelical churches flourished. In every community the evangelical church came to represent respectability, and with that came a stake in the preservation of slavery.[37]

Growth and formalization was a double-edged sword. On the one hand early evangelicals despised outward displays of power and authority. The very nature of the open, egalitarian practice stressed an individual relationship with God that did not require a more formal structure. On the other hand, church growth required better organization and funding if churches wanted to keep the converts made at camp meetings. McCurry found that evangelicalism, while continuing to appeal primarily to "the socially marginal and the politically disfranchised, particularly to women and slaves," gained adherents among white male planters and yeomen.[38] Absorption into the center of southern culture meant melding religious impulse with elite white values.[39] These white males were not egalitarian. In the South Carolina upcountry, particularly among the very influential Baptists, organizational formalization was a process that diminished individualism and egalitarianism, putting women back in their place and eliminating the strong antislavery sentiment among Separate Baptists.

After many joint conferences the Regulars and Separates merged in the early nineteenth century, although certain Separate ideals, both those Regulars admired and those they did not, remained. As late as the 1840s, the upcountry Bethel Baptist Association posed the moral question of whether Christians could own slaves and found they could not answer it. The members also sanctioned slave families and recommended that "Christian masters use utmost care to prevent . . . separation" of slave families. Asked if slave owners were justified in whipping slaves, the association responded that church discipline could fall on those who abused their position over slaves, but whipping was permissible in certain circumstances.[40] Clearly, matters of conscience remained, but formalized proceedings served as an effective outlet without posing serious problems to the dominant culture. As the evangelical ethos came to be the popular faith, it relied more on the status quo than on diversity and tolerance. Evangelicals increasingly stayed away from controversy and no longer questioned larger societal problems, instead concentrating on how an individual or family could become more pious.

The formalization of evangelical practices, a means to foster church growth, was also a form of social control. The initial, uncontrolled character of mass conversions in camp meetings threatened structure, and preachers wanted to channel that religious energy. Modifying social behavior became important in converting, and church membership stressed responsibility. Church discipline was based on the evangelical sense of community and on "a desire to create a culture rooted in otherworldly compassion."[41] Churches positioned themselves to be the arbiters of social discord. Congregations forbade drinking, dancing, illicit sex, spousal abuse, poor church attendance, lying, and libeling a fellow congregant. In one Baptist church the members agreed that races and chicken fights were "altogether against the religion of Jesus" and that it was wrong to attend them.[42]

Evangelicals understood vigilance was required to continue in God's will; humans were subject to backsliding. In 1833 Edgefield District's Bethany Baptist Church was so caught up in the need for rigorous behavioral rules that their minister discouraged them from adopting particular rules of decorum and urged them instead to follow the New Testament. The tension remained until 1840, when they adopted a formal rule book.[43] Called before a church's discipline committee, a person could feel the sting of public humiliation. Ignoring a call usually meant expulsion and isolation from an intimate community. The substantial obligations the church required brought the evangelical ethos into family daily life. Single members were expelled for fornication; married members for adultery. Men were excommunicated for neglecting their families or for beating their wives. A woman could be excommunicated for not keeping a tidy, orderly house. The Sweetwater Baptist Church recorded many disputes during the antebellum period. A Mr. Rhodes was charged with beating drums for slaves to dance; a Mr. Thorn was cited for swearing at his neighbor; and a Mr. Roper was investigated for harsh words spoken against a Mr. Cooper. Equality before God meant that all whites in the church were judged as equals. One church disciplined a planter for having a fight with his overseer. The same church was sensitive about slavery and excommunicated Brother Whatley "for saying that there would be War soon and the Negroes would be all free."[44]

Slaves also faced discipline committees. Some evidence suggests that African Americans, as much as the whites, subscribed to the discipline system. Of the enslaved people expelled, most petitioned for readmission and were usually accepted back.[45] Slaves used these committees to exercise some power. When, in 1858, Rev. B. F. Corly spent a day at Edgefield Courthouse, he likely thought his actions would go unnoticed by his congregation back at Siloam Baptist Church in Abbeville District. Corly did not realize that some African Americans, likely slaves and members of his church, noticed him when he bought a bottle of brandy and visited, "2 Houses on the road that he ought not to have stopped at with an improper motive & had conversation with some women that was not becoming to a Christian, especially a minister of the Gospel." His case was almost dismissed as false rumor spread by blacks, but the rumors persisted. Corly invoked all the privileges granted his race and gender. He called together the congregation's white men to hear his confession, asked and was granted forgiveness in a private meeting. Not everyone was satisfied with

Corly's restoration, however, and he was forced to face a council of ministers from neighboring churches. Within the confines of this white male assemblage, Corly fared worse, and for a period of several months he was removed from both his pulpit and membership in the church.[46] Although the power and authority determining Corly's fate resided in other white males, Corly's case arose from the testimony of black members of his congregation.

Church discipline and the process of public and semipublic church hearings were fodder for discussions around the cracker barrel and across fence rails, and church records demonstrate that congregations grew more sensitive to the public airing of personal laundry. Many churches made discipline proceedings private while others ceased to hold them altogether. Nevertheless, this established process of maintaining public order helped to bring evangelical values into the everyday life of the community.

Such strictures went only so far. Although the church forbade drunkenness, drinking was something communities had integrated into their collective behavior long before evangelicalism, and many individuals were not willing to give it up. The South as a region proved more resistant to temperance efforts than the North, one estimate stating that in 1831, while 44 percent of the nation's population resided in the South, fewer than 10 percent of Southerners advocated temperance. Evangelical outreach had limits even as evangelicalism was becoming an integral part of community life. The religious call for temperance never overcame the idea that the church should not interfere in civic matters. And noninterference in civic matters, of course, meant churches should not question slavery.[47]

Just as evangelicals had to accommodate slavery, another egalitarian impulse of evangelism had to be channeled; they were forced to accommodate patriarchy as well. The tradition of male dominance came with the first colonists and was well developed by the nineteenth century. In *The Mind of the South* (1941) W. J. Cash characterized the mentality to preserve white male supremacy the "Savage Ideal." Anything that might cross paths with southern white males had to conform to the Savage Ideal or face eradication. Preservation of the patriarchy—a social, political, and legal system favoring white males—was an increasingly incisive feature of the antebellum South. Before becoming second nature to Southerners, the evangelical ethos had to conform.[48]

The image of God in conversion narratives was understood as a male. Whereas women understood God as a father or friend, white male evangelicals employed the metaphors of governmental power, a ruler, a "king." One convert wrote in a letter, "Everything appeared perfectly right in the divine government; I felt submissive, and rejoiced that God was on the throne." Men struggled with the idea of personal revelation partly because there was no qualification for grace or human comprehension of why or how God saved an individual. Men feared an unjust or arbitrary God. Men most often preferred to see this struggle as a fight on legalistic or justifiable grounds. Male conversion narratives recount a search for the rules and the utter frustration in this effort, a frustration only alleviated through divine truth. Men often came to realize they needed help, sometimes from their wives, often from other men, who pushed them along their journey.[49]

White males, including the earnest evangelical and the skeptic, safely invested in religion as long as it came to function through male terms of power and authority. Evangelicalism embraced the relinquishment of free will, but it included a paradox: through this relinquishment of self, men actually gained power and agency. This was exactly the recipe white males needed to comprehend and secure their privileged position. Evangelicalism was a both a process and a tool for this dominant group to employ.

Denominational structures integrated men into all leadership positions. The roles of deacons, elders, and ministers were positions for men as were the later antebellum positions in the conferences, synods, and associations. White male authority was not absolute in either the religious or the secular world, but it was dominant. The church allowed women and enslaved and free blacks a status improved from their secular position, but it held them to severe accountability. Women might vote in church meetings, and enslaved African Americans might gain autonomy to meet away from whites, but such allowances could be revoked. Before any merger between the Separate Baptists and the Regulars, the Separates had to forego their women deaconesses and elderesses. Church leadership was for the white-male laity. The standard format was to invite the congregation to attend church business after worship, but to allow only white male members to speak.

Methodists, Baptists, and Presbyterians all acknowledged southern patriarchy and shaped expectations for proper living through lines of male authority. The patriarchal domain was the community, and white males guarded their position. Antebellum tombstones reflected this legacy. Whereas mothers were praised for motherhood, fathers were praised for leadership. Thomas Wainwright Blease died leaving a large family of seven children, but rather than remembering him as a loving father, his epitaph praised "his integrity of purpose, independence of character, and pure moral worth." Blease was not alone in leaving such inscriptions; antebellum males often left messages touting their citizenship, service, and honor.[50]

Bringing the evangelical impulse under control, churches of the mid–nineteenth century changed in emphasis. Where early evangelicalism emphasized personal conversion as the foremost goal, the later version focused on ministering to believers. Churches were places for making sense of the world. Growth in membership and formalization of doctrine gave ministers renewed authority to advise their congregants. Within this new leadership role, ministers held an improved status and could even become members of the elite. Most elite ministers were Episcopalians, but a few, such as William Bullein Johnson, spoke from Baptists pulpits. Johnson was the minister for Edgefield's Village Baptist Church and was elected the first president of the newly organized Southern Baptist Association in 1849.[51]

As the Baptists, Methodists, and Presbyterians grew away from their rural success, and denominations became more institutionalized, part of the formalization of religion was education. Academies and their less aristocratic counterparts, field schools, were often denominational. At the best academies, a prominent minister such as William Bullein Johnson or Iveson Brooks was in charge. Before becoming a minister, Abiah Cartledge taught in a field school and recalled, "it was my custom to open the school with the reading of a passage of Scripture, and prayer. I also frequently made some remarks to the pupils, in connection with the passage of Scripture read."[52] As education rose in importance, the antebellum elite made sure their sons went to local academies that offered training for admission to colleges, especially South Carolina College, where attendance was a means of entry into elite professions and society. The need for an educated and trained clergy merged with the desire for an educated populace, and denominational colleges developed and thrived. Furman (Baptist), founded in 1826, and Erskine (Presbyterian), founded in 1839, received their charters in 1850. Wofford (Methodist) was chartered in 1851 and Newberry (Lutheran) in 1856. These colleges were for males. Female colleges were chartered also: Greenville Female Baptist College in 1855, Columbia Female College (Methodist) in 1859, and Due West Female College (Presbyterian) in 1860.[53]

With formalization, education, and compromise on issues, evangelicalism increasingly pervaded antebellum life in the South. Across class and race to some extent, and in harmony with the southern gender hierarchy, the values of the churches both reflected and molded the community's mores. Persistence rates in the community also reflected membership in the church; those not belonging were more likely to move on. Among rural social networks one's religious reputation might well be a deciding factor in getting work or credit. A typical example of the integration of religion into the personal lives of the citizenry is James Ouzts, an antebellum farmer of middling means. When he recorded his experiences as an overseer and farmer in a diary, religious themes predominated. A devout Methodist, he often gave praise and thanks to God. He also regularly participated in church conference meetings, traveling at his own expense.[54]

Combining sociability and authority, ministers regularly visited the homes of their congregations. John Cornish, an Episcopal minister in Aiken, recollected that he often called on families, both rich and poor, and visits were congenial and friendly. Baptist minister Abiah Morgan Cartledge noted similar visits, and Methodist minister H. A. Roggins of McKendree Methodist made it a point to visit his new congregation soon after taking his post.[55] Such outreach reinforced the evangelical perspective that religion was not only a Sunday morning ritual but a way of life.

While Methodists and Presbyterians had some members uncomfortable with these formalized changes, upcountry Baptists, typically located in rural areas and with poorer congregations, most forcefully resisted formalization and outreach. When larger organizational bodies, such as the South Carolina Baptist Convention (formed in 1821), directed efforts toward foreign and domestic missions, religious educational development, and other forms of outreach, some Baptist congregations objected to these new directions. Old School, or Primitive, Baptists as they were named, found no biblical instruction for outreach and believed Baptist congregations must maintain strict autonomy in order to fulfill their congregational responsibilities. Primitive Baptists broke from regional associations and became a separate denomination. Saluda, Twelve Mile River, Reedy River, Broad River, Bethel, and Moriah Associations remained independent groups during much of the antebellum period. Within the Primitive Baptists, as within the Baptist denomination as a whole and in other denominations at this time, consensus on various issues of slavery was hard to come by. Individuals might disagree with a church decision; churches might disagree with their association. When the Saluda Association, for example, adopted the state association's mission to slaves and free blacks, five churches within the Saluda Association objected.[56]

Disagreements, though often imbued with religious zeal, were possible without being destructive. The tradition of religious toleration in South Carolina, which began with the proprietors' religious protection, grew with the evangelical ethos. Evangelicalism cemented a tradition of religious pluralism in South Carolina because Christianity held as its core the protection of an individual seeking accord with God. This core necessitated a space for other forms of worship and other religions. Evangelicalism championed the idea of a personal relationship with God, thereby honoring an individual's choice in whether or not to accept God's call. The evangelical ethos encouraged freedom of conscience and discouraged religious suppression. Within this theology, issues such as opposition to slavery or women's role in the church were matters of conscience and not matters to be decided by majority rule.

The evangelical ethos has continued to place a consistent focus on the individual and that person's relationship with God. With each ebb and flow of the revival movement, however, church denominations sought better control of their growing membership. A growing membership brought organization and formalization as well as certain compromises demanded by the white elite. The church moved from a position outside the general social flow, where it criticized the secular world, to the center, where it reflected elite values. As evangelicalism matured, it became increasingly conservative, compromising on the issues of women and of slavery, eventually becoming the loudest voice for proslavery advocates. Southern Protestant transition to a proslavery stand came at the cost of removing evangelical activism in civic matters. Evangelicals had to strike a balance between spontaneity and structure as they negotiated the relationship between spirituality and power. They could not approach matters in terms of societal problems because they would inevitably clash with their own slave society.

Religious tolerance across denominations was secure, but tolerance regarding abolitionist thinking was prohibited. Although some denominations, such as the Primitive Baptists, remained uncompromisingly opposed to South Carolina Baptists' formalized relations and outreach, any denomination remaining in the South had to compromise on slavery. By the late antebellum period the evangelical ethos included defense of slavery and the protection of male supremacy, two fundamental features garnering the white male support necessary to flourish in South Carolina's slave society. With these compromises on slavery and patriarchy, the evangelical wave flooded the culture, and religion became an integral part of daily life in nineteenth-century South Carolina.

Notes

1. Thomas Lowndes to the Secretary of Lords of Trade, February 16, 1728, in *The Colonial Records of North Carolina*, ed. William Saunders, vol. 3 (Raleigh: P.M. Hale, 1886), 10.

2. Walter Edgar, *South Carolina: A History* (Columbia: University of South Carolina Press, 1998), 35.

3. Robert M. Weir, *Colonial South Carolina: A History* (Millwood, N.Y.: KTO, 1983), 178. See also Charles Reznikoff, *The Jews of Charleston: A History of an American Jewish Community* (Philadelphia: Jewish Publication Society of America, 1950), and Samuel S. Hill, "The South," in *Encyclopedia of the American Religious Experience*, ed. Charles H. Lippy and Peter W. Williams, vol. 3 (New York: Scribners, 1988), 1493.

4. Edgar, *South Carolina: A History*, 43, 60, 91, 259; Jo Anne McCormick, "The Quakers of Colonial South Carolina," Ph.D. dissertation, University of South Carolina, 1984.

5. John Boyd to the Society for the Propagation of the Gospel in Foreign Parts, undated, circa 1733, in *The Colonial Records of North Carolina*, ed. Saunders, 3:394.

6. Mr. Lapierre to the Bishop of London, October 9, 1733, in *The Colonial Records of North Carolina*, ed. Saunders, 3:530.

7. Alexander Garden to the Bishop of London, September 7, 1737, in *The Colonial Records of North Carolina*, ed. Saunders, 3:264.

8. Samuel S. Hill ed., *Encyclopedia of Religion in the South* (Macon, Ga.: Mercer University Press, 1984), 841.

9. Phillip G. Clarke Jr., *Anglicanism in South Carolina, 1660–1976* (Easley, S.C.: Southern Historical Press, 1976), 14. William H. Kenney III, "Alexander Garden and George Whitefield: The Significance of Revivalism in South Carolina, 1738–1741," *South Carolina Historical Magazine* 71 (January 1970): 14–15. Edgar, *South Carolina: A History*, 184.

10. Conversion was problematic as the doctrine of salvation through faith undercut Anglican clergy's insistence on good works. The Bryan family proved much more threatening when they began teaching slaves about Christianity. Eventually Hugh Bryan's efforts at following evangelical Christianity suggested God might inspire slaves to rebel. See Harvey H. Jackson, "Hugh Bryan and the Evangelical Movement in South Carolina," *William and Mary Quarterly* third series 43 (October 1986): 594–614; Alan Gallay, *The Formation of the Planter Elite: Jonathan Bryan and the Formation of the Colonial Southern Frontier* (Athens: University of Georgia Press, 1989), 41–47.

11. Robert M. Calhoon, *Evangelicals & Conservatives in the early South, 1740–1861* (Columbia: University of South Carolina Press, 1988), 1.

12. Thomas J. Little, "'Adding to the Church Such As Shall Be Saved': The Growth in Influence of Evangelicalism in Colonial South Carolina, 1740–1775," in *Money, Trade, and Power: The Evolution of Colonial South Carolina's Plantation Society*, ed. Jack P. Greene, Rosemary Brana-Shute, and Randy J. Sparks (Columbia: University of South Carolina Press, 2001), 367–75.

13. Rainsford Diary, August 27, 1833, 21; family possession.

14. Susan Juster, "'In a Different Voice': Male and Female Narratives of Religious Conversion in Post-Revolutionary America," *American Quarterly* 41 (March 1989): 35–37.

15. Calhoon, *Evangelicals & Conservatives,* 9.

16. Philip Gatch and James Jenkins, quoted in Christine Heyrman, *Southern Cross, The Beginnings of the Bible Belt* (Chapel Hill: University of North Carolina Press, 1997), 80–81, 82–86.

17. Calhoon, *Evangelicals & Conservatives,* 151.

18. Orville Vernon Burton, *In My Father's House Are Many Mansions: Family and Community in Edgefield, South Carolina* (Chapel Hill: University of North Carolina Press, 1985), 22.

19. Francis Asbury, *The Journal and Letters of Francis Asbury,* ed. Elmer T. Clark, J. Manning Pitts, and Jacob S. Payton, vol. 2 (Nashville: Southern Methodist Publishing House, 1858), 591.

20. Petitions of Benjamin Busbee and subsequent petitions of his wife, 1810; January 1, 1815; November 29, 1815; and December 5, 1815; petitions of Benjamin and John Ryan, December 12, 1816; 1820; November 15 and December 1823; 1824; all in Petitions to the General Assembly, Legislative Papers, South Carolina Department of Archives and History, Columbia. See also Burton, *In My Father's House,* 23–28.

21. Calhoon, *Evangelicals & Conservatives,* 125.

22. See Janet Duitsman Cornelius, *When I Can Read My Title Clear: Literacy, Slavery, and Religion in the Antebellum South* (Columbia: University of South Carolina Press, 1992).

23. Hammond Plantation Diary, December 8, 15, 16, 1831. Luther P. Jackson, "Religious Instruction of Negroes, 1830–1860, with Special Reference to South Carolina," *Journal of Negro History* 15 (January 1930): 81. Charles Cotesworth Pinckney, *An Address Delivered in Charleston before the Agricultural Society of South Carolina at its Anniversary Meeting* (Charleston: A. E. Miller, 1829), 9–13.

24. Walter H. Brooks, "The Priority of the Silver Bluff Church and Its Promoters," *Journal of Negro History* 7 (April 1922): 172–218; Iveson L. Brookes, *A Defence of Southern Slavery* (Hamburg, S.C.: Republican Office, 1850), 17–18; available at the South Caroliniana Library, University of South Carolina, Columbia. For a discussion of slavery and religion in Edgefield, see Burton, *In My Father's House.*

25. George P. Rawick, ed., *The American Slave: A Composite Autobiography* (Westport, Conn.: Greenwood, 1977), 4:660, 551; 2:185; XII: 231.

26. Eugene D. Genovese, *Roll, Jordan, Roll: The World the Slaves Made* (New York: Vintage, 1972), 162.

27. Sylvia R. Frey and Betty Wood, *Come Shouting to Zion: African American Protestantism in the American South and British Caribbean to 1830* (Chapel Hill: University of North Carolina Press, 1998), 82.

28. *Edgefield Advertiser,* March 13, 1851; John A. Chapman, *History of Edgefield County from the Earliest Settlement to 1897* (Newberry, S.C.: Elbert H. Aull, 1897), 328; see also Burton, *In My Father's House* for more on the community of Edgefield.

29. Loulie Latimer Owens, *Saints of Clay, The Shaping of South Carolina Baptists* (Columbia: R. L. Bryan, 1971), 40–43.

30. Stephanie McCurry, *Masters of Small Worlds: Yeoman Households, Gender Relations, and the Political Culture of the Antebellum South Carolina Low Country* (New York, Oxford University Press, 1995), 137.

31. Lewis P. Jones, "South Carolina," in *Religion in the Southern States: A Historical Study,* ed. Samuel S. Hill (Macon, Ga.: Mercer University Press, 1983), 274.

32. Edgar, *South Carolina: A History,* 181, 261, 294.

33. David Duncan Wallace, *Historical Background of Religion in South Carolina* (Columbia: South Carolina Historical Society, 1917), 17, 25. In-depth treatment is also found in Peter Clarke, *A Free Church in a Free Society: The Ecclesiology of John England, Bishop of Charleston, 1820–1842: A Nineteenth Century Missionary Bishop in the Southern United States* (Hartsville, S.C.: Center for John England Studies, 1982). Bermingham Diary, November 3, 1860, Bermingham Papers, St. Mary's Church, Edgefield, S.C.

34. Richard Furman, *Exposition of the Views of the Baptists Relative to the Colored Population of the United States in a Communication to the Governor of South Carolina* (Charleston: A. E. Miller, 1823), 15–16.

35. Calhoon, *Evangelicals & Conservatives,* 127.

36. Edgar, *South Carolina,* 230.

37. Calhoon, *Evangelicals & Conservatives,* 9.

38. McCurry, *Masters of Small Worlds,* 169.

39. Calhoon, *Evangelicals & Conservatives,* 154.

40. Bethel Baptist Association Minutes, Annual Report for 1845, Baptist Historical Collection, Furman University, Greenville, S.C.

41. Calhoon, *Evangelicals & Conservatives,* 111.

42. For more on church discipline committees, see Burton, *In My Father's House,* 58–59, 137, 155, 244.

43. Bethany Baptist Church Records, March 24, 1833, May 23, 1840, South Carolina Department of Archives and History, Columbia.

44. Burton, *In My Father's House,* 59.

45. Horn's Creek Baptist Church Records, June 1838, April 1852; Sweetwater Baptist Church Records, November 1863 and January 1864; Big Stevens Creek Baptist Church Records, November 1826, May 1810. These are typical of the Edgefield Baptist Church Records, Furman University, Greenville, as well as McKendree Methodist Church Records, South Caroliniana Library, University of South Carolina, Columbia.

46. Siloam Baptist Church minutes, Abbeville District, quoted in Kimberly R. Kellison, "Coming to Christ: The Impact of Evangelical Christianity on Upcountry South Carolina, 1830–1890," Ph.D. dissertation, University of South Carolina, 1997, 103–4. For more on the exercise of African Americans' power over whites, see Judith N. McArthur and Orville Vernon Burton, *A Gentleman and an Officer: A Military and Social History of James B. Griffin's Civil War* (New York: Oxford University Press 1998).

47. Big Stevens Creek Baptist Church Records, February 1839, Baptist Historical Collection, Furman University, Greenville. Ian R. Tyrell, "Drink and Temperance in the Antebellum South: An overview and Interpretation," *Journal of Southern History* 48 (November 1982): 485–510. David Duncan Wallace, *The History of South Carolina,* vol. 3 (New York: American Historical Society, 1934), 85–87.

48. Wilbur J. Cash, *The Mind of the South* (New York: Knopf, 1941).

49. Juster, "In a Different Voice," quote on page 42.

50. Willowbrook Cemetery, Edgefield.

51. Edgefield Village Baptist Church Records, January 1831 through January 1853, Baptist Historical Collection, Furman University, Greenville. Hortense Woodson, *Giant in the Land: A Biography of William Bullein Johnson, First President of the Southern Baptist Convention* (Nashville: Broadman Press, 1950). The creation of denomination associations in the upcountry shows the extent to which the evangelical ethos had reached in South Carolinian everyday life.

52. Cartledge Autobiography, 8, Cartledge Papers, South Caroliniana Library, University of South Carolina, Columbia.

53. Edgar, *South Carolina: A History,* 300.

54. Ouzts Diary, Ouzts Papers and McKendree Methodist Church Records, both South Caroliniana Library, University of South Carolina, Columbia.

55. Cornish Diaries, Cornish Papers, Southern Historical Collection, University of North Carolina, Chapel Hill; Cartledge Papers, South Caroliniana Library, University of South Carolina, Columbia; McKendree Methodist Church Records, South Carolinian Library.

56. Most of these churches eventually came to adopt missions and outreach as a responsibility (Kellison, "Coming to Christ," 39–40).

"Your liberty in that province"

South Carolina Quakers and the
Rejection of Religious Toleration

W. Scott Poole

ZACHARIAH DIX, ALMOST PHYSICALLY OVERCOME with a vision of impending apocalypse, harangued the crowd of farm families, warning them of the wrath to come. The background of this Quaker itinerant preacher is uncertain, though it is known that he began preaching to South Carolina's Bush River Meeting in 1804 with a certificate of license from the North Carolina Yearly Meeting. Rumored to be a gifted prophet, he was said to have visions prophesying war, which came to him in nightly dreams, and the Quakers of Newberry and Laurens districts had listened in terror as he told of a coming apocalyptic war. Some remembered that Dix's revelations had a less otherworldly tone, though no less apocalyptic in their own way. These reports insist that the Quaker prophet warned of an impending slave uprising and lavishly illustrated his predictions with bloody tales of the recent slave revolt in Saint (Santo) Domingo.[1]

Whatever the exact message the prophetic preacher carried into the South Carolina upcountry in the early nineteenth century, it triggered a massive migration of Quakers out of the Palmetto State. By 1807 almost all the Friends of South Carolina had departed for points north, with the largest group moving en masse to Miami, Ohio. The Bush River Meeting, the Quaker society that had formal supervisory capacity over the entire state by the nineteenth century, was not formally disbanded (or "laid down" in Friends' terminology) until 1822, but for all practical purposes it had ceased to operate by 1807. South Carolina Quakerism, always a small part of the state's surprisingly diverse religious admixture, became truly a marginal phenomenon after the departure of the Newberry County Quakers. Their departure represented the end of a delicate dance South Carolina Quakers had engaged in over the previous one hundred and thirty years, a dance with a society whose commitment to slavery grew evermore complete. The Quakers of South Carolina, because of their state's peculiarity as much as their own, found their religious identity incompatible with their identity as South Carolinians.

The experience of South Carolina Quakers has been all but ignored both by historians of the religion in America and by chroniclers of the Friends. The Charles Town Meeting spent much of its one-hundred-year existence being rebuked by fellow Quakers for worldliness, and it has fared little better at the hands of historians. In *The Quiet Rebels: The Story of the Quakers in America* (1999) Margaret Hope Bacon dismisses the Quaker meetings of South Carolina and Georgia, writing "Quakerism never flourished in these colonies, and some of the meetings they established vanished." Hugh Barbour and J. William Frost, two of the most important interpreters of the Quaker movement, ignored the South Carolina meetings in their 1988 book, writing of "a large Quaker settlement in North Carolina" and, tacking on as if by afterthought, that "a few Friends lived in Charleston." In Frederick B. Tolles's classic work *Meeting House and Counting House* (1963) the South Carolina Friends make an appearance only as a community that received alms from the larger Philadelphia Meeting.[2]

It is unfortunate that the South Carolina Friends have been so frequently ignored. The Quakers offer us an important case study for understanding how religious toleration operated in South Carolina, particularly with regard to the struggles of a faith that, while it suffered little or no legal proscriptions, held to an ethos that clashed profoundly with the surrounding society. Such a study, in turn, opens up larger questions about the nature of tolerance and consensus in American religion. Most studies of American religion that reflect on the meaning of religious toleration and the fate of Dissenting groups focus heavily on how such groups are absorbed, co-opted, or rejected by dominant religious majorities. The Quakers of South Carolina allow us to turn the issue upside down. Their story is not that of a Dissenting group making its peace with the larger culture or being stamped out by the religious majority. Ultimately, it's the story of a religious minority that prospered in an officially tolerant but culturally hostile society, finally choosing of its own volition to reject that society and leave it behind.[3]

The Society of Friends came to Carolina carrying a long tradition of conflict with the larger social order. Born out of the religious ferment of the English Civil War, the Society of Friends dates its beginnings to 1652, when George Fox, the son of a Puritan weaver, began preaching and gathering "seekers" around him in Yorkshire, England. The theology developed by Fox and the new community represented a reaction against the authoritarianism of Fox's own Puritan background and stressed the individual's ability to experience the divine without the mediation of religious authority. The idea of the "inner light," the identifying peculiarity of Quaker theology, emerged from this emphasis on spiritual subjectivity. Like most sectarian movements, the followers of George Fox regarded their new faith as a return to a primitive Christianity, untainted by centuries of religious and political authoritarianism. This self-conception led these early Friends, who called themselves "the children of light," toward a countercultural standard of conduct rooted in a literal reading of the ethical teaching of the New Testament.[4]

Fox's followers soon found themselves on a collision course with English authorities both secular and religious. Believing that the teachings of Jesus counseled pacifism, Fox was imprisoned for his refusal to take a captaincy in Oliver Cromwell's "New Model Army." As disturbing to the established order, the Friends' profound spiritual equalitarianism resulted in a radical critique of power and hierarchy. In a world where rituals of social etiquette created and confirmed class distinctions, the "children of light" refused to use titles of distinction or to remove their hats in the presence of their social "betters." Believing that the standard of simplicity in speech disallowed the swearing of oaths, Fox and his followers refused to take oaths in court or to swear to the 1655 Oath of Abjuration, which required English subjects to confirm that they were not Catholic (resulting in the belief among some in Commonwealth England that these radical Dissenters were, in fact, secret Catholics). The early Friends would even be accused of sexual immorality. Rejecting the idea of sacramental marriage and the authority of what they called "hireling ministers," while seeking to keep themselves separate from the world, early Friends practiced endogamous marriage in simple ceremonies with no officiate.[5]

Persecution, not surprising given their countercultural ethos, became a part of the Friends' identity from the beginning. In fact, the popular use of the nickname "Quaker" arose from an incident in which George Fox, hauled before the magistrates of Derby, informed them peremptorily that they should "Tremble before the word of God!" and was in turn told by one outraged official that, "You are the quaker, not I." Fox was far from the only "Quaker" brought before the courts of England in the first decades of the society's existence. Before the 1689 Act of Religious Toleration, thousands of English Quakers were imprisoned, at least briefly, for their beliefs. and as many as 450 died in prison. Quakers faced persecution as extreme in the new colonies of British North America, in Puritan New England and in Anglican Virginia. Two female Quaker itinerants, Anne Austin and Mary Fisher (later Mary Fisher Crosse), were driven from Puritan Boston in 1656. The Massachusetts General Court soon thereafter passed a series of laws that fined a ship's captain one hundred pounds for bringing a Friend into the colony and fined citizens five pounds for possession of one of the "erroneous books and hellish pamphlets" of the Quakers. Quakers faced public whipping and imprisonment should they come to Boston. Between 1659 and 1661, Boston officials went even further and hanged four Quaker itinerants, including the famous Mary Dyer, who had been a disciple of Anne Hutchinson.[6]

Virginia Friends faced persecution almost as extreme as their New England brethren. In 1660 an Act for Suppressing Quakers sought to drive from the Anglican colony what it called "an unreasonable and turbulent sort of people commonly called Quakers." The series of acts that followed proved effective in driving Quaker meetings into North Carolina and Maryland, including an act "against refractory soldiers" that penalized Friends for their absence from militia musters.[7]

By the time of the founding of the Carolina colony in 1670, Quakers faced legal proscription and popular disdain throughout much of the British Atlantic. By 1664 no fewer than 224 theological and political diatribes against the Society of Friends circulated from London to Boston to Bridgetown. The name of one such 1657 pamphlet, *A Sad Caveat to All Quakers, Not to Boast Anymore that they have God Almighty by the Hand when they Have the Devil by the Toe,* perhaps gives something of the flavor of the rest.[8]

The arrival of the Society of Friends in the Carolina colony produced no such tales of persecution. In fact, other than Pennsylvania and Rhode Island, no other colony proved such a welcoming haven for the Friends or for Dissenting groups more generally. The Lords Proprietors, English investors who received their charter from Charles II to found the Carolina colony—and particularly their leader, Anthony Ashley Cooper, Lord Ashley (later Earl of Shaftesbury)—viewed freedom for Dissenters as a way to attract settlers who might otherwise be dubious of the unhealthful climate. Even more important, the proprietors came to view Dissenters as the core of a "proprietary party" that would support their ambitions against more restive and recalcitrant Anglican settlers. Thus the Fundamental Constitutions of Carolina allowed any group made up of at least seven members who agreed to meet and state their doctrine publicly to worship freely even if they were "heathens, Jews or other dissenters." Lord Ashley apparently had a special concern to bring Quakers to the colony, as the Fundamental Constitutions contained a provision that allowed Friends to "bear witness to the truth" by "any other Sensible way" rather than swear an oath.[9] Moreover, Lord Ashley hoped to set aside at least twelve thousand acres in what is now Colleton County for a Quaker township. The township did not materialize, but by 1681 enough Friends had come to Carolina to begin a Charleston meeting.[10]

The Friends could not only come to Carolina and worship in safety, they could also come and prosper. Many of the early Quaker arrivals became some of the more prominent men in the colony. Joseph West, one of the early proprietary governors may have been a Quaker, as his will left much of his estate for the aid of Quaker immigrants. Jacob Wayte (sometimes spelled Wait) proved one of the more prosperous of the early Friends, owning two lots on Oyster Point, the peninsula bounded by the Ashley and Cooper rivers that later provided the site for Charleston. Wayte used his considerable wealth, as did many of the early prosperous Quaker settlers, to fund the arrival of more Friends.[11]

Many of these new Quaker immigrants did not come from England. Like so many of the colony's first settlers, they came to Carolina by way of Barbados. The first British plantation economy in the New World, the slaveholding society on Barbados earned a well-deserved reputation for brutality. The harsh slave code imposed by the Anglican planters who ruled the tropical island's sugarcane fields made its way to Carolina and became the basis for Carolina's brutal system. Ironically, the West Indian island exported a small, but significant, number of Quakers to Carolina along with its brutal slave code.[12]

The Barbadian Friends left the island under a cloud of suspicion, shadowed by rumors that they had sought to encourage a slave revolt. George Fox himself had visited the island and was accused of fomenting rebellion because he had encouraged the religious instruction of slaves and raised the possibility that African slaves should, like indentured servants, have a set term of service. In 1671 William Edmundson, an Irish Quaker itinerant, went to Barbados and was also accused of plotting with the slaves. Edmundson's meetings were broken up by Anglican mobs, crying that the Friends were "heretics, blasphemers and traitors." An Anglican clergyman even made use of the old accusation that the Quakers were secretly Catholic, referring to Edmundson as "an Irish Jesuit in disguise." Throughout the 1670s Barbadian Quakers faced a growing list of proscriptions that caused them to search for a new home in the Atlantic world. In fact, by 1680 Quaker meetings were officially outlawed on the island.[13]

South Carolina became the place of exile for many Barbadian Quakers. In fact, some of the most prominent Quakers in the new Carolina colony had Barbadian connections. John Ladson, originally a merchant of Northampshire, arrived in Carolina in 1679 after having spent some time on the island. The most prosperous Quaker of the colonial period, the founder of one of the South Carolina lowcountry's great dynasties, also arrived from Barbados in the seventeenth century. Thomas Eliot Sr. had been a prosperous carpenter on the Caribbean island. He arrived in Charleston in 1690 and, through the acquisition of land and slaves, became a local notable with impressive holdings, owning seven thousand acres and a lot with a wharf along the Charleston Bay by 1711.[14]

Meanwhile, Quakers had arrived in what is now North Carolina as early as the 1660s; they had little connection, ultimately, to the Charles Town Meeting. When William Edmundson, while on the itinerant circuit that would eventually take him to Barbados, traveled to the mouth of the Albemarle River in 1671, he found living on its banks a family of Friends who had fled persecution in New England. Edmundson's journey led to many conversions ("convincements" as the Friends called them), and North Carolina became a Quaker stronghold in the eighteenth century, with strong infusions in the 1730s and 1750s from Pennsylvania and Nantucket respectively. The story of the North Carolina Quakers has a very different arc from that of their South Carolina brethren, as does the trajectory of the state itself. After 1691 North and South Carolina split in two for all practical purposes when the Lords Proprietors allowed a deputy governor to be appointed for the northern half of the Carolina colony. A separate governor for what would be called North Carolina was officially appointed in 1712.[15]

South Carolina Quakers, in the interim, continued to grow in numbers, wealth, and political strength in the new colony. It is important to note that they never became more than a significant minority in South Carolina. In fact, in a colony that included about four thousand white settlers, there were only about one hundred Quakers by 1700. Nevertheless, Anglican ministers had become concerned enough about their numbers to request pamphlets from England to aid in their conversion. Some of the first Quaker meetings were held in private homes, although at some time in the early 1680s, John Archdale (later proprietary governor in 1695–96) gave land for a meetinghouse on what would later be called King Street.

The wealth of the early Carolina Quakers is significant, considering the future direction of the Society of Friends at large and of the Carolina Friends in particular. Much of the growing wealth of the society rested on slaveholding. Thomas Elliot Sr., at the time of his death, owned twenty-six slaves, who he left to his estate. Ralph Emmes, a substantial Quaker planter in Colleton County, owned no fewer than fifty-three slaves. It is important to note that the Society of Friends had no proscriptions against slaveholding in this early period. In fact, only after the 1750s did the American Friends begin the process of "purifying their Society" of the taint of slaveholding and then only slowly, with qualifications. Not until after the American Revolution could Quakers be said to have anything like a strong antislavery witness. The early Carolina Quakers certainly gave little thought to the moral implications of slaveholding. In fact, Mary Fisher Crosse, the famed Quaker itinerant who had settled in Charleston and became the driving force behind the founding of the town's meeting, owned as many as ten slaves, both Africans and Indians.[16]

Quakers in South Carolina also aspired to and attained public office in the colony's early years. Thomas Eliot Sr. served many terms in the colonial assembly as did other Quaker leaders, such as John Ladson and James Stanyarne. In her study of Quakers in South Carolina, Jo Anne McCormick found that at least ten of the fifty-one adult males in the Society of Friends held public office in 1700. John Archdale was without question the most important Quaker political figure in colonial South Carolina. Archdale became one of the Lords Proprietors in 1678, purchasing the share of Lord John Berkeley. Archdale was a substantial landowner on Oyster Point and, as mentioned above, gave the land and provided the funds for the first Quaker meetinghouse. In 1694 he came to Charleston; he was named governor on November 24, 1695. He proved one of the most capable governors of the proprietary era, bringing at least a respite to the intense struggle that had developed in the 1680s between the Lords Proprietors and many of the settlers. South Carolina Friends welcomed him, and in one undated document from the Archdale Papers (thought likely to be from the beginning of his governorship) the Charles Town Meeting praised the prosperity of the colony and of their fellowship under his leadership. Archdale acted on the peace principles of the Friends, working for the passage of an act that allowed Quakers exemption from the colonial militia muster.[17]

Archdale's example holds true for many of the other South Carolina Quakers who entered politics in the first generation of the settlement. Entering the political structure, the Friends brought their Quaker principles with them even when, unlike Archdale, they kept them to their hurt. Wealthy Quaker notable John Stanyarne was excluded from the colonial Assembly for his refusal to swear an oath, showing that often the Fundamental Constitutions were honored mostly in the breach. A provision in 1692 called on members of the Assembly to remove their hats when addressing the speaker, a clear reference to the equalitarian Friends refusal to show "hat-honor."[18]

These incidents show that, despite their prosperity and the important roles they assumed in this new colony, South Carolina Quakers early on experienced a profound tension with the surrounding culture. The society being shaped by slavery in the South Carolina lowcountry put a heavy emphasis on hierarchy and deference to the established order, values obviously antithetical to the Quaker ethos. Though the colony was in no way unique in this regard, the emphasis on mastery and order that grew out of the political economy of slavery gave the idea of deference a special place in South Carolina society. This perhaps explains why, when Quakers did suffer disabilities in the colony's political life, they came about largely because of refusals to recognize the etiquette of power. Governor Archdale's uniqueness in this regard can largely be explained by the position that he held, both as proprietor and proprietary governor. Indeed, his ability him to act according to his religious scruples provides yet another example of the crucial importance of deference to authority in the early colony. The same can be said for the success of notables such as Thomas Eliot, whose wealth and prestige sheltered him from persecution.[19]

These examples aside, the South Carolina Friends had a surprisingly easy time of it in the early colony. The wealth of some of the early settlers, their willingness to serve —according to their consciences at least—in the emerging political structure, and the general acceptance of Dissenters in the colony made colonial South Carolina a welcome refuge for the Society of Friends. In fact, outside observers of the same principles worried that the Charleston Quakers might be seduced by their own success. George Fox even worried that his Carolina brethren might be prospering too much because of, what he called in a 1683 letter, "your liberty in that province." Fox was apparently responding to an earlier letter from the Charleston Friends, in which they gave an account of the size of their meeting and spoke of the favorable political climate. Fox's return letter reminded them that to forget their principles would be the same as "abusing that liberty or losing the savor of the heavenly salt."[20]

If Fox felt that political toleration would lead to spiritual apostasy, he would have been pleased by turn of events in Carolina in 1700. In April 1697 John Grenville, Earl of Bath, assumed leadership among the Lords Proprietors. Grenville, a dedicated Anglican, led the revision of the Fundamental Constitutions that deleted provisions seeming to favor Dissenters. Following Grenville's death in 1701, he was succeeded by his son, also named John Grenville, described by one historian of South Carolina Anglicanism as "a staunch, almost fanatical tory." During the second Grenville's tenure, Dissenters faced their greatest challenge of the colonial period. The 1704 exclusion act ostensibly banned Dissenters from participation in the colonial Assembly while the 1706 Church Act officially established the Anglican Church in the colony.[21]

Too much could easily be made of the effect of the exclusion and church acts on the life of the Friends in the colony. The acts were largely the result of factionalism and distrust among the proprietors, and no truly severe persecution resulted. Some Quakers continued to be elected to the Assembly. A 1706 letter to John Archdale from a supporter in the colony noted, "Churchmen gave the opportunity last election to change what Assemblymen they pleased." In the English parliament, repeal of the exclusion act came quickly, along with the assertion that the Anglicans in the Carolina colonial Assembly had allowed the passage of an act described as "repugnant to the laws of England, contrary to the charter granted to the Proprietors of that colony, . . . an encouragement to atheism and irreligion, . . . destructive of trade and tends to the depopulation and ruin of the said province."[22]

The briefly triumphant Anglicans did manage to pass a new militia act aimed at taking away the rights the Friends had won under Archdale. This act, however, merely fined, rather than imprisoned, those who refused to bear arms in the militia. In 1706 the Quaker physician Charles Burnham was arrested for suggesting that the exclusion act made the Assembly illegitimate. In 1707, however, the same Charles Burnham actually served as speaker of the Assembly. As the Quakers of Charleston entered one of colonial Carolina's most tumultuous decades, they appeared as strong as ever.[23]

The events of the 1710s, however, had a withering effect on the Charleston Quakers from which they would never completely recover. No event seemed more catastrophic for white Carolina than the Yamassee War of 1715, in which most of the white settlements south of Charleston were destroyed. At one point in the conflict English settlers were backed into a defensive perimeter that included little more than the city itself. Carolina Quakers came under suspicion because of their unwillingness to fight, and the coming of the war can be said to have introduced the first serious round of persecution.

Quaker settlers found themselves pressed, literally, between their English brethren and the South Carolina Indians in the southwestern corner of the state. The home of many Friends, Colleton County, where Lord Ashley had hoped to see a Quaker township, lay sandwiched between Charleston and Beaufort, and it saw some of the bloody conflict's worst fighting. Meanwhile, most Carolinians looked on the Quaker refusal to take up arms with disdain, particularly since the struggle seemed to be for the very life of the colony. Thomas Kimberly, a prosperous Quaker merchant, was fined fifty shillings for his refusal to appear for militia muster in 1716. A year later, when he again refused to bear arms, he had property confiscated by the militia captain. Suspicion of the Quakers continued to grow during these years, so much so that in 1719, with the emergence of an antiproprietary movement that led to South Carolina becoming a royal colony in 1720, a rumor circulated that the Lords Proprietors, in a last ditch effort to salvage their financial interest in the colony, planned to sell the colony to Quaker merchants who in turn planned to split the colony's holdings into shares and stock job them out to other investors. No such plan ever seems to have been discussed, but the fact that such a rumor circulated at this time provides a gauge for the degree of suspicion in which most Carolinians then held the Quakers. Far from becoming strong enough to take over the colony, the Society of Friends in Charleston continued to weaken throughout the eighteenth century. The Charleston Meeting, its already small numbers much diminished by intermarriage into the Anglican majority, seems to have all but disappeared by 1800. Even before this final collapse of the Quakers in Charleston, the records of the meeting are spotty, especially after 1750. In the late eighteenth century the meeting appears to have been made up primarily of a few merchants who were transient visitors to the port city.[24]

Harsh demographic realities had much to do with this decline. Small in numbers, the second and third generations of Quaker families found it almost impossible to maintain the discipline of endogamous marriage. Unfortunately, most interpreters have viewed the disappearance of the Charleston Quakers in terms of "spiritual declension." The few historians who have registered impressions of the Charleston Quakers in this period have viewed the Friends through the jeremiads of Quaker itinerant preachers. These itinerants combined their general disgust with the rather dissolute life of the city's planter class with stinging rebukes of the Charleston Friends, who had allegedly made themselves too comfortable in the midst of iniquity. Mary Paisley, who visited Charleston in 1753, offered that the city was little more than a "refuge for the disjointed members of our Society, where they may walk in the sight of their own eyes, and the imagination of their own hearts, without being accountable to any for their conduct, and yet be called by the name of Quaker." Mary Paisley at least benefited from the hospitality of the Charleston Meeting, despite her low opinion of their spiritual health. During her stay, the Quaker merchant John Sinclair provided her with, by her own admission, "much civility and hospitality." Sinclair had, however, done as had so many in the tiny community and married outside of the faith, a failing that led Paisley to inform her host that she was "ashamed to walk the streets with one under our name, who deviated so much from our principles as he did."[25]

Paisley's comments could easily lead, and in fact have led, to some dismissing the Charleston Quakers in this period and viewing them as jettisoning their own convictions in order to blend with the larger society. In truth, the story is far more complex. The story of Sophia Hume is perhaps most representative of the relationship between the Charleston Quakers and the Anglican-planter culture that surrounded them. Hume was the granddaughter of Mary Fisher Crosse, "Mother Crosse." Hume was not be raised in the faith of her grandmother but as an Anglican. This in itself shows how common intermarriage had become, as even the daughter of "Mother Crosse" could not find a partner within the faith. Sophia's mother, Susannah Bayley, married Henry Wigington, who served as deputy secretary of the province and represented the top tier of the colonial power structure.

Sophia also married an Anglican, Robert Hume, and lived a life in which she was, as she later described, "a lady of fashion." A personal crisis, however, led to a return to her ancestral faith. Robert Hume fled to England in 1731 because of a financial scandal, and the resulting embarrassment seems to have led Sophia back to her grandmother's faith. She herself lived in England after her husband's death in 1737, but she made two return trips to Charleston as an itinerant preacher in 1747 and 1767.[26]

Hume, like most itinerants who came to Charleston, came to view her former home as a morass of dissolution. Following her 1747 visit, she published a pamphlet entitled *An Exhortation to the Inhabitants of the Province of South Carolina.* Evidence from this work suggests that she had met with scorn from many in Charleston. (She described how she received "the smile of contempt" during her visit.) She focused her preaching on Charleston's subservience to "the Tyrant Custom" and the pleasures of the ballroom and the punch bowl. She wrote little about the Charleston Meeting itself, perhaps because of its small numbers.[27]

Choosing to exile herself from her native land, Sophia Hume became the paradigm for many South Carolina Friends. While she faced no legal proscriptions in South Carolina, she viewed the surrounding culture as utterly antithetical to her spiritual life. Moreover, she could not find it within herself to praise the Friends who remained part of the Charleston Meeting in the midst of what she saw as a very wicked city. Nevertheless, it is worth remembering that the vital spiritual experience that galvanized Hume had the Charleston Meeting, her grandmother, and perhaps mother as its starting point. Small and scattered, overshadowed and yet not completely extinguished by the larger Anglican community, the Charleston Quakers were a flickering flame, but a flame nonetheless. Though given official toleration from the beginning, cultural pressures combined with frequent intermarriage to decimate the community.

Demographic changes thus provide no thermometer for the spiritual intensity of the tiny lowcountry meeting. It is worth noting that a few Charleston Friends apparently freed their slaves in 1790s, showing that these lowcountry Quakers had a greater commitment to the "discipline" of the meeting than even other eighteenth-century Quakers supposed. Wealthy merchant Thomas Wadsworth, for example, declared his slaves "all emancipated and set free" in his will of 1799, setting aside for them fifty acres apiece in the South Carolina backcountry and putting them "under the special care and protection of the Friends or Quakers residing at Bush river, Newberry county." The meetinghouse remained on King Street until 1838, when it was razed in an effort to halt the spread of one of Charleston's many disastrous fires. The meeting itself had dissolved before that time. In the 1820s the "Quaker meeting" in Charleston apparently consisted of two elderly men whose personal dislike of each other prevented anything resembling amicable relations.[28]

In the interim the South Carolina backcountry had become the home of a vibrant community of Friends that had little contact with the Charleston Meeting. The first of these backcountry meetings was held near the settlement known as Pine Tree Hill and was known as the Wateree Meeting. This small meeting did have a connection to the Charleston friends through Robert Milhouse, a lowcountry Quaker who migrated to the backcountry in the 1750s and organized Irish Quaker settlers who seem to have had some connection to William Edmundson. The meeting at Pine Tree Hill, known as Camden by the 1760s, did not last very long and was laid down by 1784. The historian of the Friends in colonial South Carolina has suggested that the community was submerged by an increasing number of Anglican settlers. A better explanation for the disappearance of this meeting is that the core membership, mostly interrelated Irish families, migrated to the Bush River region of South Carolina and joined with the more substantial Quaker settlement there.[29]

The Bush River Meeting, located in what is now Newberry and Laurens counties, became one of the strongest communities of Friends in the colonial South. The greatest influx into the area came from the southward movement of Quakers from New Jersey and Pennsylvania, many of whom also settled in the Pee Dee region and began a series of meetings in what is now Marlboro County. By the 1760s enough Quakers had made their way to forks of the Broad and Saluda rivers to hold thirteen weekly meetings and the single, supervisory, monthly meeting that became known simply as the Bush River Meeting.[30]

The Friends meeting at Bush River maintained a stringent discipline over its members, expelling anyone who married outside the meeting. In one typical monthly meeting in 1775, the Bush River Friends expelled one Samuel Chapman for having "gone out in marriage" with "a woman not of our Society." They further maintained active contact with the Philadelphia Yearly Meeting, as well as meetings in Virginia. In 1789 the Philadelphia Yearly Meeting recommended that the Bush River Quakers take the troublesome Charleston Meeting under its wing, underscoring the strength of the backcountry settlement of Friends. A visitation committee visited Charleston, but apparently it was sharply rebuffed by the independent Charlestonians.[31]

The Bush River settlement likely found it easy to maintain Quaker simplicity in the rough, frontier conditions of the backcountry. Quakers were likely the majority in the Bush River District during the 1750s and 1760s, and many of their neighbors were Baptist and Presbyterian small farmers, who likely had more amicable relations with the Quakers than the Anglican planters of the lowcountry. Farming primarily for subsistence, these backcountry Quakers did produce some flour, butter, cheese, and tobacco that they traded with Charleston factors. In this yeoman farmers' world, the Friends faced few of the temptations of wealth, but they certainly can be described as prosperous. In fact, Newberry District, later made up largely of plantation agriculture, could be described in the late eighteenth century as "dotted with small, self-sufficient family units, with small grist mills located on the streams and with artisans plying their trades as coopers, cobblers, cabinetmakers, distillers and weavers."[32]

Two issues did, however, upset the peace of these backcountry Quakers, creating a crisis that ultimately led to the end of the Quaker presence in South Carolina. In both of these crises, the Friends found themselves in conflict with mores of the larger community, which continued to give official, in fact, constitutional toleration of the Friends while simultaneously exerting enormous cultural pressures on the Quakers to conform to the majority ethos. Perhaps most significant, the Friends by the end of the eighteenth century found themselves living in a state in which legislative and judicial power buttressed an institution that the Friends inner light found morally and theologically repugnant.

The imperial crisis with England represented the first major test of the Bush River Meeting. In general backcountry Quakers tended to pay little attention to the mounting crisis with the mother country until 1775. Some of the remaining Charleston Friends took an active role in the emerging conflict, though they seem to have left their Quaker principles rapidly behind. The London Yearly Meeting asked that the American Friends remain above the fray. While there were a number of exceptions, the Friends in the backcountry generally attempted to follow this course, a decision that convinced many South Carolina Whigs that their Quaker neighbors were Loyalists.

The backcountry Friends weathered the crisis of the Revolution remarkably well, at least in terms of maintaining Quaker discipline. Most acts of discipline came late in the Revolution, as the bloody conflict moved to the front doors of the Quaker settlers. Ellis Cheek, disciplined at the monthly meeting in October of 1781, is one typical example of a Friend who faced "disownment" for being "guilty of taking up arms and going out in a warlike manner, this being contrary to the peaceable principles of Friends."[33]

During the course of the conflict, the Bush River Meeting disciplined twenty-seven members for going to war. South Carolina Quakers that did choose to enter the conflict were more likely to join the Whigs, though an almost equal number cast their lot with South Carolina Loyalist regiments. Those Quakers who rejected "the testimony of peace" were relatively few in number and, much as in the Yamassee conflict, the South Carolina Friends managed to largely remain a people apart. Moreover, their isolation in the backcountry prevented them from facing the kind of social pressures, or the persecution, Friends had endured in and around Charleston after the Yamassee War.[34]

The backcountry Friends emerged virtually unscathed by the American Revolution and indeed benefited from it. The state's 1778 Constitution officially disestablished the Church of England. The 1778 Constitution and the 1790 Constitution tipped their hats to Quaker sensibilities by allowing officeholders' oaths to be taken by "affirmation."[35]

The second crisis that the backcountry Quakers faced in the latter half of the eighteenth century, however, was far more serious than the difficulties of the Revolutionary era, leading to an almost wholesale departure from the new state of South Carolina. The decision of the backcountry Society of Friends to reject slavery does much more than reveal the strength of discipline in the Bush River Meeting. In their rejection of slaveholding, the Friends rejected the kind of society that South Carolina was becoming. At the very moment when the Friends felt themselves surrounded by an emerging culture of cotton and slavery, they exiled themselves beyond its reach.[36]

South Carolina Friends had owned slaves from the very beginnings of the colony. In this, they differed little from Friends throughout British North America. Meetings in Pennsylvania and New Jersey, the centers of the Quaker life in the American colonies, had banned participation in the slave trade as early as 1696. Almost eighty years passed before the Philadelphia Yearly Meeting ruled solidly against the ownership of slaves. Jean Soderlund, in one of the more complete studies of colonial Quakers and abolition, argues that this gradualism entwined with only a very slow recognition of the equality of African Americans. Soderlund notes that even many antislavery reformers refused to accept black members until the 1790s.[37]

Criticisms such as these aside, the emergence of a Quaker abolitionist movement can fairly be characterized as one of the great moral achievements of eighteenth-century America. Remarkably, Quaker meetings in the South arrived at an antislavery position at close to the same speed as their northern brethren, despite living in societies where the profitability and practicality of slaveholding remained strong. The North Carolina Yearly Meeting took a strong stand on the matter of slave ownership by the time of the American Revolution. Indeed, by 1782, that Yearly Meeting had made "disownment" (banishment from the meeting) the punishment for slave ownership.[38]

Backcountry South Carolina Quakers faced two dilemmas as they sought to expand their "testimony of peace" into a strong witness against slaveholding. First, a number of the more prominent backcountry Quakers continued to hold slaves throughout the American Revolution. Both Samuel Kelly and Robert Milhouse were disciplined in the 1790s for refusing to free their slaves. Only five other Friends were disowned by the meeting prior to 1806. Some of these, such as Thomas Kelly, were readmitted to the meeting after agreeing to emancipate their bondmen. The minutes of the Bush River Meeting from 1794 show that it appointed a committee with the sole purpose of looking out for the physical needs of "free negroes," an indication, as Jo Anne McCormick argues, that some backcountry Friends had emancipated their slaves and now sought to help them negotiate the difficulties of their new status. Much as they had maintained Quaker discipline during the American Revolution, the backcountry Friends also moved quickly and decisively to purge the sin of slaveholding from their midst.[39]

The second dilemma proved more daunting. South Carolina, throughout the eighteenth century, had become a slaveholder's world, in which law, judicial and customary, made slavery the cornerstone of the state's social order. A series of slave codes helped push South Carolina in this direction.[40] Indeed, freeing one's slaves became increasingly difficult and eventually, after the Quakers' departure from the state, became all but impossible. Moreover, until the closing of the international slave trade in 1808,[41] South Carolina remained perhaps the major entrepot for enslaved African people into North America, and—with the 1793 invention of the cotton gin—plantation slavery spread rapidly into the South Carolina upcountry. By 1800 all the state could be said to have crossed the line from being, in the words of historian Ira Berlin, a society that holds slaves to a slaveholding society.[42]

The Bush River Meeting boldly challenged the direction taken by the new state in the 1780s. The meeting believed that it was not enough to purge individual Friends of the sin of slaveholding and sought to address the political and economic power of slavery that gradually structured life in the state. In a 1785 communication to the quarterly meeting the Bush River Monthly Meeting expressed frustration over inability to alleviate the bane of slavery. It wrote: "Dear Friends, Bush River further adds, a concern having rested on the minds of friends in respect of the poor enslaved Africans of the difficulty that seems to arise in respect of a law being procured in their favor & likewise of putting a stop to the importation of them into these colonies and also of the distressful usage which many are liable to."[43] In 1786 the Bush River Meeting sent an antislavery memorial to the South Carolina legislature.[44] The memorial was not simply rejected; it was actually ignored completely. This event, perhaps more than any other, laid the groundwork for the Quakers' eventual abandonment of the state.[45]

In the seventeen years that followed the rejection of Bush River's antislavery memorial, enormous changes came to the community nestled in the forks of the Broad and Saluda rivers. Historian Lacy K. Ford has described the backcountry in the eighteenth century as "a backwater region isolated from the main currents of South Carolina society." All that would change in the 1790s. The cotton gin made possible the spread of the hardy, short-staple cotton into the South Carolina backcountry. This spread of cotton culture meant the spread of slaveholding throughout the state. The true travail of South Carolina Quakerism had come.[46]

The arrival of Zachariah Dix in 1803 thus became the trigger for an out-migration from the state that had likely been considered by the Quakers for the last decade. Some discussion of leaving South Carolina had occurred in the early 1790s, though the motivations for the move are very unclear. In fact, two prominent backcountry Quakers, Abijah O'Neall and Samuel Kelly, both purchased land in Ohio in the late 1790s. Dix's arrival would, however, was certainly the trigger for the flood of Quaker out-migration. Dix, apparently an elderly man at the beginning of the nineteenth century, had long held a reputation as a seer, allegedly having predicted the Battle of Guilford Courthouse during the American Revolution. The records of the Bush River Meeting become increasingly fragmentary from the time of Dix's visit until the meeting was officially laid down in 1822. As early as 1806, some monthly meetings were taken up entirely with the business of handing out certificates to Quaker families resettling in Ohio, who hoped to become a part of the meetings in the Miami Valley.[47]

This great out-migration was followed by exactly the kind of changes the Quakers had feared. The spread of the cotton and slavery frontier overtook the old Quaker settlements of Newberry. At the time of Dix's arrival, Newberry District's population was 16 percent enslaved. By the time of the Civil War, 60 percent of the population was enslaved Africans, and small farms had been replaced by plantations. South Carolina law changed along with these changing economic and social conditions. If the Quaker community had stayed until 1820, they could not have manumitted slaves without the express permission of the State Legislature. In an act of 1841, it became illegal for slaves to be sent beyond the borders of the Palmetto State for the purpose of setting them free.[48] It is very likely that, given these conditions, South Carolina Friends would have faced serious persecution for their antislavery witness had they chosen to remain in the state.[49]

The experience of the two most-famous Quakers of nineteenth-century South Carolina gives further evidence that leaving had become the best option for Friends serious about pursuing their faith. Sarah Grimké and her younger sister Angelina came from one of the South Carolina lowcountry's great dynasties. The Grimké family owned an elegant home in Charleston, as well as an upcountry cotton plantation and numerous slaves in Union District. Sarah Grimké began to detach herself from this world of wealth after 1820, when her father's death prompted her to leave her ancestral Anglican faith, spending some time as a Presbyterian and eventually becoming a committed Quaker. Her sister soon followed in her footsteps. Notably, Sarah Grimké encountered the tenets of the Friends, not in South Carolina, but in Philadelphia while caring for her ailing father. Neither of the sisters found an outlet for the faith in antebellum Charleston and indeed faced social ostracism. Both women left South Carolina forever in the early 1830s to become stalwarts in the Quaker abolitionist movement. Like the Quakers of the Bush River Meeting, they felt it necessary to sever their relationship to South Carolina in order to preserve their religious identity.[50]

By the time of the American Civil War, the Quaker presence in South Carolina was negligible, though strong meetings remained in North Carolina. North Carolina Friends had become, however, largely marginal to the state's life and culture by the nineteenth century. This is not because North Carolina Quakers faced legal disabilities in that state, but because the North Carolina Yearly Meeting itself banned Friends from running for public office after 1809. Following the Civil War, many North Carolina Quakers became submerged into the evangelical religious culture that surrounded them. Quaker meetinghouses began to look more like Baptist or Methodist churches, and revivalistic methods aimed at winning new converts replaced the silent meeting. South Carolina Quakerism remained moribund throughout much of the twentieth century.[51]

A small revival of the Society of Friends came to South Carolina in the late twentieth century. The 1967 Fourth World Conference of Friends, held on the campus of Guilford College near Greensboro, North Carolina, was a major turning point for southern Friends, rejuvenating the movement. The contemporary meeting in Columbia, South Carolina, dates its beginnings from this year. The Friends grew in strength among younger, college-educated "seekers" in the South of the late 1960s because of, rather than in spite of, their strong "peace testimony" during the Vietnam era. The South Carolina meetings, in fact, became havens for white southern progressives concerned for issues of peace and justice, very much at odds with the conservative nature of white South Carolina's politics and culture. Their numbers remained small, however. In 1980 South Carolina had five Quaker meetings and seven by 2003 with one of the larger of these meetings having about thirty in attendance for "First Day" services. Small numbers aside, modern South Carolina Quakers have maintained their strong social witness with a focus on international peace, economic justice, and the abolition of the death penalty.[52]

The story of the Friends of South Carolina suggests that religious life in America does not have to be studied from the perspective of the dominant religious majorities who set the terms of religious discourse. South Carolina Quakers, at a number of points in the life of the colony and then the state, set the terms of their relationship to the larger society. The prosperous Friends of the Charleston Meeting carved a place for their community in the emerging life of the colony, seeking to use the social and political power they held in colonial society to maintain a discrete religious identity. In so doing, they created a vibrant , if small and isolated, movement amidst an Anglican majority who held values deeply antithetical to the Friends'. Nevertheless, the struggles they faced in Carolina underscore how cultural pressures can prove as dangerous to dissident religious identities as legal proscription.

The experiences of the Society of Friends in the backcountry illustrate the same points. The Bush River Meeting prospered, but the Friends knew that changes occurring in their social world, specifically the spread of cotton culture and slaveholding into the backcountry, would likely overwhelm their young community. The protections granted them in the 1778 and 1790 Constitutions meant little in the face of such pressures. Ultimately the Quakers of South Carolina rejected the toleration offered to them in the Palmetto State. They decided that there was much about South Carolina society they could not tolerate.

Notes

1. Jo Anne McCormick, "The Quakers of Colonial South Carolina, 1670–1806," Ph.D. dissertation, University of South Carolina, 1984, 196–97. McCormick's research, if not her interpretations, are very thorough and complete. This essay is very much in her debt. For more on the rather shadowy figure of Zachariah Dix, see Thomas Pope, *The History of Newberry County, South Carolina* (Columbia: University of South Carolina Press, 1973), 112.

2. Margaret Hope Bacon, *The Quiet Rebels: The Story of Quakers in America.* (Wallingford, Pa.: Prendle Hill Publications, 1999), 40; Hugh Barbour and J. William Frost, *The Quakers* (New York: Greenwood Press, 1988), 89; Frederick B. Tolles, *Meeting House and Counting House: The Quaker Merchants of Colonial Philadelphia, 1682–1763* (New York: Norton, 1963), 71. A slightly more positive view comes from Sydney Ahlstrom, who does describe the Friends as "fairly numerous" in early Charleston. However, Ahlstrom connects them with Dissenting groups more generally in the young colony, groups he refers to as "scattered and disorganized." Ahlstrom gives little or no attention to South Carolina Quakers, indeed to southern Quakers in general, after the earliest period of settlement, even on the question of slavery; see Ahlstrom, *A Religious History of the American People* (New Haven: Yale University Press, 1972), 198, 650, 699.

3. Many of the most important studies of religious diversity in American religion have focused heavily on the strength of "mainline" religion in shaping the terms of acceptance into the American religious milieu. Will Herberg's *Protestant, Catholic, Jew: An Essay in American Religious Society* (Garden City, N.Y.: Doubleday, 1955) serves as the best example of this "consensus" approach. Even when scholars such as Ahlstrom have affirmed the continuing strength of sectarianism, they have done so by placing sects in relation to the dominant religious paradigms. William Hutchison, a student of Ahlstrom's, has taken this a step further and argued for what he calls a "Protestant Establishment" that sets the terms of discourse for American religion and defines the boundaries of toleration and marginality; see "Protestantism as Establishment," in *Between the Times: The Travail of the Protestant Establishment in America, 1900–1960,* ed. Hutchison (Cambridge: Cambridge University Press, 1989).

4. Adrian Davies, *The Quakers in English Society, 1655–1725* (Oxford: Clarendon Press, 2000), 15

5. Barbour and Frost, *The Quakers,* 41–47.

6. Bacon, *The Quiet Rebels,* 25–33.

7. Jay Worall Jr., *The Friendly Virginians* (Athens, Ga.: Iberian Publishing, 1994), 25–41.

8. Ibid., 23.

9. Fundamental Constitutions, 1669, sec. 90 (version of July 21, 1669), cited in *The Colonial Records of North Carolina,* ed. Mattie Erma Edwards Parker (Raleigh, N.C.: Carolina Charter Tercentenary Commission 1963), 149.

10. M. Eugene Sirmans, *Colonial South Carolina: A Political History, 1663–1763* (Chapel Hill: University of North Carolina Press, 1966), 14; McCormick, "The Quakers of Colonial South Carolina," 15–19.

11. McCormick, "The Quakers of Colonial South Carolina," 20–22.

12. Jack P. Greene, "Colonial South Carolina and the Caribbean Connection," in *Imperatives, Behaviors and Identities: Essays in Early American Cultural History* (Charlottesville: University Press of Virginia, 1992), 68–86. See also Richard Dunn, "The English Sugar Islands and the Founding of South Carolina," *South Carolina Historical and Genealogical Magazine* 72 (1971): 81–93.

13. William Edmundson, *Journal of the Life, Trials Sufferings and Labour of Love in the Work of the Ministry* (London: J. Sowle, 1715), 73–75. Thomas E. Drake, *Quakers and Slavery in America* (New Haven: Yale University Press, 1950), 6–10.

14. Drake, *Quakers and Slavery in America,* 29,30.

15. Robert Weir, *Colonial South Carolina* (Columbia: University of South Carolina Press, 1997), 68.

16. McCormick, "The Quakers of Colonial South Carolina," 32; Jean R. Sonderlund, *Quakers and Slavery: A Divided Spirit* (Princeton, N.J.: Princeton University Press, 1985); Crosse became known as "Mother Crosse" among Charleston Quakers for her role in spiritually nurturing the early meeting. On her career as a transatlantic itinerant, see Rebecca Larson, *Daughters of Light: Quaker Women Preaching and Prophesying in the Colonies and Abroad, 1700–1775* (Chapel Hill: University of North Carolina Press, 1999), 26, 65, 67.

17. Document no. 47: "Archdale Named Governor," Document no. 48: "Friends Expectation in the Military Act," and Document no. 33: "Letter from Carolina Friends," John Archdale Papers (microfilm), South Carolina Department of Archives and History, Columbia.

18. McCormick, "The Quakers of Colonial South Carolina," 40–41.

19. Robert Olwell analyzes what he calls a "culture of power" in colonial South Carolina in *Masters, Slaves and Subjects: The Culture of Power in the South Carolina Low Country* (Ithaca, N.Y.: Cornell University Press, 1998).

20. Fox, quoted in James Bowden, *The History of the Society of Friends in America,* vol. 2 (New York: Reprint Edition, 1973), 414–15.

21. S. Charles Bolton, *Southern Anglicanism: The Church of England in Colonial South Carolina* (Westport, Conn.: Greenwood Press, 1982), 21–28. Act No. 222 of 1704, 2 S.C. STATUTES AT LARGE 232 (Cooper 1837); Act No. 225 of 1704, 2 S.C. STATUTES AT LARGE 236–46 (Cooper 1837). See the essay in this volume by James Lowell Underwood titled "The Dawn of Religious Freedom in South Carolina: The Journey from Limited Tolerance

to Constitutional Right," which discusses the controversy over the exclusion and establishment laws and the debate that resulted in the order in council declaring them null and void.
See also Act No. 255 of 1706, 2 S.C. STATUTES AT LARGE 281 (Cooper, 1837); Act No. 256 of
1706, 2 S.C. STATUTES AT LARGE 282 (Cooper 1837).

22. Document no. 12: "A Letter dated January 30 1706" and "The Humble Address of the
Right Honorable, the Lords Temporal and Spiritual in Parliament Assembled" in John Archdale Papers (microfilm), South Carolina Department of Archives and History, Columbia.
McCormick suggests that the Society of Friends "never achieved the organizational or
numerical strength necessary to maintain a meeting during the tumultuous period of the
establishment controversy." She does not, however, advance any evidence for this claim and,
in fact, her own research seems to prove the contrary.

23. McCormick, "The Quakers of Colonial South Carolina," 60.

24. Ibid., 60–70.

25. Rebecca Larson, *Daughters of Light: Quaker Women Preaching and Prophesying in the
Colonies and Abroad, 1700–1775* (Chapel Hill: University of North Carolina Press, 1999),
206–7.

26. McCormick, "The Quakers of Colonial South Carolina," 100–103.

27. Sophia Hume, *An Exhortation to the Inhabitants of the Province of South Carolina*
(Dublin: Isaac Jackson, 1747), 5, 70.

28. Thomas Wadsworth, 2 MS dated September 14, 1799, Manuscript Division, South
Caroliniana Library, University of South Carolina, Columbia; Mark Perry, *Lift Up Thy Voice:
The Grimké Family's Journey from Slaveholders to Civil Rights Leaders* (New York: Viking,
2001), 78.

29. "2nd Month, 1775," Minutes of the Bush River Monthly Meeting, Society of Friends
(transcript), 1772–1820, South Carolina Department of Archives and History, Columbia;
McCormick, "The Quakers of Colonial South Carolina," 107–9, 118–19.

30. McCormick, "The Quakers of Colonial South Carolina," 130.

31. Ibid., 131–34.

32. Pope, *The History of Newberry County,* 113.

33. "10th Month, 1781," Minutes of the Bush River Meeting, Society of Friends (transcript), 1772–1820, South Carolina Department of Archives and History, Columbia.

34. A few backcountry Friends had homes and farms pillaged and destroyed by both
Whig and Loyalist forces. Quaker testimonies of these events sometimes made the claim
that these represented examples of Quaker "sufferings." However, it seems more likely that
these are examples of the general chaos and the extreme violence of the Revolution in the
South Carolina backcountry. See Pope, *The History of Newberry County,* 51.

35. S.C. Const. of 1778, arts. 38 and 36, in 1 S.C. STATUTES AT LARGE 144 (Cooper, 1836);
S.C. Const. of 1790, art. 4, ibid., 190; James Lowell Underwood, *The Constitution of South
Carolina,* vol. 3: *Church and State, Morality, and Free Expression* (Columbia: University of
South Carolina Press, 1992), 66–68, 77.

36. McCormick, "The Quakers of Colonial South Carolina," 176–203.

37. Sonderlund, *Quakers and Slavery,* 173, 177.

38. McCormick, "The Quakers of Colonial South Carolina," 186.

39. Ibid., 186–90.

40. For the slave codes and laws passed in South Carolina during this period, see John Belton O'Neall, *The Negro Law of South Carolina* (Columbia: John G. Bowman, 1848), 7–49.

41. U.S. Constitution, Art. 1, sec. 9.

42. Ira Berlin, *Many Thousands Gone: The First Two Centuries of Slavery in North America.* (Cambridge, Mass.: Harvard University Press, 1998), 7–13.

43. Newberry County, South Carolina transcript (not literatim) of Men's Minutes, Bush River Monthly Meeting, Religious Society of Friends, 1772–1820, 1st Month, 1785, 2:29; available on microfilm at the South Carolina Department of Archives and History, Columbia. McCormick, "The Quakers of Colonial South Carolina," 187.

44. Men's Minutes, Bush River Meeting Religious Society of Friends, 1772–1820, 4th Month, 1786, 2:55–56; available on microfilm, South Carolina Department of Archives and History, Columbia. McCormick, "The Quakers of Colonial South Carolina," 187.

45. McCormick, "The Quakers of Colonial South Carolina," 187.

46. Lacy K. Ford, *Origins of Southern Radicalism: The South Carolina Upcountry, 1800–1860* (New York: Oxford University Press, 1988), 5–7.

47. John Belton O'Neall, *The Annals of Newberry, Historical, Biographical, and Anecdotal* (Charleston: S. G. Courtenay, 1859), 34–35; "7th Month, 1806," Bush River Minutes, South Carolina Department of Archives and History, Columbia.

48. Act No. 2836 of 1841, 11 S.C. Statutes at Large 168–69 (Republican Printers 1873).

49. Pope, *The History of Newberry County,* 112–15.

50. Perry, *Lift Up Thy Voice,* 45–48, 132–33.

51. Damon D. Hickey, *Sojourners No More: The Quakers in the New South, 1865–1920* (Greensboro: North Carolina Friends Historical Society, 1997), 35–47.

52. J. Floyd Moore, "Quakers in the South," *Encyclopedia of Southern Religion,* ed. Samuel S. Hill (Macon, Ga.: Mercer University Press, 1997), 629–30; see also www.palmettofriends .org for information regarding contemporary Friends.

Bishop John England and the Compatibility of the Catholic Church and American Democracy

Peter Clarke and James Lowell Underwood

WRITING IN 1835, AFTER AN EXTENDED VISIT TO AMERICA, Alexis de Tocqueville made the surprising observation that not only did he not consider Catholicism antithetical to democracy, he considered that church in the United States to be "one of the most favorable to equality of conditions."[1] He argued that this was because the church made no ranking of lay members; only the priests were set above the members, and in America Catholic clerics focused on their religious duties and did not seek political power as had sometimes been the case in Europe.[2] American priests concentrated on "revealed dogmas" and believed that political truth is open "to the free inquiries of men."[3] The American Catholic was faithful to his religion, but he was also "the most independent of citizens."[4] This made the operation of the Catholic Church consistent with the American concept of the separation of church and state. John England, whose tenure as bishop of Charleston in South Carolina overlapped with de Tocqueville's American visit, provided much of the intellectual and practical underpinning for this harmony. Bishop England argued, "We look upon Republicanism to mean, that no man has, that no set of men have any inherent natural rights to take precedence of their fellow men; and that all power to regulate the public affairs of individuals, united in the social compact, must be derived from the public will freely expressed by the voice of the majority of individuals."[5]

England was a man of varied achievements. John Tracy Ellis saw England's greatest worth in the founding of the first regularly published Catholic weekly, the *United States Catholic Miscellany*.[6] Some might see his written *Constitution for the Diocese of Charleston* (1826), with its annual conventions of clergy and lay delegates, as a far-sighted model of church organization, looking even beyond the Second Vatican Council.[7] Richard Rousseau lists England's greatest achievement as the development of a theory of church-state relations that accepts a free church in a free state.[8] Joseph O'Brien calls him "the never-wearying Apostle to American Democracy."[9] In a 1993 article about England as a Catholic spokesman and southern intellectual, R. Frank Saunders Jr. and George A. Rogers wrote that "John England's career seems almost fictional."[10] This essay tells the story of England's respect for the U.S. Constitution, the compatibility of the Catholic Church with the government of the United States, the compatibility of the U.S. Constitution with the teaching of the Church, and the contribution that the Church makes toward achieving a virtuous electorate.

England was born in Cork, Ireland, on September 23, 1786.[11] At first he studied law, but his heart turned to the priesthood, and he entered Carlow College for theological studies to prepare for ordination.[12] England was born in a time when Catholics were subjected to oppressive measures limiting their right to hold property and receive an education.[13] But education restrictions were relaxed as England was growing up.[14] The British government permitted Catholic seminaries to open, so that it could closely monitor the courses of study of those preparing for the priesthood. Priests educated in the Irish colleges on the Continent often returned to Ireland with dangerously democratic ideas. In Ireland, John England saw firsthand the harm that could come from state preference for one religion. Tithes for the State Church were collected by law, and people were imprisoned for not paying the tithe. Catholics had to support their own institutions by voluntary contributions over and above the tithe already paid to support the State Church.[15] An observer of the tithe-collection system noted that it was deeply resented by Catholics and Dissenters alike because it was "collected for the support of a Clergy, which has no spiritual relation to the bulk of the inhabitants of their parishes."[16] The method of collection was particularly galling since the clergymen for whom the exaction was levied usually contracted with "tithe proctors," who often used thuggish tactics to enforce the levy.[17]

The long history of persecution of Catholics in Ireland must have been the seed that gave growth to England's beliefs in religious freedom and the separation of church and state. This persecution was not an abstraction to England. Close family members had their lives severely disrupted. In an 1839 letter to the Reverend Richard Fuller, England looked back forty-five years to his childhood, when his grandfather had shown him the room where he had been imprisoned for four years "in consequence of the injustice to which the Catholics of Ireland were subjected in those days."[18] During the imprisonment, the family's home was seized, and England's grandmother died in a neighbor's house.[19] The bishop's father, Thomas, the eldest child, tried to contribute to the support of his brothers and sisters by teaching "some propositions of the sixth book of Euclid to a few scholars."[20] Charges were brought against him for violating the restrictions on the education of Catholics. Because of his youth, he was offered an opportunity to avoid the sentence of transportation if he recanted his beliefs "in the doctrines of transubstantiation, of penance, and of the invocation of saints" in front of a Protestant bishop.[21] He refused.[22] He fled to the mountains, where he lived as a fugitive for more than a year.[23] When enforcement of these harsh laws was relaxed, Thomas was able to return, obtain the release of his father, and reestablish the family.[24] The bishop told Reverend Fuller, "It is his eldest son who has the honour to inform you that he has good reason to feel anguish of soul at his own recollection of the oppression of Ireland."[25] It is small wonder then that freedom of religion loomed large in his mind and that he concluded that separation of church and state was desirable because of the abuse visited on Catholics from the entwined British government / Anglican Church establishment.

Conditions had improved by the time England was studying for the priesthood.[26] The Catholic Church was flourishing as it moved out of hiding. Religious groups of men and women were being formed for education and social good. England was ordained in 1808 by Bishop Francis Moylan, a brother of Gen. Stephen Moylan, who had served as aide de camp to Gen. George Washington.[27] The young priest was assigned to the North Presentation Convent in Cork, where he was soon involved in a wide variety of ministries and projects that foreshadowed his later multifaceted ministry as bishop of Charleston.[28] He took charge of a new seminary for the training of candidates for the priesthood. He edited a newspaper and founded a religious magazine.[29] England felt the breath of a church unfettered by government interference. He embraced freedom of religion and the separation of church and state on both intellectual and practical levels. He collected material for a book about Arthur O'Leary, an influential advocate of freedom of religion.[30] England fought attempts by the temporal authorities to insinuate themselves into what were traditionally church prerogatives, even if the Holy See appeared to acquiesce in the government maneuvers. When a grateful Pope Pius VII was willing to give the British monarch (whose government had been instrumental in obtaining the pope's release from imprisonment in France) a veto over the naming of Irish bishops and the British government was able to gain approval of this veto from the Irish Catholic hierarchy by offering to fund Catholic seminaries in Ireland and to pay the salaries of Catholic priests, John England was active in the campaign that defeated this government meddling in internal church affairs.[31] His Irish ministry also illustrated his deep commitment to serving often-ignored groups on the fringes of society, who would otherwise have little or no access to religious aid. A good example of this commitment is seen in his efforts to provide priests for the Catholics in the penal colony of Australia. When a priest he had urged to go to Australia was deported from that country because of a lack of official sanction, England successfully lobbied members of Parliament to seek approval for admitting two other priests to minister to the Australian penal colony Catholics.[32]

In 1820 England was named bishop of Charleston. Ordained in Cork, Ireland, on September 21, 1820, he refused to take the customary oath of allegiance to the British king and declared his intention to become a U.S. citizen.[33] England experienced the burden of the union of church and state in Ireland. The established church was not his church. His own Catholic Church was supported not by the state but by the voluntary contributions of the people and was free of government domination and interference in its offices and structures and in much of its activity.[34] The seeds of acceptance of the doctrine of the separation of church and state were planted in his mind in Ireland and grew to maturity in the United States.

Reconciling the Church and the Constitution

England arrived in Charleston on December 30, 1820. On January 21, 1821, he sent his first pastoral letter to Catholics scattered over the new diocese of Charleston, which embraced North Carolina, South Carolina, and Georgia.[35] Writing that he had long admired the excellence of the U.S. Constitution, the new bishop encouraged them in their devotion to the interests of their country and in their determination to fulfill their duties as citizens; England added, "But do not deem it presumption in us, who have not yet the honour of being an American citizen, to have adverted to the topic; for were it necessary, it would have been our solemn duty to call upon you for the preservation of the public peace, and the maintenance of those liberal institutions by which you are so well protected."[36]

The environment of religious freedom in which citizens of different beliefs could worship and the neutrality of the government, which provided a peaceful atmosphere in which a variety of religions could coexist, became keystones of England's philosophy of government. England needed to communicate his appreciation of the United States to the Catholic people in his diocese, and he also needed to persuade other Catholic bishops that the U.S. Constitution's First Amendment was not opposed to the teachings of the Catholic Church in allowing for freedom of religion and separation of church and state. It was also necessary for the new bishop to address the countrymen of his adopted land, because many Americans would have agreed with the sentiments expressed in an 1821 Independence Day speech of John Quincy Adams, in which he referred to the Catholic Church as "that portentous system of despotism and of superstition which, in the name of the meek and humble Jesus, had been spread over the Christian world."[37] Adams's remarks did not make direct reference to the Catholic Church of his time. Instead he focused on its historical role as he viewed it. Still, the address contained damaging stereotypes that could have retarded the acceptance of Catholics in America. Especially stinging were his remarks that the Protestant Reformation was necessary because the church refused to recognize the "single, plain, and almost self-evident principle—that a man has a right to the exercise of his own reason."[38] Later in this essay we shall see how England refuted these remarks in a Christmas 1825 sermon in St. Patrick's Church with Adams in the audience, in an early 1826 address to Congress, and in an 1831 letter to the Catholics of Charleston, in which he emphasized the freedom of the Catholic citizen to search independently for political truth without ecclesiastical or governmental dictation. Many Americans knew of the Catholic Church only from its enemies. England wanted to make known the Catholic Church as he knew it.

In 1821 the bishop plunged into his duties by touring Georgia, South Carolina, and North Carolina, visiting small groups of Catholics and challenging them to meet each Sunday for worship and instruction. He provided them with a missal and a catechism in English, and he commissioned lay leaders to lead worship and to give instruction.[39] These acts refuted stereotypes of the church as a cloistered mystery. Suspicions born of ignorance were abated. The increased emphasis on lay participation did not turn the church into a democracy, but it helped to make it compatible with the surrounding democratic political system. Returning from a visit to Baltimore for the consecration of the new bishop of Boston, England stopped in Washington and was "kindly received" by President James Monroe and Secretary of State John Quincy Adams.[40]

In June 1822 England began the weekly publication of the *United States Catholic Miscellany,* the first Catholic newspaper in the United States. The paper was distributed throughout the United States, Ireland, and Europe. The *Miscellany* published not only news of the diocese but also Catholic news from around the United States and from Europe. It included articles about Catholic teaching from Rome and other European sources. Articles from the *Miscellany* were reprinted in European papers.[41] In describing the needs of Catholics in the United States, England wrote to his friend Judge William Gaston, "I do not know a greater temporal one than the want of some common organ of communication."[42] On June 5, 1822, the first issue of the *Miscellany* pledged to embrace "simple explanation and temperate maintenance of the doctrines of the Roman Catholic Church" in the hope "that many sensible persons will be astonished at finding they have imputed to Catholics doctrines which the Catholic Church has formally condemned, and imagined they were contradicting Catholics, when they held Catholic doctrine themselves."[43] The *Miscellany* also promised that "for the purpose of better discharging which duty, communications and periodical publications from Rome, Paris, London, Dublin, Canada, South-America, the various parts of the United States, and other portions of the world will be obtained, and are solicited."[44] The linking of the country and the church in the title might seem insignificant, but it was a weekly public statement that the Catholic Church and the United States were compatible. England chose as the motto for his newspaper the religious clause of the First Amendment: "Congress shall make no law respecting an establishment of religion or prohibiting the free exercise thereof."[45] This motto appeared on the masthead of every issue of the *United States Catholic Miscellany* as a weekly proclamation of England's affirmation of a free church and a free state.[46]

In a report to Rome, England said the "genius" of the United States was "to have written laws, to have these laws at hand, and to direct all their affairs according to them."[47] England published his *Constitution for the Diocese of Charleston,* available for Catholics and other citizens, so all could see how the Catholic Church was governed. This forthright description of the church's method of operating further reduced stereotyping and suspicion and increased acceptance of the church by the general public. The constitution also had a modest degree of dispersion of power that included laymen in some parts of the decision-making process. Matters relating to religious doctrine were exclusively in the hands of the clergy, especially the bishop, but even he could not alter religious truths that church doctrine identified as revealed by God.[48] Laymen participated in decisions with regard to property as members of the general trustees, as vestrymen elected by lay members, and as elected members of the annual convention.[49] Lay participation reassured the community at large that the Catholic Church, though not a democracy per se, was compatible with a democratic society. Lay participation also anticipated the emphasis given to it in later documents, such as the "Decree of the Apostolate of the Laity (Apostolicam Actuositatem)," promulgated by Pope Paul VI on November 18, 1965, as a result of the Second Vatican Council.[50]

The constitution England wrote forthrightly adopted the doctrine of the separation of church and state as a system that protected spiritual and temporal power from encroachment by each other. It stated:

> 3. We do not believe that our Lord Jesus Christ gave to the civil or temporal governments of states, empires, kingdoms, or nations any authority in or over spiritual or ecclesiastical concerns.
>
> 4. We do not believe that our Lord Jesus Christ gave to the rulers of his Church any authority in or over the civil or temporal concerns of states, empires, kingdoms, or nations.[51]

It is notable that this constitution rooted the separation of church and state in the teachings of Christ, which made it harder for opponents to contend that the doctrine of separation was motivated by hostility to the church.

The Catholic Church in America and Separation of Church and State

On Christmas Day 1825, when Bishop England was in Washington, D.C., preaching in St. Patrick's Church, he used the opportunity to respond to John Quincy Adams's 1821 Independence Day attack on the Catholic Church.[52] Adams's speech, given while he was secretary of state, had also been delivered in Washington.[53] Adams, now president, was in St. Patrick's that Christmas Day to hear John England. Describing the occasion to his friend Judge William Gaston, England wrote: "Without seeking for the occasion, or feeling myself upon the topics until I had gone too far to recede, & then, & only then, my eyes rested upon Mr. Adams, I on Christmas day met foot to foot the 4th of July oration in which he so unkindly assailed us four years since. I then as cooly & as firmly as I could did my utmost, & I am told by many, with sufficient success."[54] England went on to tell Gaston that he visited the president on Wednesday and was invited to dinner with Adams on the following Saturday.[55] Two weeks after the sermon at St. Patrick's, on Sunday, January 8, 1826, England addressed the U.S. Congress with President Adams in attendance.[56] In 1950 Anson Phelps Stokes wrote: "Of all the addresses at the Sunday services so long held . . . in the House of Representatives probably none is more significant than that of the Catholic Bishop of Charleston, the widely respected John England. . . . Bishop England's statement is of special value both because of its occasion and his high standing."[57] England was an immigrant, not yet a citizen, but a chaplain of another faith had given him the opportunity and the challenge of being the first Catholic clergyman to address the Congress. On request of twenty members of the audience, he reconstructed the speech for publication.[58]

Why did England think that it was necessary to deliver this address? Bishop England felt that Catholics still confronted the legacy of suspicion and misinformation that led to a view of the church as a malevolent force rather than as the agency for good he knew it to be. Among the historical examples of this suspicion was a 1696 Carolina statute that contained a generous grant of religious freedom for a variety of Christian faiths except "Papists."[59] England believed that some Americans of Huguenot descent still hated the Catholic Church because of abuse their ancestors had suffered at the hands of Catholic authorities in France.[60] In 1749 rumors abounded that Jesuits and French agents in Mobile were scheming to attack South Carolina.[61] Charles Woodmason, an Anglican missionary to the backcountry, expressed the belief in a 1768 journal entry that Catholics were so disliked they had to conceal their religious affiliation.[62] A misunderstanding of the British Quebec Act of 1774 rekindled fears of Catholics.[63] The act recognized the right of Catholics in Quebec to practice their religion and created what was in effect a dual establishment of Protestant and Catholic faiths. It acknowledged the right of the Catholic clergy to receive their traditional emoluments but only from those who professed the Catholic religion. Government financial support was given to Protestant, but not Catholic, churches. Despite this, the law raised fears that Britain would dispatch a Catholic army from Quebec to subdue malcontents in the colonies to the south. The South Carolina Constitution of 1776 expressed alarm at this attempt to "over-awe and subdue the colonies."[64] England observed that at the time of the Revolutionary War there were few Catholics in Charleston, and those few were often unwilling to identify themselves as adherents.[65] A 1775 edict of the Committee of Public Safety of the Provincial Congress of South Carolina ordered the disarming of Catholics, Negroes, and Indians.[66] England recounted a 1775 incident in which Catholics who had complained about the disarmament and were accused of working against "the Protestant interest" had been stripped, tarred, and feathered and "carted through the streets of Charlestown" pursuant to an order of a "secret committee of five" acting at the behest of the Committee of Public Safety.[67] The South Carolina Constitution of 1778 required that many key officials be Protestant.[68] Article 38 of that Constitution expanded the right to incorporate to include not just Anglican churches but also other Protestant churches meeting certain belief standards. Catholic churches and Jewish synagogues still could not incorporate.[69]

Despite incidents of shabby treatment during the Revolution, Catholics proved to be dedicated to the struggle for American independence. David Ramsay, a physician, prominent South Carolina political figure, and historian, concluded in an 1809 book that the exemplary conduct of Catholic citizens in the defense and government of their country had shown that there was no basis for prejudicial treatment of Catholics.[70] This positive attitude was mirrored in Article 8 of the Constitution of 1790, which recognized, "The free exercise and enjoyment of religious profession and worship, without discrimination or preference."[71] Since the government could no longer favor Protestant groups, the Catholic Church in Charleston was able to incorporate in 1791 and hold its property directly rather than through trustees.[72] The new

Constitution made open celebration of the Mass possible.[73] These developments showed real progress. But England felt that events such as the John Quincy Adams speech meant he still had much to do in interpreting Catholicism and American democracy to each other to show that they were compatible.

England's address to Congress was a forceful refutation of charges that the Catholic Church was antidemocratic because of its hierarchical structure and disloyal to the United States because it owed allegiance to a foreign power: the papal state.[74] His philosophy was rooted in the doctrine of revealed religious truth.[75] God has revealed religious truth to the church as his agent and to individuals.[76] When the church exceeds the dimensions of the religious truth revealed to it by God and speaks to political issues, it becomes a mere human not a divine instrument. An individual church member is not obligated to follow these human dictates.[77] The church member is free to inquire personally into political truth aided by God and God-fostered reason.[78] This approach—which places political truth seeking in the hands of individuals participating as electors, rather than in the hands of a governmental or ecclesiastical hierarchy—is compatible with the American view of democracy and the separation of powers.[79] Neither the government nor the church can persecute anyone for his religious beliefs.[80] Such persecution does not serve Godly ends; it serves a merely human quest for power.[81] One could be both a good Catholic and a good American citizen. The bishop from Ireland became a citizen of the United States on February 6, 1826, a month after his address before Congress.[82]

As well-crafted and persuasive as it was, England's speech did not expunge the attitude against which he warred. Nearly ten years after the address, Lyman Beecher, a renowned clergymen and father of Harriet Beecher Stowe and Henry Ward Beecher, delivered a lecture called *A Plea for the West* (1835).[83] In this speech Beecher said he had no objection to extending full religious freedom to Catholics along with practitioners of other religions. But he argued that they would not be content with equality. They wanted to dominate and to use the civil authorities to enforce their beliefs on others. Beecher was a nativist, who feared a flood of immigrants would be manipulated by their priests to vote for the interests of European powers, with which he viewed the Catholic Church as allied.[84] England disdained the exercise of such political power by priests as contrary to the doctrine of the separation of church and state.

Richard Rousseau sees the development and advocacy of a theory of church-state relations that accepts a free church in a free society as John England's greatest achievement. Rousseau gives the basic principles of England's theory:

1) People are the source of political power in a democracy. . . . 2) Social in origin, democracy demands a commitment to the common good on the part of the citizen if it is to survive and flourish. 3) Clergymen must remain out of the political processes in a democracy. . . . 4) Though the Catholic Church has not always lived up to its own ideals, it is not opposed to the principles of democracy. On the contrary, it has historically fostered those concepts of the dignity of the human person and of social justice that were and are the well-springs of modern democracy. Its own structures can be seen as balancing the hierarchical with the collegial. 5) The

duty of government is to preserve public peace and order. It has no business entering into religious beliefs. The American Constitution expressly forbids it. 6) A commitment to truth in faith implies a recognition of the freedom of each human person to seek the truth. It implies as well an obligation to respect each person's freedom. Final judgment in such matters is to be left to God. 7) The ideal situation, therefore, is the proper separation of Church and State, an example of which is found in the American Constitution.[85]

For England, the separation of church and state not only protected the civil government from church attempts to dictate policy in temporal affairs, it protected the church from interference by the state in matters of ecclesiastical government and spiritual doctrine. These beliefs were not mere rhetoric to England. He acted on these principles. An example is a controversy occurring between 1828 and 1830, in which England argued against interference by the U.S. State Department in the pope's prerogatives with regard to the assignment and disciplining of priests.[86] In an effort to calm a dispute that roiled the Catholic Church in Philadelphia, Pope Leo XII ordered Fathers Harold and Ryan to leave the city and report to their Dominican general in Cincinnati, Ohio. Father Harold wrote the secretary of state toward the end of the administration of John Quincy Adams and requested "the protection of the President against this novel and unauthorized invasion of my private rights."[87] The result was a July 9, 1828, letter from Daniel Brent, a State Department official, to James Brown, U.S. minister to France (there being no U.S. envoy at the Vatican), asking him to request the Vatican to review the action taken against Harold and Ryan.[88] The letter cautioned the envoy to avoid creating any impression that the U.S. government was trying to interfere with the internal affairs of the Catholic Church in America. The approach to the Holy See was to be merely a polite request for a review.[89] Still, England considered this letter to be a serious breach of the separation of church and state. In a September 26, 1830, letter to President Andrew Jackson, England argued that the State Department action was an "attempt to overawe this head of the Church in the exercise of his spiritual and ecclesiastical authority."[90] Since Congress was forbidden by the First Amendment to engage in such action, it logically followed that "no officer of the general government" could act in that fashion either.[91]

A recurring church-state issue is whether religious organizations should accept state financial aid. England believed that the acceptance of such aid by the church was a dangerous practice. The state always demanded a quid pro quo for any fiscal assistance.[92] These conditions could lure the church away from serving the needs of parishioners and implementing God's will onto the path of satisfying the demands of the government in order to keep the government largesse flowing.[93] The issue arose during England's Irish ministry when one of the British government's inducements to get the Catholic authorities to give the king a veto power over the appointment of Irish bishops was that in return the government would pay the priests' salaries. England opposed this proposal as an opening wedge that would result in state control of church internal affairs. England was concerned that not only would such a practice make the priests cater to the whims of the government grant maker, it would also fracture the intimate relationship between priests and parishioners that existed when the latter were the source of the priests' salary.[94]

A major influence on John England's views of the separation of church and state was Arthur O'Leary (1729–1802), a Franciscan priest and combative pamphleteer. When John England's duties made it impossible for him to write the life of O'Leary that he had planned, England's brother Thomas took up the project and published a biography in 1822.[95] Thomas England described O'Leary as believing that Christ assigned church and state to separate spheres of operation. The church had the responsibility for spiritual matters. To carry out its responsibilities in this area, the church should give moral guidance to its members rather than enlisting the coercive powers of the state. Conversely, the state should not regulate spiritual matters. Instead, it should focus on the domain given it in Christ's plan and under the social compact; that is, it should concentrate on safeguarding the rights of life, liberty, and property.[96] Only when each keeps to its divinely ordained jurisdiction can church and state prosper. In his 1781 "Essay on Toleration" O'Leary observed:

> He [Christ] has furnished them [his followers] with no other means of making proselytes to his religion, but persuasion, prayer, and good example. The theocratical government is no longer confounded and interwoven with civil and political institutions. The kingdom of Jesus Christ is not of this world. He leaves the rulers of the earth the full enjoyment of their prerogatives, whether they know him, or whether they blaspheme his name: and he leaves their subjects in full possession of their rights, as men.[97]

Thus in 1814 John England urged in the *Cork Mercantile Chronicle* "adherence to the Divine Precept, of giving unto Caesar the things which are Caesar's, and of giving unto God the things which are God's."[98] To O'Leary and John England the separation of church and state was not antireligious; it was ordained of God.

England augmented these spiritual insights with constitutional interpretation. The First Amendment's prohibition of the federal government's regulating individual conduct in order to aid the church in achieving its goals was rigorous. He observed: "I do know that our General Government has not power either to enact that we shall abstain from meat on Friday or Saturday, nor that we shall eschew whiskey on Sunday; nor has it the power to lay an excise tax of one cent per hogshead upon the said whiskey, for the purpose of giving the said cent to aid the education of a missionary, either for Virginia or Liberia, or Otaheite, or Ceylon, or China."[99] These prohibitions are not specified in First Amendment text but are derived from the general principles of the Free Exercise and Establishment clauses.[100]

Joseph Lawrence O'Brien called England "Apostle to American Democracy."[101] England was an apostle of the Catholic Church to the United States and helped Catholics to see themselves and their church as participants in this American experiment. It can truly be said that England was an apostle of democracy to the Catholic Church. England was the first Roman Catholic bishop to see democracy, freedom of religion, and separation of church and state as strengthening religion by removing the need for the church to curry the favor of civil authorities, an act that corroded the purity of its religious message. England's philosophy laid the foundation for re-marks John F. Kennedy made in his September 12, 1960, address to the Greater Hous-ton Ministerial Association to demonstrate that he would not be under the sway of Catholic authorities if he were elected president. He said:

> I believe in an America that is officially neither Catholic, Protestant, nor Jewish—where no public official either requests or accepts instructions on public policy from the pope, the National Council of Churches, or any other ecclesiastical source —where no religious body seeks to impose its will directly or indirectly upon the general populace or the public acts of its officials—and where religious liberty is so indivisible that an act against one church is treated as an act against all.[102]

In developing the philosophy of the separation of church and state that prepared the way for mid-twentieth century Catholics such as Kennedy to be faithful to their reli-gion and independent decision makers on civil matters, Bishop England acted boldly. Papal attitudes of his time were skeptical of a strong doctrine of separation of church and state. In his August 1832 encyclical, *Mirari Vos,* Pope Gregory XVI stated: "Nor can We predict happier times for religion and government from the plans of those who desire vehemently to separate the Church from the state, and to break the mutual concord between temporal authority and the priesthood. It is certain that that con-cord which always was favorable and beneficial for the sacred and the civil order is feared by the shameless lovers of liberty."[103]

A keystone to England's view of the separation of church and state was the voter as an independent decision maker who was not under the thumbs of secular or ecclesiastical authorities. As guidance to the voter, England did not give instructions on how to vote on specific issues but urged the voter to approach his task with an attitude oriented toward making choices for the common good rather than personal gain. To achieve this goal, he developed a model: the virtuous citizen.

The Virtuous Citizen

England was not an adherent to the philosophy that democracy works through each individual voting his self-interest, which blends with the self-interest of the other voters to achieve a greater common good. To him the survival of a "republic is only to be found in the virtue of its citizens."[104] In an 1841 Boston speech observing a day of fasting on the death of President William Henry Harrison, the bishop said that in a democracy, if in voting, "the people look to their own individual and private inter-est, more than to the fitness of him who is chosen, ... then indeed, republicanism is near its end. It cannot subsist where there is no virtue ... and thus the regarding [of] the private good of each and not the public good of all, on the part of the citizens, is the principle which will destroy the institutions of republicanism."[105] The voter must cast his ballot with a "generous disposition," which can be found by seeking truth through religion.[106] "Religion teaches man to love his neighbour as himself, and, con-sequently, to uphold himself those institutions which confer the most happiness on the whole."[107] To England voting was not a casual exercise to be based on a momentary whim of the elector because "his fate for eternity is bound up with his due discharge of his duty as a citizen."[108]

In preparing to cast his ballot the voters should ask himself what motive prompts his choice? Was it "the benefit of the people at large, the safety of the Constitution,— or was it from a wish for place, a bargain with one, or a chaffer with another? Was it from hatred, or malice, or revenge, or ambition, or from a sincere wish to discharge my duty?"[109] In an August 24, 1831, letter, "To the Roman Catholic Citizens of Charleston," Bishop England urged his parishioners to vote as Americans and South Carolinians and not from the narrower perspective of membership in the Catholic Church or of any particular ethnic background, such as that of an Irish immigrant.[110] They should resist those who ply them with drinks, money, conviviality, and preferment and vote strictly on the merits of the candidate. This was at the heart of what England called the principle of "distributive justice" by which officers should be selected on the basis of what they can contribute to the good of the entire polity rather than that of particular individuals or special interest groups.[111] The duty of a citizen in a democracy to vote for officials on their merits is as great as the duty reposed in a single monarch or a small governing body such as a senate.[112]

To England the citizen could not justify casting a vote based on corrupt motives just because he was one of many electors. The individual's responsibility was not dispersed. Although it may have been difficult to pinpoint the corrupt or selfish elector, a voter could not dodge his responsibility to cast an informed and honest vote by hiding in the crowd. The right to vote was not a duty-free entitlement. "The abuse of this power [to vote] would be not only a violation of the [voter's] contract with the people, that every effort should be made to attain these ends [merit selection of officers], but moreover, a high offence to that God by whom society is sanctioned, and government upheld."[113] In other words, the right to vote was an important ingredient of freedom that could not be dictated by ecclesiastical or government authority but must be exercised with responsibility because not only was that the only way a citizen's freedom could be preserved but also because of his duty to God and his fellow citizens.

Even though in his 1831 letter to Charleston Catholics, England disavowed any authority to instruct his parishioners how to vote, and in a September 17, 1840, circular letter he asserted that he had "kept aloof" from "political movements," England had not consistently held himself above political struggles.[114] In Ireland he had proven himself to be a shrewd and skillful political tactician.[115] In 1818, while still in Cork, John England served as one of the campaign managers for Christopher Hely Hutchinson, a parliamentary candidate.[116] England was credited with organizing the Catholic voters in support of Hutchinson, especially the "forty-shilling freeholders," by urging them to register and go to the polls.[117] This campaign was but one facet of England's participation in the larger movement to free the Irish Catholics from the harsh penal laws that repressed their civil liberties and had only been partially repealed at that stage. Perhaps England's role as an Irish political activist can be somewhat reconciled with his later statements that priestly aloofness from politics was the proper posture. The movement to bring about Irish Catholic emancipation from the draconian penal laws could succeed only by exercising a strong influence over parliamentary elections. Political involvement was not an idle pursuit that could be shuffled off for philosophical reasons. Instead it was a necessity to achieve equal treatment for his parishioners. In other words, the seriousness of the issues involved, together with no effective alternatives to electioneering, made political involvement crucial. By contrast, in America the rights sought by the Irish Catholics had already been attained even though sharp nativist resentment remained and resulted in harassment. This reduced the need for further priestly activism.[118] Furthermore the American tradition of separation of church and state encouraged clergymen not to meddle in secular government affairs. However, in his 1840 circular letter England somewhat obliquely admitted being outspoken on public issues, including defending the administration of President Martin Van Buren. The admission was in the form of a complaint that he and other Catholics had been subjected to harsh criticism for such statements and that this criticism betrayed a lack of American commitment to equal free speech rights for Catholics.[119] When public issues touched areas in which he thought he had a duty of moral leadership, England would speak forcefully, combining the skills of a theologian and debater. A good example is the bishop's opposition to dueling as a means of defending a gentleman's honor. He viewed dueling not as an act of honor and courage but as one of false bravado that sought the selfish end of protecting one's reputation while violating God's prohibitions of murder and suicide.[120]

The Slavery Question

The generally salutary doctrine of separation of church and state becomes most problematic when a minister or priest is confronted with a serious moral wrong that is fostered by an intricate network of laws. Should the priest attack the evil headfirst or should its demise be left to the legislature that has in the past aided and abetted it? Nowhere is this dilemma more starkly posed than the quandary facing the church in the antebellum South with regard to slavery. It is with regard to this issue that John England's considerable moral force became a muted trumpet.

England was as strongly motivated to minister to his black parishioners, including slaves, as he was to attend to his white charges.[121] Entries in his journal for late January and early February 1821—made during visits to Savannah, Augusta, and Locust Grove—reveal that he baptized slave and free blacks and tried to save the marriage of a slave couple.[122] England's friend William George Read observed, "If there was a portion of his flock he served with more than ordinary tenderness, it was his humble Africans."[123] This included educating them in the precepts of Christianity.[124] At the cathedral blacks were admitted to segregated seating in church services as well as to a separate service devoted to them alone.[125] South Carolina had a long tradition of laws prohibiting the education of slaves.[126] England steered around the prohibition on teaching slaves to read and write and opened a school for free blacks in Charleston in early 1835.[127] Students quickly filled the school.[128] Unfortunately the school was swept up in the violent resentment in Charleston of abolitionist literature that had been sent to the post office there.[129] Even though the school was educating only free blacks, it was viewed as a possible breeding ground for slave insurrection.[130] A tense confrontation occurred at the seminary between an anti-abolitionist mob and England and Irish members of the militia who arrived to guard the seminary.[131] England acted as ad hoc commander and negotiator. A "respectable committee of citizens" called on England and asked him to close the school.[132] He reluctantly agreed to do so but only on the condition that similar schools operated by other denominations also be closed.[133] In insisting on this condition, England seems to have exacerbated the harm to the education of free black people, even though that was certainly not his intent. Thus England's dedication to ministering to blacks was sometimes frustrated by the turbulent times.

England's appreciation of the needs of blacks is also seen in an act that grew out of his role as papal legate to Haiti. He conducted an intensive search for a priest to go to Haiti to minister to the people.[134] His choice was a "colored and well-educated" man who had been attending a seminary in Ireland.[135] England ordained this priest, George Paddington, on May 21, 1836, in the Church of Port au Prince.[136] This not only demonstrates the considerable value England placed on the souls of black people but also his belief that an educated black man of good character could be a fine priest. This ordination, far from being a routine act, is believed by the authors to have been the first instance of the ordination of a black priest by an American Catholic bishop.

The larger question is whether England should have directly attacked slavery rather than merely deploring it and working to ameliorate its harshness. England called slavery "the greatest moral evil that can desolate any part of the civilized world."[137] But he went on to say that "I am content with my lot and with my surroundings."[138] England did not severely rebuke slave owners. He distinguished between those who initially reduced persons to slavery and those who were heirs to an ongoing system of slavery. To him the former were subject to the most severe censure, but the latter were enmeshed in a system that was not of their creation.[139] These views represent England's interpretation of a December 3, 1830, apostolic letter of Gregory XVI that condemned the slave trade. England viewed the pope's letter as not dealing with those who inherited rather than initiated slavery.[140] Owners who inherited or continued a system of slavery were in England's opinion caught in a web of rules that would make immediate emancipation difficult. England failed to appreciate the full sweep of the pope's condemnation of slavery. Not only did the pope admonish Christians not to engage in the slave trade, he also directed them not "to extend help or favour to others who perpetrate such things against them ['negroes']."[141] Surely continuing the institution of slavery by owning and working slaves on a plantation, even if the operator was not actively involved as a buyer or seller, aided the slave trade by perpetuating the slave-dependent economic system that was a prerequisite to the market.

England argued that the decentralized nature of government in the United States left the national Congress impotent and placed the slavery question under control of individual states and that the southern states were determined to continue the system.[142] This does not explain why, if the state governments were the bodies with control over the issue, England did not press them for abandonment of slavery. Perhaps such a gesture appeared so unlikely to succeed as to be quixotic. Near the end of his life, England observed that "I have been asked by many, a question which I may as well answer at once, viz.: Whether I am friendly to the existence or continuation of slavery? I am not–but I also see the impossibility of now abolishing it here. When it can and ought to be abolished, is a question for the legislature and not for me."[143] This hands-off attitude with regard to a great moral issue may reflect an extreme view of the separation of church and state, one in which the church and state power structures are not intermixed, and the church does not even use moral suasion to influence civil authority.

Rather than launch a frontal assault on slavery, which he viewed as probably futile, England tried to civilize the relationship of master and servant. One might argue that this approach was unrealistic given the extreme power imbalance between the two sides. In a March 9, 1821, entry in his journal, England noted he had just issued a catechism that he had compiled from similar documents but had had to adapt to the "peculiar circumstances" of his diocese.[144] One of the circumstances requiring adaption of the catechism may have been the institution of slavery.[145] This document spoke of the broader categories of "master," "servant," and "apprentice" rather than specifically of master and slave.[146] But the terms were broad enough to encompass the master-slave relationship. The catechism stated that a master's duty to his servants was to lead them to God by "word and example" and "to treat them with justice and humanity, and to correct and reprove them when necessary."[147] Masters were admonished that they "should do to your servants that which is just and equal; knowing that you also have a master in Heaven."[148] Servants were obligated to be "obedient, respectful and faithful" to their masters, "diligent in their work" and protective of their master's property.[149]

But England's effectiveness as a reformer of the harshness of slavery was impaired by a failure to grasp the severely repressive nature of the institution and how vulnerable to abuse it left the powerless slave. In one passage he made slavery sound like a preferred state. He called slavery an "evil" but went on to say that "no labouring people upon the face of the globe have, comparatively speaking, less severe tasks, or greater physical comforts."[150] He then described the institution as a sort of social-security system in which the slaves received the "best medical attendance." He wrote that under it the slaves "know no want, have no fear for dereliction in old age, never anticipate any destitution for their children."[151]

Thomas Paul Thigpen concludes that one reason England did not take a strong abolitionist stance was because he believed that antislavery activists often advocated nativist anti-Catholic positions.[152] England's *United States Catholic Miscellany* asserted that at an 1839 abolitionist conclave in Albany, New York, the rallying cry was

"Down with slavery and popery! Down with the Papist and the slaveholder, who are bringing the country to ruin!"[153]

Perhaps the most puzzling feature of Bishop England's stance on slavery, given his condemnation of that institution as the greatest evil, is the fact that he had a slave as a servant. David Heisser found a reference in the 1830 census indicating that a slave resided in the household headed by England.[154] Heisser describes the slave as "a manservant named Castalio, a coachman and factotum who accompanied that prelate [England] on his 1831 visitation of the diocese."[155] How England obtained this slave, whether by purchase, gift, inheritance, loan, or other means is not clear. It is notable that Castalio was usually referred to in *United States Catholic Miscellany* as a servant rather than as a slave.[156] Castalio was apparently a good man to have around in the event of a carriage breakdown on a lonely stretch of unfinished road, such as often confronted the bishop on his tours of the diocese.[157] Archival records also show that Bishop England made an October 1835 purchase of "a certain negro man slave named Joseph" from Antonio Della Torre for four hundred and fifty dollars in his capacity as trustee for the Ursuline nuns of Charleston.[158] Heisser notes that England's successors, Ignatius Reynolds and Patrick Lynch, were also slaveholders but on a larger scale.[159] Commenting on Lynch's ownership of slaves, Heisser observes, "The Bishop of Charleston was essentially in line with his fellow Catholic clergy and with the clergy of other Christian denominations in the South" during the antebellum period.[160]

The picture that emerges of slavery is quite different when the point of view of the slaves is considered. *Slave Narratives* (2000), compiled by William L. Andrews and Harry Louis Gates Jr., creates a montage of slave women who are defenseless when subjected to sexual assault, of families who are broken up by their members being sold to separate masters, of suppression of slave education, and of random cruelty.[161] In his study of slave-labor conditions, Kenneth M. Stampp cautioned against generalization, noting that much depended on the attitude of the master.[162] He noted that "the labor of the vast majority of slaves ranged from what was normally expected of free labor in that period to levels that were clearly excessive. It would not be too much to say that masters usually demanded from their slaves a long day of hard work and managed by some means or other to get it."[163]

The labor conditions confronting slaves could depend on a variety of circumstances, such as whether they were field hands, house servants, or skilled artisans, whether they worked on a plantation or in an urban setting, and whether, if field hands, they worked under a regimented gang system or a looser task system, permitting cessation or a change of labor once a task was completed.[164] Peter Kolchin observed that "the basic pattern of field work was one of long hours of work at a less-than-frantic pace, punctuated by short bursts of intense activity and relieved by opportunities throughout the year for rest and revelry."[165] He noted that being subject to a master's whim, a slave could work under circumstances that varied drastically over the course of a lifetime since he or she could be "sold, inherited, hired out, moved from one region to another, taken from countryside to city and back again, assigned new occupations."[166] Yet, although conditions varied, the slave did not have the freedom to choose an indulgent over a harsh employer. Stampp concluded, "The records of the plantation regime clearly indicate that slaves were more frequently overworked by calloused tyrants than overindulged by mellowed patriarchs."[167] These findings indicate that England's views on the condition of slaves were not fully informed.

Conclusion

Bishop John England developed the intellectual and practical reconciliation of the concepts of the faithful Catholic and the virtuous citizen with each other and with the American doctrine of the separation of church and state. He argued that the church has a divine commission to be God's instrument for revealing his message on religious matters to human beings. The good Catholic is faithful to the church's teaching on these matters. But the delegation of divine authority to the church is limited, just as government power may be limited by a constitution. England contended that when a church official strays beyond the scope of the power delegated to him by God and attempts to dictate to members how they should act with regard to civil matters, his legitimacy ends, and the member is not obligated to obey him. The individual is free to seek political truth on his own, but he should have the guidance of God in this search. This political truth is not properly supplied by the church as a set of neatly packaged instructions. The virtuous citizen casts his ballot only after carefully weighing his motives. Is he assessing the candidate as he should in light of the candidate's likely contributions to the polity as a whole, or is he casting the ballot guided by self-interests such as lust for office, ambition, greed, or revenge?

The distinction between the proper role of the church with regard to religious truth and its lack of authority with regard to political truth is deceptively easy to state but difficult to apply. Does the church as moral standard bearer not have a duty to speak out on crucial issues of good and evil even though they may be enmeshed with civil legislative and executive action, the usual domain of government not the church? Bishop England confronted this dilemma on the slavery issue. His deep commitment to minister to blacks can not be doubted. He did not devalue their souls in comparison to those of whites. The school he started for blacks challenged the prison of ignorance to which they had been consigned. He retreated only in the face of violence. He condemned slavery as an unmatched evil. Yet he threw up his hands, concluded that challenging it in the antebellum South would be fruitless, and consigned any abolition of the system to civil rather than spiritual authorities. Rather than directly challenging the system of slavery, he attempted through devices such as his catechism to curb brutal treatment of slaves. Perhaps he was merely being pragmatic. The rest of his ministry may have been fiercely resisted had he charged uphill against the fortifications defending slavery. Perhaps it would have been one fight too many; he was struggling to gain acceptance of Catholics as citizens committed to America on political issues and not under the sway of a distant power. A challenge to slavery by a leading Catholic may have made them appear too different for acceptance by Southern society.

His argument that the issue was in the sphere of civil rather than spiritual powers may be a reflection of his strong belief in the separation of church and state. But such a legalistic rationalization does not satisfactorily resolve the moral issues posed by slavery. He finessed the issue rather than confront it directly. But with respect to most aspects of his life and ministry Bishop John England was a man of luminous intelligence and courage who labored with energy and compassion for fair treatment.

Notes

1. Alexis de Tocqueville, *Democracy in America,* trans. Harvey C. Mansfield and Delba Winthrop (Chicago: University of Chicago Press, 2000), 276.

2. Ibid.

3. Ibid., 276–77.

4. Ibid., 277.

5. "Review of the strictures upon the letters of the Right. Rev. Dr. England, and the Rev. J. McEncroe," *United States Catholic Miscellany* (Charleston), January 28, 1824, pp. 50–51. See also Patrick Carey, *An Immigrant Bishop: John England's Adaptation of Irish Catholicism to American Republicanism* (Yonkers, N.Y.: U.S. Catholic Historical Society, 1982), 109.

6. John Tracy Ellis, "The Diocese of Charleston in American Catholic History," *Catholic Banner* (Charleston), December 4, 1960, 8A: 1–3.

7. John England, *The Constitution of the Roman Catholic Churches of the States of North-Carolina, South-Carolina, and Georgia; Which are Comprised in the Diocess of Charleston; and Province of Baltimore* (Charleston: Office of the Seminary, 1826). A second edition of the Constitution is printed in *The Works of the Right Rev. John England, First Bishop of Charleston,* 5 vols., ed. Ignatius Reynolds (Baltimore, Md.: John Murphy, 1849), V, pt. 4: 93–108, and in *American Catholic Religious Thought,* ed. Patrick Carey (New York: Paulist Press, 1987), 74–92. The 1826 version of the Constitution will be used for reference in subsequent endnotes.

8. Richard W. Rousseau, "The Greatness of John England," *American Ecclesiastical Review* 168 (March 1974): 203.

9. Joseph L. O'Brien, *John England—Bishop of Charleston: The Apostle to Democracy* (New York: Edward O'Toole, 1934), 215.

10. R. Frank Saunders Jr. and George A. Rogers, "Bishop John England of Charleston: Catholic Spokesman and Southern Intellectual, 1820–1842," *Journal of the Early Republic* 13, no. 3 (Fall 1993): 306.

11. Peter Guilday, *The Life and Times of John England, First Bishop of Charleston (1786–1842),* 2 vols. (New York: America Press, 1927), 1:41.

12. Ibid., 58–60.

13. Examples of restrictions on the property-holding rights of Roman Catholics in Ireland include 2 Ann. c. 6 [Irish Parliament 1703], which made it illegal for papists to get interest in land that exceeded thirty-one years and which also sought to avoid big concentrations of property in the hands of individual Catholics by decreeing that the property of

a deceased papist did not descend entirely to the eldest son but to all sons, share and share alike unless the eldest son was a Protestant, in which case he could take all the land; the law also prohibited a papist from owning a house in Limerick or Galway unless certain bonding requirements were met; and 9 Will 3, c. 3 [Irish Parliament 1697], which sought to block Catholic men from gaining property by intermarrying with Protestant women. A major educational disability is found in 7 Will 3, c. 4, sec. 9 [Irish Parliament 1695], which forbids persons of papist religion from instructing youth. See also Catholic Relief Act of 1791, 31 Geo. 3, c. 32, sec. 13, stipulating that Roman Catholics who meet certain oath requirements are not subject to prosecution for teaching youths. See also Roman Catholic Relief Act of 1829, 10 Geo. 4, c. 7, sec. 2, recognizing the right of Roman Catholics to sit and vote in Parliament, and sec. 5, recognizing the right of Roman Catholics to vote in parliamentary elections.

14. See Guilday, *The Life and Times of John England*, 1:46–59, describing a series of measures adopted in 1778–93 that improved the educational opportunities of Roman Catholics. See Catholic Relief Act of 1778, 18 Geo. 3, c. 60; Catholic Relief Act of 1791, 31 George 3, c. 32, sec. 13, protecting Roman Catholics from prosecution for teaching if they met certain oath requirements. For a complete listing of Catholic Relief Acts, see *Memoirs and Correspondence of Viscount Castlereagh, Second Marquess of Londonderry*, ed. Charles Vane, 4 vols. (London: Colburn, 1850), 3:158–60. But even the liberalizing acts such as the Catholic Relief Act of 1793, 33 Geo 3, c. 21 [Irish Parliament] did not treat Irish Catholics on a completely equal basis concerning education. One commentator contended that public schools were still not open to Catholics and the private Catholic schools could not be endowed and were thus in dire financial straits. See Denys Scully, *Statement of the Penal Laws, Which Aggrieve the Catholics of Ireland: With Commentaries*, vol. 5 of *The Catholic Question in Ireland, 1762–1829*, Irish History and Culture (1812; reprint, Bristol, U.K.: Thoemmes Press, 2000), 271–78. Catholics still were not permitted to be members of Trinity College, Dublin.

15. Guilday, *The Life and Times of John England*, I:41, 59–65, 65, 73–75. Guilday provides the most complete biography of John England. Shorter biographies are Carey's *An Immigrant Bishop: John England's Adaptation of Irish Catholicism to American Republicanism* (cited above in note 5); Jeremiah J. O'Connell, *Catholicity in the Carolinas and Georgia: Leaves of its History* (1879; reprint, Spartanburg, S.C.: Reprint Co., 1972), 37–104; Richard C. Madden, *Catholics in South Carolina: A Record* (Lanham, Md: University Press of America, 1985), 31–49; Richard C. Madden, "England, John," in *New Catholic Encyclopedia* (New York: McGraw-Hill, 1968), 5:352. first edition; Peter Clarke, "England, John" in *The Encyclopedia of American Catholic History*, Michael Glazier and Thomas J. Shelley, eds. (Collegeville, Minn.: Liturgical Press, 1997), 489–92.

16. Robert Stewart (Viscount Castlereagh), "Suggestions for the Improvement of the Tithe System in Ireland," in *Memoirs and Correspondence of Viscount Castlereagh*, 4:206.

17. Ibid.

18. John England to the Reverend Richard Fuller, October 10, 1839, reprinted from *the Charleston Courier*, October 10, 1839, in *Works of John England*, ed Reynolds, III, pt. 2, 98.

19. Ibid.

20. Ibid.

21. Ibid.

22. Ibid.

23. Ibid.

24. Ibid.

25. Ibid. The letter's oblique wording has created some confusion as to whether it was the bishop's father or grandfather who was charged with teaching Euclid. See O'Connell, *Catholicity in the Carolinas and Georgia,* 38, saying it was the bishop's grandfather who was imprisoned for teaching Euclid; but see Guilday, *The Life and Times of John England,* 1:38–40, implying that it was the father who was charged with teaching geometry. Although the matter is not free from doubt, a careful reading of the bishop's letter indicates that the charge was lodged against his father.

26. See Guilday, *The Life and Times of John England,* 1:59, noting that the 1793 removal of the prohibition of Catholics entering the professions opened the way for England to attend the seminary to study for the priesthood.

27. Ibid., 70–71.

28. Ibid., 77–97.

29. Ibid.; Patrick Carey, *Immigrant Bishop,* 13, notes that England edited the magazine *Religious Reportory.* Guilday was not able to locate copies of this magazine and mistakenly identified it as *Repository* (see Guilday, *The Life and Times of John England,* 1:457).

30. Guilday, *The Life and Times of John England,* 1:40n5. Bishop England started work on the research, but gave his notes to his brother when he left for America. His brother mentions this history in the preface to Thomas R. England, *The Life of the Reverend Arthur O'Leary, including Historical Anecdotes, Memoirs, and Many Hitherto Unpublished Documents, Illustrative of the Condition of Irish Catholics, During the Eighteenth Century* (London: Longman, Hurst, Rees, Orme & Brown / Keating, Brown & Co., 1822); available at Pitts Theology Library, Emory University, Atlanta, Georgia.

31. Reynolds, ed., *Works of the Right Reverend John England,* 1:3–4. This part of the Reynolds work is taken from a biography about Bishop England published in the *Dublin Catholic Directory.* For a detailed discussion of England's role as an outspoken opponent of giving the British monarch a veto over Vatican appointment of Irish bishops see Carey, *Immigrant Bishop,* 15–24, discussing the pope's gratitude to the British as a motivating factor in securing his assent to the veto. He also hoped that by agreeing to the veto he would induce the British to restore Irish Catholic civil rights.

32. Peter Clarke, *A Free Church in a Free Society: The Ecclesiology of John England, Bishop of Charleston, 1820–1842; A Nineteenth Century Missionary Bishop in the Southern United States* (Hartsville, S.C.: Center for John England Studies, 1982), 416–19.

33. William George Read, "Memoir of Bishop England," in *Works of John England,* ed. Reynolds, 1:11, 4–20.

34. Clarke, *A Free Church in a Free Society,* 204–5.

35. John England, "First Pastoral Letter of Bishop England," in *The Works of the Right Reverend John England, First Bishop of Charleston,* 7 vols., ed. Sebastian G. Messmer (Cleveland, Ohio: Arthur H. Clark, 1908), VI, pt. 5: 233–38.

36. Ibid., VI, pt. 5: 237–38.

37. John Quincy Adams, "Address delivered at the request of a committee of the citizens of Washington, on the occasion of reading the declaration of independence, on the fourth of July, 1821," *Baltimore Niles' Weekly Register,* 8 [20], no. 21 [515] (21 July 1821): 326–32.

Adams did not directly use the term "Catholic Church" in his speech but the historical references he made indicate that the church was the object of his critical remarks. See also Guilday, *The Life and Times of John England*, 2:50.

38. Adams, "Address at request of citizens of Washington," 327.

39. John England, *The Roman Missal, Translated into the English Language for the use of the Laity, to which is Prefixed, an Historical Explanation of the Vestments, Ceremonies, & c. Appertaining to the Holy Sacrifice of the Mass* (New York: William H. Creagh, 1822); John England, *A Catechism of the Roman Catholic Faith; Published for the Use of his Flock, by the Right Reverend Father in God, John, Bishop of Charleston* (Charleston: Burges & James, 1826).

40. Guilday, *The Life and Times of John England*, 2:49.

41. Ibid., 2:453–73, describing the founding of the *Miscellany* and providing a brief history of the newspaper.

42. John England to William Gaston, Charleston, February 18, 1822, quoted in Guilday, *The Life and Times of John England*, 1:456. See also John England, "Letters from the First Catholic Bishop of Charleston, South Carolina, to the Honorable William Gaston, LL.D.," *Records of the American Catholic Historical Society of Philadelphia* 18, no. 4 (December 1907): 380–81.

43. "Prospectus," *United States Catholic Miscellany*, June 5, 1822, p. 1.

44. Ibid.

45. Ibid.

46. Guilday, *The Life and Times of John England*, 1:455, 471.

47. John England, "Bishop England's 'Constitution,'" *Records of the American Catholic Historical Society of Philadelphia* 8, no. 3 (September 1897): 458–59.

48. England, *Constitution of the Roman Catholic Churches*, tit. 7, sec. 1, 36–37, parts of the Constitution consisting of doctrines revealed by God that are not subject to amendment are to be identified by the bishop; ibid., tit. 6, sec. 3, 34, convention consisting of the bishop and clergy and lay delegates had no jurisdiction over issues of religious doctrine or ritual.

49. Ibid., tit. 3, sec. 4 pt. 3, 20, general trustees consisting of bishop, vicar, three clergymen (chosen by the clergy), and six laymen (chosen by the lay delegates to the annual convention); ibid., tit. 2, sec. 2, 11, vestry of district to consist of clergy and laymen chosen by the lay members of the district church; ibid., tit. 5, sec. 2, 11–12, vestry powers.

50. See "Decree of the Apostolate of the Laity, Promulgated by His Holiness, Pope Paul VI on November 18, 1965," Catholic Information Network, available on-line at http://www.cin.org/v2laity.html (last visited January 23, 2004).

51. England, *Constitution of the Roman Catholic Churches*, tit. 2, sec. 1, 6. The Constitution was adopted on September 25, 1822, and then sent to the Vatican so a decision could be made as to whether it was compatible with the rules of the universal church.

52. John England, "Letters from the First Catholic Bishop of Charleston, South Carolina, to the Honorable William Gaston, LL.D. 1821–1840," *Records of the American Catholic Historical Society of Philadelphia* 19, no. 1 (March 1908): 105.

53. Guilday, *The Life and Times of John England*, 2:49.

54. John England to William Gaston, Fayetteville, N.C., January 29, 1826, quoted in Guilday, *The Life and Times of John England*, 2:52.

55. Ibid.

56. Ibid. The Messmer version of Bishop England's works includes the text of the speech before Congress, an introduction by England, and the letter requesting copies of his talk in (VII, pt. 6: 9–43); Clarke, *A Free Church in a Free Society,* 25.

57. Anson Phelps Stokes, *Church and State in the United States,* vol. 1 (New York: Harper, 1950), 502–504.

58. John England, "Address Before Congress," in *Works of John England,* ed. Messmer, VII, pt. 6: 9–10.

59. Act No. 154 of 1696, 2 S.C. Statutes at Large 133, para. 6 (Cooper 1837); England refers to this incident as evidence of distrust of Catholics in England; "The Republic in Danger," in *Works of the Right Reverend John England,* ed. Messmer, IV, pt. 4, 433.

60. John England, "The Early History of the Diocese of Charleston," in *Works of John England,* ed. Messmer, IV, pt. 3: 300.

61. John Wesley Brinsfield, *Religion and Politics in Colonial South Carolina* (Easley, S.C.: Southern Historical Press, 1983), 47.

62. Charles Woodmason, *The Carolina Backcountry on the Eve of the Revolution: The Journal and Other Writings of Charles Woodmason, Anglican Itinerant,* ed. Richard J. Hooker (Chapel Hill: University of North Carolina Press, 1953), 42.

63. Quebec Act, 14 Geo. 3, c. 83 (1773).

64. S.C. Const. of 1776, pmbl.

65. England, "The Early History of the Diocese of Charleston," 302.

66. Brinsfield, *Religion and Politics in Colonial South Carolina,* 89–90. See also John Drayton, *Memoirs of the American Revolution,* vol. 1 (Charleston: Printed by A. E. Miller, 1821; reprint, New York: Arno Press, 1969), 300–302.

67. John England, "The Republic in Danger," in *Works of John England,* ed. Messmer, IV, pt. 4: 436–37. See also Drayton, *Memoirs of the American Revolution,* 1:273–75, 300.

68. Article 3 stipulated that the governor, lieutenant governor, and privy council members be "all of the Protestant Religion." Articles 12 and 13 required that members of the Senate and House be Protestant. S.C. Const. of 1778, art. 3, art. 12, art. 13.

69. S.C. Const. of 1778, art. 38.

70. David Ramsay, *History of South Carolina, From Its First Settlement in 1670 to the Year 1808,* vol. 2 (Charleston, S.C.: David Longworth, 1809), 37–38.

71. S.C. Const. of 1790, art. 8, sec. 1.

72. Act No. 1515 of 1791, 8 S.C. Statutes at Large 161 (McCord 1840).

73. Brinsfield, *Religion and Politics in Colonial South Carolina,* 47, concludes that the first legal mass in South Carolina took place in Charleston in 1790. Another commentator found that a Father Ryan, who had been sent to South Carolina by Bishop John Carroll, had conducted masses beginning in 1788. See Peter Guilday, *The Life and Times of John Carroll* (New York: Encyclopedia Press, 1922), 736.

74. England, "Address Before Congress," 9–43.

75. Ibid.

76. Ibid.

77. Ibid.

78. Ibid.

79. Ibid.

80. Ibid.

81. Ibid.

82. Guilday, *The Life and Times of John England*, 2:67; Clarke, *A Free Church in a Free Society*, 25.

83. Lyman Beecher, *A Plea for the West* (1835; reprint, New York: Arno Press, 1977).

84. Ibid., 54–74. See also Vincent Harding, *A Certain Magnificence: Lyman Beecher and the Transformation of American Protestantism, 1775–1863* (Brooklyn, N.Y.: Carlson, 1991), xvii, 297, 361, 401.

85. Rousseau, "The Greatness of John England," 204–5.

86. See Reynolds, ed., *Works of John England*, 5:213–28.

87. William Vincent Harold to Henry Clay, Washington, D.C., July 2, 1828, in *Works of John England*, ed. Reynolds, 5:215.

88. Daniel Brent to James Brown, Washington, D.C., July 9, 1828, in *Works of John England*, ed. Reynolds, 5:218–19.

89. Ibid.

90. John England to Andrew Jackson, Georgetown, D.C., September 26, 1830, in *Works of John England*, ed. Reynolds, 5:227.

91. Ibid.

92. Carey, *Immigrant Bishop*, 53–64.

93. Ibid.

94. Ibid., 15–24, 63–64, citing the *Cork Mercantile Chronicle*, May 10, 1813, and June 6, 1814.

95. See England, *Life of Arthur O'Leary*.

96. Ibid., 93–99.

97. Arthur O'Leary, "An Essay on Toleration, or Mr. O'Leary's Plea for Liberty of Conscience," in his *Miscellaneous Tracts*, second edition (Dublin: John Chambers 1781), 345; available at Pitts Theology Library, Emory University, Atlanta, Georgia. See generally ibid., 330–45.

98. *Cork Mercantile Chronicle*, May 20, 1814; quoted in Carey, *Immigrant Bishop*, 59. England was referring to Matt. 22:21.

99. John England, "The Republic in Danger," in *Works of John England*, ed. Reynolds, 4:49.

100. *Lemon v. Kurtzman*, 403 U.S. 602, 612–13 (1971), discussing historic principles underlying the establishment clause but not explicitly found in the language of the clause. But see James L. Underwood, "The Proper Role of Religion in the Public Schools: Equal Access Instead of Official Indoctrination," *Villanova Law Review* 46, no. 3 (2001): 515n129, discussing criticisms of such analysis.

101. Joseph L. O'Brien, *John England–Bishop of Charleston: The Apostle to Democracy* (New York: Edward O'Toole, 1934), 215.

102. John F. Kennedy, "Speech to the Greater Houston Ministerial Association, September 12, 1960," in *A Patriot's Handbook: Songs, Poems, Stories, and Speeches Celebrating the Land We Love*, ed. Caroline Kennedy (New York: Hyperion, 2003), 256. See also Robert Dallek, *An Unfinished Life: John F. Kennedy, 1917–1963* (Boston: Little, Brown, 2003), 283–84.

103. Gregory XVI, "Mirari Vos: Encyclical of Pope Gregory XVI on Liberalism and Religious Indifferentism, August 15, 1832," in *The Papal Encyclicals, 1740–1878*, ed. Claudia

Carlen Ihm (Raleigh, N.C.: McGrath, 1981), 239. See also William J. La Due, *The Chair of Saint Peter: A History of the Papacy* (Maryknoll, N.Y.: Orbis Books, 1999), 234. Pope Gregory XVI did speak out against secular interference, whether by civil governments or ambitious laymen, in setting of church doctrine or the conduct of church operations. See Gregory, "Commissum Divinitus: Encyclical of Pope Gregory XVI on church and state, May 17, 1835," in *Papal Encyclicals,* ed. Ihm, 253–57.

104. John England, "Pastoral Letter for Easter, 1838," in *Works of John England,* ed. Messmer, VI, pt. 5: 306.

105. John England, "Address on American Citizenship," in *Works of John England,* ed. Messmer, VII, pt. 6: 68–69.

106. Ibid., 69.

107. Ibid.

108. Ibid.

109. Ibid., 70.

110. John England, "Letter on Civic and Political Duties to the Roman Catholic Citizens of Charleston," in *Works of John England,* ed. Messmer, VI, pt. 5: 352–73.

111. Ibid., 362–63.

112. Ibid., 361.

113. Ibid., 361–62.

114. Bishop John England, Circular Letter, September 17, 1840; available at South Caroliniana Library, University of South Carolina, Columbia.

115. Carey, *Immigrant Bishop,* 25.

116. Ibid.

117. Ibid.

118. See England to Henry Conwell, Charleston, October 4, 1822, in *Works of John England,* ed. Reynolds, 5:144–45, wherein England explained the need for more involvement by priests in political affairs in Ireland than in the United States by noting: "The state of unfortunate Ireland is not like that of America. Here [America], although the Roman Catholic Religion labours under several disadvantages, there is no state persecution, and hence the Catholic clergy are not called upon to interfere in state concerns. As similar causes to those in Ireland are not here found, similar acts would not here be regarded as becoming in a clergyman. Hence, too, what may be here unbecoming, was there justifiable."

119. England, Circular Letter, September 17, 1840.

120. England, "Discourse Delivered Before the Anti-Dueling Society of Charleston, S.C.," in *Works of John England,* ed. Reynolds, V, pt. 4: 64–77.

121. Clarke, *A Free Church in a Free Society,* 159, 406–13.

122. England, "Diurnal of the Right Rev. John England, First Bishop of Charleston, S.C.," *Records of the American Catholic Historical Society of Philadelphia* 6, no. 1 (March 1895): 38–42.

123. Read, "Memoir of Bishop England," 14; Clarke, *A Free Church in a Free Society,* 407–8.

124. Read, "Memoir of Bishop England," 14.

125. Ibid., 14–15.

126. See Act No. 670 of 1740, 7 S.C. STATUTES AT LARGE 413, para. 45 (McCord 1840), 397, 413, prohibiting teaching slaves to read; see Act No. 2639 of 1834, 7 S.C. STATUTES AT

LARGE 468, para. 1 (McCord 1840), prohibiting free persons of color and slaves from teaching free persons of color or slaves to read or write and prohibiting free white persons from teaching slaves to read or write. See also John Belton O'Neall, *The Negro Law of South Carolina* (Columbia: John G. Bowman, 1848), 23, sec. 41–42, describing and criticizing the law prohibiting teaching slaves to read as being contrary to Christian doctrine because it prevented them from being able to read the Bible; Janet Duitsman Cornelius, *"When I Can Read My Title Clear"*: *Literacy, Slavery, and Religion in the Antebellum South* (Columbia: University of South Carolina Press, 1991), 39–58, discussing the legal and social pressures and violence directed at those who attempted to educate blacks in pre–Civil War South Carolina, especially noting the Charleston violence of the mid-1830s; *Bullwhip Days: The Slaves Remember, an Oral History,* ed. James Mellon (New York: Grove Press, 1988), 197–200, contains anecdotal accounts of the brutal punishment imposed on slaves who attempted to become educated.

127. Clarke, *A Free Church in a Free Society,* 407–8.

128. Ibid.

129. England to Paul Cullen, Charleston, February 23, 1836, *Records of the American Catholic Historical Society of Philadelphia* 8, no. 2 (June 1897): 219–20; See also England, "Addresses Before the Church Conventions of South Carolina," in *Works of John England,* ed. Messmer, VII, pt. 6: 151.

130. England to Cullen, 219–21.

131. Ibid.

132. Ibid.

133. Ibid.

134. Clarke, *A Free Church in a Free Society,* 437–40.

135. O'Connell, *Catholicity in the Carolinas and Georgia,* 72. See also Clarke, *A Free Church in a Free Society,* 438.

136. George Paddington to Pierre Toussaint, 25 July 1836, Pierre Toussaint Papers, Manuscripts and Archives Division, New York Public Library; Arthur Sheehan and Elizabeth Odell Sheehan, *Pierre Toussaint: A Citizen of Old New York* (New York: P. J. Kennedy, 1955), 205–6.

137. England, "Report of Bishop England to the Cardinal Prefect of Propaganda," *Records of the American Catholic Historical Society of Philadelphia* 8, no. 3 (September 1897): 328–29.

138. Ibid.

139. These sentiments are expressed in the *United States Catholic Miscellany,* a periodical operated by England. See the March 14, 1840, issue, compiled in *Works of John England,* ed. Reynolds, III, pt. 2: 112.

140. Pope Gregory XVI's letter is reproduced in ibid., III, pt. 2, 108–12, and is also found in *United States Catholic Miscellany,* March 14, 1840, p. 281.

141. Pope Gregory XVI, "Apostolic Letter of Our Most Holy Lord Gregory XVI, By Divine Providence, Pope Concerning the Not Carrying on the Trade in Negroes," in *Works of John England,* ed. Reynolds, III, pt. 2: 112.

142. John England, "The Early History of the Diocese of Charleston." Messmer, IV, pt. 3: 317. This pamphlet about the diocese of Charleston was written by England during an 1832 visit to Ireland. See Clarke, *A Free Church in a Free Society,* 390–406.

143. John England to the Editors of the *United States Catholic Miscellany,* February 25, 1841, in *Works of John England,* ed. Messmer, V, pt. 4: 311.

144. England, "Diurnal of John England," 43–44.

145. Clarke, *A Free Church in a Free Society,* 399–401.

146. England, *Catechism of the Roman Catholic Faith Published for the Use of His Flock, by the Right Reverend Father in God, John, Bishop of Charleston* (Charleston: Burgess and James, 1821), 42.

147. Ibid.

148. Ibid.

149. Ibid.

150. England, "The Early History of the Diocese of Charleston," 318.

151. Ibid.

152. Thomas Paul Thigpen, "Aristocracy of the Heart: Catholic Lay Leadership in Savannah," Ph.D. dissertation, Emory University 1995, 599–600.

153. Ibid., 599, 622n60, citing *United States Catholic Miscellany,* October 5, 1839, p. 110, and October 10, 1835, p. 118.

154. David C.R. Heisser, "Bishop Lynch's People: Slaveholding by a South Carolina Prelate," *South Carolina Historical Magazine* 102, no. 3 (July 2001): 241, 241n12, citing Census, 1830, Charleston District, S.C., 102; *United States Catholic Miscellany,* May 14, 1831, p. 366; ibid., May 21, 1831, p. 274; Thigpen, "Aristocracy of the Heart," 621. Heisser also notes that the 1840 census contained no reference to England's having slaves. A more conservative reading of the 1830 census shows that a slave resided within the household of which England was the head. That he owned the slave is a reasonable, but not an inevitable conclusion. See Census, 1830, Charleston District, S.C., 102.

155. Heisser, "Bishop Lynch's People," 241.

156. *United States Catholic Miscellany,* May 21, 1831, p. 374.

157. Ibid.; May 14, 1831, p. 366.

158. Bill of sale recorded October 23, 1835, available on microfilm at the South Carolina Department of Archives and History, Columbia. The authors would like to thank Nick Green for finding this document.

159. Heisser, "Bishop Lynch's People," 241–43.

160. Ibid., 238.

161. William L. Andrews and Harry Louis Gates Jr., eds., *Slave Narratives* (New York: Library of America, 2000), 684–718.

162. Kenneth M. Stampp, *The Peculiar Institution: Slavery in the Ante-Bellum South* (New York: Knopf, 1972), 75–77.

163. Ibid., 77.

164. Ira Berlin, *Many Thousands Gone: The First Two Centuries of Slavery in North America* (Cambridge, Mass.: Harvard University Press, 1998), 310–17, dealing with slavery up until about the end of the eighteenth century; Peter Kolchin, *American Slavery, 1619–1877* (New York: Hill & Wang, 1993), 99–111, dealing with antebellum conditions.

165. Kolchin, *American Slavery,* 106.

166. Ibid., 110.

167. Stampp, *The Peculiar Institution,* 81. In Eugene D. Genovese, *Roll, Jordan, Roll: The World the Slaves Made* (New York: Pantheon, 1974), 4. Genovese ascribes a complex form of

"paternalism" to southern antebellum slavery. It consisted of reciprocal obligations between master and slave but formed a dependence of the slave on the master for protection and sustenance. Genovese notes, "It did encourage kindness and affection, but it simultaneously encouraged cruelty and hatred."

Contributors

W. Lewis Burke is a professor of law and chair of the Department of Clinical Legal Studies at the University of South Carolina School of Law. He is the author or coeditor of three books, including *At Freedom's Door: African American Founding Fathers and Lawyers in Reconstruction South Carolina* (with James Lowell Underwood, 2000) and *Matthew J. Perry: The Man, His Times and His Legacy* (with Belinda Gergel, 2004), as well as numerous scholarly articles and chapters on legal history. He is a graduate of Mississippi State University and the University of South Carolina School of Law.

Orville Vernon Burton, professor of history at the University of Illinois, is the author of many books on southern history. Among these are *In My Father's House Are Many Mansions: Family and Community in Edgefield, South Carolina* (1985) and *"A Gentleman and an Officer": A Military and Social History of James B. Griffin's Civil War* (with Judy McArthur, 1996). Dr. Burton received his Ph.D. from Princeton University.

Peter Clarke received his sacrae theologiae doctoratus from the Pontifical Gregorian University. He is the author of *A Free Church in a Free Society, The Ecclesiology of John England Bishop of Charleston, 1820–1842: A Nineteenth-Century Missionary Bishop in the Southern United States* (1982). He served as a parish priest in South Carolina for many years.

Walter Edgar is the Claude Henry Neuffer Professor in Southern Studies and the George Washington Distinguished Professor of History at the University of South Carolina, where he is also director of the Institute for Southern Studies. He is the author of many books, including the acclaimed *South Carolina: A History* (1998) and *Partisans and Redcoats: The Southern Conflict that Turned the Tide of the American Revolution* (2001). He is currently superintending the compilation of an encyclopedia on South Carolina. Dr. Edgar received his Ph.D. from the University of South Carolina.

Belinda Gergel was chair of the Department of History and Political Science at Columbia College. She is coauthor of *In Pursuit of the Tree of Life: A History of the Early Jews of Columbia, S.C., and the Tree of Life Congregation* (with Richard Gergel, 1996), author of numerous articles and chapters, and most recently coeditor of

Matthew J. Perry: The Man, His Times and His Legacy (with W. Lewis Burke, 2004). She earned her Ph.D. at Duke University.

Richard Gergel is a partner in the law firm of Gergel, Nickles & Solomon, P.A., in Columbia, South Carolina. His published works include *In Pursuit of the Tree of Life: A History of the Early Jews of Columbia, S.C., and the Tree of Life Congregation* (with Belinda Gergel, 1996) as well as a number of history articles and chapters. He has been an active leader in the bar and community, serving as president of the South Carolina Supreme Court Historical Society and the Jewish Historical Society of South Carolina. He earned his bachelor's and law degrees from Duke University.

David Herr received his Ph.D. from the University of Illinois in 2003. He is a professor of history and chair of the Department of History at St. Andrews Presbyterian College in North Carolina. He is the author of *Compassion and Excellence: A Brief History of Pinehurst Surgical Clinic* (2003).

Alexander Moore received his Ph.D. from the University of South Carolina. He is acquisitions editor at the University of South Carolina Press and is the author of books and articles on South Carolina history and coauthor of *A History of Beaufort County, Volume I* (1996) with Lawrence Sanders Rowland. Moore was assistant and associate editor of *The Papers of John C. Calhoun* from 1978 to 1989 and 1992 to 1994; and he published editions of *Nairne's Muskhogean Journals: The 1708 Expedition to the Mississippi River* (1988) and *The Historical Writings of Henry A. M. Smith* (1988). He has contributed essays on South Carolina people and places to the *South Carolina Encyclopedia*, the *New Dictionary of National Biography*, and the *Dictionary of American National Biography*.

W. Scott Poole published *Never Surrender: The Lost Cause in the South Carolina Upcountry, 1850–1903* (2003). He teaches at the College of Charleston. Dr. Poole received his Ph.D. from the University of Mississippi.

Bernard E. Powers Jr. is the author of *Black Charlestonians: A Social History 1822–1885* (1994). He is associate editor of *The South Carolina Encyclopedia* (2006). Dr. Powers received his Ph.D. from Northwestern University.

James Lowell Underwood received his L.L.M. from Yale University and his J.D. and B.A. from Emory University, where he served as editor-in-chief of the *Emory Law Journal*. He taught at the University of South Carolina School of Law for thirty-seven years and is currently Distinguished Professor Emeritus of Constitutional Law. He is the author of a four-volume set, *The Constitution of South Carolina* (1986, 1989, 1992, 1994); the coauthor and coeditor of *At Freedom's Door: African American Founding Fathers and Lawyers in Reconstruction South Carolina* (with W. Lewis Burke, 2000); and the author of law review articles on religious freedom.

Index